I0817466

SAUDI ARABIA

SAUDI ARABIA

A Modern History

DAVID COMMINS

YALE UNIVERSITY PRESS
NEW HAVEN AND LONDON

Translations of Nabati poetry used with permission of University of California Press, from *Nabati Poetry: The Oral Poetry of Arabia*, Saad Abdullah Sowayan, 1985; permission conveyed through Copyright Clearance Center, Inc.

For information about this and other Yale University Press publications, please contact:
U.S. Office: sales.press@yale.edu yalebooks.com
Europe Office: sales@yaleup.co.uk yalebooks.co.uk

Set in Minion Pro by IDSUK (DataConnection) Ltd
Printed and bound in the UK by Bell & Bain Ltd, Glasgow

Library of Congress Control Number: 2025931212
A catalogue record for this book is available from the British Library.
Authorized Representative in the EU: Easy Access System Europe, Mustamäe tee 50, 10621 Tallinn, Estonia, gpsr.requests@easproject.com

ISBN 978-0-300-25805-9

10 9 8 7 6 5 4 3 2 1

Contents

Illustrations

Plates

Maps

Acknowledgments

It is a pleasure to acknowledge the support I have received in the course of writing this book. In the first place, I owe thanks to Joanna Godfrey at Yale University Press for suggesting a fresh look at the history of Saudi Arabia. It took me quite a bit longer to accomplish than expected and I very much appreciate Joanna's guidance and patience at all steps of drafting and revising. This work also benefited from the talents of the team at Yale University Press: Rachael Lonsdale, Robert Davies, Katie Urquhart, Frazer Martin, Lucy Buchan, Kristy Leonard, and Chloe Foster. I am grateful to Marcel Kurpershoek for permission to cite his translation of the eighteenth-century Arabian bard Humaidan al-Shuwayʿir, and to Chip Rossetti, Editorial Director of the Library of Arabic Literature at New York University Press, for facilitating that permission. Likewise, I appreciate permission from the University of California Press to cite the Saudi scholar Saad Sowayan's translations of Nabati poetry.

James Gelvin and two anonymous readers made insightful suggestions from the proposal stage to the complete draft. Dickinson College has provided an academic home and steady support for my research for more than thirty years. For this project, I owe provost Neil Weissman and the Faculty Personnel Committee for granting a sabbatical leave in spring 2022. I am also indebted to others in the Dickinson community: to Ann and John Curley for their generosity and confidence in my work. To Madeline Brown for indispensable administrative support. To Stephen Weinberger, Matt Pinsker, and other members of the History Department. To Andrew Farrant, Ebru Kongar, Nicky Tynan, and Ed Webb for sharing their expertise on matters of economics and political science. For their love over many years, I am grateful to my family: my mother Marcia Faye Commins, my daughter Marcia Zakeeya Kavulich, and my brothers Steve, Gary, and Neil Commins. My beloved wife Susan Lindt has endured, and hopefully enjoyed on occasion, my endless chatter about Saudi Arabia's past. Colleagues in Riyadh have been essential in shaping my perspective on the history of their country and inspiring me to start writing about it. Without their warm welcome during the tumultuous months after 9/11, it is hard for me to imagine ever having much to say about their country's history. I hope they find this American's version of it a worthy reflection of our conversations over the years.

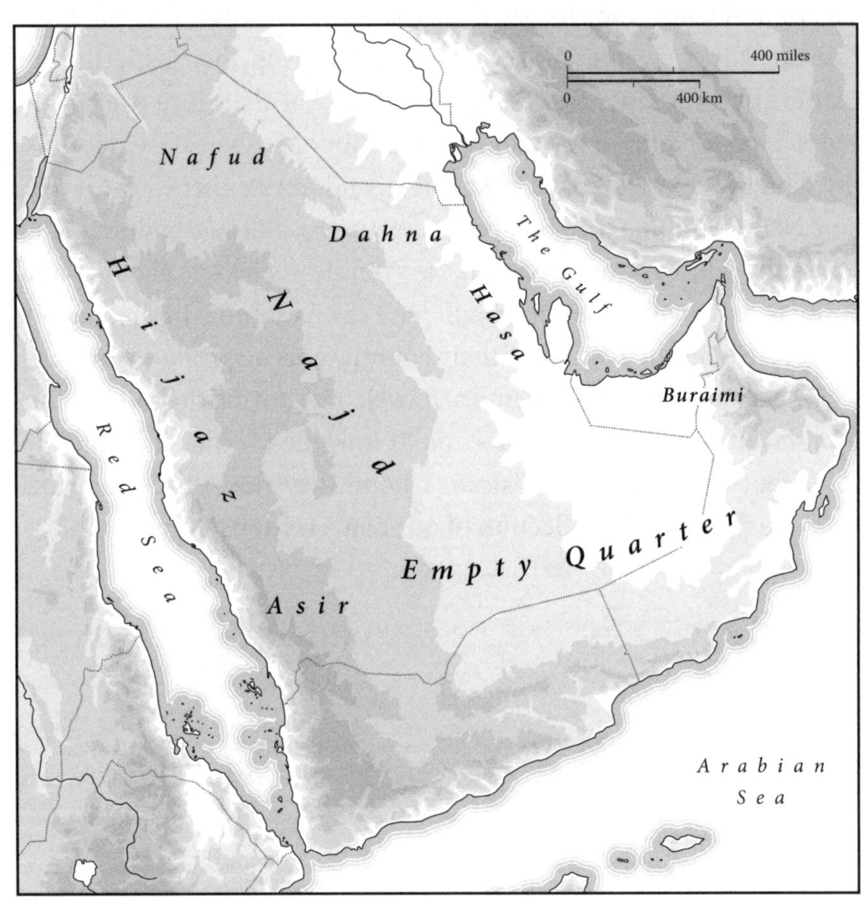

1. Physical map of Arabia.

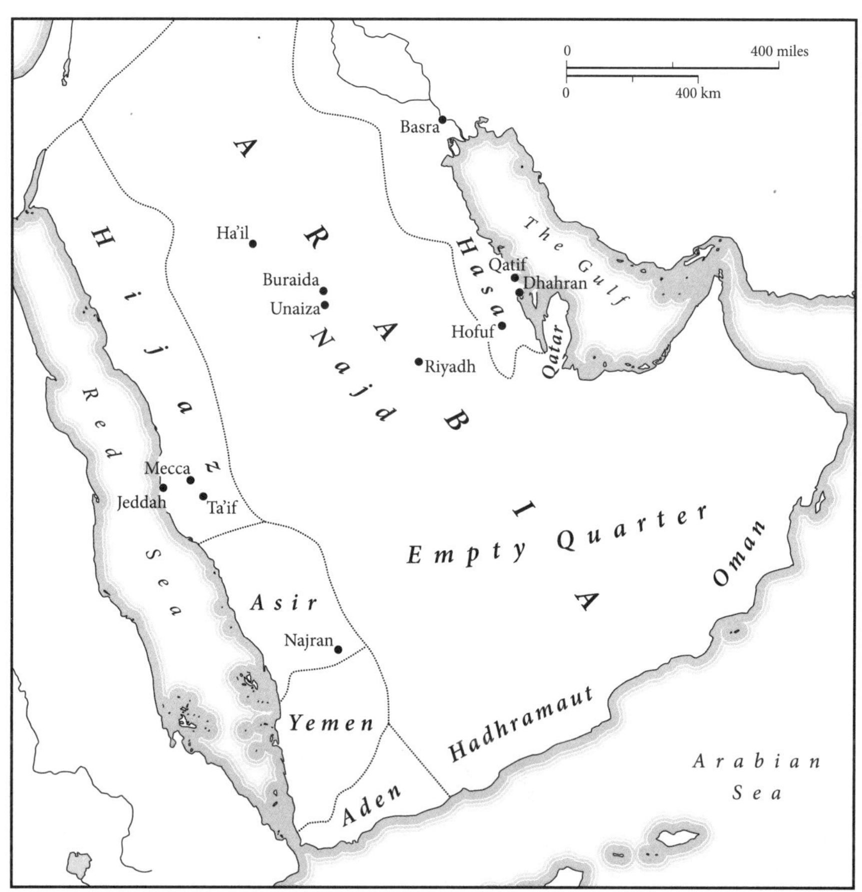

2. The main zones in Arabia.

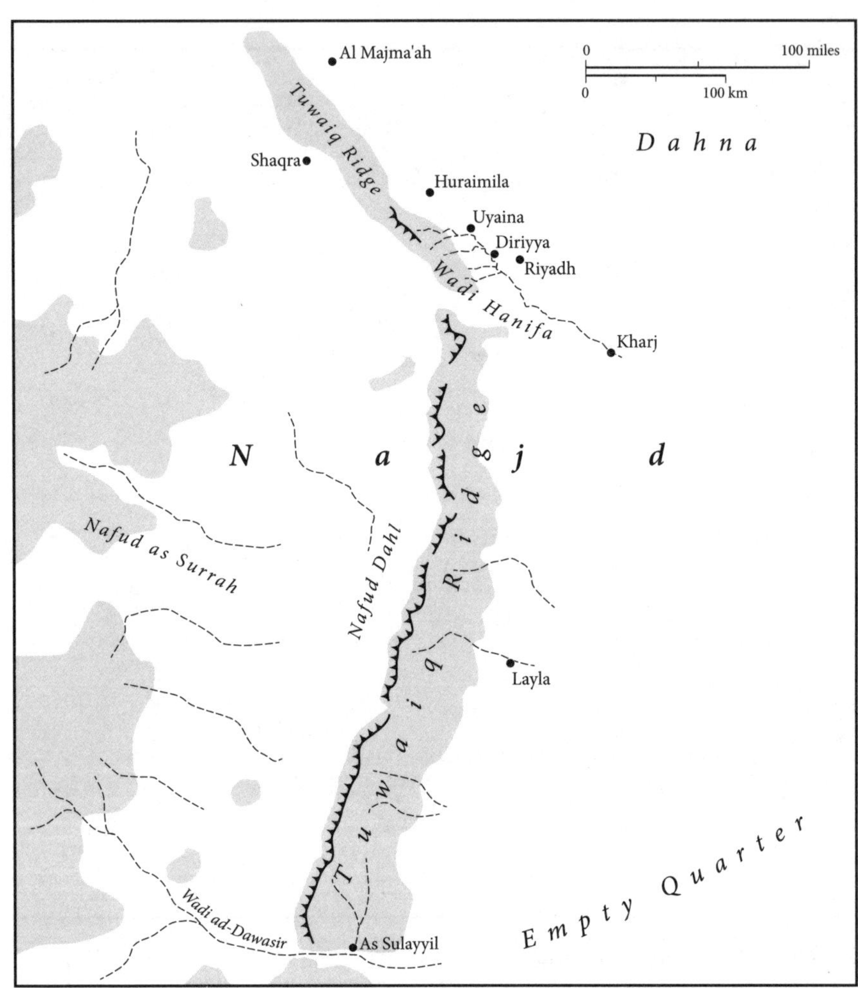

3. Tuwaiq Ridge.

Introduction

Two events in October 2023 painted starkly different scenarios for the future of the Middle East. At the southeast corner of the Mediterranean, war erupted between Israel and Hamas. The savage attack carried out by Hamas and the crushing Israeli military response implied the cycle of violence more than a century old would keep its grip on the region. Meanwhile, 900 miles away, in the heart of Arabia, some 6,000 bankers and senior executives from 90 countries flocked to Riyadh for an international summit for investors, dubbed "Davos in the Desert." The seventh annual conference held by Saudi Arabia's Future Investment Initiative was part of the kingdom's drive to break from the past and chart a path to regional prosperity and stability.[1] Under the leadership of King Salman and his son Crown Prince Muhammad, the kingdom was staking a place in the leading ranks of the global economy, part of the ambitious plan to transform the country's economy and society, as laid down in "Saudi Vision 2030." To achieve its audacious aims will entail overturning patterns and structures rooted in layers of history dating to the rise of Saudi power in the 1740s. This book recounts that history, tracking changes in politics, religion, culture, economy, and society, from one generation to the next, through the interactions among dynastic leaders, clerics, townsmen, Bedouin, workers, and activists of different stripes.

In the early 1700s, the vast region known as Najd that occupies the center of Arabia was not under a single political authority. It was divided between many independent oasis towns and nomadic tribes. One small oasis town called Diriyya was ruled by the Saud clan. By forming an alliance with the Wahhabi religious movement, the Sauds were able to conquer and unite Najd. In the early 1900s, the Saudi leader, Abd al-Aziz, bolstered his power by forming an alliance with Great Britain, inaugurating an enduring strategic relationship with Western powers. Economic strains threatened to undermine his power until he signed an oil concession with a consortium of United States companies in 1933. The oil industry had paradoxical effects. It filled the royal purse, but it also brought forth modern labor protest and connected the Saudi kingdom to dissident movements in the Arab world. Under pressure from domestic unrest and regional adversaries, in the 1960s, the monarchy took steps to gain popular consent by pledging to use oil revenue to safeguard the population's material welfare. To do so, it established effective government agencies capable of spreading the benefits of oil wealth. The revolution in the world oil market in the early 1970s then made it possible to undertake comprehensive, rapid national transformation.

At each step, Saudi rulers overcame scarcity of one kind or another (symbolic legitimation, funds, military power) by taking advantage of different external resources.[2] In large measure, the history of Saudi Arabia is the story of how its leaders shored up their position by tapping material and symbolic resources, and how in doing so, they changed internal dynamics in ways that brought forth new challenges. In the 1740s, Muhammad ibn Abd al-Wahhab's religious purification mission brought a symbolic resource no other emir in central Arabia possessed. In the first 150 years of Saudi history, conquest justified by the religious mission met fiscal demands through plunder, tribute, and taxes. In the twentieth century, Saudi rulers augmented the mission's symbolic legitimation with an assortment of external resources: expertise in foreign relations, media, education, and administration from foreign Arab advisers; funds and arms from Britain; oil revenue from the American oil company; strategic protection from the United States government; transnational religious influence from foreign Muslims; labor from an expatriate workforce. In all historical phases, Saudi power hinged on external sources for funds: booty, pilgrim taxes, foreign aid, and oil sales.

Strategic and economic ties with Western states and companies made it possible for the monarchy to conquer Arabia's Bedouin tribes, coopt provincial notables in annexed territories, project national authority throughout the country, improve living standards, and subject the religious purification mission to mundane calculation of state interest. Those same ties with the West also generated two chronic political problems. First, ties with the West conflicted with the religious purification movement's hostility toward the non-Muslim world and with popular sympathy with Muslim causes. Second, ties with the West brought political agendas for accountable government that are incompatible with absolute monarchy. The upshot has been a state of tension between the monarchy and dissident groups since the first labor protests against the American oil company in the 1940s. Dependence on external resources created other contradictions. Importing foreign Arab expertise in the early 1900s eroded the religious purification mission's hegemony and spawned dissident religious movements. In a different vein, importing an expatriate workforce in the 1970s that grew to comprise one-fourth of the country's population demobilized Saudi-Arab working-class movements and produced an economic structure that privileges Saudi nationals, a structure the economy can no longer support.

The history of religion in Saudi Arabia also involves the interplay between dynasty, local population, and external forces. It is noteworthy that resistance to the religious movement associated with the monarchy, the Wahhabi mission, goes back to the 1700s. In fact, resistance to Muhammad ibn Abd al-Wahhab's mission is what drove him to the Saud clan's oasis in the first place. The effort to convert the Sunni Muslim population to his conception of Islam was a long, violent struggle that was never complete. The Shiite Muslim population, conquered by the Sauds three different times, remained loyal to its traditions in the face of discrimination and doctrinal hostility. The annexation of Hijaz incorporated a cosmopolitan Sunni population and the shoots of a modernist current that injected an independent streak that spread and diversified in different genres and media venues. The transition from an agrarian way of life to an extractive rentier economy drove thousands off the land to the cities, where cosmopolitan Arab nationalist and leftist parties and Islamist groups recruited followers dissatisfied with the monarchy and the religious establishment. Now the monarchy itself seems to be redefining the Wahhabi mission as an expression of "moderate Islam," to justify leisure and pastimes common in Muslim societies and to curtail xenophobic school lessons inimical to full participation in global society. It remains to be seen how the current project to remake the country will turn out. It would not be the first transformation of Arabia under the Saud clan.

1

Old Najd

The history of Saudi Arabia presents a puzzle: how did one small oasis town in the central Arabian region known as Najd conquer most of Arabia? Never before had a power in Najd overcome conditions imposed by climate and terrain that diffused population and resources along two axes. One axis was the division between the sedentary population inhabiting oasis towns and the migratory population, the Bedouin tribes, inhabiting the steppe.[1] The second axis was the independence of each oasis town and each Bedouin tribe. To grasp the scope of the puzzle of how one oasis town created an Arabian empire, we begin with an overview of conditions in "old Najd," before the rise of Saud power.

An Island Inside an Island

The cradle of Saudi Arabia is Najd, a high plateau roughly the size of France that occupies the peninsula's central region, isolated from adjacent districts by mountains and sands. To the west, the barren mountains of Hijaz stand between Najd and the Red Sea. Vast sand tracts surround the other sides of Najd. To the east, the sands of Dahna, 800 miles long and as much as 50 miles wide, separate it from the fertile coastal region of Hasa on the Persian Gulf. At their southern end, the Dahna sands trail off and vanish in the vast Empty Quarter. At their northern end, the Dahna sands converge with the Nafud sands that comprise the southern fringe of the Fertile Crescent.

Najd itself is divided into two sub-regions, Upper and Lower Najd, divided by the Tuwaiq Ridge, a 500-mile-long boomerang-shaped escarpment that runs from north to south. The western side of the escarpment is Upper Najd, a broad elevated plateau lying between the Hijaz range and the Tuwaiq Ridge. Upper Najd's thin, stony soil and its sparse supply of underground water render it unsuitable for cultivation. During the rainy season, however, spotty precipitation feeds desert plant life suitable for grazing camels. Narrow north–south sand tracts break up the plateau before the Tuwaiq Ridge rises 800 feet above the landscape.

If Egypt is the gift of the Nile, per Herodotus, Saudi Arabia is the gift of oases at the base of the Tuwaiq Ridge's eastern slope inclining to Lower Najd, a region divided into clusters of oasis settlements strung along wadi (dry riverbed) systems running down the mountain.[2] Along the banks of the creases and wrinkles radiating from the escarpment, villagers tilled alluvial soil, the bounds of cultivation growing and shrinking according to the irregular rhythm of dry spells and floods. The populations of oasis settlements rose and fell in tandem with weather fluctuations. Independent oasis towns and their satellites formed an arena of evenly matched emirs. Multiple petty emirates coexisted with the tribal domains, or *diras*, claimed and defended by Bedouin tribes. Sedentary oasis dwellers and nomadic folk pursued complementary ways of production, and shared common modes of poetic expression, values, and social distinction. For centuries, a kind of equilibrium marked by modest wealth and desperate poverty set limits on the possibilities for the accumulation of power in a region where religion was part of the common coin, religion that was an extension of how adjacent Arab regions had evolved a pluralist Muslim life where legal, mystical, and theological currents coexisted.

The desert climate alternates between the hot dry summer season and the cool winter season that sees spotty rainfall. Annual rainfall seldom reaches the minimum for rain-fed agriculture (250mm), and generally fluctuates between 100 and 150mm. Rain tends to fall in short, powerful downbursts lasting less than one hour. Half the entire year's rain may fall in a single day. Median rainfall amounts are not the norm. Thus, from 1956 to 1963, the Riyadh region topped 90mm twice whereas from 1967 to 1972, the region's annual amount ranged from 110 to 230mm.[3]

Irregular weather occupies a conspicuous place in the chronicles recording events in the two centuries before the rise of Saudi power. When drought caused pastures to wither and underground water supplies to dwindle, Bedouin and cultivators migrated to damper regions, typically to Iraq and Hasa.[4] Periods of drought, two years or longer, struck Najd seven times in the eleventh "hijri" century (1591–1687 CE) and eight times in the twelfth "hijri" century (1688–1784 CE). Locust swarms periodically devoured entire crops and pastureland. Too much rain in too short a period caused flash floods that ruined fields and destroyed houses. Epidemics rounded out the list of misfortunes that afflicted people and livestock alike.[5]

Agrarian Economy and Society

The agrarian economy of Najd depended on resourceful use of the scarce supply of water. With no lakes or rivers, and erratic rainfall, cultivators captured water in two ways. First, they dug wells and underground channels to draw from subterranean aquifers. Second, they constructed dams and basins to divert and store stormwater rushing down wadis, an ancient practice known as "rainfall catchment" or "runoff farming."[6]

Excavating and maintaining wells and subterranean channels to irrigate date groves and crops demanded extensive manpower to handle ropes and buckets that lifted water to the surface, so that two or more families might share a well to irrigate date groves, wheat fields, and vegetable gardens.[7] In a few districts, the water table is shallow enough to excavate subterranean channels called *kharaz* that carried artesian spring water and groundwater seepage to fields. Attested as early as the eleventh century, the channels resemble underground systems in Iran called *qanat*s. To maintain the channels, farmers dug shafts about 10 feet wide at intervals of 30 feet.[8] Najdi cultivators could wring enough water out of flood runoff and wells to support settlements of a few thousand souls. In the typical oasis, dense groves of date palms and vegetable gardens created a cooler, more humid microclimate in the middle of the desert. Harry St. John Philby described a typical oasis in the early 1900s: "The groves of the oasis are of very prosperous appearance containing a rich undergrowth of fruit-trees and vegetables—pomegranates . . . peaches, lemons, cotton-plants . . . egg-plants and chilies."[9]

Arabian pastoralists raising camels, horses, sheep, and goats are known as Bedouin.[10] Their way of life depended on access to wells for themselves and their animals, and access to pasture fed by rainfall. From season to season, the precise location of pasture varied because the location of rainfall was unpredictable. The Bedouin synchronized migration to the rhythm of wet and dry seasons, heading into the desert from fall through late spring, when rain turns the brown steppe green, and gathering at wells on the outskirts of oases to pass the summer. For most of the year, Bedouin life revolved around the task of moving livestock from pasture to pasture. The annual shift between desert and oasis was associated with the constellations: in late spring, when the Pleiades disappeared from the sky, the Bedouin converged at oasis wells, and spent the next three months refreshing their bonds with townsmen. When Canopus rose at dawn to mark the onset of the rainy season, the Bedouin made ready to return to the desert, sending scouts to locate fresh pasture. During the migration season, they normally rested at one place a week or so before moving to fresh pasture.[11] Bedouin women handled much of the camp work: setting up the tents upon arriving at grazing grounds and then rolling up and loading them when it was time to move on. Each tent had a curtain or blanket dividing it into men's and women's sides.[12]

The scarcity of water and pasture meant that conflict between Bedouin over access to them was an endemic feature of their way of life. If a Bedouin tribe claimed a well, it had to be ready to fight off thirsty intruders. Prolonged drought forced Bedouin to move with their herds to seek pasture outside a territory commonly recognized as their domain and encroach on another tribe's domain, leading to conflict. If a tribe failed to acquire pasture, it might settle at an oasis to take up farming, a way of life the Bedouin regarded with disdain. With a narrow margin of survival for humans and animals alike, stealing livestock in surprise raids was a regular part of desert life to replace animal losses by capturing another tribe's animals. The absence of central political authority did not mean that raids were random or lawless. They followed patterns and conformed to rules of conduct. It was honorable to raid during daylight and refrain from harming women, children, and the elderly. According to a code of valor, warriors avoided fighting to the death and did not kill captives. There was no shame in asking for mercy when one was at a disadvantage, and a victor's standing increased for granting pardon and allowing the enemy to return to his folk. In battles over pasture, women would accompany men—sometimes letting down their hair and baring their breasts, as they urged the warriors to fight—to assist the wounded. A young woman in a camel litter might call out the tribe's distinctive battle cry, exhorting men to fight for the honor of the tribe, represented by its women folk. For warriors, the raid was an opportunity to build reputations, perhaps more than booty, which should be distributed to the needy to signify one's generosity, another source of excellent repute.

Poets memorialized feats of valor in the raids and defending against raids. After a battle against an enemy tribe, a warrior-poet named Nasir ibn ʿAmir ibn Hadi composed lines that evoke fierce combat along with erotic allure.[13]

Fortunate are those who were absent the day we were attacked at Amelah (a watering hole), those who did not witness the uproar of our frightened camel herds.
The panicked beasts threw off their loads. My heart was inflamed by the urging shouts of our ladies.
When I charged the enemy lines, they met me with lances and spears; but when I fled, the lady with the beautiful eyes cried out after me.
After the spear broke I unsheathed Abu Lah, my sword, the only weapon left in my hand.
I fought in their midst until I repelled the attacking multitudes. I chased them away like the rutting male camel after she-camels in heat.
Slow down, mounted lady with thick eyelashes! I shall defend you as long as my swift mare can run.
For the sake of your eyes, I shall run down the foe, and his soul shall leave his body before reaching the ground. I shall leave him for the lame hyenas and spotted vultures to sup on.
It is my custom to risk my life on the battlefield while the cowardly run away.
These are the words of a fearless man. I am a noble hunting bird.

Merchants played essential roles in exchange inside Najd and between Najd and adjacent regions. They handled trade with Bedouin when the pastoralists gathered at oasis settlements to exchange animal products for local and imported goods. Bedouin assisted merchants by providing camels to carry goods, guides to lead caravans through the desert, and armed guards for protection against banditry. Townsmen and Bedouin tribes imported spices from India and coffee and incense from Yemen. Najdi merchant houses stationed agents in Turkey, Egypt, and Syria to sell horses, camels, and dates.[14]

Najdis thought of their society in terms of two distinct categories: settled folk (*hadar*) and nomads (*bedu*). Relationships between them ranged from conflict (Bedouin raids) to cooperation through economic exchange. Townsmen traded grain, rice, salt, sugar, coffee, and rope for the Bedouin's animal products. Settled folk and Bedouin alike organized social relations according to affiliation with a tribe.[15] In everyday life, members of a tribe divided into smaller subunits of clans and households. During the summer, Bedouin gathered at wells near oasis settlements inhabited by related clans.[16] In addition to tribal organization, settled folk and Bedouin had common conceptions of virtue. Expectations of hospitality governed reputations. The proper host offered coffee to guests and served feasts of abundant meat and rice: departing guests would wipe their greasy hands on the tent flap, and therefore a greasy tent flap was a token of prestige.[17]

Bedouin and settled folk shared a literary tradition that expressed common ideals. Popular Arabian poetry, known as Nabati poetry, celebrated valor and generosity, and evoked tokens of everyday life (migration, rains, landscapes, and animals).[18] Impressions of oasis life come to us from the farmer-poet Humaidan al-Shuwayʿir, whose life straddles the turn of the eighteenth century. In direct, simple language, his verse expresses the hopes and frustrations of toiling in palm groves:

My beloved palm trees at the well's edge,
    You lovely garden of royal trunks crowned in green;
For two miserable years I toiled there fruitlessly,
    As blistering midsummer blasted my frame;
You gorgeous row of palms in the front, shudder and sob,
    Shed tears, you branches heavy with ripe fruit!
Then I swore that I would not let you taste cool water
    From my hands, that I would leave your trunks to dessicate—
You were my proudest possession until I was betrayed
    By Time and battered by its wicked blows.[19]

Old Najd did not spawn a rich tradition of writing history. Indeed, for the two centuries preceding the rise of Saudi power, only seven chronicles have been located. Rather than weave a narrative about the past that seeks meaning or connects events, the chronicles are threadbare accounts that list skirmishes, epidemics, droughts, obituaries of notables, and origins of oasis settlements in annalistic fashion.[20] In a sense, Nabati poetry was the historical narrative for old Najd, framing events in a way that was meaningful to its audience.

In preindustrial conditions, climate and terrain placed limits on the accumulation of wealth and a cloud of uncertainty hung over cultivators and herders alike. Where material distinction was ephemeral, Najdis framed conceptions of esteem rooted in the stability of ancestry, even if ancestry was a cultural construct.[21] The Bedouin and the settled folk shared the idea that some groups possessed noble ancestry that made them natural superiors to others. Tribes distinguished for their pure descent from noble ancestors assumed and exercised a presumptive right to collect tribute from inferior tribes lacking such ancestry, that is, a line of descent from ancient Arabian tribes. The noble tribes also presumed a right to levy tribute on oasis dwellers. In this model, the pure nomadic tribes were a desert aristocracy. The distinction between pure and impure ancestry was observed by settled clans as well, and even though marriage between members of Bedouin and settled pure clans took place, the Bedouin were deemed superior to settled folk.[22]

In the mudwalled towns of Najd, the scale of ancestral purity corresponded to a division of labor that underpinned social hierarchy. Noble clans claiming pure tribal ancestry collected dues from sharecroppers in fields, groves, and irrigation works, fended off attacks by Bedouin and rival towns, organized raids to subjugate smaller oases, and fought off challenges from upstart clans in the oasis. Whether noble or commoner, Bedouin or sedentary, patriarchal rules assigned roles and rules that subordinated women to the authority of men, with significant difference in the everyday roles of men and women between settled and Bedouin populations.[23] Residents whose tribal ancestors were forgotten were called *khadiri* and worked as farmers, artisans, and traders. Some historians suggest that the *khadiris* were ancient sedentary folk subjugated by nomadic settlers. At the bottom of oasis society were slaves. Emancipated slaves and their descendants were considered part of the *khadiri* stratum.[24]

Details about slavery in Arabia are scarce. The general picture shows a long history of slavery in urban households, the urban economy, and agriculture. Historian Benjamin Reilly posits an ecological thesis for the presence of pockets of Arabians of African descent dispersed in Hijaz, Najd, the Gulf, and Oman. In groves, gardens, and fields prone to the *Anopheles* mosquito that carries malaria, Arabs put enslaved Africans to work because of their genetic resistance to the disease. Over time, when slaves and their descendants attained freedom, they did so as clients (*mawali*) of their former owners and became tenant sharecroppers. In both cases, the workers of African descent were in a servile position, at the bottom of the peninsula's social hierarchy. They performed hard tasks of digging and clearing irrigation canals, maintaining underground *qanats*, lifting water from wells, pruning and maintaining date palms.[25]

Political Conditions

Preindustrial conditions—the variability and low level of agricultural and pastoral production dispersed over a large territory—gave rise to a political terrain characterized by small-scale emirates in compact oasis settlements and Bedouin tribes in expansive desert domains whose power rested on control over land and military strength.[26] Relations between the emirates and the Bedouin tribes fluctuated between alliance, independence, and domination of one over the other. The dependence of agricultural production and pastoral herding on highly variable weather made oasis and Bedouin politics unstable: inconsistent economic surpluses made it difficult to accumulate the military resources for sustaining domination.[27]

The independence of each oasis settlement contributed to strong local attachments, giving Najdi culture a parochial flavor, marked by variations in dialect, rivalries, and reputations captured in the local lore coined and transmitted through popular poetry.[28] Each oasis had a dominant clan, typically comprising rival factions that sometimes fought for supremacy, sometimes closed ranks to fend off Bedouin tribes' efforts to reduce them to vassalage. Dominant clans used the prestige of noble ancestry to legitimize power, but they lacked symbolic and institutional mechanisms to sustain allegiance to a particular individual. Clan rivals plotted to oust emirs, and former emirs took refuge at nearby oases and obtained the support of their emirs for restoration. Few emirs enjoyed durable, stable reigns. Succession was the occasion for violence between rival factions. The chronicles are littered with the wreckage of murdered and expelled emirs. Environmental constraints on population and wealth put the oases on par with one another, giving rise to small-scale emirates able to project authority over satellite settlements, but seldom over one another.

In some towns, the ruling clan's members were the original settlers who developed fallow land. In other towns, they purchased lots to farm. And in yet others, they seized land by conquest. However they came to power, the rulers had the right to sell or lease land to other clans, which might or might not be related. A clan's strength rested on how many fighters it could mobilize to defend against marauding nomads and encroachment from neighboring towns. A powerful clan would be able to cultivate and protect a larger area that produced a larger crop. When a large share of the inhabitants came from the same tribe, their feeling of solidarity to defend their town would be more intense. When a favorable spell of weather lasted some years, clans grew in size, and contenders for leadership would multiply, and eventually internecine fighting for power took place. In some cases, an oasis settlement would be divided between two factions until one gained ascendancy and the defeated faction would have to migrate.[29]

The concept of patrimonialism captures how emirs ruled oasis settlements. A patrimonial ruler exercises authority through personal relationships with family members and clients, rather than through legal and bureaucratic rules. The emir's court consisted of his extended clan and a retinue of armed clients and slaves. Emirs governed according to custom, seldom bothering to apply religious law, in part because most towns did not have experts in the law, in part because religious law limited an emir's authority. Armed retinues carried out the emir's orders. There was no fixed rate of taxation. Some emirs collected half the harvest on land in their domain, others one quarter. Likewise, there was no fixed rule for distributing tax revenues, but the general assumption was that they belonged to the ruling clan, not to the emir. The allocation of revenues was a common source of contention between members of the ruling clan.[30]

Bedouin tribes were independent of the oasis emirates. Their mobility meant they could disperse and retreat if a band of oasis fighters gained the advantage in battle, or they could launch lightning strikes against oasis settlements. Because independence and equality were core elements of Bedouin identity, tribal leaders did not rule over fellow tribesmen. Instead, they exercised leadership by building consensus and proving able to guard the tribe's wells and pastures against rival tribes.[31] The major Bedouin tribes obtained revenue by gathering tribute (*khuwa*) from weak tribes and oasis settlements, collecting tolls from merchant caravans, and seizing booty in raids.

Between the tribes and the oasis emirs, power was fragmented and unstable, political contests a matter of short-term alliances between opportunistic partners. In the decades preceding the Saudi era, the chronicles mention eleven military conflicts: three assaults by Bedouin tribes against oasis settlements, three campaigns by coalitions of oasis emirs against Bedouin tribes, and five conflicts between alliances of Bedouin tribes and oasis emirs.[32]

Despite their divisions, the oasis settlements and tribes of Najd seldom came under the authority of an external power. Before the rise of Islam, Najd was known by a different name, al-Yamama. Its central location gave it a role in Arabian trade routes to Persia, Iraq, Yemen, and Hijaz.[33] In Islamic lore, al-Yamama is associated with Musailima, its leader in the Prophet Muhammad's last years. Because Musailima opposed the spread of Islam, his name became a byword for false religion, and Najd became known as a cradle for heresy.[34] What we know about Musailima's teachings is filtered through hostile Muslim sources, but they seemed to resemble Muslim and Christian ideas about resurrection, Judgment Day, regular prayer, and tithing.[35] Muslim armies defeated and killed Musailima in 633, and the caliphs of Medina extended their sway over al-Yamama. In the 680s, a faction of Muslim rebels called the Kharijites gained control for a decade before the Umayyad caliphate in Damascus reasserted power.[36] The Abbasid caliphs in Baghdad governed Najd for a century until the caliphs lost control over much of the empire as a result of turmoil in the imperial center. In the 860s, a rebel named Muhammad al-Ukhaydir established an independent principality that lasted about two centuries.[37] After the Ukhaydir line, Najd practically disappeared from Muslim annals. Chroniclers based in imperial courts framed al-Yamama's bids for autonomy as rebellions against belief for the sake of false prophecy, staining the reputation of Najd in the minds of other Muslims.

In the decades before the rise of the Sauds, Najd was divided between emirates and Bedouin tribes contending for power with each other. From the 1670s to the 1730s, the Banu Khalid Bedouin tribe from Hasa dominated Najd. The Banu Khalid grazed their herds in Najd during the rainy months and spent summer in Hasa. The oasis towns of Najd benefited from Banu Khalid rule because it tamped down the predations of Bedouin against the towns and secured caravan routes between the Gulf coast and the interior. Banu Khalid domination did not prevent conflict between Najdi emirates that fought over pasture, farmland, water, livestock, and satellite settlements.[38]

The most incessant fighting took place within the oasis towns. It was common for the defeated side to move to a nearby town and find assistance from relatives, who might lend support to a bid to regain power in their original town. At times, the ally would benefit by receiving a share of revenue if their side prevailed. Several instances of fighting between towns arose when a faction in one town invited intervention from another town. From 1688 to 1738, Ushaiqir saw fourteen factional struggles; Unaiza had seven; Diriyya had six. The towns often divided into separate enclaves under rival clan leaders.[39] The same period witnessed a contrary trend of consolidation where leaders defeated internal rivals and asserted control over satellite settlements.[40] The scale of political power was growing from the small, independent oasis settlement to a larger emirate where one oasis town exercised authority over more extensive territory and population. The Achilles heel was factional division in the ruling clan, a perennial source of weakness in the absence of rules or institutions to contain it, something that is true of all systems of personal, or patrimonial, power.

In the early 1700s, Uyaina was the most powerful, wealthiest town in lower Najd. The ruling clan, Al Muʿammar, had migrated to the area from Washm district in the 1400s and purchased fallow land. Under the stable leadership of the Al Muʿammar emirs, Uyaina came to dominate smaller neighbors. By the mid-1600s, it ruled all or part of three nearby districts. From around 1660 to 1725, two emirs enjoyed unusually long, stable reigns.[41] It is not clear what accounts for Uyaina's stability. Weather patterns recorded by the eighteenth- and nineteenth-century chroniclers give the impression that natural factors were not favorable. Between 1660 and 1725, famine, locust swarms, epidemics, and destructive storms are recorded in seventeen years.[42]

Whatever factors or conditions stabilized clan politics in Uyaina also may have benefited the rulers of Diriyya, the first center of Saudi power. The ancestors of the Saud clan were probably an old Najdi clan called al-Dirʿ or al-Duruʿ. At an unknown time in the past, clan members migrated to the Persian Gulf region and established a settlement that they called Diriyya. In the mid-1400s, the emir of al-Dirʿ in Najd granted land to his Persian Gulf kinsmen, who settled a new colony with the same name, Diriyya. The colony's leader was Maniʿ al-Muraidi, ancestor of the Sauds. His descendants, known as Al Muradah, became hereditary emirs. In the 1500s, population pressure in Diriyya resulted in the establishment of two satellite settlements. A struggle between two factions—Al Muqrin and Al Watban—erupted in the mid-1600s. In 1726, the leader of Al Muqrin, Muhammad ibn Saud, expelled Al Watban, who migrated to Zubair in southern Iraq.[43] In all likelihood, the rifts in Diriyya would have been as forgotten as those in other Najdi towns of that period were it not for the intervention of a remarkable religious movement.

Religion

The Muslims of Najd shared religious beliefs and practices with believers in nearby Ottoman lands who followed the Sunni tradition. In the early Islamic era, the Sunni tradition had developed multiple theological perspectives, ritual practices, and legal methods. In response to such diversity, two opposed stances evolved. The denominational stance represented a tolerant inclusive attitude toward diversity and the sectarian stance insisted on a strict exclusive attitude.[44] In both the Ottoman empire and Najd, the denominational stance was the norm, in accordance with the concept of "agrarian religion" coined by historian James Grehan.[45]

In agrarian religion, scholastic conceptions of correct belief and practice based on the canon (in the case of Islam, the Quran and the Prophetic Tradition) coexist with non-canonical conceptions popular with the illiterate majority. The canonical outlook is upheld by a small literate stratum with standing and influence in urban settings possessing the economic surplus to support religious scholars.

Participation in defining, debating, and extending theology and law demanded special training in understanding and interpreting the canon. Ordinary Muslims accorded respect to fellow believers who acquired that special training, and they recognized them as a social category known as the ulama, "those who know." While not consecrated in the manner of Christian clergy, the ulama formed something like a clerical estate.

The Sunni ulama came to recognize four "legal schools" that represented different theoretical conceptions and methodological approaches to establishing specific rules in Islamic law: the Hanafi, Shafii, Maliki, and Hanbali legal schools. In the Ottoman empire, the Hanafi legal school enjoyed official standing but the other three were respected and had followers in different regions. The least common legal school in Ottoman lands, the Hanbali, was the most widespread in Najd. In the field of theology, the Sunni tradition encompassed perspectives known as Maturidi, Ashari, and Hanbali (named for the same figure as the legal school).

The canonical Sunni tradition had a foothold in a few Najdi towns, where religious law offered a set of norms for the adjudication of land, water, and property rights. Religious law was absent among the Bedouin, who lived according to tribal custom. The religious scholars in Najd belonged to the Ottoman Sunni religious sphere in three ways. First, it was common for religious pupils from Najd to pursue advanced learning in Ottoman towns: the holy cities of Mecca and Medina, Damascus, Baghdad, and Basra. Second, Najdis acknowledged a hierarchy of religious authority that accorded prestige to Ottoman scholars. Third, the substance of the Najdi scholastic tradition was consistent with teachings on law and theology in Ottoman centers.[46] Within Najd, scholastic learning was concentrated in a few towns, especially Ushaiqir and Uyaina. A final trait of Najdi scholasticism that deserves emphasis is its preoccupation with questions of law and faint interest in theological questions. The Wahhabi mission flipped the emphasis to theology.

The scholastic tradition's teachings lay lightly on the illiterate majority. Throughout the Muslim world, rural folk and most townsmen followed non-canonical customs. Instead of divine authority emanating from revealed texts accessible to a literate few, agrarian religion sacralizes places and personalities that radiate divine power to cure illness, alleviate ailments, reconcile spouses, and help couples conceive. The sacred resided in pockets of fertility, such as springs and large trees in the midst of arid settings, and in hidden channels to the supernatural, such as grottoes and caves. Holy personalities might be bygone religious figures whose tombs emitted spiritual grace and who would offer the promise of intercession on behalf of distressed believers, or they might be living holy men known for their piety and demonstrations of spiritual powers.[47]

A denominational stance, where religious scholars seldom objected to non-canonical customs, was characteristic of religious life in the Ottoman empire, as was the case in most parts of the Muslim world. There were, however, occasions when champions of the canon attacked non-canonical religion and sought to suppress it in the name of combating illegitimate innovations (sing. *bidʿa*) in religious practice.[48] Hostility toward innovations is characteristic of a sectarian current in Sunni Islam that took shape in Syrian and Iraqi towns during the eleventh and twelfth centuries. Sectarian religious scholars asserted an idealized version of Islamic history that envisioned a unity among early Muslims that never existed. In addition, they discredited the majority of previous religious scholars and claimed that they were the ones who represented the Sunni consensus.[49] The sectarian attitude was one of "suspicious besetment"[50] arising from inflexible views on belief, and it considered intermingling with followers of other religious traditions as a threat to true belief. By contrast, the denominational attitude had broad boundaries for what counted as legitimate religious belief and practice. It counted all who prayed toward Mecca (*ahl al-qibla*) as Muslims and made room for coexistence with Shiite Muslims and non-Muslims. In Najd and other

Sunni lands, the widespread embrace of non-canonical customs made it difficult for anti-innovation campaigns to succeed.[51]

The Periphery of Najd

Even though Najd had some contact and interaction with the outside world through trade and religious study, it was the most insular region in Arabia, which comprises different regions. The Red Sea formed a highway for the western Arabian region of Hijaz to interact with Arabs and Africans on the opposite shore. The folk of both shores were "Red Sea" peoples sharing ways of life dependent on the shallow waters for food, using the same materials for boating and shelter. The main Hijazi towns were the holy cities Mecca and Medina, possessing global significance for the Muslim world, but otherwise small, unremarkable towns, and the port town of Jeddah, a commercial entrepot and the gateway to the rest of the region. All three towns had cosmopolitan social profiles thanks to the annual pilgrimage to Mecca, which contained communities from distant parts of Asia and Africa. Every year, pilgrims from all parts and keen to pursue religious learning stayed on in Medina, where they were known as sojourners (*mujawir*). Some would stay for a year or two, others would settle for the rest of their lives. The annual influx of pilgrims gave Medinan society a cosmopolitan stamp much like Mecca's.

More than any other part of Arabia, Hijaz mattered to the Muslim world. From early Islamic times, it came under the rule of a succession of powers, first caliphs in Damascus and Baghdad, then sultans in Cairo and Istanbul. Muslim rulers basked in the prestige offered by ensuring safe passage to Mecca and performance of the annual pilgrimage, and by patronizing new religious construction and renovation of old structures. Hijazi tribes and townsmen had a long history of accommodating the Muslim world's diverse peoples and dealing with outside powers; they never established an independent, unified polity.

The Hasa region and Persian Gulf coast were outward-facing as well. Since classical times, the Gulf's shallow waters had made it easy to mingle for Persians and Arabs from both shores. Divers harvested pearls that merchants exported across the Indian Ocean. The Gulf was a highway for trade between India and the Fertile Crescent. At the lower end of the Gulf, Oman had ports on the Arabian Sea, exchanging goods, people, and customs with Africa and India. The Arabian side of the Gulf was too poor and thinly populated for Muslim powers to expend the effort to annex it. The population was too dispersed to gather under a unified leadership, but at times compact polities formed in Oman and the Hasa–Bahrain region. Both areas possessed enough cultivatable land to support a settled population and their ports attracted maritime merchants seeking trading posts, warehouses, and security. Hasa lies some distance from the Gulf, but faces no natural obstacles to exchanging goods, whereas the Dahna sands shield it from Najd. It is the most densely populated part of Arabia outside Yemen, thanks to abundant artesian wells that irrigate some of the largest date palm groves in the peninsula. The waters make it possible to grow large quantities of rice, fruit trees, and vegetables. Its agricultural production made it a food source for Najd and its ports made it an important channel for interaction with the outside world. In the early modern period, the Ottoman empire conquered it in the 1520s and held it until the Banu Khalid tribe wrested control in the 1670s.

The northern reaches of Najd were an opening between Arabia and the ancient cultures of the Fertile Crescent. The lower Euphrates and southern Iraq were common destinations for migrating tribesmen and for townsmen seeking trade or milder conditions during periods of drought. For generations, Iraq saw clans migrate and settle, leaving sediment layers of folk with ancestral ties to Najd and forming cultural bridges to it.

Environmental conditions and preindustrial technologies fostered a political equilibrium between patrimonial courts and Bedouin tribes, rooted in the dispersion of productive resources. While settled folk and Bedouin pursued different livelihoods and inhabited different political domains, they formed a common culture based on economic exchange, a conception of social hierarchy based on ancestry, and the vibrant tradition of Nabati poetry. Interaction with the outside world was limited to trade, study at sites of religious authority, and seeking refuge at times of drought and famine. These patterns persisted until political unification under one oasis emirate brought about new patterns of orientation to the outside world, where pieces of Arabia became peripheries to Najd, and their ties to the Indian Ocean, Mediterranean, and Fertile Crescent took new courses.

2

The Diriyya Emirate
A Sectarian Empire, 1744–1818

In the early 1700s, there was no reason to suppose that Najd would see the rise of a power that could overcome political fragmentation. Unification proved possible under the banner of a sectarian mission allied to the ruling clan of an oasis settlement. Through conquest, conversion, and alliance, Saudi–Wahhabi forces integrated the Arabian interior and sealed it against the outside infidel world. As the Diriyya juggernaut reached the Red Sea and the Persian Gulf, it collided with superior forces that emerged during the Napoleonic era: British assertion of power over maritime routes and the rise of Mehmet Ali Pasha in Egypt.

The Sectarian Idea

Najd would never be the same after Muhammad ibn Abd al-Wahhab (1703–92) started his public mission to purify religion. His doctrine on belief redefined (or in his view, reestablished) the boundary between believers and unbelievers in a way that demanded action. If you agreed with him, you had to take action against customs he considered polytheistic. If you disagreed with him, you had to take action to defend customs against his efforts to wipe them out. It was his insistence that belief requires action that ensured that his doctrine triggered not only a war of words between religious scholars but also military combat between its proponents and adversaries. The pluralist denominational Sunni tradition of old Najd had to go because it was, in Shaikh Muhammad's eyes, guilty of allowing idolatry. His mission expressed not only the sectarian Sunni outlook, but a perspective characteristic of religious sects in general: "Because sects are schismatic groups they present themselves to the world as something *old*. They left the parent body not to form a new faith, but to *reestablish the old one*, from which the parent body had 'drifted . . .' Sects claim to be the authentic, purged, refurbished version of the faith from which they split."[1]

Shaikh Muhammad's claim to reestablish authentic belief represented an intervention in a debate over the boundary between belief and unbelief going back to the early Islamic era.[2] Some of the earliest fighting between Muslims was connected to disagreement over belief, with a group known as the Kharijites asserting that committing a grave sin made one an unbeliever. One response to violence between Muslims was to frame a minimalist doctrine of belief maintaining that as long as one professed belief in God and his Prophet and acknowledged basic religious duties, one counted as a believer, and whether the commitment of grave sins made one an unbeliever was a matter for God to decide on Judgment Day. The most famous dissenter from the Sunni consensus on belief was the medieval scholar Ahmad ibn Taimiyya (d. 1328). He claimed the cult of saints was polytheistic, but his views did not spread beyond a limited circle of his pupils until Muhammad ibn Abd al-Wahhab adopted them.[3]

Shaikh Muhammad stood out for his insistence that belief in God, *tawhid*, is not merely a matter of verbal affirmation. It requires that one show no devotion to any being apart from God. Anything less is idolatry. Examples of idolatry that Shaikh Muhammad condemned included prostrating before the tombs of holy men, visiting a saint's tomb to seek a cure for maladies, seeking a saint's intercession on

Judgment Day, and the like. He argued that the idolaters of his time were worse than the pre-Islamic Arabs because they had no excuse for not understanding the revelation in the Quran and Prophetic Tradition.[4]

By equating imperfect adherence to his own definition of belief with polytheism, Ibn Abd al-Wahhab was declaring other Muslims to be unbelievers. For a Muslim to accuse another Muslim of unbelief is called *takfir* in Arabic. While not the same as the concept of excommunication in Christianity, because in Islam there is no Church from whose sacraments a believer may be excluded, *takfir* is similar in that it is the expulsion of a Muslim from the community of believers. The consensus in the Sunni tradition held that polytheistic acts warranted excommunication only after one ignored presentation of proof that a specific act constituted idolatry. What constituted "presentation of proof" was a critical question. For Shaikh Muhammad, knowing about the Quran qualified as presentation of proof. If one knew the Quran, then one's idolatry warranted excommunication. He also endorsed "secondary excommunication," where failing to excommunicate idolaters makes one an infidel.[5]

In addition to branding other Muslims as infidels, Ibn Abd al-Wahhab asserted that belief requires one to act on the principle of loyalty to believers and enmity toward infidels: "A person's Islam is not sound even if he practices *tawhid* of God and deserts polytheism unless he is hostile to polytheists and declares to them his hostility and hatred."[6] Failing to exhibit enmity toward infidels makes one an infidel. Furthermore, if a believer is in a position where he cannot exhibit enmity to infidels, then emigration to "the land of belief" is a duty.[7]

The logic of Ibn Abd al-Wahhab's positions on belief and excommunication pointed in the direction of waging jihad against professed believers. He claimed that the pre-Islamic Arabs believed in God, but because they did not devote worship to God alone, the Prophet waged jihad against them, and the believers could slay them and confiscate their property. Shaikh Muhammad's position on jihad was calibrated according to circumstances: in Uyaina, where he had the emir's support to suppress the cult of saints, he did not call for jihad; during his first years in Diriyya, he justified fighting against rival emirates as defensive jihad; after a few years of fighting, he justified offensive jihad for the sake of wiping out idolatry.[8]

Shaikh Muhammad blamed four groups for the spread of idolatry: clerics, fake holy men, Shiites, and Bedouin. Clerics failed to perform their duty to advise rulers on enforcing correct religious belief and worship, whether from fear of angering oppressive rulers or from reluctance to confront the ignorant crowd's misguided beliefs.[9] He claimed that his clerical opponents would admit in private that his doctrine was correct, but in public they rejected his teachings for the sake of appeasing rulers, the crowd, or their own profit at the expense of the crowd.[10] Fake holy men defrauded common folk, wasting their scant resources on offerings, amulets, and talismans.[11] Shiites assigned a privileged spiritual and political position to Ali and his descendants, known as the imams, viewing them as infallible guardians of religion and the sole legitimate leaders of the community. In the eyes of Ibn Abd al-Wahhab, Shiite belief in Ali and the imams was a form of idolatry.[12] Finally, Shaikh Muhammad considered most Bedouin to be infidels whereas Najdi clerics considered them fellow Muslims even if they were lax in observing ritual duties and legal rules. Shaikh Muhammad condemned Bedouin ways for resolving disputes as "idol's judgment," and he denounced retaliation because it fostered interminable feuds. Likewise, Bedouin customs on marriage, divorce, and inheritance were violations of Islamic law.[13]

For other Muslims to feel outrage for being condemned as infidels and objects of jihad needs no explanation, but why Ibn Abd al-Wahhab broke with the denominational consensus on belief is a mystery. He came from a family known for religious learning. His grandfather was a renowned expert in religious law. His father and brother held positions as religious judges. They all adhered to the denominational spirit that Najd shared with Muslims in the Ottoman lands, and they all followed the Hanbali legal tradition. Contrary to a common refrain in Western scholarship, Shaikh Muhammad did not follow mainstream Hanbali doctrine. Indeed, most Arabian Hanbalis condemned his teachings.[14] Some historians suggest that Wahhabism resembled reform tendencies in the holy cities, India, and West Africa.[15] Others trace his ideas to teachers in Medina or to revulsion at Shiite customs he may have witnessed in Basra, where he first stirred controversy for his attacks on visiting the graves of holy men. But other religious pupils from Najd studied in the holy cities and Basra without arriving at the conviction that the Muslims of their era had backslid to idolatry.[16] He claimed to have rediscovered the true meaning of monotheism independent of any teachers.[17]

The Sectarian Mission

When Shaikh Muhammad returned from his travels to study, probably in the late 1730s, he settled in Huraimila, where his father was the chief religious judge. Shaikh Muhammad refrained from denouncing the cult of saints in his father's lifetime, out of respect for his father's convictions, but when he died in 1741, Shaikh Muhammad began his mission to revive Islam in its original form.[18] His message fell on receptive ears in nearby towns: Uyaina, Riyadh, Diriyya, and Manfuha. The presence of a Wahhabi faction in several settlements may have played a role in the Diriyya emir's decision to lend support to the mission. Wahhabi partisans gave Saudi expansion an edge in its campaigns against rival emirates because the religious message provided a common platform whereas clan loyalty was confined to a single town. The sectarian choice, "To be or not to be a believer." That was the question that divided Najd.

In 1742, Shaikh Muhammad moved to Uyaina, seat of the district's eminent Muʿammar line of emirs. He forged an alliance with Emir Uthman ibn Muʿammar by marrying the emir's aunt Jawhara. With the emir's backing, he put his agenda into action. He gathered his followers to cut down three trees believed to possess supernatural powers: the Tree of the Wolf (frequented by unmarried women wishing for a mate), the Tree of Quraiwah, and the Tree of Abu Dajjanah. These activities drew supporters from towns besides Uyaina. His entourage on the day he felled the Tree of Quraiwah included two brothers of Diriyya's emir. Shaikh Muhammad next set his sights on a more prestigious and sensitive target: the tomb of the Prophet's Companion Zaid ibn al-Khattab (the brother of the second caliph Umar). Taking aim at a vestige of Islam's early heroes struck a deep chord of resentment toward Shaikh Muhammad's mission, and Emir Uthman preempted resistance by sending a company of six hundred armed men to ensure no interference with the tomb's destruction. The shaikh also pushed for strict application of Islamic law, including a famous episode when he gave the order to punish an adulterous woman with death by stoning. The incident went against prevailing scholastic opinion that such punishment was not legal in the absence of a leader of the general Muslim community.[19]

It did not take long for Shaikh Muhammad's attacks on popular customs and sacred sites to draw attention outside Najd. Religious scholars in the holy cities, Hasa, and Basra composed treatises to discourage people from following him by accusing him of unbelief. A Basra scholar called him "satan's deputy" and reminded believers that Najd was the cradle of the false prophet Musailima.[20] One scholar in Mecca urged the authorities in Najd to stop him from preaching while two others called for confining him if he turned out to be insane, but if he was a heretic, he should be put to death for spreading heresy.[21] In 1749, the sharif of Mecca called the attention of the Ottoman court in Istanbul to the Wahhabi threat. The sultan replied that Shaikh Muhammad had to be advised to change his views, or else face attack.[22]

One of Shaikh Muhammad's most determined foes was his own brother Sulaiman, who had followed their father as the religious judge in Huraimila. Sulaiman ibn Abd al-Wahhab started issuing epistles against his brother's teachings in 1751 and continued for a quarter-century until he was captured and taken to Diriyya, where he died in 1794.[23] In one treatise, Sulaiman argued that Shaikh Muhammad cited Ibn Taimiyya as an authority but misunderstood his writings, in particular the distinction between greater and lesser forms of polytheism. Sulaiman and other clerics argued that the sorts of popular customs that Ibn Abd al-Wahhab condemned were instances of minor polytheism deserving blame but not excommunication.[24]

The authors of anti-Wahhabi treatises represented religious authority in old Najd, the centers of learning that had been destinations for religious pupils, repositories of religious knowledge and expertise. One of the common accusations against Shaikh Muhammad was that he was spreading ideas that no religious scholar supported: that is, he was breaking with established authority. In an epistle to one of his critics, he admitted as much, declaring that none of his teachers knew the meaning of the testimony of belief ("there is no god but God") and that he had arrived at a correct understanding independently through a divine blessing. In response to that claim, his critics accused him posing as a prophet.[25]

Early religious controversy over Shaikh Muhammad's teachings generated a repertoire of criticisms and an image of the "fanatical Wahhabi" that would endure. It was, after all, a rare moment in the history of Muslim societies for the Sunni tradition to produce a cleric who accused other Sunnis of unbelief. Some adversaries dedicated thick treatises to detailed explanations of Shaikh Muhammad's serious errors in his assertions about belief and unbelief. Other adversaries belittled his learning and invoked Prophetic traditions (the "horns of Satan") and episodes in early Islamic history that associated Najd with heresy (the "false prophet" Musailima). It was common to compare his followers to the Kharijites for their granting permission to shed Muslims' blood and seize their property. Ottoman religious scholars coined the term "Wahhabi" to indicate that they considered Ibn Abd al-Wahhab's teaching to be his personal, eccentric opinion, beyond the pale of the Sunni consensus, and they came to believe that Wahhabi teachings provided a religious pretext for Bedouin violence against townspeople.[26]

After two years of preaching in Uyaina, Ibn Abd al-Wahhab's enemies persuaded the Banu Khalid emir of Hasa to have his vassal, Emir Uthman ibn Muʿammar, either kill or expel Shaikh Muhammad. By this time in 1744, his mission had gained influential converts in Diriyya among members of the ruling Saud clan: two of the emir's brothers, and one of his wives, Mudi bint Abu Wahtan.[27] According to one Saudi chronicle, Mudi told her husband Muhammad ibn Saud, "This man was driven to you by God as booty to be laid hold of, so show him honor."[28] A detailed account of a compact between Muhammad ibn Saud and Shaikh Muhammad in one of the Saudi chronicles reports that the shaikh asked that the emir support his mission and that he forfeit the customary levies that oasis emirs collected because they were illegal under Islamic law. The shaikh promised that plunder from jihad would more than compensate for the levies. In turn, the emir asked the shaikh for steadfast support in the fight for the mission to establish monotheism. The earliest Saudi chronicle does not give this detail, and recent historians believe that the terms of the relationship unfolded over a number of years based on the concept that rulers heed the advice of clerics on correct Islamic governance.[29]

The Conquests

Shaikh Muhammad turned his haven into a base for spreading his mission, by word and by conquest. He devoted his first two years in Diriyya to preaching and composing epistles calling for the suppression of polytheism, rebutting defenders of the cult of saints, and defending himself against criticism. His expulsion from Huraimila and Uyaina taught him that he could not achieve his aim through persuasion. The military path was necessary to establish the abode of belief, according to his conception of monotheism. That path proved long and hard.

The Saudi conquests took sixty years to reach their greatest extent, with Diriyya holding sway over most of Arabia and launching raids against Ottoman Syria and Iraq by 1810. Overcoming resistance to the Wahhabi mission and Saudi authority hinged on Shaikh Muhammad's unwavering commitment to his doctrine, strategic patience, and a degree of unity in the Saud clan rarely seen in Najd. Persistent military pressure wore down resistance in one oasis settlement after another.[30] When a town entered the Saudi fold, its leaders declared allegiance to the Wahhabi mission. Diriyya sent preachers to spread the mission and to judge according to Islamic law, collect zakat (the religious tithe), and ensure communal performance of five daily prayers in mosques.[31] At times, chronic factionalism in ruling clans presented opportunities for alliances. It also posed threats against consolidating power when defeated factions plotted revolts that ended in massacres of allies and sympathetic clerics. Reconquest brought harsh punishment to the vanquished: confiscation of horses and weapons, seizure of date groves, and expulsion of entire clans.

Subjugating the Emirates of Southern Najd, 1746–73

It took nearly thirty years to conquer southern Najd, a line of oases stretching about 100 miles along Wadi Hanifa, from the districts of Sudair and Washm in the north to Riyadh in the south. The call to purify religion resonated in Wadi Hanifa oases, including Riyadh, a mere ten miles down the wadi, where the Saud–Wahhabi alliance encountered one of its most determined adversaries. The first military clashes erupted in 1746, after the emir of Riyadh, Dahham ibn Dawwas, punished residents who accepted Shaikh Muhammad's teachings.[32] Muhammad ibn Saud reacted by launching an attack against Riyadh and there ensued a series of raids and counterraids. Two of Ibn Saud's sons were killed defending Diriyya against

Dahham's forces. In 1746/7 alone, Riyadh and Diriyya fought half a dozen times.[33]

In the first decade of fighting, Shaikh Muhammad sought to bring Uyaina and Huraimila into the fold. In 1750, Uyaina's annexation was achieved in the fashion of oasis factional violence when residents supporting the mission assassinated the Mu'ammar emir in the main mosque. Shaikh Muhammad then hastened to Uyaina, and, without denouncing the murder, chose another member from the Mu'ammar clan to become the new emir.[34] The struggle for Huraimila pitted Shaikh Muhammad against his own brother, Shaikh Sulaiman, a critic of the Wahhabis for fighting fellow Muslims. In 1752, Shaikh Sulaiman led a faction that took over Huraimila. A Saudi expedition took the town three years later and forced Shaikh Sulaiman to flee.[35]

The struggle for power in southern Najd entangled outside forces. In 1764, the Ajman Bedouin tribe beckoned military support from the Ismaili Shiite leader of Najran, a fertile district more than 500 miles south of Diriyya. In the first encounter between the Najran leader and the Saudis, the latter suffered 500 dead. Diriyya's enemies then formed a larger coalition: Riyadh's Emir Dahham persuaded the Banu Khalid leader in Hasa to march against Diriyya, but coordinating forces from across Arabia proved too difficult. Before the Banu Khalid fighters arrived, the Najran forces returned south. Nevertheless, a coalition of Najdi factions under Banu Khalid command besieged Diriyya. The defenders held out for three weeks before their enemies retreated.[36]

Riyadh was the toughest obstacle to Diriyya's aspiration to subjugate neighboring towns. In the end, years of pressure wore down Emir Dahham. When two of his sons were killed in a skirmish in 1773, he decided to retreat 100 miles south to Dilam in the Kharj district. Many of Riyadh's townspeople evacuated the town as well, leaving it undefended. Saudi forces plundered it and returned with a large amount of booty for the treasury. Altogether, according to the chronicles, in the course of twenty-five years, the conflict cost Riyadh 2,300 lives and Diriyya 1,700 lives.[37]

Subjugating Qasim and Kharj, 1773–87

With the unification of the core region surrounding Diryya, the Saudi domain stretched 100 miles from north to south along the spine of the Tuwaiq Ridge, making it about the size of Lebanon. The next target for expansion was the district of Kharj, the site of ancient underground water channels. Dilam was the main town in the district and its leader, Emir Zaid ibn Zamil, resisted Diriyya's advance for a decade. In 1774–5, he tried forming a military coalition with the emir of Najran and the Banu Khalid of Hasa, but the anti-Saudi alliance stumbled on mistrust and weak coordination.[38] At one point, Emir Zaid retreated south, only to retake Dilam with the support of allies from the Murrah Bedouin tribe and several other towns. He died in battle against Saudi forces in 1783, and his clansmen fought over succession, leaving Dilam vulnerable to Saudi conquest at the end of 1785.[39]

To Diriyya's north, the Qasim district had a relatively rich agricultural sector, and its merchants played an important part in trans-Arabian trade. The two main towns, Buraida and Unaiza, suffered the typical factional rivalry. Buraida was the scene of intrigue between factions bidding for outside support from Diriyya and the Banu Khalid emir. The Saudis were able to cement control of the town in 1787 as a result of infighting among the Banu Khalid.[40]

Conquest of Hasa, 1785–93

The annexation of Qasim and Kharj completed the unification of Najd under the Diriyya emirate, whose military frontiers extended 600 miles from Jabal Shammar in the north to Wadi Dawasir in the south. New horizons for conquest lay east to Hasa, north to the Fertile Crescent, west to the holy cities, and south to Oman and the Persian Gulf.

Hasa was a tempting economic and strategic prize. It is Arabia's largest oasis. Cultivators tapped underground springs to irrigate date groves, orchards, and vegetable gardens. Merchants handled a lively export trade in locally woven woolen cloaks and a renowned breed of donkey. Hasa's location along the Persian Gulf made it a transit point for goods entering and leaving Najd, a suitable location for a ruler to station a tax collector to gather customs duties. Possession of Hasa would give Diriyya a strategic position to launch raids against Bahrain, Qatar, and Basra.[41]

Hasa's population was divided between Sunnis and Twelver Shiites, who shared close religious and cultural ties with coreligionists in Bahrain. The Shiite tradition developed from disagreements between early Muslims over the question of who should lead them after the Prophet. Some believed that leadership, represented by the office of the caliph, should be decided according to consensus. The consensus principle became the foundation for the tradition that became known as Sunni (people of tradition and community). Other Muslims believed that the Prophet had proclaimed that leadership belonged to his kinsman Ali and Ali's descendants, known to their followers as imams. This group became known as Shiites. Conflict between partisans of consensus (Sunnis) and descent from Ali (Shiites) took different forms: civil war in the seventh century; Shiite rebellion against caliphs in the eighth century; communal strife in the tenth century. In general, Sunni–Shiite conflict in Muslim societies has been intermittent and local, not continuous and general.

Branches in the Shiite tradition arose over disagreement on the identity of the imam: how would followers know which of two or more sons of the imam was the next one? The Twelver Shiite tradition evolved in Iraq in the late ninth and early tenth centuries among followers who believed that the twelfth imam went into hiding for safety from harm at the hands of the Sunni caliph and that God would have the twelfth imam return as a messianic figure to abolish tyranny and establish justice. In the imam's absence, Twelver Shiite clerics had the responsibility to preserve the teachings of the imams and to serve as his collective deputy to adjudicate according to their legal tradition and to receive religious alms for distribution to the community.

Before the Wahhabi mission, a denominational religious attitude prevailed in Hasa. Most Sunni theologians disapproved of the Twelver Shiite tradition but did not consider them infidels. Hasa's Shiites were accustomed to paying dues to Ottoman and Banu Khalid Sunnis. In Muhammad ibn Abd al-Wahhab's eyes, Twelver Shiites were idolaters. Sectarian enmity toward Twelver Shiism accounts for the more intense violence inflicted on Hasa's Shiites compared to the fighting in Najd and the conciliatory treatment of Sunnis in Hijaz.[42]

In the early 1700s, the Banu Khalid tribe dominated Hasa and asserted its sway over the oasis settlements of Najd. The first half-century of Saudi expansion was in part the story of a Najdi emirate contesting the Banu Khalid for supremacy. In the early days of Shaikh Muhammad's mission, it was the Banu Khalid leader who ordered the emir of Uyaina to kill or expel him. Diriyya's first major raid into Hasa in 1762/3 foreshadowed a pattern of merciless wrath against Shiites. The Saudi chronicles describe massacres in the Mubarraz oasis, where the raiders slaughtered seventy defenseless residents.[43] The conquest of Hasa came soon after the pacification of Najd. In 1789, a large Saudi force repeated the earlier raid's wantonness: hundreds of men in a village called Fudul sought refuge in a house, and when they were discovered, they were slaughtered. The following year, the Banu Khalid, the former masters of Najd, weakened by factional strife, were reduced to vassalage, leaving the region's large Shiite population subject to Wahhabi rule.[44]

The Holy Cities, the Fertile Crescent, and the Persian Gulf

The Wahhabi drive to wipe out polytheism was bound to make Mecca an object of conquest. After all, Mecca is the cradle of Islam, the Prophet grew up and started his mission there, and it is the geographical focal point for two of Islam's five pillars: when believers perform the five daily prayers, they face Mecca; and Muslims journey to Mecca to perform the pilgrimage. Throughout Islamic history, political control of the holy city lent prestige and legitimacy to a Muslim ruler. For the Saudis to add Mecca to their realm would boost their standing and give the Wahhabi mission a platform to proselytize to the annual influx of pilgrims.

In the Diriyya emirate's early years, its relations with Mecca had three facets: religious controversy; participation in the pilgrimage; and military conflict. Meccan religious scholars were some of the first to condemn Muhammad ibn Abd al-Wahhab's teachings: the muftis of the four Sunni legal traditions denounced his views in 1743, when he was still in Uyaina.[45] A few years later, in 1749, the sharif had a band of Wahhabi pilgrims thrown into prison for trying to spread Shaikh Muhammad's ideas; some of them perished there.[46] Contacts between Diriyya and the head of the Meccan religious estate, the sharif of Mecca, were sporadic. In 1771, Diriyya sent an official delegation to Mecca, including a Wahhabi cleric who debated Meccan scholars about theological issues dividing the sectarian mission from other Muslims: excommunication, erecting tombs over graves, and seeking the intercession of dead saints. Diriyya sent proselytizing missions in 1790 and 1796, but Meccan scholars refused to meet with Wahhabi counterparts.[47]

Military tensions between the sharif of Mecca and the Saudis escalated in a series of skirmishes in the late 1790s. Tribal leaders around Mecca and members of the sharif's clan were starting to jump on the Saudi bandwagon.[48] In 1803, Emir Abd al-Aziz (r. 1765–1803) ordered tribal allies to march on Ta'if and as the force gathered, the sharif withdrew from the town, leaving it defenseless. The account by a later Meccan chronicler conveys the assault's intense violence and informs the perception outsiders had of Saudi fanaticism and brutality:

> When they entered al-Ta'if, they killed people without discrimination: the old, the young, the servant, the nobleman, and the pauper. They slaughtered the suckling at its mother's breast and went up to

> the houses, bringing out and killing those in hiding. They found a group studying the Qur'an and killed them to the last man. They massacred all those [who remained] in their houses. Then they went and slaughtered everyone in the shops and mosques. They killed men in the mosque who were kneeling and prostrating [themselves in prayer] . . . The Bedouins would enter al-Ta'if every day to gather the booty and take it out. They plundered money, foundations and furniture . . . As for books, they tossed them in the alleyways and markets to be ravaged by the wind; among them were thousands of copies of the Qur'an, the [*Sahih*s] of Bukhari and Muslim, and other books of *hadith*, law, grammar, and many books on different sciences. They trampled on the books with their feet for days while no one dared to lift up a single page.[49]

In April, as pilgrims were celebrating the annual hajj, a band of Saudi warriors chased the sharif out of Mecca. The Wahhabis then imposed a new religious regime on the holy city. Attendance at prayer was compulsory. Domes over the graves of holy men were razed. Tobacco was banned. The first Saudi occupation of Mecca was brief. The invaders retreated in the face of a well-armed Ottoman relief force.

Plans to regain control over Mecca were delayed by the assassination of Emir Abd al-Aziz in November 1803. The assassin was either a Shiite seeking revenge for the Kerbala massacre (see below) or a Kurdish agent of the Ottoman governor of Baghdad. The late emir's son Saud succeeded, in accordance with Shaikh Muhammad's design fifteen years earlier. In 1805, Emir Saud led an expedition to conquer the holy cities. In the face of superior force, the sharif did not resist. Saudi forces took over Medina in late 1805 and Mecca in February 1806. The sharif became a vassal to Diriyya.[50] Control over the pilgrimage rested with the Saudis, who now collected the lucrative tax on pilgrims. Caravans arriving from Ottoman lands were turned away, but the Saudis did not interfere with pilgrims coming from Yemen, Africa, and India. At that moment, with Istanbul in turmoil, there was no Muslim power capable of displacing the Diriyya emirate's control over the holy cities.[51]

Hijaz was not the only weak point on the Ottoman frontier with Arabia. The Ottoman governors in Iraq relied on Bedouin allies to deal with the Saudi threat. In 1797 and 1798, the Ottomans joined with a Bedouin tribe in expeditions to dislodge the Saudis from Hasa, but both attempts failed.[52] A devastating lightning Saudi raid in 1802 revealed the Ottomans' inability to defend the frontier. The Shiite shrine town of Kerbala was a tempting target for Wahhabi warriors. The shrine contains the tomb of Imam Hussein, the Prophet's grandson and the martyr of an uprising against the Damascus caliph in 680. In Wahhabi eyes, Imam Hussein's shrine was a conspicuous expression of polytheism. In addition, the shrine held abundant treasures donated by Shiite rulers and merchants to honor the imam. The raiders massacred men, women, and children, and spent half the day looting the shrine. In the words of the Saudi chronicler:

> They killed most of its people in the markets and homes; they destroyed the tomb erected above the grave of al-Ḥusayn (as claimed by those who believe in it); they took what was inside and around the shrine; and they took the monument that was placed above the grave and studded with emeralds, rubies, and jewels. They took all the various possessions that they found in the place—weapons, vestments, household effects, gold, silver, heavy manuscripts, and other things—such that cannot be counted. They remained there only one morning, leaving with all the possessions before midday. 2,000 of its inhabitants were killed.[53]

The atrocities became part of collective Shiite memory and a cause of enmity toward Wahhabism throughout the Shiite world.

Diriyya extended its sway southward as well. In the 1790s, military expeditions to the lower Gulf encountered a fluid political situation, with two regional powers contending for supremacy: the Qasimi shaikhs at Ra's al-Khaima and the Al Bu Said sayyids at Muscat. From the Strait of Hormuz to Bahrain, they fought a maritime war for control over Gulf ports and islands that served as bases for military and commercial activity. The Saudis became embroiled in the rivalry as allies of the Qasimis. In doing so, they clashed with Muscat's ally, the British, who became entangled because the conflict threatened maritime commerce between India and the Gulf. Diriyya helped the Qasimi shaikh assemble a fleet to raid commercial vessels in the Gulf and the Indian Ocean that were trading with Muscat. A share of the loot seized from ships as far as Zanzibar made its way to Diriyya, now growing rich from maritime raids as it long had from attacks on Bedouin and caravans.[54]

Inside the Sectarian Empire

The Diriyya emirate transformed Najd's religious and political landscapes. It polarized townsmen and mobilized supporters for a protracted conflict that lasted a half-century. The demand to give allegiance to a sectarian idea and a ruling clan was a knife blade that divided the sedentary population and ended with purges, expulsions, and migration to Ottoman territory. In place of Najd's denominational religious life and polycentric political map, a combination of religious and political power became the framework for a unified regime. The framework, however, was never seamless: dissident clan factions laid low and bided their time for opportunities to break away; Bedouin tribes were fair-weather friends; and pockets of believers faithful to the denominational spirit persisted. Nevertheless, the Diriyya emirate did create a new historical situation, with Najd emerging as a regional power, integrated under the leadership of the Wahhabi mission and the Saud clan.

Shaikh Muhammad's goal of abolishing polytheism allowed for no gray zone. Religious scholars opposed to him were committed to the denominational outlook and they supported emirs who resisted

Saudi power. As their towns surrendered, they abandoned their homes to resettle in Iraq and Hijaz. Diriyya replaced them with men loyal to Shaikh Muhammad's sectarian doctrine. The judges, preachers, and teachers in Najd no longer looked to scholars in Ottoman lands as repositories of the authoritative scholastic tradition. Instead, they came from the ranks of pupils who studied under Shaikh Muhammad and his sons, who became the progenitors of a hereditary caste of religious authorities known as "the Shaikh's family," or Al al-Shaikh, and who served as guardians of the mission. The Wahhabi mission thus severed religious ties to historical centers of Sunni learning; it established a new center of religious authority—the Shaikh's family at Diriyya—and it invented a new canon, the works of Ibn Abd al-Wahhab.

His works did not, however, provide a blueprint for organizing a state. In fact, it is not clear that Shaikh Muhammad planned to direct an expansionist enterprise when he began his mission.[55] In its very early stages at Huraimila and Uyaina, before he moved to Diriyya, followers gave him an oath of allegiance, or *bay'a*, that signified conversion to his doctrine but not political allegiance, as is normally the case in the Sunni tradition. Strong opposition to his message made him realize that he needed a political patron, and in pragmatic fashion, he took it from any backer, first the Mu'ammar clan, then the Saud clan. Diriyya's emirs had no special claim to leadership before they offered a haven to Shaikh Muhammad. In return for political support, he elevated Muhammad ibn Saud above other emirs, putting a stamp of religious sanction on his authority to collect taxes and to wage expansionist warfare. The arrangement conformed to a common Sunni political model where the ruler takes advice from religious scholars, and as long as the ruler does not command believers to violate Islamic law, then believers owe the ruler obedience.[56] The acquisition of a political patron led to a change in the oath of allegiance to include Muhammad ibn Saud along with Shaikh Muhammad.[57]

Ibn Abd al-Wahhab's influence extended well beyond symbolic legitimation for the Diriyya emirate. It was he, not the Saudi emir, who declared offensive jihad in 1746.[58] He supervised the disbursement of zakat revenues and the allocation of plunder.[59] He also may have been responsible for managing relationships within the ruling clan, a perennial source of disruption in oasis politics. The Diriyya emirate had three smooth successions, in 1765, 1803, and 1814.[60] Shaikh Muhammad decided that Saud would succeed Abd al-Aziz (1718/19–1803).[61] After the conquest of Riyadh in 1773, the shaikh retired from most public affairs, and from that point, Saudi emirs took the reins. For example, Emir Abd al-Aziz and then his son Emir Saud (1748–1814) took over Shaikh Muhammad's role of sending letters inviting leaders to embrace the Wahhabi mission.[62] Furthermore, Emir Saud started using the title of imam, with the connotation of possessing religious legitimacy greater than an emir, the title used by the first two Saudi rulers. Later Saudi rulers continued to use the title of imam until the twentieth century, when Abd al-Aziz ibn Abd al-Rahman adopted the title of sultan.[63]

As the emirate expanded, it developed the same kinds of administrative, military, and fiscal mechanisms as other conquest regimes rooted in patrimonial courts. Diriyya built alliances with ruling clans and sometimes solidified them with marriage.[64] In some places, trusted lieutenants from Diriyya were dispatched to govern entire districts. Appointing someone from Diriyya had the advantage of sidestepping entanglement with local factionalism.[65] With expansion beyond the core districts of Wadi Hanifa, Diriyya's agents acted as regional viceroys possessing military and administrative authority.[66] Whether local emirs or deputies of Diriyya, agents of Saudi power performed a limited set of functions: collecting taxes, keeping order, mobilizing military forces, and supporting the mission.

Saudi military power depended in the first place on levies from oasis townsmen. There was an expectation that the emirs in every oasis settlement would dispatch fighters upon receiving the summons to wage jihad.[67] Bedouin seldom fought with Saudi forces before the subjugation of Qasim in the 1780s; then they became more frequent partners, drawn by the prospect of plunder. Indeed, Diriyya's military forays frequently had the purpose of amassing resources: weapons, livestock, and other goods. In 1759–61, for example, the Saudis mounted ten raiding expeditions to plunder towns in the districts of Washm, Kharj, and Sudair, as well as small Bedouin encampments.[68] Battlefield leadership rested in the hands of Saudi emirs. Abd al-Aziz and his son Saud demonstrated their qualifications for rulership by commanding men in combat on many occasions, proving they possessed courage and tactical judgment. Abd al-Aziz began leading expeditions when he was around thirty years old. Saud started to lead expeditions in his early twenties.

The Saudis were like other rulers in preindustrial societies who had three sources for revenue: taxation, plunder, and tribute. In much of the world, agricultural production was the largest and most stable source of revenue. That is why early kingdoms originated in river valleys where the supply of water for crops made possible regular taxation of the harvest. Commodities exchanged in long distance trade were also taxed. In addition to taxation, rulers went to war for plunder and to impose tribute on conquered territories.[69]

Najd's arid conditions posed a natural obstacle to accumulating much revenue from agricultural surplus. Plunder and tribute offered richer potential for ambitious emirs. According to one of the Saudi chronicles, Shaikh Muhammad persuaded Muhammad ibn Saud to stop collecting "illegal taxes," that is, taxes unsanctioned in Islamic law. The shaikh assured the emir that plunder from jihad would more than compensate for revenue from such taxes.[70] The sources do not give a breakdown for revenues from plunder and taxes, but accounts of plunder figure prominently in the Saudi chronicles, which enumerate the booty acquired in military expeditions, from lightning raids to mass mobilizations. Booty included livestock (camels, horses, sheep, goats), weapons, and assorted personal and household belongings.[71]

In addition to the spoils of war, the Sauds collected punitive indemnities from towns that resisted conquest and from rebellious towns.[72] When Dilam capitulated, Diriyya's treasury took possession of the town's palm groves and confiscated livestock, weapons, food stores, and belongings, then sold them back to the residents.[73] The chronicles mention collection of zakat, but there are no records that provide details on how much revenue was gathered. Each year, squads consisting of assessors and armed guards supervised zakat collection from townsmen, villagers, and Bedouin.[74] The scattered references on Diriyya's expenditure indicate that the lion's share went to the Saud clan and allied emirs. The treasury provided food for widows, orphans, and the poor, categories defined as recipients of charity in the Quran. Other treasury expenditures included religious instructors, hospitality to strangers, and maintaining mosques and wells.[75]

The most visible sign of the emirate's splendor was Diriyya's growth and the court's exhibition of wealth. The Saudi capital consisted of a string of settlements 5 miles long hugging the banks of Wadi Hanifa. At its height, its residents numbered around 13,000.[76] The palaces surpassed previous Najdi standards by covering customary mudbrick walls with stone coated with mud plaster for a smoother outward surface. The mudbrick and mortar used in buildings erected during the later decades were of higher quality than ordinary materials and made it possible to build tapered walls. The most notable structures were Emir Saud's four-story audience hall, the treasury, the royal mosque, and palaces of other members of the dynasty. A mosque named after Shaikh Muhammad's daughter Mudi stood out for its two-story columns.[77]

Descriptions of Diriyya date to Emir Saud's reign in the early 1800s, and therefore they reflect conditions at the emirate's height. Whatever simplicity or austerity prevailed in its early years had been jettisoned in favor of a court that ostentatiously displayed its wealth. Emir Saud's four wives were said to dress in fine Indian fabrics and to sport exquisite jewelry. The emir's retinue counted a small army of slaves, concubines, and servants. Honored guests attended feasts that offered heaping servings of rice, sheep, and camel. The emir and his sons maintained stables for pedigree horses seized in raids and collected as zakat from Bedouin subjects. The central treasury kept stores of gifts to shower visiting emirs and Bedouin shaikhs, and funds for the poor, equipping soldiers and stocking garrisons, and keeping mosques and wells in good repair.[78]

For centuries, Muslim dynasties sponsored court historians to set down the record of their achievements. Emir Abd al-Aziz appointed one of Shaikh Muhammad's students, Hussein ibn Ghannam (c.1739–1810), to chronicle the rise of Al Saud and the Wahhabi mission. Ibn Ghannam's works departed from the annalistic tradition of old Najd chronicles by imputing universal significance to events. He developed a version of Saudi history that likens believers in the Wahhabi mission to the early Muslim followers of the Prophet Muhammad: believers waging jihad against unbelievers, undertaking emigration (*hijra*) to the abode of belief, and suppressing apostate rebellions.[79] The stark difference between the spotty annals of old Najd and Ibn Ghannam's work points to Diriyya's ambition to occupy the central role in a normative narrative going back to the Prophet's career.[80]

The Diriyya emirate transformed political and religious conditions in Najd, but its effects on society and economy were marginal. When a Bedouin tribe embraced the Wahhabi mission and acknowledged Saudi authority, it had to perform correct worship, pay zakat, abandon tribal custom in favor of Islamic law, cease raids against other Bedouin and caravans, and stop collecting tolls on caravans. Entering Diriyya's fold in some instances meant sharing the bounty of a victorious expedition but it did not ensure steady loyalty. When a tribe renounced allegiance, Diriyya would dispatch a punitive attack. In general, Bedouin tribes' allegiance was conditional.[81] Wahhabi teachings may have had different, unintended effects on men and women because they abolished religious practices at shrines frequented by women and they banned amulets and charms that women used in healing customs. Furthermore, Wahhabi authorities corralled believers to the mosque, where women were allowed to attend the congregational Friday prayer, provided they remained in the back, separate from men. With other forms of worship banished, women found their options for religious observance severely limited.[82] The Diriyya emirate's effects on the economy varied. During phases of conquest, sieges dampened agricultural production by destroying date palm groves and hurt trade with raids on caravans. After the pacification of Najd, conditions were more secure. Clashes between oasis towns ended and Bedouin usually respected safe passage for caravans. Security may have favored growth in agriculture, livestock, and trade, but evidence for economic activity is patchy.[83]

Collision with Superior Powers

While the Diriyya emirate was imposing unitary rule over central Arabia and Hasa, adjacent regions were undergoing transformative changes that limited expansion. In the Persian Gulf, three tendencies intersected to produce an era of British domination. First, the East India Company strengthened its grip in the western Indian Ocean. Second, the British thwarted an attempt by the French to gain a foothold in the Arabian Sea. Third, naval conflict escalated between Arab powers in the Persian Gulf. The resolution of these trends was the decisive pacification of the Gulf through British naval strength.

Around the same time, European rivalries in the Mediterranean region spilled into the Red Sea and Hijaz. Napoleon Bonaparte led a French invasion of Egypt in 1798, aiming to disrupt Britain's communications with India. Three years later, the British lent support to the Ottoman empire's expedition to expel French forces from Egypt. Istanbul then looked to one of the expedition's military commanders to restore authority. The commander, Mehmet Ali, had the political guile and vision to make Cairo the scene of the Middle East's first experiment in adopting European advances in economic production, military organization, and administration. He also harbored the ambition to make Egypt the core of an empire straddling the Eastern Mediterranean and the Red Sea, including Hijaz. Conflict with the Saudis over control of Hijaz was unavoidable.

When the Saudis seized the holy cities, the Ottomans were too disorganized and weak to undertake an expedition to recapture them, so they turned to Mehmet Ali to deal with the upstart Arabian power. The pasha of Egypt appointed his son Tusun Pasha to command the expedition. In 1811, Egyptian forces came ashore at Yanbu, the Red Sea outlet for Medina. In the first military encounter, Saudi fighters thrashed Tusun's troops, who retreated in panic. Tusun prudently prepared for a second campaign by distributing funds to Bedouin tribes and Hijazi towns to ensure their cooperation. With his flanks secure, Tusun Pasha seized Medina in October 1812 and evicted the Saudis from Mecca in January 1813. The Saudis learned to avoid open field warfare, where they could not prevail against the pasha's artillery. Their strengths were ambushes and defensive sieges behind the dense walls of mudbrick forts impervious to shelling that afforded perches for showering gunfire on attacking forces. Familiarity with the terrain enabled the Saudis to whittle down invading troops searching for water sources. In one early battle, three-quarters of the 2,000-strong Ottoman force perished.[84]

The war produced an Arabian heroine, Ghalia, the widow of a Bedouin shaikh. She used her claim to her late husband's slave retainers, food stores, and horses to lead resistance to an Egyptian foray near Ta'if. Prior to hostilities, she sent a confident letter to the pasha threatening to rout his army. In a five-hour battle in January 1815, the pasha prevailed, and Ghalia retreated with the Saudi army south to Bisha for a last stand in Hijaz. Egyptian artillery scored a lucky direct hit on a command post, and the Saudi fighters, including Ghalia, retreated to Diriyya. With momentum turning against the Saudis, Bedouin tribesmen began to side with the Egyptians, but they lacked sufficient troops and the supplies to launch military operations in Najd. The Saudi side needed a respite from the fighting and agreed to a truce that included renouncing any claim to the holy cities and a declaration of loyalty to the sultan.[85]

During the truce, Emir Abdallah (r. 1814–18) punished emirs in Qasim who had not put up a fight and Bedouin tribes that went over to the Ottoman side. Back in Cairo, Mehmet Ali appointed his son Ibrahim Pasha commander in Arabia. He took two years to get ready for an invasion of Najd that showed he absorbed the hard lessons of Arabian warfare. He commanded troops better trained in siege warfare and better prepared to treat battle wounds. He continued Tusun Pasha's practice of paying Bedouin tribes for their support. Ibrahim's first target was al-Rass in the approaches to Qasim. The well-fortified town withstood the besieging army for three months before surrendering in October 1817. By year's end, Ibrahim had conquered Qasim. Bedouin shaikhs and the old Najdi ruling clans joined the Egyptian bandwagon as it advanced toward the Saudi capital and laid siege to Diriyya with a force of 5,600 infantry and 2,000 cavalry. The invaders arrived in April 1818 and Diriyya held out until early September. Emir Abdallah surrendered on September 11. Ibrahim Pasha sent him with other prisoners to Cairo, where Mehmet Ali granted a respectful audience before dispatching the Saudi emir to Istanbul, where the sultan had him beheaded in December 1818.[86]

It is easier to describe than explain the rise of Saudi power because the historical sources are so sparse, episodic, and partisan. We can trace the unfolding of religious controversy from its genesis, but the details of political and military events are recorded in hindsight by authors partial to the Saudi–Wahhabi cause. European travelers and consuls reported what they heard from their sources, but we seldom know who their sources were and where their sources got their information.[87] Nevertheless, historians have put forth explanations that emphasize different combinations of religious, social, and economic factors. In the context of the premodern Middle East, the Diriyya emirate's mingling of a religious movement with group solidarity, *ʿasabiyya*, roughly fits the historical sociology of the renowned fourteenth-century Arab historian Ibn Khaldun: "Small fragments of a following on a tribal name, sometimes on that of a religious figure, sometimes on that of a tribal shaykh—but all overlap and can combine to form a powerful enthusiasm given the right setting."[88]

One set of scholars considers Wahhabism a binding force that unified settled populations coping with chronic political violence.[89] Other scholars suggest that changes in trading patterns or the spread of firearms underpinned the Saudi conquests.[90] Whatever brought about the Diriyya emirate, it achieved historical transformation of Najd by mobilizing and integrating the sedentary population under a sectarian vision. In doing so, it devised a formula to end political fragmentation, cohere around a single center of power, dominate most of Arabia, and extend its sway in all directions. Unification did not encompass the Bedouin tribes, who remained independent into the twentieth century. The rise of Najd coincided with political shifts in adjacent lands, primarily the arrival of British power in the Gulf and the appearance of a modernizing Ottoman pasha in Cairo able to project power to the Red Sea. Together, the British and the Ottomans halted and reversed Saudi expansion. As a political matter, the defeat of the Diriyya emirate restored the status quo ante: Najd was on the fringes of empire, too remote and poor for the major powers to conquer, too fragmented to pose a threat.

3

The Riyadh Emirate
A Sectarian Enclave, 1821–91

At the end of 1818, Diriyya was in ruins, its political and religious leadership scattered between captivity in Cairo and distant Arabian confines as far as Ra's al-Khaima on the Gulf. The prospects for revival were dismal, and yet regional circumstances created an opening for reconstituting Saudi–Wahhabi power, albeit on a tenuous, reduced scale, with a new seat at Riyadh. The revived emirate's modest achievements commonly get short shrift in accounts of Saudi Arabian history, but it played an indispensable part in sustaining Saud power and entrenching Najd as a sectarian enclave.

The war with Mehmet Ali was part of the wider historical arena where the Ottoman and British empires encroached on Arabia, with two effects on Najd. First, they strengthened defenses against Najdi expansion and raids. In doing so, they reduced the resources a Najdi emirate might accumulate through plunder and tribute. Second, Najd had to rely more on its own resources to support political consolidation. Under conditions of political containment and predatory austerity, two modes of consolidation developed: a rump Saudi emirate in Riyadh based on southern Najd towns, sanctified by a religious estate in defensive posture; and a Rashidi emirate in Ha'il, based on tribal affiliation and security for townsmen. Both Riyadh and Ha'il negotiated with the imperial powers. Neither one solved the challenge of clan fission. Neither one succeeded at incorporating the prosperous Qasim district.

The Revival of Saudi Power at Riyadh, 1819–65

After destroying the Diriyya emirate, Mehmet Ali had no strategic reason to keep troops in Najd indefinitely, and his forces withdrew in summer 1819. In the struggle to fill the power vacuum, members of the Saud clan who had escaped the invasion returned to Diriyya and were poised to succeed; therefore Mehmet Ali sent an expedition to reoccupy Najd in fall 1820.[1] For the next four years, one Egyptian commander after another tried to tame the region with punitive measures. The Egyptians ordered Diriyya's residents to evacuate, with the promise of resettlement elsewhere, and then led them into an ambush where 230 men were massacred. There followed a reign of terror: destruction of palm groves, plunder of property, extortionate taxation, imprisonment, and execution.[2] Nevertheless, resistance did not wilt. Bedouin raiders harassed Egyptian supply columns, and hostility from townspeople kept the garrisons penned up in their strongholds. In 1823, a Saudi emir, Turki ibn Abdallah, rallied old allies to join a campaign against the Egyptians.[3] Rather than wage an endless fight in Najd, Mehmet Ali had his men negotiate safe passage. They left in summer 1824. With Diriyya in ruins, Turki made Riyadh his seat of power.[4]

During Emir Turki's ten-year reign (1824–34), he was able to consolidate power over core districts in Najd and in Hasa. His son Emir Faisal used Hasa as a base to exert military pressure on Bahrain. Saudi forces also gained control over the Buraimi oasis, which straddles routes to the Arabian Sea and the Gulf, making it a natural forward position for probes in both directions. The British thwarted efforts to subjugate their treaty partners in Trucial Oman and Muscat.[5] London's position in the Gulf and Mehmet Ali's grip on

Hijaz put hard limits on the Riyadh emirate's opportunities for expansion and plunder.

In Najd and Hasa, Emir Turki's rule rested on a consensus among oasis emirs and Bedouin shaikhs rather than universal obedience. His speech to a gathering of emirs and shaikhs indicates that material interest and fear of punishment, not political loyalty or religious conviction, bound them to Riyadh:

> "Verily, whenever my order reaches you, you are happy about it because you find something in it for yourselves. You are like those who watch a palm tree and rejoice when a strong wind blows because more [dates] fall. Now know that I shall not allow you to take anything from the people. He among you who commits injustice toward his flock, his punishment will not be dismissal but exile from the country." Then he said to the people, "If any amir oppresses you, inform me of it." Then the governor of Buraidah, ʿAbd al-ʿAziz ibn Muhammad ibn ʿAbd Allah ibn Hasan, stood up and said, "O Imam of the Muslims, be specific and not general, in your speech. If you have been angry at any one of us, tell him of his deeds." Then Turki said, "The speech refers only to you and those like you who believe that you possess these districts by your swords, while [actually] they were taken and subdued for you by the sword of Islam and because you agreed on an imam."[6]

If the Riyadh emirate's sinews were as tenuous as Turki's speech suggests, the Saud clan's cohesion was even weaker. For on May 9, 1834, a distant relative, Mushari ibn Abd al-Rahman, gunned the emir down as he left the palace mosque after Friday prayer. Three years before, the assassin had plotted against Turki and fled to Hijaz. Turki allowed him to return and paid the price for trusting his kinsman. Mushari immediately proclaimed himself ruler.[7]

Emir Faisal was leading a military expedition in Hasa when he got word of the assassination. In short order, Faisal marched to Riyadh, captured Mushari, and had him put to death. The assassination did not destabilize the emirate, but the outlook for the Riyadh emirate worsened when Mehmet Ali decided to add Najd to his empire, which by then included Syria. His plan was to install a young Saudi emir, Khalid ibn Abdallah, son of the last ruler of Diriyya. As Egyptian forces advanced in early 1837, Faisal retreated to Hasa and Khalid took over in Riyadh, essentially a puppet of Mehmet Ali's commander, Khurshid Pasha. Faisal did put up a fight, establishing a stronghold in Kharj that withstood siege for several months before he surrendered at the end of 1838 and went into exile in Egypt.[8]

At the beginning of 1839, it seemed possible that Mehmet Ali would annex much of Arabia. Khurshid Pasha eschewed the earlier occupation's harsh measures in favor of steps to improve the economy. To that end, he had experts conduct a survey of agriculture in lower Najd, Qasim, and Hasa.[9] He did not have enough time to see if a different strategy would placate the population. The Ottoman empire was able to gain the support of the British and the Habsburg empire to expel Mehmet Ali's forces from Syria and compel him to withdraw from Arabia. Emir Khalid lost a power struggle against a distant relation, Abdallah ibn Thunayan, and moved to Hijaz to retire on an Ottoman pension. Ibn Thunayan barely had time to consolidate his position before Emir Faisal reappeared in 1843 after escaping confinement in Egypt. Most of the central districts sided with him, and rather than resist, Ibn Thunayan surrendered.[10]

The two decades of Emir Faisal's "second reign" were the Riyadh emirate's most stable period. The main challenge to his authority came from the restless townsmen of Unaiza and Buraida in Qasim. He experimented with different approaches to managing them. He appointed emirs from local lineages, one of his brothers, and a notable from the Riyadh district, but the district's townspeople launched one uprising after another: in 1849, 1854, 1859, and 1862.[11] Factional strife within each town and rivalry between them put any sort of equilibrium beyond reach.

Faisal's efforts to expand in the Gulf collided with the British commitment to protect its treaty partners. Strife in Bahrain's ruling Khalifa lineage provided an opening to meddle and press for tribute, but British readiness to intervene spared the island a Saudi invasion on two occasions. In 1861, London decided to make a formal commitment to Bahrain's independence in a treaty known as the "Friendly Convention." Faisal understood the wisdom of respecting the superior power's insistence that he leave Bahrain alone.[12]

Events in the lower Gulf followed a similar pattern whereby Emir Faisal sought to either expand his domain or exact tribute from weak neighbors. The British shored up their clients and blocked Saudi expansion. In 1845, Faisal's commander in Buraimi raided Omani ports and demanded tribute. The British responded by sending gunboats to Muscat, whereupon the Saudis agreed on a modest tribute of 5,000 Maria Theresa (MT) dollars from the sultan of Oman. In the early 1850s, the Saudis again threatened Oman in an attempt to raise the amount of tribute to 60,000 MT dollars. The British intervened once again to shield their client, who agreed to pay 12,000 MT dollars. Saudi possession of Buraimi was contested by the shaikh of Abu Dhabi. Control over the oasis changed hands in the late 1840s and early 1850s, and opposing claims persisted into the twentieth century.[13]

Saudi Civil War, 1865–91

It took the Riyadh emirate just a few years after Faisal's death in 1865 to start unravelling, as clan strife and external challenges drained Riyadh's power. Faisal had designated his son Abdallah to succeed him, but another son, Emir Saud, revolted. In the first contest between Saudi brothers, Abdallah's forces defeated Saud, and the rebellious emir took refuge in Oman.[14] The sultan of Oman exploited Saudi dissension by withholding tribute and drove the Saudis out of Buraimi.[15] With strife at the center, the Saudi realm was beginning to fray at the edges.

In fall 1870, Saud mounted a new challenge. He recruited two powerful Bedouin tribes (the Murrah and Ajman) to help him seize control over Hasa, which he used as a base to build his strength to the point that Abdallah decided to leave Riyadh rather than face the coalition his brother had assembled. When Saud took charge in Riyadh, Abdallah resorted to a strategy that went against the grain of his clan's alliance with the Wahhabi mission: he summoned military assistance from the Ottoman governor of Basra, an official who represented polytheism from the perspective of Wahhabi doctrine. An Ottoman expedition seized Hasa, but did nothing else to help Abdallah. The dynastic war raged on, with Riyadh changing hands several times before Saud died of smallpox in January 1875. His death, however, did not end the fighting. Saud's three sons combined to fight Abdallah and his brother Abd al-Rahman.[16]

Protracted strife in the Saud clan presented an opportunity to a powerful vassal in northern Najd, Muhammad ibn Rashid (r. 1869–97), to expand his power at Riyadh's expense. Ibn Rashid's ancestors belonged to the Shammar tribe, whose members included nomadic and sedentary elements. The Diriyya emirate had conquered the Shammar's main oasis settlements by 1780, but never established a firm grip on the region, known as Jabal Shammar. While the Sauds were recovering from the Egyptian occupation, the Rashid clan established power in Ha'il under two brothers, Abdallah and Ubaid. Under their rule, Ha'il developed into hub for trade between Iraq and Hijaz, reviving the ancient route known as Zubaida's Road. To promote this route, the Rashidis created a police force to protect Ha'il's market. To draw wealthy Shiite merchants from southern Iraq, they established a reputation for religious tolerance, allowing tobacco and silk clothes, in contrast to Riyadh's exclusion of Shiites and its puritanical climate.[17]

The Rashidi emirate owed its strength to local support from Shammar tribal shaikhs and to friendly ties with Istanbul. To ensure the allegiance of the shaikhs, the Rashidi emirs paid them subsidies and performed regular displays of generosity with public feasts.

Maintaining strong relationships with Ottoman governors in Mecca, Medina, and Baghdad required occasional gifts in the form of outstanding Arabian horses; at times, the emirs paid annual tribute to the pashas of Damascus and Medina.[18]

During the Saudi civil war, Muhammad ibn Rashid took over Qasim, Sudair, and Washm. By 1887, he was in a position to determine the outcome of the Saudi civil war. He killed Saud's sons in battle and "invited" Abdallah to be his guest at Ha'il, essentially as an honored hostage. Two years later, Ibn Rashid permitted a very ill Abdallah to return to Riyadh. Three days after he got back in November 1889, he died. His brother Abd al-Rahman was now the leader of the Saud clan. He attempted to throw off Ibn Rashid's control by forming an alliance with anti-Rashid tribes and townsmen in Qasim. Muhammad ibn Rashid mobilized Shammar and tribal allies. In January 1891, the two sides fought the Battle of Mulaida. It was a catastrophic defeat for Abd al-Rahman and his allies. He and his family were forced to abandon Riyadh to the Rashidis and to go into exile. Saudi power vanished again.[19]

The Wahhabi Mission

The Egyptian invasion devastated the Wahhabi mission. Some clerics were killed in the fighting, others were put to death. Three of Shaikh Muhammad's sons were exiled to Cairo, where they perished. Some fled for their lives to Iraq and the Gulf. And yet, when Emir Turki secured his position in Riyadh, there were enough survivors to reconstitute the network of judges, teachers, and preachers. In 1825, the Egyptians allowed the most prominent member of Al al-Shaikh, Abd al-Rahman ibn Hasan, to return to Arabia. For the next forty years, he advised Saudi emirs and presided over the Wahhabi mission's revival and consolidation, appointing judges and teachers, and composing epistles against the mission's detractors. His descendants supplied religious leadership well into the twentieth century.[20]

Under the Diriyya emirate, the Wahhabi mission purged Najd of religious opponents, but traffic along pilgrim and merchant caravan routes left the region open to infiltration by men harboring the Ottoman denominational outlook. Riyadh's guardian shaikhs feared religious backsliding might overtake Najd, much like it had done in Muslim societies in earlier times. Political support from the Sauds made it possible to consolidate the mission as the distinctive religious orientation in Najd, based on three pillars: cohesive leadership, a scholastic estate shaped by the leadership, and mechanisms to exclude outside influences.[21]

The mission's leadership came from the descendants of Muhammad ibn Abd al-Wahhab, collectively known as Al al-Shaikh. In the Riyadh emirate, Shaikh Abd al-Rahman ibn Hasan, his descendants, and other branches of Al al-Shaikh had a tight grip on religious leadership, which lasted until the 1970s. In a society where kinship influenced relationships and status in both nomadic and settled spaces, the continuity of religious leadership in a single lineage bolstered its authority. Anchoring the mission's doctrine required a cadre of lieutenants to preach and teach it. Members of the provincial cadre typically spent time at Riyadh, much as Diriyya was the hub for ambitious religious pupils some decades before. Young men from the districts descended on Riyadh to attend lessons with one or another member of Al al-Shaikh to obtain a certificate (*ijaza*) attesting to mastery of the doctrine.[22]

To prevent contamination by outside religious influences, the mission's leadership excluded and censored dissident voices. This meant subjecting a prospective judge to close scrutiny because he spent ten years in Damascus where he studied with a scholar known for opposition to the mission.[23] It also meant examining the manuscript collection of a famous scholar when he died. Abd al-Rahman ibn Hasan inspected the contents of the deceased scholar's collection, where he found "harmful" treatises that criticized Wahhabi doctrine and removed them from circulation. Guarding against religious contamination depended on loyal agents throughout the realm. Lax vigilance gave religious opponents the opportunity to spread anti-Wahhabi ideas. During the early years of Faisal's restoration, a Sufi shaikh from Baghdad named Daud ibn Jirjis al-Naqshbandi visited Unaiza, and held religious lessons in which he disputed Wahhabi doctrine.[24] The religious leadership in Riyadh dispatched a letter rebuking Unaiza's townsmen for hosting Ibn Jirjis and demanded the names of the townsmen who invited the visitor to share with Emir Faisal, who had ordered that Ibn Jirjis be banished.[25]

Emir Faisal's inability to establish authority over Qasim had a parallel in the religious sphere. Remnants of the old Najdi religious tradition in accord with Sunni denominationalism persisted in Buraida and Unaiza under their independent-minded emirs. One indicator of religious nonconformity was the choice of religious pupils to pursue learning in Iraq or Hijaz rather than Riyadh. Unaiza in particular hosted a handful of clerics known for hostility toward the Wahhabi mission and for loyalty to the old Najdi spirit of pluralism.[26]

The clerics mostly succeeded at shielding the sectarian enclave against idolatry, but they were ineffective in the political arena. Wahhabi political doctrine assumes the presence of a ruler committed to the mission and capable of keeping order. During the Diriyya emirate, Wahhabi clerics did not confront the effects of prolonged clan strife ensuing from contested succession. As a matter of fact, Sunni political theory does not have a principle for succession, whether it be in a caliphate, a sultanate, or another form of authority. Consequently, the conflict between Abdallah and Saud that erupted after Emir Faisal died presented Wahhabi clerics with a question for which their doctrine had no answer. Their tendency was to pay allegiance to the ruler, no matter how he came to power.[27]

When Saud rebelled against Abdallah, the leading cleric, Shaikh Abd al-Rahman ibn Hasan, denounced him because Emir Faisal had named Abdallah his heir and the people had declared allegiance to him. When Abd al-Rahman died in 1869, his son Abd al-Latif followed him as head of the religious estate. He faced a test in 1870 when Saud forced Abdallah out of Riyadh. Even though Abd al-Latif had condemned Saud's rebellion, he now recognized Saud as the legitimate ruler on the grounds that Islam requires communal solidarity, which in turn depends on the presence of a legitimate ruler to whom believers owe obedience.[28]

Religious leaders faced a new dilemma when Abdallah regained power with support from the Ottoman empire. According to standard Islamic principles, Abdallah forfeited political legitimacy because he violated the rule against seeking assistance from idolaters, and in the Wahhabi view, the Ottomans were idolaters. Abd al-Latif adopted an uncompromising stand against Abdallah's alliance with the Ottomans, distributing epistles that condemned loyalty to infidels as a clear violation of divine law and charging Abdallah with apostasy for inviting infidels to Muslim lands. At that point, division in clerical ranks surfaced: a Wahhabi cleric justified Abdallah's cooperation with the Ottomans on the basis of exceptions to the prohibition against seeking assistance from idolaters.[29]

To steer the community of believers through civil war, Abd al-Latif sought firm mooring for communal solidarity, but Sunni political thought offered only expediency—whoever has the power to uphold religion is the legitimate ruler. In the end, he became a casualty of clan strife in late 1876. He had just ended the afternoon prayer in Riyadh when a Saudi pretender shot a rival in the mosque. He apparently suffered a heart attack and died a few days later.[30] In spite of his efforts, the civil war bared the poverty of Wahhabi political doctrine: in face of severe crisis, it failed.

While the Wahhabi clerics endured political and religious challenges in Najd, there were glimmers in the Muslim world of greater acceptance for their teachings. In a few Ottoman Arab cities, reformist religious scholars established common ground with the Wahhabi mission based on opposition to the cult of saints and interest in reviving the legacy of Ibn Taimiyya. A cluster of religious scholars in

Baghdad, Damascus, and Cairo dissented from Ottoman hostility toward the mission and developed the idea that Wahhabis belonged in the mainstream Sunni fold. These scholars maintained that the Wahhabis had an undeserved reputation based on fabrications about their beliefs; that the Wahhabis actually followed the Quran, the Sunna (the Prophetic Tradition), and the Sunni legal schools; and that they were merely upholding the Hanbali legal school.[31]

In South Asia too a religious current emerged that was in harmony with Wahhabi doctrine. The Ahli Hadith, or Hadith Folk, espoused a purification of religious beliefs and practices along lines similar to the Wahhabi mission, with strict condemnation of popular customs (visits to saints' tombs) they regarded as illegitimate innovations, intolerance toward other Muslims, and fascination with the writings of Ibn Taimiyya. Its clerics diverged from the Wahhabi mission on Islamic law. Whereas Wahhabis considered it legitimate to follow the four Sunni law schools, the Ahli Hadith insisted on disregarding them altogether and relying only on the Quran and the Sunna. Nevertheless, there was enough common ground for Ahli Hadith and Wahhabi scholars to correspond with each other, and for Wahhabis to travel to India to attend lesson circles with Ahli Hadith scholars, starting in the 1880s.[32]

The Riyadh Emirate

The Riyadh emirate took a pragmatic approach to exercising authority that replicated the Diriyya emirate's ways. In most places, it relied on district emirs from local ruling lineages, and to oversee strategic frontiers in Hasa and Buraimi, it appointed regional viceroys from loyal clans, continuing a practice from the late Diriyya period to appoint military commanders over frontier districts. Faisal appointed his cousin Ahmad al-Sudairi emir of Hasa oasis and Qatif. Sudairi and his son Turki later became emirs in Buraimi.[33] Some clans that were prominent in the Diriyya emirate's military and provincial leadership reappeared as pillars of the Riyadh emirate. Three men from the clan of Ibn Ufaisan served as military commanders and governors.[34] Former slaves and their descendants held important positions. Salim ibn Bilal al-Harq was commander of Diriyya's military expedition that annexed the Buraimi region and became its governor. His son Bilal ibn Salim had a distinguished career under the Riyadh emirate, as a military commander in Hasa and governor of Qatif.[35] During the second phase of Emir Faisal's rule (1843–65), he tended to replace local ruling lineages with patrimonial networks radiating from his entourage in Riyadh. This was the case in the southern districts of Kharj, Aflaj, and Wadi Dawasir.[36] Faisal's ability to install his men was a measure of his authority. In Qasim, where the ruling lineages of Unaiza and Buraida resisted subjugation, he experimented with different approaches. Placing Unaiza under his half-brother Jalwi ended in revolt and Jalwi's expulsion.[37] Faisal tried to govern Buraida with an ally from Manfuha, but that ended with an uprising as well.[38]

Relations between the Riyadh emirate and Bedouin tribes were highly variable. When Riyadh held firm control over core territories in southern Najd and Hasa, the Bedouin tended to respect its authority, although extracting taxes often required armed expeditions.[39] During the Egyptian occupation and the Saudi civil war, the Bedouin ignored Riyadh. In brief, the Bedouin did not feel attached to Saud authority.[40] Some tribes did embrace Wahhabi beliefs and practices, but most followed tribal custom instead of Islamic law.[41] From the perspective of sedentary Arabia, they were untamed. From their own perspective, they preserved their freedom.[42]

Assessments of the Riyadh emirate's population, revenues, and expenditures depend on a single report by Lewis Pelly, Britain's Political Resident in the Persian Gulf, who visited in 1865.[43] He put the ratio of settled population to Bedouin at five to one (115,000 to 20,000), with commensurate contributions to the treasury (692,000 MT dollars to 114,000 MT dollars).[44] Roughly half the revenue came from Hasa (400,000 MT dollars).[45] Four tribes accounted for half the revenue from Bedouin.[46] Sources of revenue included a transit fee charged to pilgrims and the canonical zakat levied on livestock, harvests, trade, and gold and silver holdings.[47] Local tax collectors gathered revenue from settled areas, and roving teams taxed Bedouin tribes, gathering horses and livestock. In return, Bedouin chiefs received robes of honor.[48] Altogether, taxation yielded around 810,000 MT dollars and Riyadh exacted another 20,000 MT dollars in tribute from Bahrain, the Trucial shaikhs, Muscat, and Jabal Shammar. Pelly estimated pilgrim fees could have been as high as 2 million MT dollars. Emir Faisal believed it possible to increase agricultural production using mechanical pumps and arranged with Pelly to have some imported, but Faisal died a few months later, and the import of pumps did not materialize for nearly eighty more years. Faisal may have been the first Saudi leader to envision a future where the Bedouin settled and improvement in water management could lead to a more prosperous agrarian economy.[49] Pelly's rough estimate of expenditures divided them into one-quarter for the royal family, one-quarter for allowances to governors, clerks, religious officials, and charity, and half for military costs.[50]

Military expeditions served different purposes: to conquer, to exact tribute, to suppress revolts, and to punish Bedouin raids. Oasis settlements and Bedouin tribes supplied fighters and animals (horses and camels) to join expeditions when called upon. Fighters received a share of booty, divided according to Islamic law, one-fifth for the treasury, the remainder for fighters. The only permanent armed units were the emir's personal retinue, estimated to number 200, and two garrisons posted to Hofuf and Buraimi, which were costly to maintain.[51]

History and Nabati Poetry

The Riyadh emirate kept alive the impulse to memorialize the Saudi venture in history writing. Hamad ibn La'bun (c.1767–1844) had served the Diriyya emirate in its later years as a tax collector and acted as an imam under the Riyadh emirate. His chronicle added a new wrinkle by incorporating material from the pre-Saudi chronicles. The major historical work from the Riyadh emirate is *The Sign of Glory in the History of Najd* by Uthman ibn Bishr (1795–1873). In 1835, he completed the first volume of his chronicle that concludes in 1821, on the eve of the Riyadh emirate's revival. At some point, he joined Emir Faisal's court and under his patronage composed the second volume that ends in 1850, completing it in 1854. In his work, he emphasized how Saudi rule brought order and security in contrast to Ibn Ghannam's focus on the Wahhabi mission.[52]

The persistence of old Najdi political patterns had a cultural counterpart in the realm of Nabati poetry and celebration of the warrior ethos exalting the heroic knight boasting triumphs over enemies. One renowned warrior-poet was Ubaid al-Rashid, brother of the emir of Ha'il. According to a western visitor to Ha'il in the late 1870s, Ubaid's ode commemorating his tribe's triumph over the townsmen of Qasim in 1841 was still on men's lips:

> We, the settlers and nomads of Jabal Shammar, advance in two columns, encouraged by fair maidens with long black locks.
> We came to the field in the morning and found the enemy ready for a fight. The smoke of our gunpowder veiled the skies above.
> We thank our lord, the Almighty, the Just; the Qasimis and the sons of Wayil [of the Anazah tribe] were routed.
> My gallant comrades quenched the thirst of their sharp swords.
> The hard ground of Bagʿa flowed with the blood of our enemies.
> We follow our shaikh Abu Mitʿib; he is the feast of the hungry, the spring of the poor, the protector of the weak.
> As for me, ninety of the enemy I slew with the edge of my sword, and I fear not those who yearn to avenge them.[53]

When Unaiza's Emir Abdallah ibn Salim retaliated against caravans and villages in Ha'il's orbit, Ubaid responded with verbal shrug, followed by bravado and barbed taunts insulting his foe's manliness:

So what, Ibn Slem, if you attack our outlying settlements? Such bluff and pretense will not be to your advantage.
When we attack, we slay our enemies by the thousands, and our loot is thoroughbred mares.
When we attack, we attack the seat of the chief, and not the outlying villages; our war drums have been sounded in many a shaikhly camp.
Were we to hear a cry for help coming from the top of a high knoll, our sorties would come through any mountain pass to give assistance.
We drench our swords in enemy blood in defense of our country, riding our shod mares.
Do not let the blind amir of Buraidah lead you astray; and do not be deluded by the war dances of butchers in the market of your town.
Your brother was thrown from his horse in the battlefield; he was slain by those who perfume their swords with the blood of their enemies.
If you want my advice, keep to your trade, and count your coins and small change.
Work for the price of a bed for your pretty wife, and sleep with her; and perfume yourself with the smoke of incense burners.[54]

Late Ottoman Arabia

The withdrawal of Mehmet Ali's forces from Hijaz in 1840 paved the way for the restoration of Ottoman authority at the dawn of the Tanzimat era, when Istanbul adopted measures to strengthen control over population, territory, and resources. In the late 1800s, the wave of Ottoman reform reached Hasa and Hijaz, introducing mechanisms of modern governance, albeit incrementally, in a fashion that deepened the differences between conditions there and in Najd. New institutions spread gradually from the center to the provinces.

Administrative bodies such as councils for municipal affairs and education appeared in Istanbul and nearby towns in the 1840s, but they did not come to Hijaz until the 1880s.[55] Education reform arrived in the 1870s and 1880s with the first public schools. The official imperial education agenda dovetailed with the outlook of Jeddah merchants and donors from India who funded private schools offering curricula that blended religious and modern topics. In 1883, the government imported Mecca's first printing press and published works in Ottoman Turkish, Arabic, and Malay.[56]

Jeddah was the main commercial port for Hijaz, an outpost of the Red Sea–Indian Ocean world of maritime trade.[57] Its merchants supported Ottoman political authority by lending funds to pay for military expeditions. Mecca's prestige in the entire Muslim world made it the political and symbolic center of Hijaz and the natural location for Ottoman government headquarters. Istanbul rotated governors every two to three years, and consequently they wielded less influence than the local religious aristocracy: the sharifian families recognized for descent from the Prophet. They held leading roles in the economy, law, and public safety, but their division into factions gave Ottoman governors leverage to favor one or another contender for the post of emir of Mecca.[58] The sharifian clans owned some of the only productive agricultural lands in Mecca's vicinity in Wadi Fatima and around Ta'if. The sharif controlled the storage and distribution of food supplies that came from Cairo and Istanbul. He had sway over markets with power to appoint the market inspector and the heads of guilds. In addition, he commanded a small armed retinue of slaves, retainers, and clansmen. Notwithstanding their extensive influence, the Meccan sharifs, and Hijazi townsmen in general, depended on the Ottomans to compensate for the province's perennial food deficit by ensuring delivery of stocks, primarily from Egypt. In addition, the Ottomans paid allowances for staff at the holy places and managed endowments to keep religious sites in good repair. Together the governor and the sharif bore responsibility for ensuring safe passage of pilgrim caravans through Bedouin domains. The organization of the pilgrimage was a complex operation and the occasion for Bedouin and townsmen to profit. Pilgrims hired Bedouin guides and rented camels for the journey. Meccans leased rooms in their homes, supplied food, and sold sacred souvenirs.[59]

The holy cities formed the hub of the Muslim world, a symbol of unity, where pilgrims and sojourners from distant lands assembled to mingle, to share inspirational moments of worship, and to enrich their spiritual repertoires. For some, it meant coming to believe that customs at home represented departures from canonical practices. For others, it meant augmenting customs with prayers and rituals introduced by pilgrims from other lands. The Ottomans upheld a denominational climate in matters of Islamic law and worship. The Hanafi legal tradition was the official one throughout the empire, but the other Sunni legal traditions were respected. Ottoman authorities had a laissez-faire attitude toward Sufi brotherhoods. More than twenty Sufi brotherhoods linked the holy cities to the far reaches of the Muslim world: Southeast Asia, India, Africa, and central Ottoman lands. The numerous Sufi lodges were physical expressions of the brotherhoods' diversity and influence.[60]

The return of Ottoman authority to Hasa in 1871 coincided with Istanbul's revision of provincial institutions framed in the 1864 "Vilayet Law." The new template for a province was to establish a governor at a capital, to post officials answerable to the governor at district centers, and to set up local councils to handle administrative tasks. The Ottomans chose Hofuf to serve as the provincial capital and they designated Qatif and Mubarraz as district centers. At first, Istanbul appointed imperial officials with experience in other Arab provinces to collaborate with local notables to keep order and collect taxes. In Hofuf and Mubarraz, Shiite landowners and merchants served as district officials and members of an agricultural council responsible for tax assessment and collection. Their counterparts in Qatif held posts as members of a Civil Administrative Council. The

Ottomans set up a chief religious court that adjudicated according to Hanafi law at the same time allowing other schools of law, Sunni and Shiite, to adjudicate for believers adhering to them.[61]

While Istanbul gave official support to Sunni traditions, Hasa's Shiite religious institutions persisted. In Qatif, Shiites comprised a large majority of the population and made up the landowning and merchant elite. By contrast, in the Hasa oasis, the population was about evenly divided between Shiites and Sunnis, and the Sunnis were the major landowners. The material basis for Shiite religious institutions was twofold: income from endowed agricultural lands and the religious tithe (*khums*) paid to clerics. The income from these sources paid for ceremonial halls (*husainiyas*) for religious gatherings.[62]

Shiism in eastern Arabia was not a monolithic tradition and it did not wholly conform to Shiite traditions in Iran and Iraq, where the Usuli tradition held a dominant position in the seminaries and mosques. Qatif was the major center for the Usuli tradition in eastern Arabia. Elsewhere the Akhbari scholastic tradition had a foothold in the village of Awwamiya. In addition, Hasa was the birthplace of the Shaikhi scholastic tradition, which had arisen in the early 1800s and gained a following in Iraq and Kuwait.[63] The Shaikhis continued to have a following in Hofuf and Mubarraz, where they had a mosque, a school, and a husainiya, funded by a wealthy Shiite merchant of Qatif, Mansur ibn Jumʿa.[64]

The division of eastern Arabia's Shiites between scholastic traditions reflected starkly different conceptions of clerical authority. According to the Usuli tradition, legal scholars possessed the authority to use personal interpretation in order to arrive at legal rulings, and lay believers had a religious duty to follow the rulings of legal scholars. By contrast, the Shaikhi tradition denied the validity of personal interpretation and assigned authority to clerics endowed with mystical inspiration from the Hidden Imam. In secular terms, the scholastic schism mattered when it came to forming networks of clerical authority. The Usuli clerics of Iran and Iraq would not have any sway with Shaikhi clerics and their flocks in eastern Arabia. A fragmented scholastic tradition hindered the formation of a unified Shiite community in the Gulf region.

The Diriyya emirate's integration of southern Najd's oasis towns paved the way for the Saud clan to reestablish power at Riyadh. The townsfolk in Qasim and Hasa seldom paid ready allegiance. Instead, we find submission under compulsion in Hasa and tensions with Qasim's internally divided towns. The emirate's lieutenants in Buraimi were able to collect only grudging tribute from Oman. The Rashidis of Jabal Shammar accorded recognition to Saudi authority with regular military support but did not pay taxes or tribute. The upshot was a sectarian enclave vulnerable to rebellious vassals and under pressure from external powers, at times compelled to acknowledge British and Ottoman supremacy in the respective spheres. Such acknowledgment marked an end to the Diriyya emirate's hostile stance toward the outside world as a realm of idolatry and the beginning of Saudi Arabia's integration into the international political system, a very slight opening to the outside world.

4

The Opening of Najd, 1902–32

The first two Saudi emirates relied on the material and symbolic resources of Najd. The third phase of Saudi power added external resources and foreign strategy to secure its position. At the turn of the twentieth century, the Saud clan was in exile in Kuwait and political conditions in the Gulf were in flux in the midst of a contest for power and influence between local shaikhs, the Ottomans, and the British. From the many stratagems Arab shaikhs used, the shaikh of Qatar hit on one that worked for others, including the Sauds.

In 1893, the Ottoman governor of Basra attempted to push Istanbul's authority down the Gulf coast and install a garrison at Doha as part of the empire's efforts to strengthen its frontiers. The shaikh of Qatar, Qasim ibn Thani, used the peninsula's hostile terrain to exhaust the small detachment. The Ottoman pasha agreed to withdraw the garrison in exchange for Shaikh Qasim recognizing the sultan's authority and adopting a nominal appointment as district governor (*qa'im-maqam*). A future ruler of Kuwait, Mubarak al-Sabah, accompanied the abortive Ottoman expedition and witnessed how well Shaikh Qasim played a weak hand. Mubarak adopted similar tactics to establish Kuwait's autonomy a few years later. In Kuwait, a young Saudi emir, Abd al-Aziz ibn Abd al-Rahman, may have absorbed the ways of the clever Gulf shaikhs who used geographical distance to negotiate with Istanbul.[1]

The revival of Saudi power took place in two stages. In the first stage, Emir Abd al-Aziz reenacted Emir Turki's establishment of the Riyadh emirate: he gained control of the clan's old seat of power and revived the alliance of southern Najdi oasis settlements. Next, through persistence and adroit tribal diplomacy, he gained control over Qasim. Then he exploited the fortuitous preoccupation of the Ottomans with crises closer to Istanbul to seize Hasa. In little more than a decade, he ruled a domain that largely corresponded to Emir Turki and Emir Faisal's emirate.

In the second stage, Abd al-Aziz conquered the Rashidi emirate at Ha'il, the Hashemite Kingdom of Hijaz, and autonomous emirates in Asir. To achieve these gains, he innovated to gather additional assets for expansion. First, he mobilized Bedouin tribesmen who joined a new movement, the Brethren, that settled nomads in agricultural colonies, embraced Wahhabi doctrine, and waged jihad. Second, he formed an alliance with Great Britain that provided strategic protection, funds, and weapons. In order to manage the first Saudi alliance with a Western power, Abd al-Aziz relied on foreign Arab advisers versed in Western languages, politics, and diplomacy.

Sectarian mobilization of Bedouin tribesmen, borrowing the Gulf emirate strategy of allying with Britain, and importing foreign Arab expertise, provided the means to defeat Arabian rivals. It proved impossible, however, to move from military expansion to political consolidation without resolving the contradiction between sectarian mobilization and alliance with "infidel" Christians and "idolatrous" Arabs.

Expansion: Phase One

Ten years after the Sauds surrendered Riyadh to the Rashidi emirate, Abd al-Aziz led a band of fighters to raid Rashidi tribal allies in southern Najd. His forays turned out to be the start of the second revival of Saud power. On January 15, 1902, he led a surprise attack on Riyadh and regained the seat of the Saudi emirate. When his father Emir Abd al-Rahman came from Kuwait a few months later, he named Abd al-Aziz the new leader of the Sauds.[2] Their perennial allies in the Tuwaiq Ridge oasis towns helped expel Rashidi allies and in short order the towns of Sudair and Washm were back in the Saudi orbit.

Gaining control over Qasim was the next step in expansion. The four-year struggle over the region involved multiple adversaries: factions in the main towns, the Rashidis, and the Ottomans. In spring 1904, Abd al-Aziz plotted with local factions to seize Unaiza and Buraida, but Istanbul was not ready to concede the hub of central Arabian trade and sent an expedition to regain Buraida.[3] The conflict over Qasim turned into a stalemate, and the two sides worked out a *modus vivendi* in talks between Emir Abd al-Rahman and Ottoman officials in Basra.[4] Istanbul recognized him as the district governor (*qa'im maqam*) of Najd and paid him a monthly stipend provided he agreed to station a garrison of imperial troops in Buraida. Abd al-Aziz considered the arrangement a temporary convenience and waited for the hardships of occupation to have their effects: disease took a toll on troops and Bedouin raids on supply lines whittled down Istanbul's willingness to send reinforcements. Abd al-Aziz bolstered his forces and rather than directly confront Ottoman forces—after all, he was officially a provincial deputy to Istanbul—he attacked the sultan's ally, the Rashidis. In a battle in April 1906, the Rashidi emir got separated from his forces and landed in the midst of Saudi fighters, who cut him down. Abd al-Aziz then seized control in Buraida and, without consulting Istanbul, appointed a local ally to govern the town. By this point, the Ottomans had exhausted their capacity to provision and rotate troops. They agreed to an orderly withdrawal.[5] Shortly, Qasim's propensity to buck outside rule resurfaced. The Buraida emir threw off allegiance to Abd al-Aziz and joined forces with a powerful shaikh from the Mutair tribe, Faisal al-Duwish, to assert his independence of Riyadh. Abd al-Aziz defeated them on the battlefield in September 1907 and overwhelmed the last resistance from Buraida townsmen to his rule some months later.[6]

To regain Riyadh and nearby districts, Abd al-Aziz relied on the same resources and tactics as his ancestors. He and his father added to the political repertoire willingness to enter the Ottoman fold, in the manner of Emir Abdallah in 1870, and of Arab warlords elsewhere. The annexation of Qasim brought two benefits to Abd al-Aziz. First, the region's caravan trade bolstered revenues. Second, it gave him strategic depth against the Rashidi emirate. Nevertheless, his position was vulnerable, with the Ottomans in possession of Hasa and Hijaz, while British power blocked expansion toward the lower Gulf.

Abd al-Aziz believed that he needed British backing if he were to drive the Ottomans from Hasa. In 1903, he sent an emissary to the British agent in Bahrain[7] to find out if the British would block an Ottoman expedition to expel him. The British turned away his overture and a second probe three years later. In 1911, Abd al-Aziz held his first meeting with a British official, Captain William Shakespear, the political agent in Kuwait. He pledged to respect the integrity of Gulf shaikhdoms under British protection if the British promised to protect him from an Ottoman effort to regain Hasa. At that time, London wanted to avoid provoking Istanbul, so the talks did not lead to a treaty, but they framed the contours of such a treaty four years later.[8]

Conditions for a Saudi takeover ripened in 1911–12, with unrest mounting in Hasa's towns and Bedouin raids on caravan trade while Istanbul was occupied with one military emergency after another. In October 1911, Italy invaded Ottoman Tripoli (Libya). In October 1912, Balkan states attacked and threatened the imperial capital.[9] Istanbul redeployed imperial forces to defend against European enemies and recalled troops from Baghdad, Basra, and Hofuf, leaving its Gulf possessions weakly defended. The Hasa garrison shrank from

2,000 men in 1900 to about 400 men. In March 1913, Abd al-Aziz met again with Captain Shakespear and this time he got the impression that the British would not oppose a move into Hasa. On May 4, 1913, Abd al-Aziz led an 8,000-man force against the fortress at Hofuf. The outnumbered Ottoman defenders negotiated a surrender and evacuation. Eleven days later, Abd al-Aziz seized the ports of Qatif and Uqair.[10]

For the region's Shiite majority, the prospect of Saudi annexation was unnerving. In early 1913, Shiite notables contacted British officials in Bahrain to request protection. After the Saudi takeover, they again sought protection, claiming they were Bahrainis, sharing the same culture and enterprises in pearling as islanders. The British, however, would not alter their long-standing policy of refraining from asserting influence beyond the treaty shaikhdoms. With little chance for successful armed resistance, opponents to Saudi rule departed: several hundred Shiites migrated to Bahrain and Iraq. A wealthy pearl merchant who urged the Ottomans to return was executed. Other traders hoped that Abd al-Aziz would prove more effective than the Ottomans at containing Bedouin raids.[11]

The fall of Hasa coincided with the conclusion of protracted talks between Istanbul and London on the political status of the Arabian shore. The imperial powers signed a draft treaty two days after Abd al-Aziz began his march on Hasa (May 6, 1913) whereby Istanbul relinquished claims to Bahrain and Qatar, Kuwait was defined as an autonomous Ottoman district, and Britain recognized Hasa as an Ottoman possession.[12] The lightning Saudi invasion would have rendered the treaty's provision about Hasa irrelevant if Abd al-Aziz had not proclaimed loyalty to Istanbul and offered to serve the sultan as his governor. The Ottomans knew better and threatened to reoccupy the district. Abd al-Aziz reached out to British officials to renew his bid to join their network of protected rulers, but London was not willing to alienate Istanbul for his sake. In order to secure his position, then, Abd al-Aziz made an agreement with Istanbul in May

1914 whereby he became the hereditary governor. For the time being, he would fly the Ottoman flag, use Ottoman mail, and apply Ottoman customs regulations.[13]

Abd al-Aziz still had to deal with Ottoman vassals in Ha'il and Mecca who posed threats to his grip on Qasim. As long as he had to rely on resources at hand, his position was precarious. In the next few years, he innovated in two critical ways to amplify his power. He leveraged external resources by forming an alliance with Britain, firmly attaching his dynasty's fortunes to the Western powers. He also leveraged internal resources, mobilizing Bedouin tribesmen in a novel movement that had them settle in colonies, converted them to the Wahhabi mission, and recruited them for battle. These steps helped him get through the years of the First World War, put him in a position to defeat his Arabian rivals, and transformed the political landscape by using an external power to augment the authority of a sedentary ruler enough to end, once and for all, Bedouin autonomy.

A Treaty with London

In December 1914, Captain Shakespear met Abd al-Aziz in northern Najd, where he was leading an expedition against the Rashidis. The Ottoman sultan had recently declared war against Britain, and Shakespear was dispatched to persuade the Saudi leader to join British forces fighting pro-Ottoman tribes in Iraq. A treaty with London seemed to be within reach that would place Abd al-Aziz in London's network of protected Arabian rulers if he agreed to have no dealings with any other foreign power. Before Shakespear could report to headquarters in Basra, he was killed in a battle between Saudi and Rashidi forces, leaving Anglo-Saudi relations in limbo.[14] Abd al-Aziz could have used British assistance to deal with the serious threat to his rule in Hasa from Bedouin tribes. The Ajman and Murrah tribes refused to pay taxes to the Ottomans, and they proved unwilling to submit to Riyadh. At a battle in June 1915, some 20 miles west of Hofuf, the Ajman shredded a Saudi force, injuring Abd al-Aziz and killing his brother Saad. He retreated to Hofuf to recover from his wounds while the Ajman raided nearby oases.[15] At this low stage of his fortunes, Abd al-Aziz reached agreement with the British on terms for a treaty, signed at a meeting with Percy Cox on Darin Island, off the coast of Qatif, in December 1915.[16] Britain recognized Abd al-Aziz as the ruler of Najd and Hasa and promised it would prevent an attack against his territory by land or by sea. Abd al-Aziz agreed to respect Britain's protected Gulf shaikhdoms.[17] The treaty also committed him to refrain from contact with foreign powers, from granting concessions to foreigners, and from selling or leasing any territory. Cox agreed to assist Abd al-Aziz against the Ajman by supplying arms (1,000 rifles) and money (£20,000).[18]

The treaty marked a new departure for the Sauds: formal integration with the Western-dominated global political order in a way that foreshadowed future relationships with Western powers, where neither party was completely satisfied with the other. London wanted Abd al-Aziz to strengthen an anti-Ottoman coalition that included Sharif Hussein, while Abd al-Aziz wanted Britain to fortify his position against Arabian rivals that included the pro-British sharif and the pro-Ottoman Rashidis. The British, however, believed their defense obligation applied only to non-Arabian powers.[19] In a bid to bolster Abd al-Aziz's military capacity against the Ottomans, Percy Cox met him at Uqair in November 1916. Cox promised arms and a £5,000 monthly payment in return for the Saudis posting a force of 4,000 men in Qasim as a strongpoint against potential Rashidi maneuvers against Hijaz or Mesopotamia.[20] The monthly allowance, which London paid until March 1924, was a substantial addition to his treasury, estimated at the time to collect £100,000 annually.[21] Yet the amount paled in comparison to Sharif Hussein's £200,000 monthly allowance.[22]

The Brethren Movement[23]

Alliance with London was a new twist in Saudi strategy that marked a departure from the Wahhabi principle of bearing enmity to infidels. As such, it clashed with a second new twist in Saudi strategy that turned Bedouin into warriors for jihad. The religious mobilization of Bedouin worked up to a point and then it foundered for a few reasons. First, the neophytes took the sectarian outlook too far, even by Wahhabi standards. Second, they did not respect customary limits on waging jihad. Third, their pursuit of agriculture proved insufficient for subsistence, so they relapsed to raiding. Fourth, their settlement in colonies and conversion to the mission did not translate into obedience to the ruler and respect for his agreements to adhere to borders. The experiment was a success in harnessing Bedouin to military conquest, but a failure in yoking them to a sedentary political authority. When they rose in revolt, Abd al-Aziz crushed them.[24]

In 1913, a Baghdad publication reported the establishment of an agricultural colony populated by Mutair and Harb tribesmen.[25] In the next decade, Bedouin tribesmen settled more than 100 colonies, known as hijras, the Arabic term for both emigration and a place where emigrants settle. In the history of Islam, the original hijra was the relocation of the Prophet and the believers from Mecca to Medina in 622. During the Riyadh emirate, Wahhabi authors encouraged true believers to flock to their realm, the land of belief, for according to a Prophetic tradition, emigration will not cease until repentance ceases, and repentance will not cease until the sun rises in the west.[26] The Brethren movement represented migration from ignorance to true belief imparted by Wahhabi instructors in the colonies.

To help former Bedouin take up farming, Abd al-Aziz allocated land, seed, and equipment, but the perennial challenges of Najdi agriculture meant that the colonists frequently depended on subsidies.[27] It became customary for the emirs of the colonies to descend on Riyadh to collect payments for the settled tribesmen. Rank-and-file fighters received annual payment and were eligible for funds to cover weddings, house construction, food, and livestock.[28] The Brethren colonies became havens for dogmatic exclusion rooted in the sectarian principle of enmity toward polytheists. That the Brethren avoided folk who visited Kuwait was in accord with Wahhabi teachings, but their aggression toward followers of the Wahhabi mission is hard to explain.[29] To tamp down the Brethren's excessive zeal, Abd al-Aziz had extremist preachers expelled from colonies and Wahhabi clerics distributed treatises correcting wayward Brethren.[30]

In the wake of continued raids on oases and nomads, Abd al-Aziz convened clerical leaders in 1919 to endorse his authority over the zealous neophytes. They did his bidding, issuing a declaration: "He [the Muslim] should not be hostile or friendly except to those that the legal ruler orders. He who contravenes this goes against the way of the Muslims."[31] This verdict broke with Wahhabi doctrine that had defined unbelief according to religious practice and did not allow the ruler a voice in the matter. In 1919, the religious leaders in Riyadh met with Brethren leaders to discuss religious questions, most notably whether people who chose to persist in nomadism were unbelievers and whether the customary Bedouin headgear (the *ʿiqal*) was a sign of idolatry. The Brethren insisted that tribal sections must abandon nomadism, and they felt justified to attack them when they did not settle in colonies, or in their eyes, emigrate to the land of belief. Some Brethren rejected the Wahhabi leaders' authority, claiming they compromised religious principles for the sake of placating Abd al-Aziz in return for material rewards.[32]

The rift over religion extended to the battlefield, where the Brethren abandoned Bedouin conventions that minimized killing and viewed attacks on non-combatants as cowardly. The Brethren became infamous for slaughtering their captives and for massacring women and children, against the orders of Abd al-Aziz. From the Brethren's perspective, their enemies were infidels, and according to the rules of jihad, infidels had to convert or die.[33] One contemporary observer suspected the Brethren were not truly driven by religious ideals; rather, they twisted religion to justify plundering oases and caravans.[34]

Expansion: Phase Two

Notwithstanding the Brethren's occasional defiance of Abd al-Aziz, they were instrumental in his military campaigns to subjugate the Rashidi emirate at Ha'il and the Hashemite kingdom in Hijaz that Sharif Hussein declared in 1916, when he launched his revolt against the Ottoman empire. The Rashidi emirate was riven by violent clan strife, with three emirs murdered by kinsmen in an especially turbulent phase before one faction stabilized the situation in Ha'il for a decade. Then, in April 1920, yet another palace murder indicated to Abd al-Aziz that the Rashidi emirate was ripe for conquest.[35] Momentum was on the Saudi side, bolstered by Brethren proselytizing to the Shammar tribe. Abd al-Aziz also applied economic pressure by restricting access to markets in Qasim, Hasa, and Kuwait to Shammar sections that switched their allegiance from the Rashidis to him.[36] In March 1921, he laid siege to Ha'il. At first, Emir Abdallah ibn Mitʿab rejected terms of surrender, but he relented under pressure from townsmen wishing to avoid destruction. At that point, opponents to Saudi rule rallied to another member of the Rashidi clan, Emir Muhammad ibn Talal. The final resistance to Abd al-Aziz held out against a Saudi siege until November 1921, when Emir Muhammad surrendered.[37]

After defeating the Rashidis, Abd al-Aziz turned to the conquest of Hijaz. He held two advantages in his contest with Sharif Hussein: he had strong support from the Brethren, and he proved a superior player in international and tribal politics.[38] The Saudi leader whittled away at tribal support for the sharif in the borderlands between Hijaz and Najd. As tensions mounted, in 1924, Sharif Hussein announced that Najdis were barred from the pilgrimage. Infuriated Brethren demanded Abd al-Aziz take action, and in July 1924, he announced his intention to seize Hijaz. As a large Brethren force approached Ta'if, a highland town outside Mecca, sharifian forces slipped away, leaving it undefended. The Brethren went on a ferocious rampage of looting and slaughter, massacring more than 300 townsmen.[39] Reports of the massacre spurred a panicky exodus from Mecca. To spare the holy city Ta'if's fate, town leaders persuaded Sharif Hussein to abdicate in favor of his son Ali.[40] On October 18, 1924, Saudi forces entered the holy city without opposition. Abd al-Aziz fully understood that he had to prevent a repeat of the Ta'if atrocities if he wished to elevate his standing in the Muslim world. The Brethren attacked domed tombs and ransacked coffeehouses where they smashed water pipes, but there was no loss of life. Abd al-Aziz gained the cooperation of Mecca's merchant and religious dignitaries who formed a consultative council to manage the pilgrimage and other local matters.[41]

In the meantime, Sharif Ali held out in Jeddah and the city's merchants formed the Hijaz National Party that called for the establishment of a constitutional government. They supported Sharif Ali's attempt to build up a defense force but all he could manage was the import of a few rickety armored cars and aircraft piloted by White Russian refugees. As time passed, the merchants' confidence in Sharif Ali waned. Some began to send family members across the Red Sea to Port Sudan for safety, while others secretly contacted Abd al-Aziz to negotiate terms of surrender.[42] Sharif Ali ran out of funds to pay troops in early December 1925. As he made plans to withdraw from Jeddah, a delegation of merchants went to Abd al-Aziz's camp on the outskirts to negotiate the terms of surrender. He agreed to safeguard private property and promised to retain officials in their civil posts. On December 20, Sharif Ali departed on a British steamer. Three days later, Jeddah's notables proclaimed allegiance to Abd al-Aziz and proposed that he establish the Kingdom of Hijaz as a separate realm distinct from Najd. The composite realm became known as the Kingdom of the Hijaz and Najd and its dependencies.[43]

The last Arabian territory to come under Saudi rule was Asir, a rugged mountainous region tucked between Hijaz and Yemen. When Ottoman forces withdrew at the start of the First World War, the region became divided between two emirates, each one fending off larger neighbors: Imam Yahya of Yemen and Abd al-Aziz. For more than a decade, Yemeni and Saudi forces maneuvered for advantage, with the Saudis cementing their hold over Abha, the main town in Asir, and the Yemenis occupying the strategic port of Hodeida. Imam Yahya strengthened his position by forming an alliance with Italy, which was striving to make its stronghold in Eritrea the base for a Red Sea sphere of influence. In 1934, Italian forces came to Imam Yahya's assistance and blocked a Saudi offensive. Armistice talks led to the Treaty of Ta'if, which recognized Saudi rule in Asir and Yemen's possession of Hodeida.[44] Lax enforcement of border control prevented disruption of economic and social life and made it easy for Yemenis to live and work in districts that suddenly became the sovereign territory of Saudi Arabia.[45]

Determining international borders was part of the Saudi realm's integration into a regional political system largely defined by treaties and the European mandates imposed on former Ottoman Arab provinces in Iraq and Syria, as the epoch of conquest states gave way to international diplomacy. Treaties offered security against attack by hostile neighbors and they were instruments to assert claims over populations in newly defined frontier zones. Different conceptions of the relationship between people and international lines haunted efforts to establish a firm boundary between Saudi Arabia and Iraq. The British and the Iraqi government wished to draw a clear enforceable line while Abd al-Aziz favored shared border areas to ensure Bedouin access to wells and pasture. It took years of negotiation to reach an understanding to form neutral zones in recognition that fixed lines do not work for migratory livelihoods.[46]

That Abd al-Aziz recognized the utility of borders is evident from his desire to reach an understanding with the British that delineated the exact extent of his territory, as stipulated in the 1915 Treaty of Darin. He had to wait until November–December 1922, when the British decided it was time to determine the borders of Najd, Iraq, and Kuwait. By that time, London and Paris had divided Ottoman Arab provinces, with approval from the League of Nations, into Syria, Iraq, and Palestine, and the British had further separated Transjordan from the rest of Palestine. The 1922 Uqair Protocols were not determined by the respective Arab leaders but by British High Commissioner for Iraq Percy Cox. Abd al-Aziz wanted recognition over territory up to the Euphrates River and the delegate for Iraq claimed land deep into Najd. Cox drew borders that favored Iraq's claims, and then compensated Abd al-Aziz by giving him land claimed by Kuwait, reducing it in size by approximately two-thirds. In recognition of multiple tribal claims to access wells in northern Arabia, the protocols provided for two neutral zones, one for tribes from Saudi Arabia and Iraq, another for tribes from Saudi Arabia and Kuwait.[47]

In late 1925, the British and Abd al-Aziz held talks to settle the boundary between Najd and Transjordan and to clarify provisions in the Uqair Agreement covering the border with Iraq. After the conquest of Ha'il, the Saudis advanced toward Transjordan and annexed the Sakaka and Jawf oases. Soon Brethren warriors were raiding within 15 miles of Amman.[48] The Hadda Agreement between Abd al-Aziz and Transjordan confirmed Saudi possession of Wadi Sirhan and Transjordan's annexation of Aqaba.[49] Both the Hadda Agreement and the Bahra Agreement with Iraq provided for binational tribunals to investigate Bedouin raids and to compensate their victims. The two agreements also acknowledged the rights of nomadic tribes to cross international lines to graze their herds.[50]

The treaties did not ensure smooth relations across borders. Kuwait's rulers resented the way the Uqair Protocols gave a chunk of disputed territory to Abd al-Aziz. The Saudi leader was frustrated that the Kuwaitis did not establish border control to collect customs duties on trade on his behalf. To put pressure on Kuwait, he tried to impose a blockade, with partial success. He did not have the resources to patrol thinly inhabited territory, nor did he have the support of all Najdi tribesmen accustomed to regular trade with Kuwait. In the mid-1930s, the prospect of oil in the Saudi–Kuwaiti neutral zone brought about negotiations to end the blockade, but the two sides did not reach a formal agreement on border regulation until 1943.

On the sidelines of the 1922 Uqair Conference, Abd al-Aziz for the first time entertained a proposal to grant an oil concession to a Western company. Major Frank Holmes represented a British firm, the Eastern and General Syndicate, that prospected for concessions to sell to oil companies.[51] Percy Cox opposed Holmes because he wished to secure a concession for the Anglo-Persian Oil Company. Even though Abd al-Aziz learned about Cox's ulterior motive and liked Holmes's proposal, he did as Cox wished and turned him away. A few months after Holmes left Arabia empty-handed, he learned that Britain was going to stop paying subsidies to Abd al-Aziz. He returned to Arabia and reached agreement with Abd al-Aziz on a concession. Eastern and General made annual payments until 1927, when it let the concession lapse in favor of pursuing oil in Bahrain.[52]

The Treaty of Jeddah

By the end of 1925, circumstances in and around Arabia had evolved to the point that both Abd al-Aziz and the British had reasons to negotiate a new treaty. The Treaty of Darin's restriction on contacts with foreign powers mattered little when Abd al-Aziz ruled a compact domain in Najd and Hasa. Now that he controlled Mecca, thousands of pilgrims would arrive every year from lands under French and Dutch colonial rule; therefore it was fitting that his government have official relations with the European powers. For their part, the British wanted to avoid stirring unrest among the large Muslim population in India by appearing to have undue influence over the holy cities. In addition, the British desired good ties with Abd al-Aziz for the sake of stability in Transjordan and Iraq, and to keep him out of the orbit of the Soviet Union and Italy.[53]

The two sides reached agreement on the Treaty of Jeddah in May 1927. Abd al-Aziz shook loose from restrictions on the conduct of foreign relations and the granting of commercial concessions. The British won his pledge to refrain from interfering in the mandates and the Trucial shaikhdoms. The treaty gave Saudi Arabia independent standing at a moment when most of the Arab world chafed under imperial control, but it did contain a stipulation that Abd al-Aziz accept "consular manumission," a practice that went back to the Ottoman period whereby the British consul in Jeddah had the authority to manumit fugitive slaves.[54] The consular manumission clause implied Saudi Arabia's integration into a global moral campaign that anticipated the era of calls to safeguard human rights.

By 1927, the Western abolitionist movement was more than a century old. Britain passed the Act for the Abolition of the Slave Trade in 1807, and in subsequent decades, the British pressured Muslim rulers to sign treaties that empowered the Royal Navy to search merchant vessels for slaves and to confiscate them for manumission. In 1847, the Ottoman empire accepted those terms for the Persian Gulf.[55] The increase in global demand for dates and pearls from the Persian Gulf starting in the 1860s spurred renewed demand for slaves. With widespread evasion of British patrols, in the early 1900s, slaves comprised as much as one-fourth of the population in the Trucial shaikhdoms and Qatar.[56] British pressure on Istanbul to suppress slavery became a sore point in Hijaz, where Ottoman officials were torn between local slaveowners wanting to capture runaway slaves and the antislavery lobby in Britain.[57] After Abd al-Aziz conquered Hijaz, slavery became a sensitive issue in Anglo-Saudi relations, fueled by abolitionist sentiment in Britain and the United States. For instance, in 1927, *The New York Times* published an article criticizing the European powers for allowing the slave trade to persist.

The article also reported that Abd al-Aziz's bodyguard included 120 slaves and that he planned to form a battalion of slave soldiers.[58] According to the Treaty of Jeddah, Abd al-Aziz would assist British measures to suppress the slave trade and agreed to manumission for slaves who reached the British legation in Jeddah. The treaty's inclusion of slavery reversed Riyadh's self-image of its moral posture in the world. Long accustomed to lecturing other Muslims to meet Wahhabi standards, Riyadh was now on the receiving end of lectures from infidels about the evils of slavery.

During the twelve years that the treaty clause on slavery was in force, more than 200 slaves—190 men and 72 women—took refuge at the British legation, with all but eight returning to their homes in Africa. Fugitives typically fled under cover of darkness and entered the legation before dawn. British officials expedited exit visas and issued manumission certificates.[59] Enslaved women mostly served in households as washerwomen and concubines.[60] Enslaved men were put to work in diverse ways: as household servants, chauffeurs, shepherds, shop assistants, soldiers, sailors, porters, and camel drivers. Slave owners allocated tasks according to a slave's origin. Thus, Ethiopians frequently wound up in households and Sudanese people in agriculture.[61]

When slaves arrived at the legation, an official interviewed them and filled in a form with details about their lives and reasons for seeking consular manumission, typically one kind of abuse or another: beatings, withholding food, or separation of families: husbands and wives, parents and children.[62] A slave sometimes passed from one owner to another. A twenty-five-year-old man named Salem was the son of a member of the Abyssinian royal bodyguard:

> Salem states that he was kidnapped when a boy of 10 or 12 years by means of a trick in Addis Ababa & was taken by train to Jibouti and sold there to a Dankali named Musa, who took him by dhow via Tajura to Hodeida and sold him to a Medi merchant named

> Muhammad. His master took him to Medi and sold him after 5 days to Abdullah El Sindi, of Mecca. He remained with Abdullah El Sindi for 18 months and was then sold to a Beduin named Sultan Ibn Hilal, with whom he remained for about 6 years. He was then sold to Amir Muhammad Abdurrahman, a brother of H.M. King Abd al-Aziz. He remained 5 years with his late master and escaped this year while the Amir was in Mecca performing the pilgrimage.[63]

A member of the king's guard, also named Salem, heard that his father was searching for him. By the time the palace learned the British legation was seeking information about him, he had been freed and gotten married. To alleviate his father's concerns, the king had Salem go to the legation to inform the British that he was leading a comfortable life and did not want to leave his position at the palace.[64]

The Brethren Revolt

The Treaty of Jeddah was part of Abd al-Aziz's pivot from conquest to consolidation. His primary challenge was how to square cooperation with London and the powerful Brethren movement. The Brethren jeopardized three prongs of his strategy to consolidate power: stabilizing authority in Hijaz, pacifying the desert, and maintaining correct relations with Great Britain. In the case of Hijaz, Abd al-Aziz minimized Brethren influence to win local and international Muslim support for his rule. To pacify the desert, Abd al-Aziz issued an order forbidding intertribal raiding and attacks on villages and towns, leaving the Brethren colonies to subsist on unreliable harvests. The order turned a customary part of the warrior ethos into a criminal act.[65] He also declared the abolition of tribal domains that divided Arabia's pasture and wells.[66]

Maintaining correct relations with British authorities in Iraq proved to be the thorniest issue. When Abd al-Aziz conquered Ha'il, some tribal sections in northern Najd consented to pay him tribute and others migrated to Iraq. The latter became known as "Brethren refugees," and they became embroiled in cross-border raids into Najd.[67] As border violence escalated, the British increased armored car and air patrols, especially after an attack in March 1924 killed hundreds of Brethren refugee tribesmen.[68] The Saudi Brethren's religious zeal was only one cause of the border violence. A second cause was the way border enforcement, a normal part of Western international relations, doomed the livelihoods of the Bedouin. For centuries, tribes obtained permission from neighboring tribes to traverse their domains for access to pastures, wells, and markets where they sold camels and purchased dates, rice, and other supplies. Drawing a border that blocked migration was tantamount to economic warfare.[69] The Brethren leader Faisal al-Duwish explained Brethren raids into Iraq: "How could we help it when our grazing grounds and wells had been taken from us and seeing that we were persistently encouraged to do so [to raid]?"[70]

Many Brethren did not accept the premise that by settling in colonies they recognized Abd al-Aziz's authority to bind them to agreements he made with the British. Indeed, leaders of major tribal sections regarded him more as a peer, not a ruler, and they expected political rewards for participating in conquests. According to one scenario, Arabia would become a confederation of tribal domains: northern Najd would go to the Anaza; Qasim and parts of Hijaz would go to the Utaiba; central Najd would go to the Mutair; districts around Medina and Yanbu would go to the Harb; and Hasa would go to the Ajman.[71]

Tensions with Brethren leaders precipitated the most severe crisis in Abd al-Aziz's reign. They accused him of violating several religious principles. Emirs Faisal and Saud went on diplomatic missions to England and Egypt, respectively, contrary to the ban on travel to the lands of unbelief. The Saudi governor in Hasa tolerated Shiite religious practices. Abd al-Aziz opened the country to motor vehicles and the telegraph, which the Brethren considered forbidden innovations, and he imposed taxes on Bedouin that were illicit according to Islamic law. In January 1927, Wahhabi clerics met with the dissidents to discuss their complaints. The clerics agreed that Shiism should be suppressed. They also agreed that some taxes were illegal, but they asserted that Abd al-Aziz had the authority to collect them and that the Brethren had no right to disobey him. Abd al-Aziz agreed to limit the import of new inventions. On the most sensitive issue, the clerics declared that only the sovereign had the authority to declare jihad.[72] The summit with clerics did not resolve the growing friction between the Brethren and Abd al-Aziz. In November 1927, a Brethren attack on a British police post in Iraq killed around twenty people.[73] The British warned Abd al-Aziz if he did not restrain the Brethren, they would retaliate. After new raids in Iraq and Kuwait, British warplanes carried out attacks on Brethren tribesmen in Najd.

Under pressure from the British and the Brethren, Abd al-Aziz called for a gathering that became known as the Riyadh Conference of Notables, held in the first week of November 1928. Thousands of townsmen, villagers, and Brethren descended on Riyadh. Armed townsmen loyal to Al Saud kept watch on the thousands of Brethren and Bedouin gathered outside the town walls in a sea of tents. Abd al-Aziz and senior members of Al Saud occupied the center of a spacious palace balcony, flanked by Wahhabi clerics and townsmen, while delegates from Brethren colonies and tribes formed rows facing the balcony. Abd al-Aziz opened the meeting with a declaration that he did not wish to rule without the consent of the people, and that if the people were dissatisfied with his leadership, he would abdicate and let the assembly choose another member of his family to lead. The clerics affirmed their confidence in his leadership and the Brethren leaders did so too, but they wanted answers to questions. Was it allowed to use the telegraph? Was he going to allow the British to maintain police posts that interfered with Bedouin migration? Was he committed to jihad? The clerics ruled that the telegraph was a permitted invention. Abd al-Aziz pledged that he would try to have police posts removed. On the question of jihad, he announced it needed further, private discussion. At the end of the conference, the notables affirmed their allegiance to Abd al-Aziz, giving him the public endorsement that he sought.[74]

The conference did nothing to placate rebellious Brethren leaders. They attacked a caravan belonging to Buraida merchants, looting the goods and slaughtering the traders; they attacked Shammar nomads and made off with livestock; and they declared jihad on tribes in Iraq. Abd al-Aziz had to respond or watch the work of a quarter-century of war and diplomacy crumble to pieces. He had strong support from townsmen eager to end raids on caravans, and from tribesmen who joined his side in return for payment in gold coin. The British supplied large quantities of rifles and ammunition, military aircraft, pilots, technicians, and fuel for military vehicles. In addition, London pressured the rulers of Kuwait and Iraq to withhold assistance from the rebels.[75]

In March 1929, Abd al-Aziz set off from Riyadh in a motorcade bound for Qasim and a decisive contest. On the morning of March 30, 1929, he rode to the plain of Sabila, not far from the original Brethren colony, flanked by his brother Muhammad and his son Saud, leading a force that outnumbered his adversaries three to one. Barely thirty minutes after he gave the command to open fire, his men, armed with a dozen machine guns, mowed down the enemy and forced a chaotic retreat.[76]

The decisive victory at Sabila did not put an end to the Brethren revolt. The Ajman tribe in Hasa in particular remained unbowed and launched a flurry of devastating raids on towns and villages. Some Brethren joined the revolt, abandoning their colonies to resume the customary way of desert raiding.[77] Other Brethren, however, stayed on the sidelines or supported Abd al-Aziz, persuaded he could not be defeated. They were right. His commanders possessed technological advantages, both on the battlefield, with machine guns mounted on armored vehicles, and off the battlefield, with telegraph communications to track rebel movements. And they had orders to give no quarter. Thus, one Saudi commander had 250 captives put to death and some 40 fugitives from the battlefield hunted down and killed. A force led by Abd al-Aziz's two sons Muhammad and Khalid cornered a second rebel band and slaughtered them to the last man.[78] The remaining rebels, desperate to survive, sought refuge in Kuwait and protection from British forces stationed there. In January 1930, the main body of rebels surrendered to British forces on the Saudi–Kuwaiti frontier. The British returned the rebel leaders to Najd in exchange for a pledge from Abd al-Aziz to refrain from executing them.[79]

Abd al-Aziz sealed his victory with a mix of punishment and rehabilitation. On one hand, dissident Brethren had their camels and horses confiscated. On the other hand, some former rebel leaders joined the royal entourage. One former rebel, Majid ibn Khathila, later accompanied Abd al-Aziz on his trip to "idolatrous" Egypt in 1945 to meet the "infidel" American president Franklin D. Roosevelt. Rank-and-file Brethren warriors joined units in a new military institution, initially called the White Army, and later the National Guard. Veterans of early military campaigns received lifetime pensions.[80]

Abd al-Aziz was able to establish the prerequisite for a modern state: the central authority's monopoly on the use of force. The official newspaper drove home that message when it reported Abd al-Aziz's declaration to religious dignitaries and military leaders after Sabila. He announced that they owed obedience to the ruler and stated that they may not "hold meetings either to discuss religion or worldly questions without permission from the monarch."[81] It was a clear statement of the ruler's supreme authority and the subject's duty to obey.

After the Bedouin Epoch

The defeat of the Brethren ended an epoch. Bedouin no longer collected tribute from villages, towns, and caravans. They no longer possessed autonomy. Instead, Abd al-Aziz dominated the Bedouin by putting limits on their migration and abolishing raids. This chapter in Arabian history is part of the story of how the modern international system of centralizing states and borders disrupted and rearranged economic, social, and political rhythms of pastoral nomadism. In the same period, Iran's Pahlavi shah was crushing nomadic power, and Hashemite rulers in Transjordan and Iraq were leveraging British funds, arms, and advisers to pacify their Bedouin. In the new global order, borderless folk were relegated to smuggling, crowding shantytowns, accepting settlement schemes, and trading independence for "development."

Nor was there room for the boastful Najdi poet of yore: "It is of no real consequence to lead an army, what is of real consequence is to be a poet like me. Here I sit peacefully by my hearth and coffee pots, yet with my words I can raise multitudes up in arms against each other for any cause I choose."[82] Abdallah al-Oni (c.1870–1923) was the last poet to weaponize Nabati verse. His career embodies the twilight of a political and cultural order where the Nabati tradition was part of struggles for power among Bedouin tribes and oasis towns. Oni grew up as a protégé of Hasan al-Muhanna Aba al-Khail, the emir of Buraida. His career mirrored the political turbulence that accompanied the collapse and revival of Saudi power. In 1891, his patron allied with the Sauds against the Rashidis in the Battle of Mulaida. With the defeat of the Saudi coalition, he fled to Kuwait. A decade later, Oni incited Emir Abd al-Rahman to expel the Rashidis from Qasim, but the 1901 Battle of Sarif was another victory for Ha'il. After Abd al-Aziz captured Riyadh the next year, Oni rallied the far-flung network of Qasimi traders and workers in Kuwait, Iraq, and Syria to join the campaign against Rashidi rule with a rousing poem that became known as *al-khaluj*, the term for "a camel bereaved of its newly born calf," because he was said to have heard a she-camel's cry outside the Kuwaiti ruler's palace. The thirty-two-verse poem presents the Qasim district as a mother suffering mistreatment, and it summons the men of Qasim to fight to restore their honor. On hearing the poem, Qasimis residing as far away as Damascus rode off to join the successful Saudi campaign to rid Qasim of the Rashidis. For a short time, Oni's former patron became emir of Buraida, but Abd al-Aziz was seeking vassals, not allies, and in short order he expelled the emir for bucking his authority. At that point, Oni moved to Ha'il to support the Rashidis against Riyadh. Upon the fall of Ha'il, Abd al-Aziz had Oni transported to Riyadh to keep an eye on him. Abd al-Aziz grew suspicious that Oni was secretly plotting with the deposed Rashidi emir Muhammad ibn Talal, also under watch in Riyadh. Worried that Oni might use his poetic talent to rouse opposition, Abd al-Aziz sent him to prison in Hofuf, where he died of tuberculosis shortly after release from confinement in 1923, thereby fulfilling the prediction of another Nabati poet: "Your poetry will bring death upon you."

Oni's passing marked the end of Nabati poetry as an element in Arabian political conflict, but the tradition persisted as part of popular entertainment. The Syrian-American writer Amin Rihani described a performance in Unaiza by a renowned elderly blind poet. He started with a recitation of verse by the eighteenth-century Nabati poet Humaidan al-Shuwayʿir, then grew more animated as he chanted his own verse, snapping his fingers, then standing up, throwing off his headscarf, beating his hand on his chest, swaying and dancing.[83]

At the same time that Nabati poetry, a token of old Najd, was in decline, literary modernism, a token of integration with contemporary regional currents, was coming of age in Hijaz. In the late Ottoman and sharifian years, educated Hijazis embraced the new genres (essay, short story, novel, theater) and styles (free verse) developing in Cairo, Beirut, Damascus, and the Syrian diaspora in North America. Newspapers, schools, libraries, and literary clubs were the platforms for modernist exchange, experiment, and expression. The memoirs of Ahmad al-Sibai (1905–1984) capture the flavor of the small cohort of men oriented to cosmopolitan conceptions of learning and literature, the feeling that inherited schooling was outmoded and stifling.[84]

Journalism came to Hijaz during the late Ottoman period. The 1908 constitutional revolution in Istanbul fueled a burst of journalistic energy throughout the empire. Mecca, Medina, and Jeddah saw a half-dozen periodicals appear.[85] During the sharifian period, a newspaper called *al-Qibla* (*The Direction of Prayer*) served as the official mouthpiece.[86] Under Hashemite patronage, Hijazi and Syrian writers imported modernist literary currents from Cairo, Damascus, and the Syrian-American diaspora.[87] *Al-Qibla* was an outlet for poems and essays lauding technical progress, criticism of traditional ways, and experimental writing. The major figure in Hijazi literary modernism was Muhammad Hasan Awwad, a pioneer in composing in free verse and incorporating mythic figures. Awwad mentored a cluster of younger poets whose works featured in publications after annexation to Saudi rule.[88]

The first Saudi newspaper came out shortly after the conquest of Mecca. In December 1924, the sharif's press was used to publish the first issue of *Umm al-Qura* (*The Mother of Cities*), a moniker for Mecca. Other early newspapers were private endeavors with religious and literary themes expressed by poets and essayists echoing the Arabic literary sphere, with the conspicuous influences from Cairo and the Syrian-American current of Mikhail Nuaima and Gibran Khalil Gibran. From 1928 to 1930, the Egyptian revivalist Muhammad al-Fiqi managed a religious publication aspiring to import Rashid Rida's blend of religious modernism in a Salafi idiom.[89]

Hijaz was not the only scene for early traces of modern literature. The commercial ties of Unaiza's merchants with Bombay, Damascus, and Cairo led many to embrace a cosmopolitan outlook that caused Amin al-Rihani to dub the town "the Paris of Najd."[90] A young educator from Unaiza, Salih ibn Salih, had studied and lived abroad, in Iraq, Kuwait, Bahrain, and Dubai. On his return to his native town, he established the al-Ahliyya private school, where he introduced live stage performance at the end-of-year ceremony in 1928. In this first modest step for theater, students acted out a dialogue between

Education and Ignorance to emphasize the value of schooling, at a time when few people believed it was worthwhile.[91]

Guardians of the Wahhabi mission strove to restrict public expressions of literary modernity, preventing public performances and performances where men and women mixed onstage. Consequently the spread of modern literary sensibility was slow and steady, and reactions against it were episodic and intense, yet over time, the population grew accustomed to performing arts and comfortable with private enjoyment to avoid public controversy.

Patrimonial Rule in the Conquest Phase

Dynastic strife plagued the Riyadh emirate and proved fatal in the end. The schism that had fueled the Saudi civil war persisted in the early years of Abd al-Aziz. His dissident cousins—grandsons of Saud ibn Faisal—refused to pay him allegiance and found refuge with maternal relatives in the Ajman tribe. Abd al-Aziz attempted to mend the clan breach through marriage, but the cousins continued to incite opposition until 1915, when he secured the allegiance of the faction's leader, known as Saud al-Kabir.[92]

Resolving one generation's rivalries did not ensure stability in the next, particularly on the question of determining the line of succession. When Abd al-Aziz decided to designate Saud, his oldest surviving son, the successor, he had to reckon with potential claims by his own brothers. His only full brother, Saad, was killed in battle in 1915. The oldest surviving brother, Abdallah, was an able military commander content to play the part of a loyal lieutenant. The next oldest brother, Muhammad, also had battlefield experience and was not ready to cede a claim to power.[93] After Abd al-Aziz announced that his son Saud was to succeed him in May 1933, Muhammad refrained from declaring his allegiance. He was probably grooming his own son Khalid to make a bid for leadership, but Khalid died in 1938. Muhammad himself died in 1943, removing the last threat to Abd al-Aziz's plan for succession.[94]

Harmonizing clan relationships served two purposes. It diminished inside threats, and it produced a corps of loyal lieutenants. In classic patrimonial fashion, Abd al-Aziz depended on sons and cousins to govern different parts of the realm. He also experimented with patrimonial practice by inviting outsiders to serve as advisers and officials. One set of outsiders consisted of northern Arabs with extensive exposure to the West: the Egyptian Hafiz Wahba, the Syrian Yusuf Yasin, the Palestinian Fuad Hamza, the Iraqi Abdallah al-Damluji, and others.[95] In recruiting these men, Abd al-Aziz drew on the Ottoman legacy of training men to handle relations with European powers. The northern Arabs comprised a cosmopolitan stratum attuned to Western manners and tastes. Another set of outsiders came from the Najdi merchant diaspora spread between Zubair, Kuwait, India, and Egypt. The roster of early ambassadors included Najdi merchants in Egypt (Fawzan al-Sabiq), Iraq (Abd al-Latif al-Mandil), Kuwait (Abdallah al-Nafisi), Bombay, (Abdallah al-Fawzan),[96] and Bahrain (Abd al-Aziz al-Qusaibi).[97] Both groups of outsiders reflected Abd al-Aziz's awareness of the imperative to keep close track of Ottoman and European developments.[98] While they brought the touch of worldly experience he sought, they also represented engagement with the infidel world—the very thing Wahhabi clerics had striven to prevent.

The annexation of Hijaz presented Abd al-Aziz with the choice between imposing an administrative regime and adapting to the existing one. He followed the common practice of expansionist empires by favoring continuity.[99] This meant incorporating late Ottoman institutions that reached Hijazi towns in the 1890s: public schools, libraries, newspapers, and the printing press.[100] He also preserved Ottoman agencies that managed the pilgrimage, public health, and education.[101] To win support from Hijaz notables, Abd al-Aziz invited merchants and clergy to join advisory bodies that he placed under the supervision of Emir Faisal.[102]

Apart from the foreign Arabs and a few late Ottoman institutions in Hijaz, patrimonial governance did not change. All power resided with one person; there was no specialization of government offices. Around 1930, Riyadh had seventeen departments that were in fact nothing but wings and rooms in the royal palace for camels, horse-breeding, motor vehicles, radio facilities, hospitality, and a clinic. The treasury was handled by Abdallah Sulaiman, a former trader from Unaiza, who shared information about finances only with Abd al-Aziz. When Abd al-Aziz traveled on military expeditions, a staff of twelve clerks and six servants accompanied him to handle all domestic and foreign affairs. In the manner of a premodern peripatetic monarchy, the court was mobile, with essential records in packed wooden chests and loaded onto camels.[103]

Public performance of generosity reflected a tacit part of the relationship between Abd al-Aziz and his subjects, captured by the declaration of his chief steward, Ibn Shilhub: "Every king in the world is supported by his people; but the people of Najd are supported by their king."[104] During his stay in Riyadh in 1922–3, the Syrian-American writer Amin al-Rihani reported that the palace prepared and distributed two meals each day to about 500 warriors and beggars. He also described a biannual distribution of 3,000 cloaks from Persia, Iraq, and Syria to the royal household and palace servants.[105] Ibn Shilhub kept a list of every visitor to Riyadh, their tribe, and the purpose of their visit. Abd al-Aziz reviewed the list to determine the distribution of clothes, goods, and money. Ibn Shilhub had a staff of four: two bookkeepers and two clerks to record allocations of food and clothes, according to his dictation. "Write in the book, Ahmad ibn Jaber of Tharmadah, 250 rupees." Rihani described the storehouse holding booty as containing "odds and ends of rusty cannons and guns, bits of rugs, metal water-cans, army boots, belts, broken swords, and whatnot are thrown pell-mell, heaped on top of each other."[106]

To afford a grand version of old Najd's proverbial greasy tent flap, Abd al-Aziz depended on the same revenue sources that earlier emirates tapped: war booty and the religious tax on crops and livestock. One estimate for annual revenues before the annexation of Hasa was

£100,000.[107] After the fall of Hasa, it took a few years to collect customs on trade passing through Qatif. By 1920, the port generated customs revenue amounting to £72,000 per year. From 1917 to 1924, the British made regular payments that contributed £60,000 per year. On the eve of the Hijaz campaign, annual revenue reached £210,000. Control of Jeddah and the holy cities brought customs on the Red Sea trade and pilgrim tolls, pushing annual revenue to £1.5 million.[108] After a few prosperous years, the onset of the Great Depression caused steep and lasting declines in the pilgrim traffic and Jeddah customs. The number of pilgrims fell from 132,000 in 1927, to around 90,000 in the next three years, and to fewer than 30,000 in 1932.[109] To meet expenses, Abd al-Aziz borrowed from private traders and the British Government of India.[110]

Sectarian Retreat

For nearly two centuries, the Wahhabi mission strove to purge traces of idolatry. The annexations of Hasa and Hijaz presented opportunities to extend the regime of godliness, but would Abd al-Aziz force Wahhabi doctrine on Hasa's Shiites and the denominational religious culture of Hijazi towns exposed to revivalist movements radiating from Egypt, Syria, and South Asia? Even parts of Najd did not yet conform to Wahhabi views on correct worship. In 1918, a Western visitor to Unaiza described men and women mingling and singing to celebrate the Ramadan feast while Bedouin women danced. At the end of the congregational prayer and sermon, women stayed in the central mosque, giving themselves up to highly emotional prayers and weeping.[111]

The mission's patrimonial authority remained intact in the hands of Al al-Shaikh, first Abdallah ibn Abd al-Latif (d. 1920) and then his cousin Abdallah ibn Hasan (d. 1958). They established the mission in Mecca, where their deputies took charge of the Grand Mosque, and appointed trusted clerics to preside over religious matters in the other provinces.[112] This generation of Wahhabi clerics quietly accepted Abd al-Aziz's compromises on religious principles.[113] Ever since Muhammad ibn Abd al-Wahhab's search for an emir to lend muscle to his message, the mission had derived its power to enforce conformity from a political leader. Therefore, while Wahhabi clerics initially objected to Western inventions, they eventually relented, sometimes after coming to see the practical benefits. For instance, they accepted the telegraph after learning it was useful for quelling revolts in Hijaz and Asir in the early 1930s.[114] In addition, Wahhabi clerics bowed to the strategies of leveraging the expertise of foreign Muslims and establishing diplomatic ties with infidel governments. Furthermore, Abd al-Aziz's drive to stabilize his realm required gaining consent from residents in newly annexed regions. Consequently, the clerics had to settle for different degrees of religious conformity, according to a political calculation. The sectarian enclave of the Riyadh emirate had depended on strict enforcement of separation from unbelief. The new political order depended on opening the enclave to outsiders and relaxing enforcement of Wahhabi norms. For the sake of avoiding provocation of Hijazi townspeople, stabilizing power in Hasa, and acquiring recognition of the Muslim world for possession of the holy cities, a dose of the denominational spirit was necessary.

The Riyadh emirate witnessed little exception to the principle of excluding infidels, having allowed only a few Western visitors late in Emir Faisal's reign. Exile in Kuwait instilled in Abd al-Aziz an open attitude toward the outside world. As a ruler, he entertained foreign Muslims and non-Muslims when he deemed it beneficial to his quest for power. The clerics, however, held onto their conviction that preservation of belief required distance from others. The Egyptian adviser Hafiz Wahba recalled an incident around 1928 when he was on the road with the head of the religious estate, Shaikh Abdallah ibn Hasan, and they encountered H. St. John Philby, Abd al-Aziz's British adviser, before his conversion to Islam. Wahba shook Philby's hand and invited him to a meal. The shaikh later told Wahba that he disapproved of friendly interaction with infidels. Wahba replied that Abd al-Aziz sometimes treated Christian visitors with honor, and the cleric retorted that the ruler often acted in ways he considered wrong.[115]

The clerics likely disapproved of the way Abd al-Aziz's cousin Abdallah ibn Jiluwi dealt with Hasa's Shiites. Ibn Jiluwi was known for brooking no challenge to his authority, whether from subjugated Shiites or zealous Brethren. While he appointed some Wahhabi judges to district courts, he allowed Shiite judges to continue operating local courts as long as they paid a special tax for exemption from military service.[116] When Brethren vigilantes came to the district in the early 1920s, they demanded that Ibn Jiluwi compel Shiites to conform to Wahhabi norms. He made clear who was in charge. He rounded up and threw thirty Brethren in prison for causing a riot when they attacked a girl for what they considered immoral dress; he had a member of the Brethren flogged for beating a girl for wearing a silk dress.[117] At the height of the crisis between Abd al-Aziz and the Brethren, Ibn Jiluwi did ban public observance of Shiite religious holidays and he placed Wahhabi clerics in control of some Shiite mosques. These measures triggered a short-lived uprising and a spate of Shiite emigration to Bahrain and Iraq. After the suppression of the Brethren, Ibn Jiluwi stood by when Shiites expelled Wahhabi clerics. The regime of quiet toleration resumed, but Shiites were not permitted to establish new religious institutions.[118]

In Hijaz, Abd al-Aziz took steps to convince three audiences that the holy cities were in good hands: the local population, foreign Muslims, and European powers whose colonies had large Muslim populations. During the Ottoman era, the denominational spirit was prevalent. The Ottomans recognized the four Sunni legal traditions, tolerated Medina's small Shiite community, and respected the region's range of Sufi orders. Under Saudi rule, Wahhabism's sectarian impulses modified but did not transform the religious climate. The Hanbali legal tradition became the official legal school, while the other legal traditions continued to be taught in the holy cities. Sufi orders were deeply rooted in Hijaz and they formed part of the holy cities' connections with distant regions: the Caucasus, West Africa, Southeast Asia, and elsewhere. Wahhabi clerics viewed the orders as havens of idolatry but were not permitted to completely suppress them. After a handful of attacks on Sufi convents caused some Sufi shaikhs to leave, a *modus vivendi* set in whereby Sufi shaikhs kept their ceremonies out of the public eye and the authorities looked the other way.[119]

On some matters, Abd al-Aziz bowed to Wahhabi demands. He allowed the clerics and their Brethren acolytes to tear down religious memorials in Medina (domes over the tombs of the third caliph and Shiite imams) and in Mecca (a minaret and dome over the Prophet's birthplace). These actions stained the reputation of Wahhabism in the Muslim world as an aberrant sect hostile toward the Prophet and the imams. In addition, restrictions were placed on public observance of the Prophet's birthday, a popular holiday in much of the Muslim world.[120] At the same time, Abd al-Aziz recognized that the Ta'if massacre had damaged his reputation, and he took steps to assure Muslim opinion that he would safeguard the holy cities and the pilgrimage. In 1926, he ordered the Brethren out of Mecca after they attacked Egyptian pilgrims.[121] He abolished the exorbitant fees charged to transport pilgrims from Jeddah to Mecca and for pilgrimage guides. To coordinate the complex logistics of the hajj—transport, food, lodging, and hygiene—he established special agencies, and he promoted the use of motorcars to ease the journey between Jeddah and Mecca. As a result, pilgrim numbers increased until the Great Depression.

In everyday life, enforcement of Wahhabi restrictions was intermittent, and many popular pastimes persisted: smoking tobacco, singing in public, playing music on phonographs, card games, and children's dolls.[122] The new rulers prohibited the annual Qays festival that women celebrated in Mecca and Jeddah during the pilgrimage when most men went to Mina and Mt. Arafat. For four days, women from different neighborhoods organized processions, donned costumes representing public authorities (the sharif, the police, the head of the quarter), and chanted bawdy songs to the beat of drums. The custom persisted in private quarters and in Hijazi villages into the 1970s.[123]

The annexation of Hijaz set up a struggle between the Wahhabi mission and the modernist current over education. When Abd al-Aziz ordered the creation in 1926 of a Directorate of Education, he sidelined Wahhabi clerics and entrusted it to Hijazi and foreign Arab advisers.[124] The measure marked the rise of a bifurcation between religious and modernist camps and an enduring tension between Wahhabi clerics and Directorate (later Ministry) of Education officials. The clerics opposed teaching foreign languages because they exposed children to infidel ideas, and they objected to classes on modern science because it sometimes contradicted religious beliefs. The Egyptian head of the directorate, Hafiz Wahba, pointed out that Companions of the Prophet spoke languages besides Arabic, and that since the country was dealing with foreigners, it was better that countrymen know their languages instead of depending on foreigners to translate. With his usual pragmatic outlook on matters, Abd al-Aziz overruled the mission's impulse to forbid and approved Wahba's education plan.[125]

In 1927, the Directorate of Education experimented with a hybrid school to bridge the divide between advocates for Wahhabi and modernist approaches to education. The Saudi Scholastic Institute was founded to train teachers and civil servants with a curriculum that included modern subjects (geography, engineering, natural sciences) and classes on Wahhabi theology.[126] The institute did not last long, but it was a step in transforming how pupils learned Wahhabi teachings. By embedding them in course syllabi and classroom tests, in essence, the institute packaged the mission for mass public education and rendered it in a format easily transported to other parts of the Muslim world. The foundation was laid for the burst of Wahhabi proselytizing in the 1970s and 1980s.[127]

While the clerics lost ground in education, they acquired new resources to monitor public behavior and regular attendance at mosque prayer in the name of enforcing the duty to command right and forbid wrong. The duty is based on verses in the Quran, but like so many matters in Islamic law, how to perform the duty is the subject of different opinions. Is a verbal reminder enough or must one use force to command right and forbid wrong? The legal experts framed the matter as a question of whether it is a duty to perform with the hand, with the tongue, or with the heart. Historical sources do not shed light on how the duty was enforced in early Saudi history. During the occupation of the holy cities in the 1800s, the Saudis banned smoking tobacco in public and made attendance at mosque prayer compulsory for men. Under the Riyadh emirate, the rulers instructed local emirs to assist clerics in performing the duty, notably taking attendance at prayer.[128] Abd al-Aziz established a Committee for Commanding Right and Forbidding Wrong in Hijaz to enforce the duty. The committees' monitors, known as *mutawwiʿa*, were on the watch for smoking, alcohol, and mingling between unrelated men and women.[129]

The mission gained a new outlet for proselytizing when Abd al-Aziz took over Mecca in December 1924, and established an official newspaper, *Mother of Cities*. The newspaper's inaugural issue carried a speech by Abd al-Aziz where he declared that the people of Najd adhered to Muhammad ibn Abd al-Wahhab's teachings only to the extent that they conformed to the Quran and the Sunna.[130] Subsequent articles tackled what their writers considered mistaken ideas about Wahhabism as a new sect, and explained that the people of Najd followed the Quran and the Sunna, without adding or omitting anything, for the sake of adhering to the way of Prophet and the *Salaf*, the Arabic term for the early generation of Muslims.[131] Dissemination of Wahhabi doctrine received another boost from treasury funding to subsidize the publication of anthologies of Wahhabi treatises. The shift from painstaking reproduction of manuscripts by hand to mass print production generated an industry of massive output.

In addition, allies in the transnational Muslim press reframed Wahhabi doctrine for a cosmopolitan Muslim audience. An influential voice in Muslim debates over Wahhabism belonged to Rashid Rida, publisher of a monthly religious magazine, *The Lighthouse*, that he founded in Cairo in 1898. By the 1920s, his publication had readers throughout the Muslim world and diaspora, and he was using it to solicit support for Abd al-Aziz as ruler of one of the few Arab lands independent of European rule.[132] Notwithstanding Rida's backing for the Saudi leader, Wahhabi clerics suspected that Rida was a political opportunist, not a sincere proponent of their creed, and they opposed giving him influence over religious affairs.[133] Abd al-Aziz ignored them and appointed men from Rida's circle to influential positions in Hijaz to reassure townsmen that he realized foreign Muslims were more attuned to their sensibilities than Najdi clerics. The foreign Muslims included a Syrian, Muhammad Bahjat al-Bitar, who played a part in setting up modern schools and religious education in Hijaz, and the Egyptian Muhammad al-Fiqi, who helped launch a publishing enterprise for religious works.[134]

Parallel to the rehabilitation of Wahhabism's reputation in the Muslim world, Abd al-Aziz cultivated a positive image to Western audiences as a progressive leader determined to drag a conservative society into the modern age. In 1928, the Syrian-American author Amin al-Rihani published *The Maker of Modern Arabia*.[135] The book reviewer for *The Daily Boston Globe* characterized Abd al-Aziz as recognizing "the value of sympathetic publicity," and the reviewer provided it, describing "the hospitable Arab king" as seeking "the liberation of the Arabs from their own lethargy and from foreign domination."[136] In a similar vein, *The New York Times* correspondent in Jerusalem called readers' attention to the "intensive work" Abd al-Aziz undertook since gaining control in Hijaz.[137] The lengthy headline imparts the flavor of the story: "King Abd al-Aziz would make Arabia great. Warlike but Benevolent Ruler Wants his Country to be the Leading Moslem Power. Favors Modern Methods. Goes in for Autos, Good Roads and Sanitation but Insists on Religious Precepts."

The reporter presented Abd al-Aziz as a modernizer, instituting sanitation measures for pilgrims, introducing cars, and constructing highways to connect Jeddah, Mecca, and Ta'if. American readers were to view him as an enlightened monarch introducing tokens of technical innovation (automobility) and social advance (settlement of the Bedouin) that form pieces in a web of signs comprising modernity.

Abd al-Aziz was a resourceful leader, searching for new assets (Bedouin converts, foreign Arabs, British arms and money) and safeguarding old assets (the Najdi coalition, religious prestige). If he believed it was necessary to make the Wahhabi mission bend for the sake of expediency, then so be it. The religious leadership proved sufficiently deft to yield at times, and to hold fast at other times. There would be no return to the sectarian enclave, but the clerics adopted new modes to defend their doctrine and to spread it to other Muslim societies that had been largely hostile or indifferent. In a sense, they lost the contest to maintain a pure godly regime and acquired instruments to wage the struggle against idolatry on a vaster scale.

Agrarian Conditions

For all the military and political energy consumed by the conquests, little changed in the towns of Najd and Hasa. Emirs still held their public meetings in the markets, the center of public life, where townsfolk, villagers, and Bedouin traded dates, wheat, and local wares for imports such as coffee, tea, and sugar.[138] In the Hasa oasis, protective walls still shielded villages and towns where commercial transactions took place through barter and multiple currencies: the Maria Theresa dollar, Ottoman coinage, the British gold sovereign, and Indian silver rupees. Glimmers of change, however, were on the horizon. Landowners were discussing the prospect of inviting an Egyptian engineer to introduce hydraulic techniques that would increase agricultural production.[139]

The most significant omen of a different future was the arrival of the first motor vehicles in Riyadh in January 1923. Two teams of eight camels hauled two cars from the Persian Gulf through the Dahna desert, a 50-mile stretch of soft sand separating Najd and Hasa. With an Indian chauffeur at the wheel, Abd al-Aziz enjoyed regular desert excursions, followed by servants and children on horseback, to a site about 10 miles from town for a picnic and horse races.[140] Abd al-Aziz imported motor vehicles to move his fighters in the campaign to suppress the rebellious Brethren. Motor vehicles replaced camels as the means to transport merchandise across the desert, ending a reliable source of income for the Bedouin who used to provide freight animals.[141]

More than automobiles, the new political dispensation wrecked Bedouin independence. International borders hindered migration. Even worse, in 1921, Abd al-Aziz imposed a blockade against Kuwait. He wished to acquire a share of customs duties on trans-Arabian traffic by diverting imports to Saudi ports at Jubail and Qatif. Bedouin tribes accustomed to trading with Kuwait were collateral damage in his drive to increase revenues.[142] The blockade was one of the Brethren's grievances with Abd al-Aziz and they found ways to dodge it, smuggling goods through Iraqi territory and landing at remote spots along the Gulf coast.[143]

In 1931, Abd al-Aziz bolstered the blockade with border patrols to intercept smugglers and confiscate their goods, but scarcity and high prices drove tribesmen in Hijaz to defy the blockade. A strong motivation for dodging the blockade was a sudden rise in food prices starting in 1929, when the finance minister devalued the riyal (Maria Theresa dollar): in two years, the riyal lost 44 percent of its value against the rupee. Tribesmen blamed Abd al-Aziz for high prices and felt forced to seek less costly food supplies in Kuwait. The hardship of Bedouin tribes was exacerbated by the way Abd al-Aziz and members of the Saud clan confiscated pasture areas to create around eighty reserves for their own camels, depriving Bedouin of an essential resource and transferring control over land from Bedouin to dynasty.[144]

The attempt to control markets and Bedouin access to them was not new. Ottoman governors in Baghdad and Basra had adopted the same measures to tax trade and assert authority over Bedouin. Merchants and Bedouin collaborated to defy Ottoman officials, sometimes abandoning markets and ports under strong Ottoman authority and redirecting trade to markets and ports beyond the reach of Istanbul's agents.[145] More effective enforcement over movement through the desert was part of the emergence of the international state system and the state's assertion of legal authority over trade inside its territory. Abd al-Aziz was carving out his realm's place in that system, using police to control access to "foreign markets." Southern Iraq and Kuwait were distant from the lower reaches of Hasa, Najd, and Hijaz, but they were never before considered foreign. The conversion of customary habits into crimes signaled the end of Bedouin independence. They were expected to submit meekly to confiscation of pasture and devaluation of currency, and to allow the state to dictate where they could exchange and purchase. Consolidating central authority entailed two processes of integration, bringing a fragmented population under a single authority and defining the unified state's place in the international system, at the expense of the Bedouin way of life.[146]

Abd al-Aziz transformed Najd and its position in the world. He mobilized the sectarian mission to enlist Bedouin for conquest, then he allied with "infidel" Britain to conquer the Bedouin for the sake of establishing stable rule. In the early 1930s, severe fiscal and economic pressures threatened to destabilize the Saudi dynasty's revival. What sources might replace the fruits of military expansion? How were the Bedouin to survive when international borders and internal pacification removed raiding as an option, and motor vehicles denied them tolls they used to earn as guides and cameleers for caravans? The transformations of political power (no more Bedouin tribal independence) and religious culture (no more sectarian enclave) did not yet have sturdy material foundations.

5

Petroleum and Its Discontents, 1932–53

The 1915 and 1927 treaties with Great Britain were turning points in Saudi engagement with the global political system. The 1933 oil concession was a turning point in the newly declared kingdom's integration with the global economy. Together, they exemplified Abd al-Aziz's strategic pivot to external resources. Singly, petroleum triggered monumental transformations. The oil industry created new fields for labor in construction, transportation, and operations. It generated the country's first modern political movement when Saudi and foreign workers went on strike to protest low pay and poor living conditions. Wave after wave of foreigners arrived to pursue oil exploration and production, and to staff oil company offices, schools, and clinics. The concentration of labor and services spawned new towns that replicated urban patterns common to oil enclaves elsewhere. The oil industry accelerated the spread of modern education and the rise of a generation of writers advancing literary forms in tune with broader Arabic literary currents. The sheer mass of wealth contributed to the end of customary modes of production and divisions of labor, and funded experiments in raising agricultural productivity and settling Bedouin.

The Oil Concession and a Multinational Industrial Working Class

Concessionary agreements between Middle Eastern rulers and Western investors go back to the mid-1800s. The concession was a vehicle "to attract capital and accelerate economic development by restricting the operation of market forces."[1] The first oil concession in the Middle East was the 1901 D'Arcy Concession for oil exploration and production in Persia. Western prospectors did not look to the Arabian shore of the Gulf until the 1920s. Abd al-Aziz's first brush with oil exploration, the 1923 concession to the Eastern and General Syndicate, went nowhere. Momentum for a second concession gathered in the wake of the May 1932 oil strike in Bahrain. It seemed likely oil lay somewhere on the Arabian shore across from Bahrain. Saudi Arabia became the arena for a contest between British and American companies bidding for a concession.

Negotiations over terms for a concession provided rulers the opportunity to pit bidders against each other.[2] Abd al-Aziz's finance minister, Abdallah Sulaiman, understood and exploited the opportunity by bargaining with a British delegation representing the Iraq Petroleum Company and an American delegation representing Standard Oil. The British firm already had abundant oil supplies through other concessions; its purpose was to keep the Americans out of the Gulf. Standard Oil had a pressing need for new supplies and consequently outbid its rival to reach agreement with the Saudis on May 29, 1933. The agreement granted a concession for sixty years and provided for a lump sum payment to the Saudi treasury of £50,000 (35,000 gold pounds), another lump sum payment against royalties upon discovery of commercial quantities, and royalties tied to annual production. It took the company some time to dispatch a crew and drilling gear. After six wells failed to strike oil, Well No. 7 at Dammam hit a gusher on March 4, 1938.[3]

The Arabian-American Oil Company (Aramco) followed the mining industry's habits of managing workers in the United States and South America.[4] Those habits included a stratification of jobs, compensation, and working conditions according to ethnic and racial categories. When transferred to oil fields in Hasa, the racist labor regime engendered worker grievances and demands for remedy. As it had done in other parts of the world, modern capitalist industry created modern political protest. In this case, the labor movement was not simply the story of the Arab worker versus the American boss. Instead, there was quartet of players: a multinational labor force, a national government in Riyadh, and the United States government in Washington pressing the oil company to adopt decent policies.

In 1940, the first year of work to create the industry's physical infrastructure, the company employed fewer than 4,000 workers, mostly Saudis (3,200), followed by Americans (371), and various other foreign nationalities (156).[5] The outbreak of the Second World War interrupted progress for a few years as the Allies directed scarce industrial supplies to wartime industries. When work resumed in 1942, demand for workers exceeded local supply and the company hired foreign workers, adding a new dimension to the country's global integration, by connecting it to labor networks. In Bahrain and Kuwait, British companies employed Indians and Persians with experience in the industry alongside local Arabs. Racial discrimination fueled labor activism and a rash of strikes in Bahrain (1942 and 1947) and Kuwait (1948–9). Racist company practices also created tensions between the rulers and the Western companies. The rulers in Saudi Arabia, Bahrain, and Kuwait recognized that rapid development of oil resources required foreign nationals with the necessary technical skills; at the same time they expected the Western companies to train and promote local workers.[6]

Harsh conditions, the mingling of nationalities, and the presence of workers with experience organizing labor to remedy grievances sparked Saudi Arabia's first modern political mobilization. A small cohort of Indian workers protested working conditions in February–March 1943 and October 1944. The company chose to replace them with workers from the Italian colony in Eritrea that had come under British occupation. The colony's skilled workers met the need for the large numbers required to construct a refinery (at Ras Tanura) to supply fuel for American military forces in the Pacific theater.[7]

The first group of eighty-eight Italians arrived in December, two months after the second Indian worker protest, and by October 1945, their number exceeded 1,500 to become the largest national cohort at work on the refinery project. It took little time for the Italian workers to protest dismal accommodations, inferior medical care, and low wages (one-third to one-half the rate for Americans performing the same jobs). On July 30, 1945, all 1,700 workers at the refinery project went on strike and requested the American consul to mediate. On inspecting the facilities, the American official urged the American company to meet workers' demands. He wanted to ensure the supply of fuel to military forces was not interrupted. The company agreed and the strike ended.[8]

Two years later, in May 1947, Italian workers again went on strike, over the same issues: housing, food, and wages. Once again, workers asked the American consul (a different one) to arbitrate. Upon inspecting the situation, he wrote a scathing report that described the squalid conditions the oil company considered normal as "a disgrace to American enterprise." The State Department got involved because of possible repercussions in Italy, where the Communist Party was gaining popularity. Both the State Department and the Italian government urged the company to improve conditions, but it resisted. Some workers were repatriated to Eritrea, others returned to work after improvements were promised.[9]

The company treated the Italians as it had the Indians, replacing them with other workers, this time recruiting from Aden and Khartoum, imagining that troublemakers were the cause of labor unrest, not miserable work conditions.[10] As if to demonstrate that

American contempt for Italian workers did not immunize the workers from exhibiting racist contempt, the Italians protested the opening of a "mixed camp" in 1953 where they were housed with Palestinians, Pakistanis, and Indians. By that time, the Italian cohort was shrinking, and the company was replacing them with foreign Arabs, especially Palestinians.[11] After the 1948 Palestine war, King Abd al-Aziz pushed Aramco to recruit Palestinians. The company opened a recruitment office in Beirut and in short order received several thousand applications. By the end of 1950, 800 Palestinians were working for the company.[12]

Shuffling nationalities did not improve relations between management and labor because the company's template for ranking jobs, wages, and living conditions according to an ethnic hierarchy put Saudi and Arab workers at the bottom. Workplace inequity amplified resentment over rules barring Saudis from Western residential compounds and forbidding workers' families from living with them, thereby creating all-male compounds. The company did respond to demands for promotion opportunities by sending a handful of Saudi employees to Beirut and Cairo for business training. The American management, however, continued to assume that Arab employees were not entitled to improved living conditions. Company housing remained segregated, assigning inferior accommodations to Arabs and other foreign workers. The company also barred Arabs from the camp cinema: a Saudi employee wishing to attend a showing of the Charlie Chaplin film *Limelight* was turned away.[13]

One slight after another moved a group of around 150 workers—Saudis, foreign Arabs, and others—to organize a petition requesting the company to fulfill its commitments. At that moment in May 1953, the Saudi government was seeking revision to the concession from Aramco, so workers had reason to believe Riyadh would back up their demands. They submitted a mass petition to Crown Prince Saud seeking his approval for a workers committee. Officials from the Ministry of Finance visited Dhahran in early October and apparently recoiled at the degree of grassroots activism. A few days later, on October 15, provincial authorities arrested the organizers. The next day, protesters staged demonstrations at the Hofuf police station, the American consulate, and the Dhahran air base. On October 17, 13,000 workers began a strike that lasted ten days. During that time, around a thousand Saudis were arrested. Repression proved effective at ending the strike, and Aramco did eventually agree to raise wages, cover some employee expenses such as uniforms, and admit children of workers to company schools.[14]

The first wave of modern political contention in Saudi Arabia followed patterns of mobilization elsewhere. Modern political contention entails an aggrieved party, in this case workers, and a target of the aggrieved party capable of addressing its concerns. The target is usually either an employer or the state. Protest movements sometimes press the state to intervene, perhaps by creating regulations that employers must respect. A triangle of workers, company, and state is precisely what took shape in Saudi Arabia's oil industry. The multinational composition of the workforce, the shifts in its national elements, and the cycles of their mobilization were part of a larger pattern in Gulf oil zones. And like other locations in those zones, the spectrum of grievances and demands later broadened to encompass anti-imperial horizons.

Slavery: Decline and Revival

At the same time as a modern working class took shape and mobilized for rights, the country's enslaved population came under new regulations governed by revisions to the Treaty of Jeddah. Before talks in 1934 to revise the treaty, the British legation undertook a review of slavery and the slave trade in Saudi Arabia. It estimated there were 40,000 slaves and their numbers were falling because of dwindling demand. Motor vehicles replaced camel caravans that relied on enslaved camel drivers; pacification of the steppe meant tribal shaikhs purchased and maintained fewer enslaved armed retainers; landowners used mechanical devices for agricultural tasks instead of slaves. The global depression had an indirect impact on the slave trade by lowering the number of pilgrims because slave traffickers used to bring enslaved children to Mecca on the pretext they were performing the sacred duty and pretending the enslaved boys and girls were their own offspring. European colonial powers conducted naval patrols in the Red Sea that targeted slave ships and reduced traffic from Africa to Arabia to a trickle. As a consequence, traders redirected traffic to Arabia through Yemen to bring enslaved Yemenis and Africans. The Meccan slave market shrank to one small shop and private exchanges.[15] The scope of slavery was contracting, but its salience as part of the trappings of power continued. Saud clan members were the largest slaveholders in the country. Abd al-Aziz alone was estimated to possess 3,000 men and women, many of them gifts from shaikhs and notables that he sometimes presented to reward loyal subjects. Ensuring they were dressed well was material evidence of the king's wealth and standing.[16]

Abd al-Aziz wanted to demonstrate to his subjects that he did not take orders from the British, and for their part, the British did not want to make him look weak in front of the Arab world. After two years of talks, the British and the Saudis agreed to new terms on slavery (October 1, 1936). The British ended consular manumission (the consul's authority to repatriate slaves). Abd al-Aziz pledged to prohibit the import of slaves for the purpose of selling them, but he would allow slave owners to enter his realm with slaves if they were acquired before 1936, when the treaty revisions came into effect. He also committed to manumit slaves able to prove they were freeborn and enslaved in violation of Islamic law after 1925. He further agreed that owners could not separate children from their mothers. London suspected Abd al-Aziz of lax enforcement. British officials in the Persian Gulf observed a redirection in the slave trade, trafficking children from the Makran coast (present-day Pakistan) to Saudi

Arabia via Dubai and Abu Dhabi. They later learned that Saudi officials in Buraimi violated the 1936 regulations by selling documents to traders that falsely attested that captives from Baluchistan were born into slavery.[17]

The founding of the United Nations changed the international context of slavery. Article Four of the 1948 Universal Declaration of Human Rights called for the abolition of slavery and the slave trade. A United Nations committee established in 1949 to study the scope of slavery encountered resistance from several national governments. Oddly, the cradle of abolitionism, Britain, shied away from shining a light on slavery in the Trucial shaikhdoms, where the Second World War years witnessed a new burst of enslavement, in part through kidnapping, in part as a result of famine conditions driving families to sell children. The British received reports that slave traders used deceit, offering to pay parents a bride price to acquire custody and then selling the "brides" to other slave traders. Baluchi girls on the market in Mecca for concubinage fetched high prices. By enriching Gulf shaikhs, the onset of oil production briefly enlarged demand for slaves. A Saudi commander of the military post in Buraimi facilitated caravans of forty to fifty slaves trekking from the oasis to Salwa (near Qatar), where agents of the Saudi royal family were the main customers. Much of this came to light after the British expelled the Saudis from Buraimi in August 1952 and they came across documents attesting the sale of slaves destined to Emir Saud's palace.[18]

Writings about slavery in Saudi Arabia and other Muslim societies often assert that slave owners commonly treated slaves in humane fashion and that Islamic law protected slaves from abuse. The apologetic tone contrasts the comfortable circumstances of domestic slaves to harsh oppression in antebellum United States plantations. An American author, Marianne Alireza, described conditions for five female slaves in one of Jeddah's wealthiest merchant families during the 1940s. One of them, Bushra, was retired from her duties and had her own lodging, along with a stipend and annual gifts of clothing and other "gratuities." A second servant, Saada, looked after the young children of the household. Insaaf came from Ethiopia when still a young girl and did kitchen chores. Baraka served the author's sister-in-law. Resistance to enslavement is implicit in Alireza's description of Murgana, aged eight or nine. Murgana found ways to appear compliant and avoid chores by conveniently disappearing when called upon. Alireza describes her as "mischievous, destructive, rebellious." Alireza's in-laws did not understand why she would not purchase a slave.[19]

The push and pull over slavery formed part of Saudi Arabia's integration into the global political order through treaties with Western powers. It represented how Western governments and social movements, here abolitionism, framed Saudi Arabia as a reluctant latecomer to accepting global norms, foreshadowing later discourses about human rights where the kingdom figured as a target of pressure and criticism.

The United States

Whatever scruples Western powers had regarding slavery, strategic interests consistently took priority. Abd al-Aziz was fortunate that geography and geology endowed his domain with strategic value. He had the judgment to read shifts in international affairs to take advantage of that value. During the Second World War, the global political order shifted. The British empire declined, the United States and the Soviet Union ascended. Saudi Arabia adapted to the new global context, with Washington and Riyadh taking their first steps toward a relationship where the Americans offered economic assistance to shore up a country possessing a strategic location and natural resources. As the war drained Britain's resources, its ability to pay subsidies to Saudi Arabia's treasury diminished, and London encouraged Washington to shoulder more of the burden to bolster an important partner for the West.

The main impact of the war on Saudi Arabia was to strain the budget. Customs duties charged to pilgrims comprised an important source of revenue. The wartime threat to navigation in the Indian Ocean caused the number of pilgrims from India and Southeast Asia to fall to fewer than 10,000 in 1940. The oil company suspended most operations and that meant lower royalty payments. At the same time, a three-year drought ravaged harvests and decimated livestock herds. Before the creation of international borders, Bedouin would have migrated with their animals to seek pasture, but that option no longer existed. To make matters worse, wartime inflation pushed food prices as much as ten times higher. Abd al-Aziz initiated relief measures in summer 1942: he had government trucks deliver rice, dates, and small cash payments to tribesmen in remote areas. He also had annual payments he normally distributed in Riyadh sent to tribesmen in their regions. He increased the number of food distribution sites for Bedouin who lost their herds to drought.[20]

Finance minister Abdallah Sulaiman informed British officials that lower revenue and higher expenditure to feed the famine-stricken country meant it needed a large increase in assistance. He estimated the 1942 budget would need £3.7 million, compared to an average £3 million per year for the previous three years; he estimated revenue at £1 million.[21] Economic and fiscal conditions got worse in 1942 and 1943, with widespread hunger and officials' salaries falling months in arrears. In the latter year, about one-third of the budget, which increased to £5 million, was allocated to providing food and payments for the poor. At that point, the British persuaded the United States to provide financial assistance.[22]

The Second World War was a turning point in the United States' rise to global power. Before the war, the United States, which established official ties with Saudi Arabia in 1931, considered Arabia part of the British imperial sphere. During the war, Saudi Arabia suddenly assumed strategic significance for Washington because of its oil reserves and convenient location for prospective airfields.[23] In 1942,

United States forces operating between the Pacific and European theaters relied on British airfields in Bahrain and Iran, but heavy military traffic strained these facilities' capacities and the Americans sought a location for a larger airfield, giving rise to interest in Dhahran, the oil company town, as an option.[24] When President Roosevelt approved Lend-Lease assistance for Saudi Arabia in February 1943, it was to obtain permission to use its territory for an airfield. The first bundle of Lend-Lease assistance that year consisted of irrigation equipment and some eighty trucks.[25] Granting Lend-Lease was a step in Washington's eclipse of London as Saudi Arabia's main Western patron. Military assistance soon followed: in 1944, the United States delivered arms and equipment, accompanied by trainers. The kingdom's growing importance in Washington's geopolitical strategy led to a meeting between Abd al-Aziz and President Roosevelt, after the Yalta summit, in February 1945. An American vessel bore the Saudi king and his entourage from Jeddah to the Great Bitter Lake in Egypt for his rendezvous with the president aboard the USS *Quincy*. The two leaders discussed the future of European mandates in Palestine, Syria, and Lebanon, and prospects for American technical assistance to develop Saudi agriculture.[26]

By war's end, Saudi Arabia's position as an oil producer and as a landing point for military and civil aviation was embedded in the thinking of the War Department and the State Department.[27] With only an airstrip completed when the war ended, the Americans dropped the military rationale and cited commercial and political reasons: now it was a matter of stabilizing a country "whose vast oil resources are now in our hands," establishing American civil authority over the airfield, and the risk of losing the king's confidence if the Americans decided not to finish the work after lobbying for it—what is typically referred to as "losing credibility."[28] The shifting rationale for an air base suggests that an imperial mindset had taken root in Washington, a reflex for seeking possible threats and means to extend power.[29]

In January 1946, the United States and Saudi Arabia reached an agreement for the Americans to build and lease the Dhahran air base for three years. In exchange, the Americans provided a lump sum payment of $10 million and a $25 million loan. Dhahran airfield was fit for large American bombers and placed under an American military commander. As the end of the lease approached, the Saudis bargained for military assistance. The talks dragged on for two years, during which the Saudis granted one-year extensions. In February 1951, the lease was renewed for five years, and Saudi Arabia received $50 million in military credits to buy arms and weapons training. The lease was renewed again in 1956 before expiring in 1962. By then, the country was firmly in the United States orbit as an ally in the Cold War, a new phase in the kingdom's integration with the global political order.[30]

The Regional Political Order

At the same time as Abd al-Aziz leveraged external powers to bolster the economic and fiscal pillars of his kingdom, he was occupied with securing his position in the regional order. Hijaz remained a sore point for Transjordan's Emir Abdallah. Domestic politics preoccupied Iraq's King Faisal. The focus for Saudi–Kuwaiti relations was how to divide customs revenue on trade bound for Najd. The common denominator for Abd al-Aziz was finding ways to avoid conflict with British-sponsored governments.[31]

In January 1930, shortly after Abd al-Aziz crushed the Brethren, he received a proposal from King Faisal of Iraq to stabilize conditions along the border. The two leaders met on board a British vessel in the Persian Gulf for two days of talks that paved the way for an agreement in 1931 to prevent raids, to set up a commission to arbitrate border incidents, and to permit tribesmen access to markets on either side of the border. In 1936, Iraq and Saudi Arabia signed a treaty of alliance adding provisions for mutual consultation if either country were to be attacked.[32]

Relations with Emir Abdallah took longer to resolve. Under the 1925 Treaty of Hadda, a tribunal reviewed claims for compensation arising from losses in tribal raids. Adjudicating claims in a consistent fashion proved practically impossible. Tribesmen raided each other with no regard for the authority of either government, and it was not always clear which government had sovereignty over which tribesmen. To make matters worse, a drought and an outbreak of locust swarms struck northern Arabia in 1931–2. In famine conditions, Bedouin tribesmen were not disposed to submit to a new political order that eliminated tried and true survival mechanisms such as raids and movement unfettered by national borders. The low point in Saudi relations with Transjordan came in May 1932, when an exiled tribal leader, Ibn Rifada, launched a rebellion in concert with Emir Abdallah and disgruntled Hijazi urban leaders. He led a force of around 800 fighters in a raid on northern Hijaz, but he found no support there, and Saudi forces easily defeated him. Emir Abdallah's plot threatened to destabilize Arabia, the exact opposite of British aims. Pressure from London made him give up efforts to subvert his neighbor and reach terms for a bilateral treaty signed in July 1933.[33]

The one area where the British failed to bring stability during the 1930s was Palestine, where Arab and Zionist national goals were impossible to reconcile. An Arab revolt against Zionist immigration and British rule broke out in spring 1936, and in response, London formed a royal commission, led by Lord William Peel, to investigate the causes of the revolt with a view to recommending steps to ease tensions between the two communities. In July 1937, the commission issued a report calling for a division of Palestine into Arab and Jewish states. A few months after the Peel Report came out, Abd al-Aziz expressed his views on the Palestine issue to a British official visiting Riyadh.[34] The king was hearing that Najdi tribesmen wanted him to break relations with Britain for the sake of the Arabs of

Palestine. He expressed the fear that the Zionists would use Palestine as a base for expanding to the Gulf and Hijaz. He did not hesitate to express religious bigotry when he called the Jews a race cursed by God for rejecting Jesus and Muhammad. He did not wish to become Britain's enemy, but, in the end, he said that his people cared only about God, the Prophet, and honor. If they lost British support, they could live on dates and camels forever.[35]

After the Second World War, the Palestine question created tensions between Saudi Arabia and the United States when President Harry Truman announced support for admitting 100,000 Jewish Displaced Persons (survivors of Nazi concentration camps) to Palestine. Abd al-Aziz let American diplomats know he felt Truman was breaking a promise that Roosevelt had made not to favor measures harmful to the Arabs of Palestine. In public, the king expressed strong support for the Arabs of Palestine and warned Washington that its interests would suffer if it supported the Zionists. In private conversations, however, he assured American diplomats that bilateral ties would not suffer.[36] In those remarks, he captured a common refrain in Arab–Western diplomatic relations ever since, where an Arab leader feels pressure from his people to act on behalf of the Palestinians and assures a Western interlocutor that alliance with the West is too important to sacrifice.

As the May 1948 deadline for British withdrawal from Palestine approached, the Arab states agreed to intervene to prevent partition, and the Saudis sent two battalions comprising 1,200 poorly trained troops under an officer whose last combat experience was in 1924, when he fought on the Hashemite side against Saudi forces in Hijaz.[37] The Saudi contingent went to the Egyptian front and deployed under Egyptian command. The Saudis also announced that if the Americans provided material support to Israel in the war, they would consider cancelling the oil concession and seizing the Dhahran air base. This may have been the first time an Arab leader resorted to control over oil production as a political tactic. During the 1948 war, the Saudis requested American military assistance, but Washington held back until the United Nations armistice took hold.[38]

The Patrimonial Court

Abd al-Aziz exhibited remarkable leadership in the drive to conquest and in dealings with the outside world. When it came to the mechanics of governance, he stuck with the tried-and-true instruments of patrimonial rule. He was an empire builder, not a state builder. Not everyone in his court believed in the emirate model anymore. Sometime around 1930, the palace treasurer, Abdallah Sulaiman, wrote to his brother lamenting the lack of organization in government offices:

> Things have been worsening year after year. The formations and arrangements, and the changing of posts, and every act we do bring no benefit since people have gotten used to this and no longer care about it or even draws their attention. The reason for this is because all the changes and formation or reorganizations were not based on the foundations that other world governments follow.[39]

Abd al-Aziz issued decrees to establish specialized government offices, but the disorganization noted in Sulaiman's letter continued to characterize Saudi administration into the 1960s. The highest body was the royal council, consisting of the king, his brother Abdallah, the two senior princes Saud and Faisal, and the treasurer Abdallah Sulaiman. Staff at the palace supervised stores and warehouses holding supplies for the extensive royal household, and they kept track of gifts and subsidies distributed to tribesmen and visiting dignitaries. Palace servants maintained the royal stables for horses, camels, and the motor pool. A rudimentary communications bureau oversaw telegraphic messages with provincial centers and provided translations of foreign news broadcasts.[40]

According to an Egyptian report in the late 1930s, the main sources of revenue, in descending order, were the pilgrim tax, the oil concession, gold mines, and zakat.[41] Collecting enough revenue to meet expenses was difficult because of widespread resistance to taxation. When the court tried to increase tax rates in the early 1930s to compensate for the decline in pilgrim revenues, revolts broke out in Asir and Hasa.[42] Abd al-Aziz resorted to borrowing from Hijazi merchants.[43] While he ordered the formation of a Ministry of Finance in 1932, it never developed a budget that covered all government departments. The one time that Sulaiman drafted a budget, in 1947, the king rejected it because it cut royal expenses.[44]

The haphazard approach to fiscal matters also applied to building a regular military force. To fight Arabian rivals and quell rebellious Brethren, it was natural for Abd al-Aziz to equip levies with modern weapons and deploy motor vehicles supplied by the British. After the Brethren revolt, he organized the former warriors into a force called the White Army, a forerunner to the National Guard, but Abd al-Aziz was not eager to develop a standing army.[45] He did not create a defense ministry until 1946.[46] The following year, British officers led an abortive military training mission in Jeddah and Ta'if. Volunteers drilled with leftover equipment from the Ottomans; desertions were common. During the Palestine War, the government boosted recruitment by offering higher pay, but nearly all of the 1,000 volunteers who turned up were illiterate. Consequently, the British advisers set up a school to prepare students for training in Britain and Egypt. The nationalist mood in Egyptian army camps proved contagious and a few years later, the Saudi trainees turned out to be some of the country's first advocates of Arab nationalism.[47]

Provincial administration continued along patrimonial lines, with clan members acting as governors. Saud was in charge in Najd and Faisal in Hijaz. The king's cousin Abdallah ibn Jiluwi turned Hasa into a family preserve, ruling the province as a fief until he died in 1935, whereupon his son Saud succeeded him.[48] Members of the

Sudairi clan were appointed to Jabal Shammar. The remote northern district of Wadi Sirhan was effectively autonomous. Because of Asir's diverse topography, it was divided into three zones: Najran, Abha, and Tihama.[49] Administration of the provinces changed little from the early Saudi emirates, with the king's family and local notable clans keeping order and collecting taxes. The only other representatives of central authority were religious judges and tax collectors, much as they had been under the Diriyya emirate.[50] The glue holding the realm together was personal loyalty. Throughout his reign, Abd al-Aziz depended on many of the same families that sided with him from his early years and that ultimately became part of the country's business elite, such as the Gosaibis from Hasa and the Alirezas from Jeddah. He was in power long enough to coopt powerful families that opposed his rule at first, such as the Dabbaghs and the Sabbans of Jeddah, who had orchestrated rebellion in collusion with Emir Abdallah of Transjordan.[51]

In Hijaz, Emir Faisal preserved much of the Ottoman–Hashemite administration, which had brought some innovations. He established a provincial court in Mecca, where he presided over departments for health and education.[52] Abd al-Aziz approved a special charter in 1926 that established a consultative council with responsibility for guilds, police, courts, local services, and public works.[53] Mecca was the center for Abdallah Sulaiman's small cadre of clerks handling financial affairs. The annual influx of foreign pilgrims and the presence of foreign consuls in Jeddah made it the logical headquarters for handling foreign relations.[54]

The administration's ad hoc character is evident in the variety of tasks that fell to Abdallah Sulaiman at different times. When Prince Faisal and his foreign affairs deputy Fuad Hamza traveled to London for talks on Palestine in 1939, the Foreign Affairs Ministry did not have staff to handle business in their absence, and the king appointed Abdallah Sulaiman to take charge, in addition to his usual duties. Abd al-Aziz felt he could rely only on Sulaiman as an all-round troubleshooter, calling upon him to arrange transportation from Jeddah to Medina for an important foreign visitor, allocating zakat funds to prominent clerics, and dispatching health workers to administer smallpox vaccines to the palace in Riyadh.[55]

The Saudi polity remained a patrimonial court, consisting of a ruler, his kinsmen, his allies from local ruling clans, and foreign Arab staff. The key to the stabilization of dynastic power, then, was not the formation of a modern state but the stream of foreign assistance: British subsidies, payments and loans from the American oil company, and Lend-Lease funds from the United States government during the Second World War. To subjugate the Bedouin tribes and provide relief for the needy, Abd al-Aziz depended on the protection of external powers. Only after the war did revenues from oil production relieve budget pressures in a lasting way.[56]

The Mission and the Opening

The country's integration with the global political and economic order, pursued to achieve internal integration under a single authority, forced Wahhabi clerics to lower the barriers of their sectarian enclave. For the sake of political expediency, Abd al-Aziz sought treaties with the British, made agreements on international borders, and recruited foreign Muslims indifferent to Wahhabi doctrine. Clerics meekly accepted their ruler's business deals with infidels and their influx into the kingdom. Around 1932, fewer than fifty non-Muslims resided in the Saudi realm, primarily in Jeddah. By 1936, the number reached around 130.[57] If the country were to adopt modern technology, which Abd al-Aziz used to defeat the Brethren revolt, it had to open the door to more foreigners, even if it grated on Wahhabi nerves.

In response to reports of foreigners roving the kingdom searching for minerals, nine clerics urged Abd al-Aziz to recall that Islamic law prohibited collaboration with Christians.[58] How he responded is not recorded. In 1944, when a cleric objected to American technicians working on an irrigation project in Kharj district, Abd al-Aziz ordered him to Riyadh. He appeared at an audience before the king, his advisers, and court clerics. He declared that the king was "selling the land, and his people, into bondage of Unbelievers, and that this course of action is contrary to his obligation as a Muslim ruler and protector of the holy places and traditions." Abd al-Aziz asked the court clerics if it was true that the Prophet himself had hired non-Muslims to perform specific tasks and they affirmed that it was. He then asked the clerics if the Prophet's example meant it was permitted for him to hire foreigners to undertake projects for the sake of the kingdom's welfare, and they again affirmed that it was. When the dissident cleric did not accept those arguments, Abd al-Aziz warned him that rejecting the learned opinions of senior clerics was grounds for punishment. At that point, the dissident cleric dropped his objection.[59] While the king affirmed support for the clerics on ceremonial occasions, he did not hesitate to overrule them on questions he considered essential to his power. At the same time, developments in the outside Muslim world opened new opportunities for the mission to exercise influence.

During the high tide of Western colonialism between the world wars, the kingdom's independence was almost unique in the Arab world and Abd al-Aziz enjoyed a favorable reputation as a nationalist leader. Arabic publications spread sympathetic accounts of Wahhabism and Saudi Arabia framed in terms of nationalism and progress, closely resembling the presentation of Abd al-Aziz in American newspapers in the late 1920s. The rehabilitation of Wahhabism in the Sunni imagination continued on the path laid down by Rashid Rida and his pupils in the 1920s, with an emphasis on its favorable attitude toward learning and technology (even though that was untrue) and with a renaming of the mission as "Salafi" in order to bury the negative reputation of religious teachings coming from Najd and to associate it with the notion of pristine, authentic teachings.[60]

The Egyptian writer Muhammad Hamid al-Fiqi's *The Impact of the Wahhabi Mission on Religious and Material Reform in Arabia and Elsewhere* praised the Saudis for bringing order to Hijaz and commended the Wahhabi mission for spreading literacy through mass education.[61] In a similar vein, *The Wahhabi Revolution* by Saudi writer Abdallah al-Qasimi cast the Saudi enterprise as a nationalist saga, with Muhammad ibn Abd al-Wahhab sparking a revolution against oppression for the sake of democracy. Qasimi wrote about the Wahhabi mission as a "Najdi Salafi mission" and a "Salafi rebirth," thus blending the era's emphasis on nationalist rebirth with the moral impulse in the religious mission.[62] The twentieth-century revival of Saudi power was a story of turning feuding emirates into a unified, independent kingdom, secure against European invasion. Qasimi also emphasized how Abd al-Aziz brought modern medicine, education, and technology to his realm with the introduction of innovations in communications (telephone and telegraph) and transportation (automobiles and aircraft). Qasimi misrepresented the Wahhabi mission as being open to new inventions. The new image of Saudi Arabia, then, appealed to readers in Arab countries striving for material progress during the years of European colonial domination, making the kingdom's political and religious leadership appear to be models for imitation.[63]

Saudi Arabia's reputation also benefited from the emergence of religious revivalist organizations in the wider Muslim world animated by a sense that Muslims were confronting threats from Western powers, and that to meet those threats, they needed to reaffirm a commitment to making religion the focus of individual and collective life. Revivalist organizations arose in urban settings where the rising literate stratum was abandoning, and in some cases attacking, agrarian religion's denominational spirit.[64] While these organizations responded to conditions outside Saudi Arabia, their religious orientations created ground for Wahhabi proselytizing and fostered a generation of foreign Muslims that would staff transnational religious institutions the Saudis set up in Mecca.

In 1926, an Egyptian cleric, Muhammad Hamid al-Fiqi (1892–1959), established an organization inspired by Wahhabi proselytizing for the abolition of illegitimate innovations. In addition to religious purification, the Helpers of the Prophetic Tradition (Ansar al-Sunna al-Muhammadiyya) combated Western intellectual currents popular with educated youth, particularly the ideas of Darwin, Marx, and Freud.[65] A member of the Helpers became a supervisor over the agency formed in Hijaz to "command right and forbid wrong," and the group's members defended Wahhabi doctrine in Egypt.[66]

The most influential revivalist movement was the Muslim Brotherhood, founded in 1928 by Hasan al-Banna (1906–1948), an Egyptian schoolteacher.[67] Banna had an ambitious program for his movement. The Muslim Brotherhood's field of action encompassed education, social welfare, physical fitness, publishing (propaganda), job training, health, and politics. Under Banna's leadership, the Muslim Brotherhood developed an elaborate organizational structure, with committees for special functions, such as finance and social welfare, and with sections for workers, students, and professionals. Members undertook activities that put into action the idea that Islam serves public welfare, with health clinics, literacy classes, and assistance to fellow Muslims in need. As befits a former schoolteacher, Banna set up clubs for youth to build camaraderie through camping trips and sports teams for wrestling, soccer, and boxing. He assigned youth sections to perform public services such as street cleaning in poor neighborhoods. The public could follow the Brotherhood's activities in its own newspaper. This modern model of religious activism thrived. In twenty years, membership in Egypt reached 500,000, and branches surfaced in Jordan, Palestine, Syria, Lebanon, Yemen, and the Gulf.

Branches of the Muslim Brotherhood were set up in several Arab countries, but King Abd al-Aziz kept it out of Saudi Arabia. He met Banna during the pilgrimage and told the Egyptian that the kingdom did not need a Muslim Brotherhood organization because Muslims in the kingdom were already brothers. Later Saudi kings viewed the Muslim Brotherhood as a partner in projects that strengthened Saudi Arabia's educational institutions and international outreach, but they mistrusted the organization's activist ethos. In addition to royal rejection of organized activism, the Brotherhood's religious orientation was at odds with the Wahhabi mission. They agreed on the threat posed by Western culture and secular political trends such as socialism and communism; and they agreed on the general idea of urging Muslims to make religion the focus of their lives; but Wahhabism's narrow theology was at odds with Banna's "big tent" approach that called for overlooking what he considered minor differences in belief and worship for the sake of Muslim unity against non-Muslim and secular Muslim adversaries. As a result of this difference, Wahhabi clerics excluded the Muslim Brotherhood from religious institutions where theological correctness mattered (such as Saudi religious institutes) but not from institutions that promoted Muslim solidarity against non-Muslim threats.

The interwar period, then, marked a turning point in the trajectory of relations between the Wahhabi mission and the Muslim world. The rehabilitation of Wahhabism as part of the Sunni fold now coupled with the rise of revivalist movements seeking allies for the struggle against the powerful tides of Western cultural influence in Muslim societies from Morocco to Indonesia. Soon after Abd al-Aziz took control of the holy cities, members of the Helpers of the Prophetic Tradition showed up and served the kingdom. Their common commitment to warn Muslims against Western cultural influence provided a foundation for cooperation in religious institutions possessing a more cosmopolitan accent than that of the Najdi mission. The result was the opening of outlets for Wahhabi outreach beyond Arabia and for outside Muslim trends to make inroads into Arabia where their independence implicitly and quietly eroded Wahhabi authority.

Reshaping Social and Natural Terrains

Abd al-Aziz's suppression of the Brethren spelled the end of Bedouin independence. For the first time, it was possible to establish unitary political authority.[68] Sedentary Arabia had the power to curtail migration to markets and pastures, forcing a restructuring of the rural economy that denied pastoralists essential resources that had always been part of their multi-resource economy. The British traveler Wilfred Thesiger pondered the future of Arabian Bedouin under modern conditions: "I knew for them the danger lay, not in the hardship of their lives, but in the boredom and frustration they would feel when they renounced it. The tragedy was that the choice would not be theirs; economic forces beyond their control would eventually drive them into the towns to hang about street-corners as 'unskilled labour.'"[69]

Having dismantled pillars of the pastoral economy, Abd al-Aziz first tried to turn Bedouin into self-sufficient cultivators in the Brethren colonies, but that did not work out. Consequently the king became a source of patronage and relief for impoverished Bedouin. Some joined the National Guard, others went to work for the oil company. It became common for Bedouin to invest wages in trucks and put their intimate familiarity with the terrain to use in the freight business, driving trucks instead of camels. Some former Bedouin put their savings into livestock herds and hired foreigners to tend their flocks.

Devising ways to provide for demobilized Bedouin was an essential pillar for a regime of law and order rooted in the outlook of sedentary folk. Livestock raids became theft. Blood feuds became violations of the king's peace. Violators of the ban on blood feuds exploited the very international borders that curtailed the old way of life to escape the law, sometimes fleeing to Iraq and waiting for the opportunity to return under an amnesty if they paid blood debt.[70] Abd al-Aziz drew on Bedouin expertise to enforce his writ to convert the Bedouin realm into orderly rural areas. In one episode of desert forensics, he engaged three brothers renowned for their tracking skills to pursue rustlers who had made off with two riding camels pasturing outside Riyadh. Royal guards placed basins over the camels' and the robbers' tracks to preserve evidence. The king then sent for Salim and Ali al-Ariq, expert trackers from the Murrah tribe, itself renowned for uncanny skill: according to their own lore, the tribe's ancient ancestor, from the days before Prophet Abraham, rescued a jinn woman from a wolf attack and her family rewarded him by permitting him to marry her. From their match issued the Murrah tribe, possessing supernatural tracking powers inherited from a jinn ancestress.[71] The Ariq brothers followed the trail of hoofprints and footprints for 250 miles before catching up with two of the rustlers. The king sentenced them to a year in prison, but the third rustler remained at large until Ali al-Ariq spotted his footprints five years later outside the chief mosque in Riyadh and notified police, who arrested him.[72]

Integration of the Bedouin under a central political authority, with assistance from foreign patrons and a foreign oil company, dissolved a historic way of life. Its customs, however, persisted through enactments that represented cultural unity between king and tribesmen, rituals that became part of the dynasty's repertoire for spreading a sense of national solidarity. A British visitor to Riyadh in 1937 described the performance of a war dance, or *arda*, at the royal palace, to honor one of the king's sons for completing lessons in memorizing the Quran. From a palace verandah, women of the royal family watched as some 700 men danced in ranks, raising and lowering their swords to the rhythm of drums, and chanting verses of war and love. King Abd al-Aziz, Emir Saud, and other princes joined the throng, gathered to mark the generational transmission of God's revelation with a ritual of swords, swaying bodies, and verse, a medley of meanings and communion to be shared by the hundreds of men with fellows for miles and years.[73] Notably absent from the tableau were the Wahhabi clerics. This was a separate space where the beats of old Najd persisted apart from the mission's oversight.

The internal combustion engine is part of this history, in the vehicles Abd al-Aziz deployed in fateful military encounters with Brethren rebels, and in vehicles that ended the camel's two-millennium domination of overland transportation in Arabia.[74] The new mode of transportation extinguished a way of life, a way of knowing, and a way of relating to the natural world. The eclipse of the camel caravan changed what counts for knowledge. During Wilfred Thesiger's 1945–6 journey with four Bedouin companions, he learned that they were able to detect a camel's traits from its tracks: if a camel had a rider or not; if a camel was pregnant; if a camel spent most of its life in sandy terrain or gravel-strewn plains (they had different soles according to the surface). They knew where a camel grazed from its droppings and how recently it had drunk water.[75] The Bedouin estimated rainfall by scooping a handful of sand to see how deep they had to reach before finding moisture.[76] The journey's slow pace was essential for the accumulation of knowledge, allowing the traveler to notice small details: an insect, a dead bird, animal tracks, a bird's nest, wind ripples in the sand. "The very slowness of our march diminished its monotony. I thought how terribly boring it would be to rush about this country in a car."[77]

The automobile turned the desert into a void to be traversed as fast as possible to arrive at a destination. It made the Bedouin's remarkable knowledge of desert ecology obsolete and rendered them illiterates requiring uplift and schooling. In one epoch, the Bedouin were experts in lore necessary to survival; in the new epoch, they were drones in a new way of drawing sustenance from beneath the desert in a form that altered the entire economic logic of the country, dependent on shipping out a vast but exhaustible resource. What had been sustained for centuries became a token of backwardness.

Even before the discovery of oil, the internal combustion engine was scarring the desert and changing the biological balance.

Missionary physician Louis Dame described a car trip he took in 1933, from the Gulf to Hijaz. When he came to the Rukba plain on the approach to Hijaz, he reported that in the king's most recent annual hunt of gazelles, gunmen riding in cars killed 400 gazelles in a single day. The slaughter was so extensive that Dame did not see a single gazelle during his crossings of the plain.[78] In a 1937 car trip from Kuwait to Riyadh, the Dicksons counted only six gazelles.[79] Around the same time, a visitor noted that using cars for hunting brought the gazelle near extinction and the slaughter of the bustard by the thousands.[80] When Thesiger made his second crossing of the Empty Quarter in 1947–8, he lamented the slaughter of wildlife enabled by motor vehicles: "Hunting-parties scour the plains in cars, returning with lorry-loads of gazelle which they have run down and butchered." He estimated it would be only a few years before the oryx followed the Arabian ostrich into extinction.[81] By the mid-1940s, wealthy urban families in Jeddah, with both men and women family members, were driving to the desert to hunt gazelle from cars.[82]

Motorized power also altered the fragile oasis environment, with mechanical pumps replacing animal power to raise water to the surface. Increasing the supply of subterranean water for cultivating food crops seemed like a good way to apply mechanization, but it did not take long before the water table fell and disturbed customary ways of allocating water between fields. Nevertheless, the king and Abdallah Sulaiman urged Aramco to bring a team of American agriculture experts to supervise the royal farms south of Riyadh. At the time, a Dutch observer foresaw mechanization would cause harm in several ways. It would accentuate social inequality by displacing workers. Over-pumping underground water would damage the soil with higher salinity and cause the water table to fall, harming poor cultivators unable to afford the equipment to dig deep wells.[83]

New technology altered urban landscapes as well, starting with royal palaces. In the mid-1920s, the royal household comprised around eighty adults. A decade later, some 800 people routinely slept in the palace. With little room for expansion in the city, the king ordered construction of a new palace a mile north of Riyadh, where he moved in 1938. Relocating the center of power outside the city walls signified confidence in stability and security. Funds from the oil concession were spent on purchasing cars for the royal garage, which created new jobs for mechanics and drivers. The wider use of cars led to construction of palaces at some distance from the old city.[84]

Riyadh underwent rapid change. In the 1940s, the population grew from 47,000 to 83,000. As the compact town expanded beyond fortified walls, new districts became identified with rank and occupation. The royal family and wealthy merchants resided in the city's north and west. The city's east and south were home to mechanics, workers, and Bedouin, whose seasonal tent encampments became permanent, with walls going up around their tents and eventually roofs over the walls. Immigration from Wadi Dawasir in the south led to a new suburb near Manfuha while the arrival of builders and tradesmen from Qasim created Hillat al-Qusman. The city's appearance began to change faster after a railway to Dammam was completed in 1951, making it easier to transport new construction materials, notably concrete, to replace mud and brick.[85] Modern inventions started arriving in the main towns, with the radio becoming commonplace, bringing music, regional news, and awareness of political developments. The Singer sewing machine spared many hours of labor formerly performed by slaves. Shops began offering imported cosmetics, soaps, and perfumes.[86]

In Hasa, the oil industry produced urban patterns characteristic of mining and plantation enterprises in Asian and African colonies, where company towns were divided between enclaves for Western staff and "native towns" for local labor. Oil company towns in Venezuela, Iran, Iraq, Kuwait, and Bahrain conformed to the pattern and the same scenario unfolded in Saudi Arabia, where Aramco built completely separate and different places for Saudi and American employees.[87] The American company's need for goods and services brought forth a corps of local merchants and contractors, some from old merchant families, some from men who started as unskilled labor. The gathering of merchants, contractors, and workers seeded urban development and careers. Unaiza native Sulaiman Olayan (c.1920–2003) went to live with relatives in Bahrain, where he learned English. In the late 1930s, he worked in the Aramco oil fields and became a labor contractor, bringing workers from Palestinian refugee camps in Lebanon for the Tapline project piping oil from Saudi Arabia to Sidon, the main Lebanese port on the Mediterranean Sea. He later expanded his business, the General Trading Company, to freight, utilities, and consumer goods. Olayan became one of the wealthiest businessmen in the country. His path from the Najdi center of the caravan trade to Bahrain, to the Eastern Province reflected the country's integration into the global economy and internal transformation under the impact of global capital.[88]

After the Second World War, Saudi government officials asked Aramco to come up with a plan for a new town to house the growing workforce. Company officials favored the suggestion because it might resolve grievances that fueled labor unrest. In 1947, the company selected a tiny fishing settlement, Khobar, whose inhabitants numbered fewer than 100 before the concession. The location was convenient for transporting industrial equipment from Bahrain to Dhahran. By 1951, Khobar had more than 13,000 residents. It would be completely different from older cities that had compact residential quarters, irregular courses for narrow streets, and a central location for mosques and markets. The planners made the streets wide enough for cars and laid out streets on a grid. The main artery, King Khalid Street, became a new kind of urban space for vendors, musicians, and shops—a setting for new "life-worlds" for consumption and leisure. King Khalid Street became known for its modern commercial profile, with banks, grocery stores, pharmacies, restaurants, and jewelry shops. The street's novel modernity made it known as the Champs-Élysées of Saudi Arabia, the route for royal motorcades to pass as well as the thoroughfare for out-of-town shoppers. The government and the oil company pointed to the oil towns as exemplars of modernity, and they became the template for modern urban development that would be replicated across the kingdom.[89]

From the perspective of Saudi optimists, there was reason to feel good about the new oil city. An article in a Medina newspaper succinctly framed the narrative promoted by Aramco that emphasized the company's contribution to the public good. Salih al-Zakir, an official in the Ministry of Finance, praised the company for building an expansive industrial framework that promised immense wealth, and for undertaking development projects, such as a new hospital and the Dhahran airport.[90] Other Saudis were gratified to see Aramco combat malaria outbreaks that were endemic in the Hasa oasis. In 1947, the disease spread so widely among the company's workforce that the American managers instituted a mosquito eradication program by spraying homes with DDT. The program worked for a few years, but by the mid-1950s, mosquitoes developed immunity to the pesticide and the company had to find a different chemical to reduce malaria infection.[91]

A symbiosis of Western culture and Arabian money gave rise to a distinctive pattern where Americans lived in isolated enclaves, Saudi royals purchased American comforts for their new palaces, and foreign contractors arrived to cater to both sets of customers. American colonies transplanted United States suburbia, complete with golf courses and swimming pools.[92] The residential enclaves formed a sealed environment in which the foreigners worked and lived and from which they were forbidden to venture except on organized outings. Within the compound, Americans might show movies in open-air settings, far from curious Saudis.[93] With rising oil income, princes adopted Western models of consumption and leisure. They engaged foreign firms to construct palaces with swimming pools and air conditioning. As reports of free-spending ways spread, European, American, and Arab businessmen flocked to the kingdom.

It was not only a matter of the world coming to Saudi Arabia. In the 1940s and 1950s, merchant families sent their sons abroad for schooling in Egypt, Lebanon, and the United States, where they came to enjoy such leisure pastimes as soccer and movies.[94] Soccer became a point of controversy between its fans and the clerics.[95] The clerics opposed the sport because it exposed men's legs in public. In 1951, however, Prince Abdallah ibn Faisal as Minister of Interior decided to permit teams, even though other princes feared they might serve as vehicles for political activity. The clerics succeeded at blocking cinemas, but members of the royal family showed movies in their palaces.[96]

Early Shoots of Modernism

In the world of letters, the outlets for writers attuned to contemporary Arabic culture multiplied. Hijaz in particular was the vanguard of a literary scene that looked to Cairo and the Arab diaspora, or *mahjar*, for inspiration. As an inlet for a modernist sensibility in the wider Arab world, newspapers in Jeddah, Mecca, and Medina were the primary venues for writers trying their hands at fiction, especially the short story. In the 1930s, Hijazis took over the government newspaper *Mother of Cities* from Syrian hands and opened its pages to Saudi writers. It was the only newspaper to last more than a few issues until Muhammad Salih al-Nasif, the scion of a leading Jeddah merchant family, launched *The Voice of Hijaz* (*Sawt al-Hijaz*) in 1932. The newspaper was a popular venue for young authors of fiction and literary reviews. The shortage of materials during the Second World War forced the newspaper to shut down, then, after the war, Nasif published a weekly literary periodical, *The Saudi Land* (*al-Bilad al-Saudiyya*), projecting a national rather than provincial Hijazi brand.[97]

The Hijazi press incubated the pioneers of Saudi literature, usually writing in the vein of themes and styles that reflected late Ottoman and Sharifian literary developments. They did not address questions about Saudi Arabia as a nation, nor did they show awareness of Najdi preoccupations. Instead, their outlook was anchored to cosmopolitan Arabic currents. Some works bore the imprint of the Syrian-American writers Amin al-Rihani and Gibran Khalil Gibran, with their introspective, meditative tone in essays and free-verse poetry. When topical essays became more popular, they exhibited a secular outlook with no reference to religion.[98] Medina entered the literary scene in 1937 when Abd al-Quddus al-Ansari launched *The Spring* (*al-Manhal*), which became the foremost outlet for poets experimenting with free verse. Ansari also published literary reviews of Saudi fiction and translations of short stories by Muslim, Asian, and Western authors.[99]

The country's first novella came out in 1930. *The Twins* by Abd al-Quddus al-Ansari (publisher of *The Spring*) is a didactic tale about two brothers whose educations demonstrate the virtuous effects of education in national schools in contrast to the pernicious moral downfall that ensues from going abroad to study. The brother who decided to pursue learning in Paris has a romance with a dance girl who spends his money and leaves him penniless. He later dies in a barroom brawl. Early short stories resembled Ansari's novel in sketching cardboard characters representing virtue and vice confronting individual moral dilemmas when coping with poverty, illness, or misfortune.[100]

Some authors injected humor into their work. *His Stolen Clothes* (1939) by Muhammad al-Maghribi gives a playful treatment of stock characters in rural Hijaz, such as an eccentric innkeeper.[101] The Algerian-born Ahmad Huhu was preoccupied with the fate of literature, perhaps echoing anxieties of European authors of the period.[102] He wrote a newspaper essay, a short story ("The Last Man of Letters," 1938), and a play (*The Literary Poseurs*, 1939) on the theme. In the newspaper piece, Huhu lamented, "The day will come when it [literature] will wane and it will be waste and madness to devote oneself to it. Thus, it will remain in isolation, buried between the covers of books. It will be [a curiosity] like an ancient coin, visited merely like a grave until its very trace is effaced and it falls into utter oblivion." The play, a biting farce, is the only written piece of drama from the period. Sometime in the future, society is indifferent to literature, yet people still value a literary reputation. An old man named Khalil offers a two-hour course promising to establish one's reputation as a man of letters. Four students respond to the advertisement he placed in the newspaper. At the start of the lesson, Khalil informs the class that attaining a literary reputation has two elements. The first is the necessary appearance: elegant clothes, eyeglasses, and a pen and notebook for jotting down ideas. The second is to memorize the names of ten famous writers and some titles of their works. One of the pupils asks if there is a faster, easier way because memorizing ten writers seems like a lot of work. Khalil responds that that is what it takes to become a major man of letters, but if you want to be an average man of letters, then four names are enough.[103]

Theater entered the literary scene through the back door of annual school celebrations that often presented skits that depicted the value of school learning as the solution to the problems arising from ignorance. A second popular topic was exemplary events and personalities in Islamic history, shared symbols that brought together the audience, performers, and school staff. In 1935, King Abd al-Aziz lent his prestige to an Unaiza school performance of a historical play about the Arabs and the Persian emperor.[104] The first performance of a scripted play took place at the Mecca high school established in 1937 to prepare pupils for advanced study outside the country.[105] The school's Egyptian teachers were familiar with theater as literary genre. At the inaugural annual ceremony, students staged two plays. One play was written by a teacher in English; the other play, in Arabic, had the usual didactic theme dealing with ignorance but was unusual in consisting of six acts.[106] Staging a play beyond school walls was another matter that did not materialize until decades later because of clerical opposition.[107]

Saudi authors whose lives straddled the eras before and after oil expressed a range of sentiments about a bygone way of life, with some lamenting the loss of closeknit community and others bidding good riddance to unceasing hardship. Mansur ben Muhammad al-Khiraiji's *Beyond the Glamour of the Job: Snaps from My Earlier Life* describes a rural childhood immersed in poverty. His father died when he was seven, leaving his mother to provide for him and his older brother Salih, with help from her brother, a landless laborer who had his own wife and daughters to look after. Khiraiji recalls chopping roots for the stove, gathering fodder for the donkey, and fetching water from wells a few miles away. His brother and uncle scoured the desert to gather firewood and then journeyed to Bedouin camps to trade their gleanings for food or other supplies. He and his brother would pick up crates of grapes from a landowner and travel half a day to reach Bedouin camps to sell them for a share of the proceeds. Khiraiji brings to life the nameless, faceless poor of the desert, and he offers an admiring portrait of his uncle's sturdy character, a man who endured hardship with equanimity and did not live to see his nephew, the author, receive a scholarship to study in the United States.[108]

Nostalgia for calmer times and a sense of community pervade *Memories of a Pliant Child* by Abd al-Aziz al-Rabee'. He describes how the people of Medina used to live amid date groves, celebrating the date harvest with local customs. He longs for the days when artisans fashioned bird cages without using nails or glue. He especially misses the days before cars: the city streets were quieter and riding animals to get around was healthier than riding in cars. He remembers that the first fatal car accident in Medina came as a shock, in contrast to recent times when death on the road became commonplace. In his youth, the only motor transport to Mecca was via post office cars that made the trip three times a month, so people would reserve seats ahead of time. The uncomfortable, bumpy road and the erratic driver of one of the post office cars inspired a local wordsmith to coin a short poem that gently poked fun. That sort of intimacy was no longer part of life in Medina, where date trees were a memory, and steel and cement buildings amplified noisy traffic jams.[109] Hasan Naseef aptly captured the sentiment in his memoir: "God bless the time before cars entered our lives, and when radio, tape recorder, electricity and all the other modern inventions were still unknown."[110]

Anxiety about rapid change was felt in the domain of veteran Brethren too. Around 1950, a former British official long acquainted with the Bedouin noted worries that princes influenced by cosmopolitanism and foreign Arab advisers were out of touch with the old ways. They were too westernized, and they were falling away from religion. The official reported that conservative Bedouin believed that Emir Saud understood them. They gave him credit for banning alcohol in Aramco compounds, but they worried about what would happen under the next king.[111]

In the two last decades of Abd al-Aziz's rule, Saudi Arabia became integrated in two external orders: the global economy and the regional culture, including its religious literary modernist currents. The oil concession brought about Saudi Arabia's integration into the global economy as a producer of a valuable raw material for the industrialized world. Abd al-Aziz sought the concession to shore up a shaky fiscal foundation for preserving stability that depended on foreign subsidies to keep hungry Bedouin and Hijazi townsmen in line. The oil industry had contradictory effects. On the one hand, oil income paid for a few projects to improve transport, communications, construction, and urban infrastructure. On the other hand, the industry spawned an industrial working class that mobilized to launch the country's first modern political movement and foreshadowed a future of contestation between the regime and activists connected to outside political currents.

The country's integration with political, religious, and literary currents in the Arab and Muslim spheres came about as a result of Abd al-Aziz's approach to ruling Hijaz, whose townsmen were part of late Ottoman Arab cultural life, and his reliance on foreign Arabs to handle foreign relations. His strategies for shoring up his power punctured the walls of isolation Wahhabi clerics had erected. They reacted to events as they came, resisting at times, retreating at times, finding new allies abroad, and unwittingly opening the country to religious currents that would later challenge the clerics and their royal patrons. Balancing fidelity to Muslim interests with growing economic and strategic ties to the United States became a chronic challenge for Saudi rulers.

6

The Age of Revolutionary Arab Nationalism, 1953–70

In the 1953 labor protests, Saudi and Arab workers challenged the oil company, imperialism, and the monarchy. Nationalist and leftist groups would soon form to pursue visions of social justice and of independence from Western political and economic domination. In the late 1950s and early 1960s, they made common cause with a faction of "Free Princes" and with kindred movements in other Arab countries. Prince Faisal led conservative princes determined to thwart the Saudi dissident current, in part by promising to deliver material benefits to the population. To fulfill that promise, Faisal and allied princes began to turn the patrimonial court into a modern government with the capacity to carry out national development.

Court Politics and the Arab Revolutionary Current

For half a century, Abd al-Aziz ibn Abd al-Rahman was the central figure in the revival and consolidation of his clan's power. He knew that sustaining its power would depend in part on preventing the kind of dispute that tore apart the Riyadh emirate. In 1933, a year after announcing the Kingdom of Saudi Arabia, he proclaimed that Emir Saud would succeed to the throne, but naming a successor did not ensure harmony between his sons. After all, the last uncontested succession in the Saud line was in 1814.

A month before he died in November 1953, Abd al-Aziz announced the formation of a Council of Ministers, but two decades after the first government ministries had been established, they were more notional than real. The king and his court still ran the country in patrimonial fashion.[1] King Saud ignored the Council of Ministers, choosing to rule through his sons and trusted commoners. Faisal and the other brothers pushed for a fraternal distribution of power.[2] The royal power struggle between King Saud and Crown Prince Faisal lasted a decade and ended in Saud's abdication, Faisal's coronation, and the creation of a bloc of allied senior princes that lasted a half-century, from 1964 to 2015, when King Salman concentrated power in his own line.

The clan contest unfolded against the backdrop of a phase in Arab regional politics dominated by anticolonial leaders and parties. Arab nationalist and leftist causes won widespread allegiance among modern social groups: industrial workers, professionals (teachers, doctors, engineers), civil servants, and military officers. The most influential Arab nationalist movement was the Arab Baath Party, founded in Damascus in the late 1940s to pursue unification of the Arab world, from the Atlantic Ocean to the Persian Gulf, freedom from imperialist domination, and socialism.[3] The platform proved popular, and branches were set up in Lebanon, Iraq, Jordan, Yemen, and the Gulf.

While the Baath had a popular platform, its leadership failed to excite the masses the way Egyptian president Gamal Abdel Nasser did. He belonged to a clandestine group of army officers who came together after the 1948 Palestine war believing Israel owed its victory to the corruption and ineptitude of Arab rulers, including the Egyptian monarchy. Calling themselves the Free Officers, they plotted the overthrow of the monarchy in July 1952. Nasser did not embrace the cause of Arab unity. Rather, he mobilized Arab nationalist sentiment in Egypt and other countries to support him as the leader of anti-imperialism. Both Nasser and the Baath leaders in Syria wished to erase Western domination, but each felt entitled to claim leadership of Arab anti-imperialism, therefore they became wary allies, then rivals, and eventually enemies. Rivalry within the Arab nationalist camp and polarization between the Arab nationalists and conservative regimes characterized regional relations in the era of the "Arab Cold War."[4]

The revolutionary camp included communist and socialist movements that had developed decades before Arab nationalism, but never became dominant, in part because Nasser and the Baath opposed them. In fact, the Arab nationalists were ruthless in crushing communists in Egypt, Syria, and Iraq. As if opposition from conservative regimes and Arab nationalists were not a big enough handicap for leftist movements, their natural ideological ally, the Soviet Union, abandoned them for the sake of gaining the support of more powerful Arab nationalist forces as part of its global rivalry with the United States.

Saudi Arabia did not come under foreign rule, but its incorporation into the modern political and economic systems came about through treaties (with London), military training agreements (with London and Washington), and a concession (with corporate oil) that defined its role as a strategic dependent and peripheral economy. From those subordinate positions, Saudi rulers, court advisers, technocrats, workers, and the educated stratum expressed, in different ways, anti-imperialist sentiment: battling London over claims to Buraimi, pressing Aramco for decent working conditions, and turning the press into an organ for voicing nationalist demands. Saudi Arabia's political opposition mirrored currents in the rest of the Middle East: workers fought for labor rights, leftists struggled against exploitation, and nationalists agitated against Western domination; they all confronted royal autocracy, Western powers, and the foreign oil company.[5] The ground for forming a unified opposition front, however, was not promising. Reflecting an early stage of national integration, activists had to cope with geographical dispersal between urban pockets in the east, center, and west, as well as the same factional feuds as in the rest of the Arab world between Nasserists, Baathists, socialists, and communists.[6]

The Saudi left, an assortment of labor, Arab nationalist, and leftist groups, developed from a transnational context: Saudis worked and studied in Egypt, Lebanon, and Iraq, whence they returned with enthusiasm for nationalist and leftist causes; Egyptian, Palestinian, and Iraqi teachers and oil workers came with welcome skills and unwelcome dissident ideas that Saudi pupils and workers picked up. The government detected the subversive threads in transnational ties and attempted to sever them. In the crackdown on the 1953 protest movement, it deported Lebanese and Palestinian workers and banned newspapers coming from Bahrain.[7] Saudi labor leaders continued to organize in the face of repression. In 1954, they set up the National Reform Front. The front advocated for a constitution, parliament, and political freedoms (legal political parties, labor unions, free press); opening public schools for girls, ending illiteracy, and promoting higher education; abolishing slavery; revising the oil concession and using oil revenue for national development; and ending the US military presence.[8]

The cradle of political opposition, the Eastern Province, was the center of gravity for movements that drew support in labor camps, the old port town of Qatif, and new oil cities such as Dammam and Jubail.[9] Sons of established Shiite notable families gravitated to opposition groups. Hasan al-Jishi (1918–1972), for example, was from a respected merchant family with roots in Bahrain and Qatif. In the early 1930s, he lived with members of his extended family in Bahrain, where he worked for the oil company (BAPCO) before moving to his native Qatif and finding work with Aramco. In the 1950s, Jishi worked to spread nationalist and leftist thinking by founding a night school, a literary club, and a theater. The authorities suspected him of using private spaces to spread subversion and closed them down.[10]

In the mid-1950s, Eastern Province newspapers enjoyed some latitude to advance progressive views.[11] *Dhahran News* highlighted economic problems: how Aramco's food imports undermined local farmers and how the oil company's wages drew young men away from tending date groves and vegetable gardens, resulting in neglect and lower output.[12] Writers called for fair distribution of the blessings of oil wealth to include the historic towns like Qatif, not just the new cities in the orbit of the oil industry. Letters to the editor expressed readers' dissatisfaction with the failure of government offices to handle garbage, sewage, and pollution.[13] The press also spread Arab nationalist views supporting the Algerian revolution and Palestine.[14]

In 1954, Saudis went to the polls to elect municipal councils in the Eastern Province, Hijaz, and Riyadh. That leftists and nationalists from both Shiite and Sunni communities won seats on the councils both in the new oil towns of Dammam and Khobar as well as the historic town of Qatif suggests the elections were reasonably fair, even though the provincial governor, Saud ibn Jiluwi, was against the elections and against allowing elected councils to exercise authority.[15] The councils offered popular movements the chance to gain a foothold in government, but the councils got bogged down in quarrels between elected councilors and the governor's appointees. No elections were held after 1960. Without a legal or constitutional foundation for representation, elections were a gift from above that the rulers could grant or withdraw at will. Demands for political representation met the same fate as demands for worker representation, and in both cases, political activism was forced underground.[16]

The brief opening for the press and elections corresponded to King Saud's early years on the throne, when he viewed Egyptian President Nasser as a possible ally confronting a common adversary: the British. King Saud resented that London sided with Abu Dhabi and Oman in their dispute with the Saudis over possession of the

Buraimi oasis. Riyadh announced a formal claim to Buraimi in 1949 and it sent troops to cement that claim in 1952. American oil companies believed the region may hold petroleum reserves and they supported the Saudi claim against Abu Dhabi and Oman. The dispute was submitted to the United Nations for arbitration. Before that body reached a decision, Britain backed an Omani military expedition that ousted the Saudi forces in 1955. Ultimately, Abu Dhabi and Oman divided the villages spread across the oasis, leaving Riyadh empty-handed.

During the Buraimi dispute, King Saud funded pro-Egyptian newspapers in Jordan, Iraq, and Syria. Nasser sent a technical team to advise the Saudis on administrative improvement and a military training mission. The Egyptian officers proved better at political sabotage than professional training. In May 1955, Saudi army officers were caught plotting against the monarchy. A new round of searching for subversive activists resulted in the arrest of a prominent figure in the Ministry of Finance office in Dammam, Abd al-Aziz ibn Muʿammar, on suspicion of stirring up labor unrest and spreading leftist ideas. The search for dissidents led authorities to Aramco camps and the arrest of Palestinian workers for membership in nationalist parties.[17]

The combination of labor unrest and anti-imperialism fueled a rash of protests when the king visited Dhahran on June 9, 1956. As his motorcade proceeded down the main boulevard, Saudis waved banners welcoming him and condemning imperialism. Two days later, a royal decree prohibited demonstrations and strikes. Then, on June 14, a disturbance broke out at the Ras Tanura Intermediate Camp over barring Saudi workers from a cinema that Pakistani and Palestinian workers frequented. Security forces dispersed the crowd and arrested the leaders. Ten men received a hundred lashes in public the next day, and then were sent to prison in Qatif where they underwent torture that proved fatal for some of them.[18] The government offered a carrot to go with the stick by announcing that it was instructing Aramco to improve workers' education, health care, and employment. At the same time, the government warned against harmful individuals sowing disruption, code for political activists it blamed for expanding political demands to include closure of the American air base. The police rounded up more than ninety men, many never to be seen again and presumably killed in detention. With security forces prowling the camps and nearby villages and a new decree making strikes illegal and punishable with lengthy sentences, most workers returned to work June 23.[19]

As happened in so many parts of the world, prison became a space for political dissidents to mingle and form new factions. Discussions among the dissidents led to polarization between Arab nationalists and Marxists, and fragmentation within both groupings: Nasserists, Baathists (later Syrian and Iraqi factions), independent Marxists, pro-Moscow Marxists. One small faction called the Arab National Liberation Front included Prince Talal, oil ministry official Abdallah al-Tariqi, and the Shiite cleric Abd al-Karim al-Humud.[20] In 1958, activists still at large created a new organization, the National Liberation Front, which operated in secrecy, printing and distributing pamphlets calling for abolition of the monarchy, ending slavery, and expelling US military forces.[21] In the following years, a former member of the National Reform Front, Nasir Said, formed a new opposition organization in Cairo. The original name of the organization was the Federation of the Sons of the Arabian Peninsula and it later adopted the name Union of the People of the Arabian Peninsula when Said relocated to Yemen on the heels of the revolution there. With Nasser's blessings, he used Radio Cairo to issue calls for abolishing the Saudi monarchy in the name of Saudi workers, students, and troops.[22]

In early 1958, economic, dynastic, and regional tensions overlapped. Factions in the Saud clan mirrored the division between conservative and nationalist-leftist poles in the regional and domestic political arenas. Mismanagement of the budget caused the Saudi riyal to fall steeply in value. One cohort of senior princes opposed the concentration of power in the king's entourage. Another cohort of progressive princes, led by Prince Talal, called for turning the country into a constitutional monarchy. The regional tide for Arab unity under republican leaders hit its peak when Egypt and Syria agreed to form the United Arab Republic. The converging pressures led senior princes in March 1958 to press Saud to put Faisal in charge of the Council of Ministers. Faisal stabilized the currency by curbing spending, including a limit on royal allowances (still a very generous sum at 18 percent of the kingdom's budget).[23] The austerity measures, however, cut too deep and brought on a recession. At that point, merchants and princes who had wanted to sideline Saud because of lax fiscal control supported his return. The progressive princes abandoned Faisal as well, disappointed that he did not enact political reforms.[24]

While Faisal and his faction managed Saudi affairs, the Egyptian–Syrian union generated new heights of enthusiasm for Arab nationalism, with Nasserist and Baathist crowds in Jordan and Lebanon calling for their governments to join the United Arab Republic. Then, on July 14, 1958, a group of Iraqi military officers, calling themselves the "Free Officers" after the Egyptian model, overthrew the Hashemite monarchy in Baghdad. Instead of throwing in its lot with the Arab nationalist cause, the revolutionary regime in Iraq pursued an independent course, repressed Nasserists and Baathists, and became hostile to Nasser. In addition, Britain and the United States sent military forces to Jordan and Lebanon, respectively, to shore up pro-Western governments. Three years later, Syrian officers expelled Egyptian officials from Damascus and pulled out of the union.

Saud had resumed full power in December 1960, and appointed three progressive princes to cabinet positions in a bid to balance Faisal's faction, but his unwillingness to reform governance cost him their support. Power shifted back to Faisal when Saud had to seek medical treatment in the United States in late 1961. After recuperating, Saud returned and left Faisal in charge of the foreign ministry. The progressive princes became convinced that whoever led the government, Saud or Faisal, would oppose their agenda. Prince Talal quit the Council of Ministers and went into exile. In August 1962, he issued public statements praising Nasser and calling for a constitution and socialist policies. His fellow progressive princes Badr and Fawwaz fled the country to join him in Egypt.[25]

A new revolutionary threat appeared on the kingdom's southern flank in September 1962, when "Free Officers" in Yemen seized control of the capital Sanaa and proclaimed the end of the monarchy. In the mid-1950s, Yemen's Imam Ahmad had gravitated to Nasser's orbit because of shared antipathy toward British imperialism, arising in the imam's case from opposition to British rule in Aden (occupied since 1839). It appeared odd when Imam Ahmad announced Yemen's adherence to the United Arab Republic. It changed nothing in the absolute monarchy, but it did assuage Yemen's Nasserist army officers. The imam's decision to withdraw from the union after Syria's secession in September 1961 angered the officers. A week after Imam Ahmad died, the Yemeni Free Officers seized power in the capital, but they were not able to get their hands on the imam's successor, his son Badr.

Faisal was in Washington when the Free Officers in Yemen took control. He immediately sought guarantees of American military support, but the United States was occupied with the Cuban missile crisis and preferred a diplomatic approach for easing tensions in Arabia. When Faisal met with President Kennedy on October 5, Kennedy told Faisal that he should initiate reforms to stabilize the kingdom and, in a nod to American protests against Saudi Arabia's exclusion of Jews, that he should allow Jews to visit the kingdom. In return, the United States would strengthen its commitment to defend the kingdom against domestic as well as foreign threats. At that time, the Cold War frame, more than oil supply, accounted for Washington's strategic support for Riyadh. Faisal indicated he would unveil a major reform program, and the Americans agreed to send a new military training mission.[26]

On returning to Riyadh, Faisal found Saud ready to let him handle the emergency in Yemen, where Egyptian military forces were arriving to shore up the revolutionary officers. The Yemen revolution represented an opportunity for Nasser to rise above rivals in Syria and Iraq. Yemen's new President Abdallah Sallal called for the overthrow of all monarchies in Arabia and received assistance from Egypt and the Soviet Union. To contain the new republican regime in Sanaa, the Saudis and Jordanians supplied arms and funds to the royalist side. The Soviet Union lent planes and crews for Egypt to transport thousands of troops to bolster Yemen's revolutionary regime. Moscow also sent two bomber squadrons with Soviet pilots to strike royalist forces' camps inside Saudi Arabia. Riyadh's attempts to defend its airspace foundered when four of its own pilots defected to Cairo in the first week of October and another seven defected in November. It turned out they were part of a conspiracy to overthrow the monarchy. Jordan's King Hussein tried to assist the Saudis, but his pilots defected as well.[27]

Instability in Yemen, intermittent labor unrest, pressure from the Free Princes, and the need to present a forward-looking image to Washington formed the backdrop to Faisal's 1962 "Ministerial Statement" setting forth an agenda consisting of ten points. The statement, issued on November 6, 1962, promised to refashion government into an engine for economic and social development.[28] It began with a commitment to framing a Basic Law, akin to a constitution, that would define the government's powers and how they were to be organized (presumably in terms of executive, judicial, and legislative functions), the relationship between the government and the population, and the rights of citizens. Three points referred to religion: the creation of a council to reconcile religious law with modern conditions, a commitment to proselytize, and steps to reform the Committees for Commanding Right and Forbidding Wrong. Three other points pledged the government would ensure social welfare in education, medicine, social security, and unemployment; facilitate economic development in industry, agriculture, and trade; and abolish slavery. The statement embodied the developmentalist vision adopted by other Middle Eastern governments and endorsed by progressive Saudi movements such as the National Liberation Front. By adopting demands to raise living standards, Faisal undermined the left's claim of royal indifference to the circumstances of ordinary people.[29] The constitutional plank, however, remained a dead letter. Faisal's aim was to update patrimonial rule, not to end it.

The abolition of slavery was a long time coming. In fact, Saudi Arabia was one of the last countries to do so.[30] Pressure for taking the step came from many directions: Nasser and the Soviet Union declared that slavery proved the Sauds were "feudal reactionaries," abolitionists in the United Kingdom published accounts of the abuse of slaves, and French authorities documented clandestine slave trading from African territories under cover of the pilgrimage. Inside the kingdom, Faisal had manumitted his slaves in 1956. The Free Princes pushed for abolition, and in August 1962 Prince Talal manumitted eighty-two slaves. Six months after the announcement of abolition, 10,000 slaves had been emancipated and their owners received 10 million Saudi riyals (SR) in compensation, although in many cases former slaves became servants for their former owners.[31] Slavery left an imprint on society: former slaves and their descendants came to form part of the lower class and made up a significant portion of the country's poor, in part because of racial discrimination that places informal bars on marriage between light-skinned and dark-skinned Saudis.[32]

The Yemen war's threat to Riyadh and other pro-Western governments brought about changes in Saudi Arabia's foreign relations. Faisal bolstered the royalist front (Saudi, Hashemite, and Yemeni) by dropping the Saudi claim to the Buraimi oasis in order to mend ties with London. The British agreed to provide private anti-insurgency advisers to the royalist side and acted as intermediaries between the Saudis and the Israelis, who delivered Russian military equipment captured from Egypt in the 1956 Suez war.[33] It is worth mentioning that including Yemen's monarchy in the royalist front had a religious dimension because it was part of the Zaidi Shiite tradition. Wahhabi clerics distinguished between different groups in the Shiite tradition and did not consider the Zaidis to be infidels.[34]

At this stage, a dominant faction in the Saud clan came into focus, with senior princes taking over levers of power they would retain for decades. Prince Fahd became the minister of interior responsible for implementing the Ten Points. Prince Sultan got the defense portfolio and managed the war in Yemen. Prince Abdallah took command of the National Guard. Prince Salman became the governor of Riyadh.[35] Saud was not content to be marginalized and in March 1964 he insisted on his right as king to resume leadership. This time, senior princes obtained a decree from Wahhabi clerics in support of Faisal remaining head of the government and a large gathering of princes met to endorse the decree.[36] Saud forced the issue once more in October. Senior princes and clerics concurred that it was time for him to go. On November 3, 1964, the king abdicated and soon after left the country for the rest of his life, moving first to Lebanon, then Egypt, and finally Greece, where he died in 1969.[37]

Accounts of King Saud tend to emphasize his spendthrift ways and erratic maneuvers in regional politics. They often overlook the expansion of access to health and education, and improvements to facilities for pilgrims that took place under his rule.[38] A revisionist interpretation of the contest between Saud and Faisal argues that Saud was open to putting the country on a progressive path marked by constitutional representational principles and independence of Western imperialism. In this view, Faisal stood for royal dictatorship allied with Western imperialism.[39] In any event, the royal alliance that formed in the early 1960s ensured stability on March 12, 1975, when King Faisal was assassinated by a nephew.[40] The assassin was avenging the death of his brother at the hands of security forces ten years earlier in a violent demonstration against the opening of Riyadh's first television station. Crown Prince Khalid became king, and Prince Fahd was named the new heir to the throne. The alliance of princes managed the sensitive moment of succession without a hitch.[41]

Nasser's decision to commit men, treasure, and prestige to the Yemen civil war turned out badly for him. In 1964, 70,000 Egyptian troops were bogged down in what became known as "Nasser's Vietnam."[42] Three years later, the Egyptian economy was sputtering, the army was still stuck in Yemen, and Nasser was taking incessant attacks from Arab rivals that eroded his standing. To regain popularity, he responded to a Soviet report in May 1967 that Israel was preparing to attack Syria with a show of bravado, demanding that United Nations peacekeeping forces, posted to the Egypt–Israel border, withdraw. Even though Israel demonstrated that the Soviet report was false, Nasser closed Israel's outlet to the Red Sea through the Tiran Straits at the southern tip of the Sinai peninsula—a move that the Israelis considered an act of war. Egypt and Syria announced a military alliance. The conservative pro-Western King Hussein of Jordan joined the alliance to placate Arab nationalist feeling in his country. When it appeared that the United States and other Western powers were not going to take prompt action to reopen navigation through the Tiran Straits, the Israeli government decided to attack Egypt, Syria, and Jordan.

On June 5, Israeli warplanes destroyed the Egyptian, Syrian, and Jordanian air forces. In the next five days, Israeli ground forces attacked on all three fronts. When a ceasefire took hold June 11, Israel had seized the Sinai peninsula and Gaza from Egypt, the West Bank and East Jerusalem from Jordan, and the Golan Heights from Syria. The Israeli attack sparked protests and riots in Saudi Arabia's Eastern Province towns. Oil workers and university students gathered at the Ras Tanura refinery, where they called on the government to embargo oil sales to the United States. A crowd of protesters mounted a demonstration at the United States consulate in Dhahran and attacked vehicles and property at the Dhahran airfield. In Dammam and Khobar, protesters attacked government offices and the homes of wealthy Saudis. The government restored order by calling in the National Guard.[43]

The stunning military defeat of Arab armies in the June 1967 war was a political catastrophe for the Arab nationalists. Nasser's ability to stoke dissent in conservative countries withered. At an Arab conference held in Khartoum in August 1967, Nasser and Faisal mended fences, agreeing to end their respective involvement in Yemen. Saudi Arabia, Kuwait, and Libya pledged to provide economic assistance to "frontline" states Egypt, Syria, and Jordan. The Saudi opposition suffered the loss of Nasser's support.[44] The war also made a lasting change to how the conflict with Israel was framed. Its conquest of East Jerusalem left it in possession of religious sites Muslims consider sacred. The Aqsa Mosque is considered the third holiest place for Muslims after the Grand Mosque in Mecca and the Mosque of the Prophet in Medina. A religious lens supplanted the Arab nationalist lens for viewing the Israeli–Palestinian conflict.

With Nasser's eclipse, the center of revolutionary Arab nationalism shifted to Baghdad and Aden. In July 1968, the Baath Party came to power in Iraq. Baghdad became the main base for exiled Saudi dissidents. The Arab world's first Marxist regime came to power in Aden when the British withdrew in November 1967. The People's Democratic Republic of Yemen supported a simmering rebellion in Oman's Dhofar region that had the potential to destabilize Arabia's hereditary monarchies. Leftists and nationalists in Saudi Arabia continued to threaten royal rule. In June 1968, the government discovered a cluster of mutinous army officers.[45] One year later, the government arrested 200–300 military officers, government officials, and oil workers for planning to assassinate King Faisal and Prince Sultan in a plot to overthrow the monarchy.[46] By 1970, the left's center of gravity was in exile.[47] When King Khalid ascended the throne in 1975, he granted amnesty to many leftists and allowed exiles to return.[48]

Labor activists, Arab nationalists, and leftists expressed a vision of effective, just governance that would have required the monarchy to share or surrender power. Royal refusal meant harsh repression. Activists met different fates: some died in prison, some languished in exile, some reconciled with the royals and gained positions in the government, lending their talents to development projects that improved material conditions. The defeat of Arab nationalists and leftists did not spell the end of political opposition. Rather, a new generation would take shape and make demands for effective, just governance, this time in the name of religion.[49]

From Patrimonial Court to Neo-Patrimonial State

The patrimonial style of rule was incapable of meeting demands from the growing segment of industrial workers and educated Saudis. Under pressure from political challenges at home and abroad, the monarchy took incremental steps to fashion formal government institutions characterized by statutory functions and dedicated staff.[50] Consequently, Saudi Arabia's patrimonial court turned into a neo-patrimonial state, a hybrid that blends two kinds of government office.[51] One kind purchased clan peace by distributing agencies among senior princes in the manner of political spoils. The princes turned "their" government agencies into fiefdoms, harvested for salaries, subsidies, and favors to share with clients, much as Abd al-Aziz used to distribute subsidies he received from the British and the Americans.[52] Contrary to Faisal's reputation for efficiency, he maintained a patrimonial network of clients, brokers, and profiteers, just like the other senior princes.[53] The political rationale for assigning government offices to members of the Saud clan is one reason why there was so much duplication and overlap in jurisdiction. Six different agencies were responsible for economic planning and three agencies for importing grain.[54] Faisal's aim was the centralization of power, not efficiency. Thus, he relied on a small group of advisers to make all significant decisions on policy.

The second kind of government office followed the model of a specialized bureaucracy. In Steffen Hertog's apt phrase, these were "islands of efficiency" in a sea of inefficient institutions. These offices performed indispensable financial and economic functions, without which the princely fiefdoms would not have the funds for their client networks. Two notably efficient offices were the Saudi Arabian Monetary Authority (SAMA) responsible for establishing a unitary national currency and functioning as a national bank; and the Saudi Basic Industries Corporation (SABIC) which laid foundations for heavy industry.[55]

The partial development of bureaucratic institutions put the Saudi government on the path from patrimonial to neo-patrimonial rule, where the latter followed a legal-bureaucratic logic in government bodies that most mattered (petroleum, finance, industry) while decisive tools of power operated on the basis of personal networks radiating from an individual or oligarchy. Saudi Arabia's trajectory from patrimonial to neo-patrimonial forms of rule had a peculiar wrinkle, namely, the sphere of religious authority that also assumed a neo-patrimonial form.

Patrimonial logic determined the shape of the country's military forces because their purpose was to protect the dynasty, in the manner of an old Najdi emir's armed retinue, rather than defend national territory. The series of plots by Arab nationalist military officers spurred suspicion in royal quarters and had two effects. First, the country created two separate military institutions, the regular armed forces under the Ministry of Defense and the National Guard recruited from trusted tribes and placed under royal command. Second, the Sauds decided not to introduce conscription. Thus, Saudi forces were small and divided between separate princes. Prince

Abdallah took over the National Guard in 1962 and made it a fiefdom that strengthened his position within the Saud clan balance of power, but making loyalty instead of competence the criterion for promotion diminished the guard's efficacy as a military force.[56]

In the early 1960s, the regular armed forces and the National Guard each had around 18,000 men, but by 1967, the National Guard was a bit larger with 31,000 troops, and the army had 25,000 troops. The tension between political need and military efficacy is one reason why the kingdom did not fulfill its military potential and had to rely on foreign powers for strategic security. After the June 1967 war, the government uncovered networks of Arab nationalist officers and carried out purges in the army and air force. Instead of imposing long jail sentences on the officers, the government released them from detention after one or two years. The monarchy used the influx of oil income in the 1970s to purchase their loyalty, or at least quiescence, with high salaries.[57]

The creation of separate military forces shielded the monarchy from mutinous officers. The bifurcated education system placated the religious estate. By following political logic, the divisions in military and educational institutions hampered national integration. Along with the division of military forces, the decision to not introduce conscription diminished the prospect for robust national defense. The growth of religious institutes meant diverting a large segment of the young, educated population from modern professions. The combined effect was to increase dependence on external resources: Western military power for national defense, foreign labor to fill technical occupations. Rising oil income afforded the dynasty the means to employ Saudis in public-sector offices; the significance of Saudi oil in the global economy meant that Western powers would ensure the country's security. In both cases, the government opened itself to criticism for failing to fully develop national potential for the sake of dynastic power.

One obstacle hindering the spread of efficiency to ministerial fiefdoms was the low number of Saudis with the right kind of education.

During the 1960s, about 8,500 students completed high school and about 1,000 graduated from secular universities. In 1970, the government had about 50,000 positions; therefore the majority of Saudis in public agencies did not have high-school diplomas. These numbers make clear why foreign Arabs were recruited. In such conditions, it was natural that employment in government offices did not require formal training or professional qualifications. Instead, hiring and recruitment took place through personal networks, allowing brokers to exploit proximity to princes for personal gain. As dependency on patronage for salaries became widespread, civil-service workers seldom quit, supervisors rarely dismissed workers for poor performance, and many offices became overstaffed; and yet other offices were understaffed due to deficient planning and poor training.[58]

Rising oil revenue made it possible to increase the scope of royal largesse channeled through government agencies: in the 1960s, the government budget quadrupled; the number of state employees doubled; and new ministries were created for petroleum, labor, information, social affairs, and the pilgrimage.[59] An indirect effect of expanding government offices was the reinforcement of perennial social patterns because they reproduced patrimonial networks of patrons and clients in the way they hired staff and distributed oil revenue. In the 1960s and 1970s, Najdi traders placed their sons in state agencies at the highest rate of any social group, taking roughly 30 percent of state positions. The educated middle class and its sons came in second at roughly 25 percent, while only 17 percent of government employees came from rural backgrounds. The traditional merchant class that used to supply goods to the royal court became petitioners for business licenses and contractors for public works. The least advantaged groups were Bedouin and former Bedouin: denied their historic autonomy and collective rights to tribal domains, they depended on stipends from Prince Fahd's Ministry of the Interior and positions in the National Guard. Few obtained posts in government agencies or integrated into the urban economy.[60]

From Wahhabi Mission to Religious Bureaucracy

The Wahhabi mission's ardor for correct belief and worship proved compatible with bureaucratic organization.[61] The proliferation of government agencies extended to the religious domain in two phases. First, in the 1950s and 1960s, the leader of the religious estate, Muhammad ibn Ibrahim Al al-Shaikh (1893–1969), took steps to reshape religious education, organize clerical authority over fatwas (juridical opinions), publications, and mosques, and preserve the independence of religious law courts. We might say he used his patrimonial authority to lay the foundations for a neo-patrimonial religious establishment. Second, after his death in 1969, the government created the Board of Senior Clerics to relocate the center of religious authority from Al al-Shaikh to a collective body.

In 1950, around 15,000 children were attending school in the entire country; rural areas had around 50 schools with 2,000 pupils; fewer than 200 Saudis were studying in Egypt; about 20 were in the United States.[62] The introduction and spread of public education meant that schools would become powerful agents of social change. The question was, change for what purpose? Government ministries and the oil company sought graduates qualified to manage public agencies and the petroleum sector, in large measure as a way to wean the country from reliance on foreign workers. The religious estate wished to make schools channels for spreading Wahhabi learning to the masses. The government's decision in the 1950s to adopt the Western education model threatened the mission's primacy in teaching children. The clerics turned to allies in Islamic revivalist movements from other countries who had developed a hybrid model that blended lessons on modern science with religion. Parallel to national public education, the clerics developed an education system based on religious institutes that spread in the 1960s, and eventually became religious universities in the 1970s and 1980s.[63] Investments in secular and religious forms of education spawned two distinct subcultures of literate Saudis, with the religious set adopting the hybrid outlook joining Wahhabi dogma with revivalist activism that would eventually comprise its own current of political activism and dissent thanks to the assimilation of Muslim Brotherhood categories and goals.[64]

One of the long-running battles between secular and religious circles in Saudi Arabia has centered on the question of codifying Islamic law, an issue that arose in other Muslim societies.[65] Religious judges customarily exercised the authority to issue verdicts based on their understanding of how general legal rules applied to specific cases. When labor unrest in the 1950s prompted discussion of drafting a labor code, Muhammad ibn Ibrahim firmly opposed it. As interaction with foreign companies increased, however, the need for legal transparency kept pressure for codification alive. In 1973, the Board of Senior Clerics commissioned a study that presented arguments for both sides. The board split, with a majority standing fast against codification and a minority finding reasons to allow it. As time passed, younger clerics accommodated to the change. In fact, the minister of justice who later ordered gradual codification in 2007 was a son of Muhammad ibn Ibrahim.[66]

Resistance to codification was rooted in principles of Islamic jurisprudence. There was no religious principle against bureaucratic offices, and Muhammad ibn Ibrahim proved an adept architect of formal religious offices. In 1953, he created an office to handle several functions, including the production of fatwas. The office replaced the individual mufti (jurist) with a collective body to handle the workload demanded by the flood of unprecedented questions arising in the rapidly changing country. The fatwa agency replicated similar councils established in other Muslim countries and concentrated clerical authority in an official body, issuing authoritative rulings on minutiae as well as on questions of national import. Muhammad ibn Ibrahim empowered the fatwa agency to supervise religious personnel (preachers, imams in mosques), and to review religious publications for conformity to mission doctrine.[67] He also energized a campaign to spread and defend the mission, by launching a journal for articles on religious law and doctrine, and by setting up a publishing house to reissue classic Wahhabi treatises and refutations of secular intellectual trends.[68]

By all accounts, Muhammad ibn Ibrahim was a formidable personality who used his sway to shield the religious sphere from dynastic interference. His death in 1969 ended hereditary leadership of the religious estate and gave an opening to the palace to absorb religious affairs into the structure of national government. A royal decree in 1971 created the Board of Senior Clerics with comprehensive authority over religious affairs: the Ministry of Justice, supervision of the holy places, religious institutes and universities, girls' education, and the Committees for Commanding Right and Forbidding Wrong.[69] The seventeen-member board divided functions among three agencies: one for legal research and routine fatwas, one for religious scholarship and preaching, and one for fatwas of political import.[70]

The government's adoption of regular, detailed budget management makes it possible for the first time to gain a clear picture of how much revenue was allocated to religious institutions. In 1973/4, the agency responsible for pilgrimage and religious endowments had the largest budget of any religious office: 120 million SR compared to 93 million SR for the Ministry of Justice, and 27 million SR for the Committees for Commanding Right and Forbidding Wrong. Wahhabi missionary activity had a negligible budget into the 1970s. Altogether religious agencies received around 3–4 percent of the budget in 1971.[71]

While the mission adapted to bureaucratic structures, its outreach to the Muslim world expanded through Faisal's efforts to build an alliance of conservative Muslim governments, his so-called "Islamic foreign policy." Leading clerics believed that Western culture and Arab nationalism posed such serious threats to religion that they had to temper the mission's sectarian posture and cooperate with other Muslims in transnational religious institutions. In short order, transnational institutions became channels for two-way influence: Wahhabi clerics used them to proselytize in other Muslim countries and foreign religious currents gained a foothold in Saudi Arabia.[72]

The Islamic University of Medina opened in 1961 for the purpose of instilling Wahhabi doctrine in students from around the Muslim world. University regulations stipulated that 80 percent of students were to be non-Saudis. Governing bodies and the faculty drew from countries as far away as Indonesia. Members of revivalist groups filled staff and faculty positions. Wahhabi clerics controlled the administration and ensured that theology courses followed Wahhabi doctrine. Over time, the university produced a network of alumni and former teachers who became agents for the distribution of Saudi funds to the revivalist movements in their home countries.[73]

The Muslim World League emerged from an international conference Faisal held in Mecca in 1962 to discuss ways to combat socialism and secularism. In India and Pakistan, the Muslim World League worked with revivalist organizations to wage a campaign of religious purification against Sufi orders and popular religious customs. In West Africa, agents of the League cooperated with revivalists to set up new religious associations to fight popular religious customs. The Organization of the Islamic Conference (later renamed Organization of Islamic Cooperation), founded in 1969, became a vehicle to raise awareness of Muslim suffering, whether in Jerusalem, Kashmir, or elsewhere. In 1972, Wahhabi clerics and revivalists established the World Assembly of Muslim Youth to shore up religious commitment among Muslim students attending Western universities (another element of global integration).[74]

Development and Society

By the 1960s, state-led development was a common strategy in the Middle East. Revolutionary Arab regimes and conservative monarchies alike strove to increase production and provide public services such as roads, hospitals, and schools.[75] In Saudi Arabia, developmentalist projects had multiple roots. In Najd, the shaikh was expected to extend generosity to the needy. The townspeople of Hijaz had long depended on outside patronage for food supplies. When Abd al-Aziz annexed the region, improvements in transportation and lodging for pilgrims bolstered the symbolic, fiscal, and commercial advantages of managing the annual pilgrimage to Mecca. The royal appetite for comfort brought modern amenities to Riyadh, while in Hasa, Aramco constructed new towns for workers and managers. In an interview with *The New York Times*, the newly enthroned King Saud stated his aspiration to increase agricultural production by extending irrigation, excavating canals, and building dams, and to integrate rural and urban populations through new communications.[76]

The adoption of central planning was a way to address political unrest in the Saud clan (the Free Princes), the military (air force defections), and the oil fields (labor). The 1962 revolution in Yemen and Egypt's intervention gave urgency to finding ways to exploit oil's potential to fund projects that would justify dynastic control over the country's wealth.[77] Faisal's Ten-Point Program promised to improve living conditions by developing education, health care, and social security. The government would take the lead in expanding highways, creating banks and industrial firms, and increasing water supply for farmers and Bedouin. The program was a blueprint for a new bargain between the dynasty and its subjects, one where the dynasty headed a government that acted as a trustee of the national treasure to spread its benefits to the population. The era of the developmentalist state had arrived.[78]

The government established agencies and passed laws to lay institutional frameworks for development. The primary agency for managing development was the Central Planning Organization, established in 1965 (converted to the Ministry of Planning in 1975). The General Organization of Petroleum and Minerals, or Petromin, founded in 1962, negotiated concessions with foreign firms to explore for and produce oil outside the Aramco concession area. The legal framework for a modern economy included the Banking Control Law (1966) to stimulate private investment, the Land Apportionment Act (1968) to revive activity in the agriculture sector, and the Labor Law (1969) to prevent unrest.[79] Foreign experts and Saudis trained in Western universities took the lead in recommending and implementing development projects.[80]

State-led development shifted the economy's center of gravity from agrarian production to petroleum extraction and allocation of revenue. The new economy altered labor (from cultivation, herding, and craft manufacture to office jobs), the gendered division of labor (displacing women from customary work), and the composition of the workforce (national and foreign). It fashioned a population unlike any in the country's history. Government control over pastureland and the introduction of machine power pushed people out of the countryside while investment in infrastructure, schools, clinics, and modern amenities pulled them to cities. Estimates for the balance of rural and urban population indicate gradual change in the early decades of oil production, with a shift from an 80:20 ratio in 1932 to a 75:25 ratio in 1962, before the pace quickened to bring rural and urban segments even in 1970. Plans to expand industrial production meant urban growth because such production demanded the concentration of labor, proximity to transportation infrastructure, and access to electricity.[81]

The oil enclave was the axis for integration with the global economy. Its wells, pipelines, and refineries drew labor from the interior and abroad, and stimulated enterprises funneling imports to the enclave and forwarding them to the interior. Integration with the global economy and the creation of a modern state had ripple effects throughout the country. Government projects supplied technology and credit to increase harvests. Imported machines displaced rural workers and spurred migration to cities, where government offices and private firms put Saudis to work as civil servants and office workers. In the new order, women's labor was expendable, replaced by foreign men, whose growing ubiquity increased moral anxiety and pressure to keep women out of sight—if not at home, then under strict covering in public, enforced by religious police.[82]

In Najd, mechanical power changed the agrarian economy. In the Unaiza region, for example, the number of irrigation pumps increased from three in 1925 to more than 500 thirty years later. The larger quantity of water along with the introduction of tractors and threshers made it possible to cultivate more land. As machines replaced human labor, women who once worked on family plots became wage workers on large landholdings while young men shifted to jobs in construction, the oil sector, and state agencies. At the same time, the backbones of Unaiza's economy—long-distance trade and local craft production—collapsed in the face of competition from inexpensive foreign imports. Men and women displaced from craft production entered the ranks of agricultural wage workers.[83]

National government offices facilitating economic transition wove Unaiza into a fabric of administrative links rooted in Riyadh. In 1954, the Ministry of Agriculture and Water opened offices, followed in the next decade by the Saudi Arabian Agricultural Bank, established in 1964.[84] One of the bank's aims was to help medium and small farmers weather the tide of food imports and to reinvigorate domestic food production by extending credit. Bank loans also helped stem a trend for indebted smallholders to sell their land and swell the ranks of rural wage workers. In its first five years, the bank made loans to around 13,000 small and medium farmers to acquire irrigation engines and pumps. The bank achieved mixed results in propping up medium and small farmers. In the long term, it represented the tendency for national government institutions to make their presence felt in all corners of the country.[85]

On the national scale, the agrarian economy's contraction and the expansion of state offices transformed the workforce. In 1962, Saudis comprised more than 90 percent of the workforce, with about three-quarters working in agriculture, including raising livestock. By 1970, even though the number of Saudi workers grew by half a million, foreign workers accounted for about one in three workers and the percentage of workers in rural areas fell under 60 percent; that figure fell under 50 percent in 1974.[86]

Saudi Arabia and the other Gulf states regulated foreign workers through sponsorship, known as *kafala*, an arrangement where private individuals acted as guarantors for foreign workers. In classical Islamic law, a *kafala* contract obliges a guarantor to take responsibility for another person undertaking a legal obligation, or surety, that could be delivery of goods, payment of debt, appearance before a court, and so on. A labor contract was not one of the kinds of obligations that came under *kafala*.[87] The modern adaptation of *kafala* to labor originated in Bahrain in the 1920s, when British officials required pearl-boat captains to assume legal responsibility for their crews. When the oil industry began attracting large numbers of foreign workers in the early 1930s, the British extended the modified *kafala* surety to them as well. Over time, sponsors became labor contractors receiving payment (classical sponsors received no compensation), obtaining work and residency permits, and ensuring foreign workers' departure at the end of their contracts. One of the significant differences between classical and modern sponsorship is that the classical sponsor was legally accountable if the sponsored person violated the contract whereas the sponsored foreign worker is penalized, not the guarantor, for overstaying or breaking another law. Guarantors have leverage over foreign workers by holding their papers, giving them the power to demand longer work hours and to withhold payment. While there is no principle in Islamic law that establishes this sort of sponsorship, the religious authorities in the early 1990s legitimized it on the grounds of the kinds of measures a ruler may enact for the sake of ensuring the general welfare of the population.[88]

Bedouin were part of the project for national development, not only in Saudi Arabia but throughout the Middle East, where governments adopted similar policies based on assumptions that defined nomads as a "problem" to solve. According to the United Nations and other international organizations, nomads made minimal contributions to national economies and their way of life harmed the environment.[89] The aims of Saudi rulers aligned with the assumptions of the international organizations, but the development script seldom worked according to plan. Instead, tribesmen drew on a legacy of adopting multiple resources for subsistence, now utilizing opportunities in the oil sector, public social services, and the Saudi Arabian National Guard.[90]

In the mid-1950s, a drought devastated livestock in much of the country. In the north, the Shararat tribe's camel herd collapsed from 50,000 to fewer than 4,000. One tribesman told a Saudi researcher that only ten camels from his herd of 100 survived the drought. Bedouin were accustomed to coping with drought by selling their animals and migrating to better pasture, but international borders limited the scope of migration. Many men weathered the drought by finding work in the petroleum sector in Kuwait and the Eastern Province.[91] Another option was to take up agriculture. One Shararat shaikh approached the district governor to request a modest land grant to establish a small agricultural settlement. The official agreed and the shaikh settled with his clan at a site they called Tabarjal that soon had a mosque, two wells, and a few houses. Other Shararat clans began to settle nearby and took up cultivation alongside animal husbandry. The government then set up a health clinic and the shaikh opened a school next to his house. Some years later, the son of another shaikh became headmaster and was able to persuade fellow tribesmen to send their sons. Then, some parents requested a school for girls: in the transition from nomadic to sedentary ways of life, families did not need girls to gather firewood, fetch water, and help weave tents; instead, they wanted daughters to "learn religion." In 1962, the national government opened a social security office. Its offer to pay subsidies in exchange for settlement enticed more nomads to settle down. The number of houses quintupled from eleven to fifty-two in the next three years. The creation of the Real Estate Development Fund in 1975 reinforced momentum for settlement by providing interest-free loans for homes and commercial buildings.[92]

The blend of private initiatives and government-funded social services was repeated across the country. Bedouin settled with fellow clansmen in villages and small towns, frequently near wells and abandoned oases. Former Bedouin villagers did not miss the hardships of their old way of life: losing livestock to disease, drought, harsh material conditions. They did not particularly like agriculture, but they appreciated that settlement gave them access to modern inventions such as sewing machines, radios, and motorcycles.[93] Signs of national integration were common: regular interaction with the provincial governor, travel to see relatives who moved to other parts of the country for work, performing the pilgrimage, attending schools, and using hospitals. Some tribal leaders became agents of the state, sometimes as commander in the National Guard of a unit of men from their tribe, turning it into part of a centralized political system.[94]

The tribal hierarchy and social organization underwent shifts in the context of the modern economy. Rather than a hierarchy of shaikh and common tribesmen, status was defined by income from modern occupations that required schooling. The economy of the extended family withered, and smaller family units became the norm. Identification with a Bedouin past, however, remained strong. Alongside tribal belonging, there emerged a generic Bedouin identity shared by members of different tribes that set them apart from Saudis descended from settled folk, pride in coming from a way of life that eschewed materialism, captured in Wilfred Thesiger's account of a Bedouin shopping spree in the 1940s. His companion Salim bin Kabina purchased "a load of grain, two pounds of coffee beans, two cooking-pots, three water-skins, a length of rope, a ball of string, two packing needles, a dozen boxes of matches, four yards of dark blue cloth for his mother, a loin-cloth for himself, and penknife." Thesiger had hoped that he would buy blankets, but Bin Kabina said, "Camels are what I want. They are what matter . . . I shall have six. Now I am rich. I am used to hardship. Cold won't hurt me. I am a Bedu."[95]

For the national government, settlement fulfilled the purpose of cementing authority over population and territory.[96] Some Bedouin, however, lamented pacification. In their eyes, it meant the destruction of a life full of meaning and satisfaction. Abdulaziz Al-Fahad recalls a man of his grandfather's generation named Dghaylib bin Khnaysir who lived into the 1950s. Settled folk "chastised him for raiding, killing other men, and stealing their property" and warned that he would pay in the afterlife, but Dghaylib replied that he did not believe God would punish him because he killed a dozen or so tribesmen at the same time King Abd al-Aziz escaped punishment even though he was responsible for killing thousands. He held the old outlook that killing a tribal enemy was no worse than killing for religion or state.[97]

Religious Activism

The import of Western goods and the adoption of Western tastes were part of the opening to the outside world greeted with enthusiasm by some, trepidation by others. The royal and religious authorities both had reason to feel apprehensive about foreign influences. In the early years of King Saud's reign, the clergy pushed for a prohibition on women driving (1957) and lobbied the throne to restrict overseas study (1955). From the royal perspective, Palestinian and Egyptian teachers were sources of labor unrest and leftist subversion to combat through deportations and by discouraging study in Arab countries.[98] In 1963, religious police determined to prohibit cigarette smoking raided cafes in Riyadh, while in Jeddah, they enlisted the interior ministry to shut down cinemas. The introduction of television in 1965 provoked violent protest.[99] That year, a band of puritans in Medina regarding Western goods and norms as threats to a godly social order went on a rampage, smashing store windows displaying female mannequins. For the religious establishment, coming to grips with consumerism, sports, television, and the like, the "smashing windows" incident underscored the challenge of fitting Wahhabi norms into the new urban space.[100]

Medina's moral vigilantes represented the mingling of Saudi and imported religious currents at the Islamic University founded a few years earlier. Among the non-Saudi faculty, nobody surpassed the influence of Nasir al-Din al-Albani (1914–1999), a renowned scholar of Prophetic Traditions. As a young boy, he moved with his family from Albania to Damascus, where he developed an original method for assessing Prophetic Traditions that put him at odds with the classical Sunni tradition.[101] When he arrived in Medina in 1961, students flocked to his courses, but his controversial views incurred the disapproval of Saudi clerics. In one treatise, he claimed that no canonical text required women to cover their faces. In another, he challenged the rules for prayer, allowing worshippers to wear shoes. His followers began to pray apart from other Muslims in their own mosques. Albani did not have a political agenda, but his refusal to accept standard views on religious rules implied rejection of Wahhabi clerical authority. At the end of his second year, the university administration let his contract lapse, and he moved to Jordan.

Albani's former students became instructors at the Islamic University and other religious institutes, where they preserved his elevation of Prophetic Traditions above the authority of clerics.[102] It was a band of his admirers who attacked storefronts in Medina in the name of fulfilling the duty to command right and forbid wrong. After the incident, five young men approached the university rector, Shaikh Abd al-Aziz ibn Baz, to approve their forming a group dedicated to upholding the duty to command right and forbid wrong. Whether Ibn Baz meant to endorse moral vigilantism or rein it in is not clear, but he agreed to sponsor them and suggested they call their association the Salafi Group for Commanding Right and Forbidding Wrong.[103]

A kindred revulsion at infidel ways drove the formation of a colony of old believers in Buraida, Qasim's provincial capital. The "Buraida Brethren," purist adherents to Wahhabi doctrine, objected to public schools offering classes on geography, astronomy, and English, preferring to educate their children in a private school. They wished to withdraw from society, eschewing the telephone, television, and other modern conveniences. The authorities accommodated them, issuing special identity cards without photographs because the Buraida Brethren considered images prohibited.[104] The pocket of old believers retreated from changes entailed by global and national integration; they just wanted to be left alone.

An activist religious current bent on converting society to its vision, known as the Awakening, began to take shape as a consequence of Riyadh's search for allies in the Arab Cold War and for personnel to manage transnational bodies and the growing education system. Saudi Arabia was an attractive destination for members of the Muslim Brotherhood enduring persecution under Arab nationalist regimes in Egypt, Syria, and Iraq. The kingdom offered employment opportunities and a culture hospitable to the Brotherhood's goal of making religion the central principle of public life. The guests in turn made dependable allies to confront secular currents, but their anti-imperialist agenda implied opposition to Riyadh's friendly ties with the West; the contradiction remained latent until the 1990 Kuwait crisis. From a long-term perspective, the Muslim Brothers had similar roots and effects with the modernists. They both represented a rising tide of outside forces seeping into the country and slowly dissolving the ramparts of Wahhabi authority with its solitary focus on purifying belief and ritual. Integration with the Muslim cosmopolitan sphere reinforced the nationalist leftist effects of instilling an activist ethos: now a politicized religious identity was taking hold among growing numbers of religious university graduates.

Muslim Brothers began coming to Saudi Arabia in the 1950s to lend talents, energies, and contacts to support transnational institutions (the Islamic University of Medina, the Muslim World League) and public education. Prominent Brothers assumed influential posts at universities while rank-and-file members by the hundreds filled positions in schools and the Ministry of Education. Muslim Brothers applied their template for blending religion with school subjects such as economics, sociology, psychology, history, and literature. Muslim Brothers also imported their division between two factions, one following the reformist emphasis on education in Hasan al-Banna's mission, and the other following the revisionist emphasis on combating secular regimes according to the writings of Sayyid Qutb, executed by the Egyptian government in 1966.[105]

Because of the government ban on independent organizations, Saudis who came under the influence of the Muslim Brothers referred to their current as "the Awakening." By keeping a low profile, they had leeway to create extracurricular programs for youth intended to shape a new generation imbued with "an Islamic culture," a consciousness of religious solidarity, commitment to supporting fellow Muslims in distress, and readiness to combat Islam's enemies: Western imperialism, Zionism, and the secular ideologies that represented Western cultural invasion. They sponsored school clubs for sports and cultural activities, weekend and summer camps on the model of scouting programs, and theatrical skits to raise awareness of Muslim suffering.

By the late 1960s, four networks of Awakening teachers and disciples informally associated with the Muslim Brotherhood crystallized, with strongholds at religious universities in Riyadh, Jeddah, and Mecca. One Awakening network set itself against the Muslim Brotherhood. It was associated with Muhammad Surur, a Syrian teacher who drifted from the Muslim Brotherhood in the late 1960s and developed his own brand of activist Wahhabi doctrine while teaching in Saudi Arabia in the late 1960s. After he left in 1973, one of his Saudi disciples made Surur's teachings popular with Awakening youth in Qasim and Riyadh.

The Awakening's activist ethos had a counterpart among Shiites in the Eastern Province, where Wahhabi influence had the unintended effect of spurring the country's Shiites to mingle with transnational Shiite networks. Pressure on Shiite religious institutions and practices drove an exodus of clerics and religious students to Iraq, leaving Shiite religious education in the Eastern Province to wither and pious Shiite youths no option but to seek advanced learning outside the country.

In the 1950s and 1960s, clerics at Iraq's prestigious seminaries in Najaf and Kerbala saw young people drawn to Western cultural influence, secular Arab nationalism, and communism. Two movements formed that asserted religion's central place in public life. The Dawa party developed in Najaf and expressed a traditionalist clerical outlook that found receptive niches in Lebanon and Bahrain. The Shirazi movement came from Kerbala and attained footholds in Kuwait and Saudi Arabia.[106] Muhammad Shirazi established the Movement of Vanguard Missionaries in 1968. His writings drew on both Shiite (the Iranian Ali Shariati) and Sunni (the Pakistani Abu Ala Mawdudi and Muslim Brotherhood) thinkers. Shirazi moved to Kuwait in 1971 to escape persecution by Iraq's Baathist regime. Kuwait did not have a tradition of religious learning, and its Shiite notables offered a hospitable reception, in the manner of smalltown elders honoring a big city celebrity. The Iraqi cleric invested charitable donations from his hosts in a chain of religious institutions that included a seminary that drew students from Bahrain, Iraq, Kuwait, and Saudi Arabia.

The Awakening and the Shirazis took shape in the waning years of Arab nationalist and leftist currents in Saudi Arabia. While the religious activists eventually challenged royal authority, they did so at different times and for different reasons. The Awakening called out the government's failures to preserve religious purity against Western culture, to manage economic and social development, and to show solidarity with Palestinians. The Shirazis protested material discrimination against Shiites and suppression of Shiite religious expression. Each one presented a challenge to dynastic power, but they could not act together because of anti-Shiite prejudice in the Awakening movement.

Upon the death of King Abd al-Aziz, tensions among the princes over succession did not destabilize the monarchy. Nationalists and leftists in concert with junior royal factions could not overcome the palace's capacity for repression and cooptation. In general, elite conflicts in patrimonial systems do not create a crisis when society is not mobilized.[107] To combat nationalist movements and leaders, such as Nasser, the Sauds joined conservative Muslim rulers to forge an anti-leftist coalition in the name of "Islamic solidarity," even though nothing in Islamic principles calls for dependence on non-Muslim powers (the United States) or for repression to censor and jail dissidents. By lending religious legitimacy to the Sauds, the Wahhabi mission proved its value as an instrument for defending the monarchy against domestic and foreign critics.[108] The solutions to the political pressures of the 1960s, namely promoting national development and forming ties with religious revivalist groups, would give rise to new sources of pressure on the monarchy in the ensuing decades.

7

The Oil Boom and Rapid Development, 1970–90

In the early 1970s, two developments put the Saudi monarchy on firmer ground. First, the decline of Arab nationalism eased external pressure from revolutionary regimes and undermined domestic political opposition. Second, the oil revolution brought a sudden influx of massive oil revenues that made it possible to accelerate the drive from austerity to affluence. The social ramifications of affluence were the focus of tension between modernist and conservative currents that grew sharper in the wake of disruptive events in 1979 that shook the region and threatened the monarchy. It responded by increasing cooperation with Islamic revivalist groups and with the United States, a strategy that worked as long as Muslim and Western partners had a common cause: the fight to expel the Soviet Union from Afghanistan. Throughout this period of opportunities and challenges, the bloc of allied senior princes sustained its cohesion, with a smooth succession to Crown Prince Khalid after the assassination of King Faisal in 1975, and a second uncontested succession to Crown Prince Fahd when Khalid died of a heart attack in 1982.

Regional Realignments

Three events in 1970 signaled the decline of the Arab left. First, in September, Jordan's King Hussein crushed revolutionary Palestinian organizations in a bloody affair that became known as Black September.[1] The fighting between Jordanian forces and Palestinian guerrilla groups ended after King Hussein and Palestine Liberation Organization leader Yasir Arafat met in Cairo, where Egyptian President Nasser mediated ceasefire terms. His death from a heart attack on September 28, the day after the two leaders departed, was the second event to signal the decline of the Arab left. Egyptian Vice-President Anwar al-Sadat took over in Cairo, and set about repairing relations with Nasser's adversaries, such as King Faisal. The third event was the overthrow of Syria's neo-Baath regime in November at the hand of its defense minister, Hafiz al-Asad. He vowed to moderate radical domestic and foreign policies in the name of a "Corrective Movement."

Stability in the Persian Gulf became a focus of concern in 1968, when London announced its decision to withdraw naval forces, leaving the small Trucial shaikhdoms to figure out their political futures and portending a scramble for advantage between Iran, Iraq, and Saudi Arabia. In 1971, six shaikhdoms formed the United Arab Emirates while Qatar and Bahrain each pursued independence. To maintain stability in Britain's absence, President Richard Nixon decided to boost the shah of Iran as the primary surrogate for the United States. The application of the "Nixon Doctrine" where Washington depended on proxies to act on its behalf proved effective until the 1979 Iranian revolution. In the meantime, Iran's Muhammad Reza Shah irritated Saudi rulers with his arrogant attitude, but he did preserve a conservative, pro-Western order.[2]

The Oil Revolution

Saudi Arabia's position in Arab politics was reinforced by a revolution in the global oil industry. The 1970s oil boom was enormously consequential. At the beginning of October 1973, a barrel of oil cost

$2.90; by March 1974, the price had quadrupled to $11.65 per barrel. Saudi Arabia's oil revenues spiked from $2.7 billion in 1972 to $22.6 billion in 1974. Oil producers in the Gulf enjoyed similar gains: Iranian revenues increased from $2.4 billion to $18 billion; Kuwait's revenues rose from $1.4 billion to $6.5 billion; and Iraq's swelled from $600 million to $5.7 billion.[3] The steep price increases stemmed from the intersection of three developments in the world economy: the push by producing countries for renegotiating oil concessions to gain control over the production and pricing of their primary source of revenue;[4] the "Nixon shock" decision for the United States to abandon the gold standard; and the increasing reliance of the United States on oil imports to meet demand.

The Iranian ruler Reza Shah was the first Middle Eastern leader to try to revise the terms of an oil concession. After a few years of haggling with the Anglo-Persian Oil Company, Reza Shah cancelled the D'Arcy Concession in 1932. The British company then agreed to increase Iran's share of oil sales and guaranteed an annual minimum royalty payment. After the Second World War, Iranian nationalists and leftists supported by labor unions dominated the elected parliament. In 1951, the prime minister, Muhammad Mosaddeq, signed a bill to nationalize the company, causing a crisis in relations with London. At first, the United States tried to mediate a resolution to the conflict, but when Dwight Eisenhower became president, his more hawkish administration ordered the Central Intelligence Agency to bring down Mosaddeq's government. Washington deemed the August 1953 coup a successful operation because it prevented Iran from "falling to communism." In the long term, it poisoned Iranian–United States relations and played a part in the hostile posture of the Islamic Republic toward the United States and its regional partners such as Saudi Arabia.

How to divide oil revenue became a point of dispute between oil-producing countries and Western companies around the world. Abdallah al-Tariqi was one of Saudi Arabia's first oil experts educated in the United States. He became the most influential voice in the country calling for better terms from the American company. In the late 1950s he joined with Venezuela's oil minister Juan Pérez Alfonzo to urge other major oil producers to establish an association to present a united front toward the Western oil companies that were able to set prices by raising or lowering production.[5] A sharp drop in oil prices in 1960 spurred Iran, Iraq, and Kuwait to join with Venezuela and Saudi Arabia to form the Organization of Petroleum Exporting Countries (OPEC). It would take another decade before conditions in the world oil market gave the producing countries the leverage to enforce their demands.[6]

The oil-producing countries fell into different camps. "Price hawks" such as Algeria, Iraq, and Libya threatened to nationalize the oil companies if they did not agree to increase producers' revenues. Iran's shah had costly industrial and military ambitions, and he sided with the price hawks demanding higher prices. "Price doves" such as Saudi Arabia and the Gulf monarchies had small populations; therefore they could meet economic development needs with moderate price increases. Moreover, they needed Western security guarantees against the Arab nationalist regimes.[7] Nevertheless, the price doves and the price hawks converged in their determination to gain control over their petroleum industries. In December 1972, Saudi Arabia and Kuwait acquired 25 percent participation in the oil companies operating in their countries and increased their share until they reached 51 percent by the end of 1982. They achieved nationalization by consent in stages.[8]

The second development in the world economy that contributed to the oil revolution was the decision by the United States government in August 1971 to "float" the US dollar, ending the gold standard. The dollar lost value, thereby devaluing dollars paid to oil producers. To avoid a loss of revenue in real terms, oil producers demanded that Western oil companies link the oil price to changes in the value of the dollar. The two sides agreed on terms in January

1972, and then when the United States devalued the dollar again in early 1973, oil producers again sought higher prices.[9]

The third development was the decline in United States oil production. It coincided with the dollar's devaluation and shortfalls in energy output from other domestic fuel sources arising from environmental restrictions on coal and slower than expected growth in nuclear power. With rising demand for oil imports, the Nixon administration ended quotas on oil imports in April 1973. Independent oil companies then competed with the major companies for oil supplies, putting additional pressure on prices. In fall 1973, oil producers and major Western companies were set to hold new talks because the prices of Western industrial goods were rising faster than oil revenues. Until that point, bargaining over oil was rooted in the economics of global trade, but it then got tangled in Middle East war.[10]

Egypt's Anwar al-Sadat tried various ways to press Israel to withdraw from the Sinai peninsula, which it seized in the 1967 war. At first, he looked to the United States to lean on Israel, but Washington was preoccupied with the Vietnam War. In spring 1973, Sadat reached out to Syrian president Hafiz al-Asad, who wished to recover the Golan Heights. For the first time in the history of the Arab–Israeli conflict, two Arab leaders developed plans for a coordinated attack. Sadat brought King Faisal into plans for war, not as a belligerent, but as a strategic partner willing to withhold oil from Western powers if they sided with Israel. On October 6, 1973, Egyptian and Syrian forces caught Israel by surprise and burst through its defensive positions along the Suez Canal and in the Golan Heights. Israeli forces retreated before the first wave of attacks and organized for a counter-offensive that turned the tables on its adversaries. American and Soviet diplomatic intervention brought about a ceasefire on October 25.

The war coincided with talks between OPEC and major oil companies, so that negotiations over oil production, sales, and prices became intertwined with the fighting. In the months preceding the war, Saudi officials warned the Americans that if the United States supported Israel in a new round of fighting, the Saudis would cut oil production. Thus, when Washington decided to rearm the Israelis ten days into the war, Arab members of OPEC announced a 5 percent cut in production. The Americans continued to airlift arms to Israel, and Saudi Arabia declared an embargo on oil exports to the United States. On October 16, Arab members of OPEC announced they were raising the price of oil by 70 percent. The end of the war did not end the confrontation between oil producers and Western companies. Price hawks pushed for more increases while Saudi Arabia and other price doves urged smaller increases. At a December meeting held in Tehran, the pro-Western shah of Iran joined with the Arab nationalist leaders in Iraq and Libya to push the price of oil to nearly $12 per barrel.

The confluence of strains over war and oil raised tensions between the United States and conservative Arab monarchies. Washington's military and diplomatic support for Israel frustrated the Arabs; Americans blamed "rich oil shaikhs" for high prices and long lines at gas stations. The Saudis ended their embargo on exports to the United States in March 1974, when Washington assured Riyadh that it would help Syria and Israel reach an agreement to disengage their military forces.

US Secretary of State Henry Kissinger formulated a strategy to de-escalate Arab-Israeli tensions and to mitigate the disruptive effects of the oil shock. In June 1974, a high-level Saudi delegation went to Washington to lay a new foundation for bilateral relations with the establishment of the Joint Commission on Economic Cooperation. The joint commission formed specialized groups to design programs to advance agriculture, industry, technology, and education in Saudi Arabia. The two governments also agreed to create a joint commission to strengthen Saudi military forces. Kissinger expected that the joint commissions would create opportunities for the United States to sell a massive volume of advanced technology products that would shrink the United States' trade deficit and that putting the relationship on

1. The first portrait of a Saudi emir, Abdallah ibn Saud, drawn by a French architect in 1818 in Cairo, while the emir was en route to Istanbul to be executed.

2. Al-Khudud is an artesian spring in Hasa, near the Persian Gulf. Pools around such springs supplied water to date palm orchards and were centers for social activities—bathing, laundry, and picnics.

3. Enslaved men and women were part of the Arabian social fabric, working for urban households, oasis farmers, and Bedouin until emancipation in 1962.

4. Bedouin made the most of natural resources, migrating with their belongings loaded onto camels to find fresh pasture, living off their camels' dairy products, and hiring them to caravan merchants in need of pack animals. Bedouin camps included Salukis, swift Arabian hounds bred to hunt game.

5. Bedouin tents pitched near oasis settlements were a sign of the symbiotic relationship between nomads and townsfolk sealed by trade, and common values and ideas about social distinction rooted in ancestry. Encampments were a familiar sight on the outskirts of Riyadh until the 1950s.

6. The Brethren—zealous Bedouin converts to Wahhabi beliefs—rebelled against Saudi authority in 1929. The rebels claimed to be faithful believers, and they refused to bow to central government authority and to respect international borders. Their defeat spelled the end of Bedouin independence.

7. The Saudi kingdom stood on a foundation of common culture and religion, including participation by the king and princes in the traditional sword dance, which was part of Bedouin and town life. This celebration at the royal palace honored a prince's memorization of the Quran, a milestone in Islamic education.

8. A narrow street, sheltered against the blistering sun, in the northwest ancient trading town of al-Ula, now the country's first UNESCO World Heritage Site.

9. The interior of a mudbrick residence in al-Ula, which was abandoned after the oil boom. Characteristic timber-and-thatch ceiling and wall decoration, including a phrase invoking God's protection.

10. The steamy Red Sea port of Jeddah was known for the merchants' multi-story houses with distinctive protruding wooden screens that afforded residents cross-ventilation while safeguarding privacy.

11. Saudi Arabia drew the attention of the public in the United States during the Second World War as a source of petroleum that could alleviate shortages and relieve gasoline rationing.

12. The first cars to arrive in Riyadh were dragged by camels and men from the Gulf coast across the Dahna sands years before American drillers struck oil in 1938.

13. Bedouin adapted to using motor vehicles as the primary mode for transportation, even moving camels, formerly used to carry freight, in pickup trucks to reach fresh pasture.

14. The new urban streetscape in a middle-class Riyadh neighborhood. Saudis who once lived in mudbrick houses moved to electrified apartment units with air conditioning and plumbing, along broad streets designed for cars instead of narrow sheltered passageways, and near playgrounds for children.

15. With the adoption of Western consumer habits, upscale stores on urban thoroughfares displayed risqué dresses on mannequins. The absence of heads was a concession to Wahhabi norms. Window shopping became a new pastime, but in 1965, puritans in Medina went on a rampage, smashing store windows.

16. Decades after the government declared it would ensure the population's material welfare, a significant proportion of Saudis and expatriate residents lived in low-income neighborhoods where houses and streets were in disrepair. In the early 2000s, the government adopted programs to alleviate poverty.

17. Even though the tenets of Islam reject racial and ethnic discrimination, the historic division of society according to ancestry is visible in the preponderance of descendants of enslaved Africans and immigrants from Africa at the bottom of the economic ladder.

18. Attacks by Al Qaeda in the Arabian Peninsula on residential compounds began a contest between terrorists and the government that lasted four years and ended in victory for the authorities.

19. The Shiite minority in the Eastern Province have mounted nonviolent demonstrations calling for the release of political prisoners, equal access to state jobs, and the end of religious discrimination.

20. Saudi Arabia and other Gulf countries employ several million Asian workers. Cases of abuse at the hands of employers have spurred demonstrations in workers' home countries demanding legal protection.

firmer ground would incline the Saudis to sustain high levels of oil production that would ease pressure on global supply and prices.[11] When it came to selling American weapons, Kissinger's scheme proved effective: Saudi arms purchases from the United States roughly quadrupled, from $450 million in 1973/4 to $1.9 billion in 1974/5. The deals were highly lucrative for US weapons makers and for Saudi brokers.[12]

The United States Treasury Department and the Saudi Arabian Monetary Authority (SAMA) agreed that Saudi Arabia would invest the massive surplus from oil income in Western and Japanese banks. In late 1974, SAMA agreed to purchase short-term treasury bonds in the amount of $2.5 billion in the first half of 1975.[13] This arrangement formed part of a larger pattern whereby Saudi Arabia and other members of OPEC lent a large portion of their surplus oil income to governments of industrialized countries. The cozy financial arrangement alleviated strains between the United States and Saudi Arabia, but friction still arose at times from Washington's ties to Israel. For instance, in 1978, Israel spurred opposition in the United States Congress to the sale of the F-15 Eagle fighter to Saudi Arabia. The Carter administration was able to gain congressional approval after Riyadh agreed not to station the planes in the north close to Israel and accepted modifications that removed any offensive capacity. It was a frustrating experience for the Saudis, especially because they were paying for the planes while Israel and Egypt received them as a reward for agreeing to sign their peace treaty.[14]

In addition to giving Saudi Arabia and the Arab Gulf states a central role in global energy, the oil revolution reshaped the Indian Ocean labor market. The massive development projects funded by oil revenues brought a huge influx of migrant workers. Combined with the decline of the Arab left, the contraction of foreign Arab labor in the Gulf contributed to demobilization of the Saudi left, along with the provision of a higher level of benefits to citizens that left non-citizen workers at the bottom of the labor hierarchy.

The Rentier State

Changes in policy and initiatives for improving governance in the 1960s paved the way for directing investment of oil revenue in the 1970s. The first two five-year plans (1970–5 and 1975–80) concentrated on laying down physical infrastructure, especially transportation and communications, expanding access to public education, and establishing a petrochemical industry.[15] The second plan addressed housing shortages in the cities and transportation capacity by enlarging ports and expanding roads to handle the import and distribution of equipment and goods. Planners set ambitious goals to vastly increase enrolment in public schools.[16] With the state taking the leading role in development, the population's welfare depended on the state to invest and allocate oil income.[17]

When scholars took stock of the reshaping of Saudi Arabia and other large oil producers during the 1970s and 1980s, they found it useful to flesh out a political and economic model that explained their distinctive features. Saudi Arabia and the other major oil producers were said to have become rentier states. Such states draw much or most of their revenue from external sources (in their cases, oil sales, but in other cases, foreign aid or worker remittances) that allow them to meet fiscal needs without taxing the population, and that allow them to direct economic development. These states have small populations and one major natural resource that is valued in global trade.[18]

According to this model, the rentier state exhibits six traits.[19] First, the state's control over oil revenue (rent) gives it a dominant role in the economy, with the power to decide how to distribute and invest revenue. Second, control over oil revenue gives the state autonomy from society. Social groups depend on the state for jobs, social benefits, and public goods; the state does not depend on social groups for loans and taxes. In the Saudi case, during the 1930s and 1940s, merchant families in Hijaz were able to exercise political influence because they loaned money to the government and their standing as provincial leaders made their support valuable. In the 1960s, the balance shifted in favor of the dynasty, with merchants depending on it for contracts and licenses to act as agents for foreign firms.[20] Third, a "rentier mentality" emerges whereby economic activity consists of seeking a share of oil revenues (rent); that situation leads to economic stratification according to the distribution of shares in rent. Fourth, by importing food and goods, the rentier state undermines domestic agriculture, livestock, and small manufacturers, but then sustains these sectors with subsidies. Fifth, there is little pressure for political representation because the rentier state provides goods, services, and jobs. Sixth, expatriate workers supply labor while local workers occupy public-sector positions that pay higher wages than private-sector work. The overall effect is the emergence of a "rentier bargain," whereby citizens obtain material comfort from the government and the government obtains political quiescence from citizens.

Critics of the rentier state model point to shortcomings. They say that it underestimates constraints set by international forces, such as shifts in the oil market. In addition, the model overestimates state autonomy in the face of demands from social groups. For example, by the mid-1980s, so many Saudis depended on the state that cutting services and salaries would have been destabilizing.[21] Nevertheless, the rentier state model is valuable for highlighting similarities among countries where control over rent gives the state the power to direct resources in ways that have rearranged where people live (from countryside to city), and that enable the state to dominate the population through reward and repression.

Social Transformation

The pace of change in Saudi society accelerated during the first decade of high oil revenue. By 1990, most Saudis lived in cities. Investments by five-year plans in health and education lowered infant mortality, extended life expectancy, trained teachers, built schools, and educated a growing percentage of children, albeit with a noticeable gender gap between boys and girls. Development took on different aspects in the various regions. In the east, the oil industry dominated the economy; Hijaz was the country's commercial hub; finance and government offices were concentrated in Riyadh; Asir and the northern regions remained largely agrarian.[22] Throughout the country, the rentier state employment pattern set in, where most Saudis held public sector jobs and the private sector depended on foreign workers. Most private sector growth was based on government spending for construction and maintenance of infrastructure.[23]

Conditions in one of the oldest Brethren colonies, Sajir, demonstrate the deep penetration of state institutions and modern economic forces into the country's far reaches, made possible by the allocation of oil income. State inputs (interest-free loans, subsidies to acquire machinery, a national road network) stimulated intensive cultivation, carried out by wage workers from Egypt and Pakistan, and integrated producers with the national economy.[24] Branches of central government agencies tied rural folk to the central state. In the early 1980s, Sajir's government offices included interior ministry agencies for the police and civil defense, a rural council for infrastructure development under the rural affairs ministry, branches of the agriculture ministry and the Saudi Agriculture Bank, a health clinic, and a social services office for social security and disaster relief. There were six schools: boys' and girls' primary schools; boys' and girls' secondary schools; a high school for boys; and a teacher training school for girls (residents hoped that education would lead to easier livelihoods than farming).[25] The rural council guided the development of more than 100 enterprises: brick factories, mechanical shops, a water bottling plant, gas stations, restaurants, and others. Local residents owned the enterprises and employed foreign workers from other Arab countries, South Asia, Afghanistan, and the Philippines.[26]

In the country's southeast on the fringes of the Empty Quarter, Murrah tribesmen relocated to permanent settlements in phases:

starting with tents in small compounds, then moving into houses while around them sprang up shops, schools, mosques, and gas stations. For tribesmen remaining in remote rural areas, the government set up clinics to deliver basic health care, and as a result, infant and maternal mortality rates declined. Families had more children, and it became normal for children to attend school.[27] Former Bedouin entered the national economy, finding work in the oil industry and establishing small businesses in freight, construction, and pipeline repair. By the late 1970s, most Murrah households owned a truck, in part thanks to a state program that offered installment payments without interest. In this way, tribesmen purchased pickup trucks and water tankers to move herds and supply them with water. The government also encouraged more cultivation by assisting with excavation of new wells and deployment of mechanical pumps to old wells.[28]

Settlement had uneven effects on gender relations. During the early phase of settlement, former Bedouin women worked on farms, then the arrival of Asian workers to perform agricultural tasks left women with little role in production and more dependent on male relatives. At the same time, they did gain material comfort. As time passed, former Bedouin assimilated stricter ideas about dress and other gender norms: requiring that women wear a black abaya and niqab and that they travel only in the company of a male relative; forbidding women to drive and to use public transport alone; and agreeing to arranged marriages.[29] In some places, fathers were reluctant to allow girls to attend school. Girls usually got married when they were fifteen or sixteen years old; fathers preferred to marry their daughters to older men with money; and polygamy was becoming more common.[30]

Responding to Social Transformation

Social change evoked different reactions. Many Saudis were eager to turn austerity into a memory. Modernist authors shed no tears for leaving behind the old times when chronic illness, high infant mortality, and hunger were the common lot. One of the pioneers in Saudi fiction, Ibrahim al-Nasser (b. 1930), sketched village life as a dark world haunted by fear of malevolent spirits. The protagonist in his short story "Mischief" comes from a younger generation that had forsaken the old superstitions and would "sneer at everything the people of our neighborhood, even our village as a whole, cling to." Villagers were consumed with belief in jinns and demons. If someone stumbled in the dark, their mother would break eggs there to "appease the jinn."[31] In Fahad al-Khlaiwi's (b. 1946) "The Remains of Memory," the protagonist imagines returning from the big city to his "little speck" of a village set in the desert vastness. He recalls moving to Jeddah, getting married, renting a house, finding a place in the civil service, and, like others of his background, adopting the relaxed attitudes of urban life. He imagines the village as "a complex of unjustifiable constrictions like being locked in a wooden box." When he tries one evening to remember the place of his childhood, the memories are no longer there.[32]

Other Saudis felt that they paid a high price for health and comfort. Fahd al-Atiq's novella *Life on Hold* chronicles a family saga that parallels three phases of twentieth-century migration, first in the early 1900s, from a Najdi village to the outskirts of Riyadh, then in the 1950s to an early extramural neighborhood, and from farmwork to office work, and finally in the 1970s, from a mudbrick house to a suburban neighborhood.[33] The protagonist recalls the old Riyadh neighborhood (Shumaisi) as a vibrant, close-knit community of extended family, the organic rhythm of time in narrow streets, and compact, one-story mudbrick houses built around courtyards. With the move to new suburbs, lives are marked by distance from relations and pervaded by malaise, boredom, and loneliness.[34]

Atiq's novel suggests that, for some Saudis, escape from material privation meant the loss of the incalculable quality of social intimacy. Some dove headfirst into suburbanity and embraced consumerism. The home of a nouveau riche family is described:

> All the walls in his house are covered in glass cabinets full of books and antiques. Can you imagine? How can they read when they spend all their time shopping or in hotels or out on the town, even if they do memorize a few intellectual phrases to make an impression when they speak in public? That house is a testament to the consumer lifestyle that has taken root among us.[35]

The narrator relates that some rejected consumerism in favor of ostentatious piety, and yet others felt stuck in between, "lost and adrift."[36] Thus, the protagonist's father "felt that life had lost its appeal since the first signs of what they called the economic boom, which had granted people loans to build new homes in the new suburbs."[37] A different sort of lament for the end of Bedouin independence was heard in the Nabati odes of poet Bandar bin Srur (1937–1984). Like many Bedouin of his generation, he no longer migrated with livestock, but from one occupation to the next: National Guardsman, smuggler, clerk, and truck driver. His verse mocked tribal shaikhs for chasing handouts like chickens scampering after feed.[38]

Ambivalence about social transformation was part of the rift between modernists and their critics. Three mutually reinforcing developments strengthened the modernist camp: the country's integration with cosmopolitan Arab literary and intellectual spheres; internal national integration through urbanization and the spread of public education; and the growth of state agencies staffed by men with outlooks shaped by study in the West and working for Aramco and for state agencies. The modernist current's ranks included former Arab nationalists and leftists that the government coopted with posts in ministries dedicated to development: industry, finance, and agriculture.[39]

The climate for modernists improved after King Faisal's assassination and Prince Fahd's growing influence. While Faisal had cracked down on independent journalism for its dissident leanings, Fahd relaxed restrictions on the press. Newspaper supplements then opened their pages to former leftists calling for individual rights and freer expression and to women writers promoting social reform. By the end of the 1970s, the Saudi intellectual (*muthaqqaf*) had emerged as a new social category, distinct from the activist, the pencil-pushing bureaucrat, and the religious cleric.[40]

The modernist current's push for change extended to modest initiatives to present theatrical performances. Until the 1970s, theater was limited to school plays that dealt with regional issues (the Algerian revolution and the Palestine cause), offered didactic sketches about the family, or staged simple comical skits.[41] The first attempt at public performance in 1960 did not come to fruition. After months of preparation on the part of a Meccan writer, an Egyptian director, and a handful of actors, the Committee for Commanding Right and Forbidding Wrong succeeded at halting production. Theater for the public waited until 1974, when Molière's *The Doctor in Spite of Himself* was staged in Riyadh. The director, Ibrahim al-Hamdan, had studied in Cairo and the United States. To adapt Molière's play for Saudi Arabia, Hamdan turned its female characters into male ones. There was only one live performance, but it was broadcast on television a number of times, and it was the catalyst for the formation of the Saudi Society for Culture and Art, with headquarters in Riyadh and branches in Jeddah, Ta'if, Abha, Dammam, Hasa, and Qasim. From 1974 to 1977, the Society produced around fifty plays that addressed pressing issues such as high housing costs caused by real estate speculation.[42]

Defenders of conservative customs in the name of safeguarding religion had more to worry about than modernist assertion in the literary sphere. The government's encouragement of girls to attend school was starting to raise the public profile of women in Saudi cities. From 1965 to 1980, enrollment in elementary schools for girls increased from 45,000 to 325,000. In the same period, the number of girls attending intermediate schools grew from 1,000 to 80,000. Teaching institutes for women saw enrollment rise from 710 to 11,000.[43] By the mid-1970s, women were managing charitable associations, women news announcers were appearing on television, with hair covered but faces bared, and women university graduates were working in medicine and journalism. Unable to prevent the changes that accompanied education and urbanization, the religious establishment developed new rules to contain them by instituting gender segregation in workplaces and blurring images of women in advertising.[44]

Tension between religious and modernist currents spilled over into retail spaces. In 1977, Riyadh had one bookstore dedicated to stocking works by Islamist authors, and in that year a merchant opened the first store in Riyadh for religious cassettes with sermons and Quran recitation. It was not long before such stores crowded out shops selling popular music recordings.[45] The contest between "Islamic cassettes" and pop music captured the way consumption was more than a matter of acquiring items for personal use, but also an expression of cultural orientation, be it a preference for Western commodities or a sign of religious fidelity.

The very presence of modernists was an affront to Wahhabi doctrine's aim to purge what it viewed as unbelief. Even though modernists were few in number, their positions in government gave them influence and legitimized the authority of a worldview inimical to Wahhabi doctrine. In the early 1970s, the religious establishment was changing shape in wake of Muhammad ibn Ibrahim's death in 1969. For the first time, the leading clerics did not come from the Al al-Shaikh lineage. Instead, two senior clerics embodied the Wahhabi mission's authority: Abd al-Aziz ibn Baz (1912–1999) and Muhammad al-Uthaimin (1929–2001). Together they presided over the expansion of religious agencies during the oil boom. The Wahhabi establishment gained resources (agencies, staffing, funds) that allowed clerics to preserve a sphere of authority, but dependence on the budget decisions of a government agency implied subordination to secular power.

One area where the clerics were able to expand their influence was higher education. The conversion of religious institutes into universities signified their determination to compete with the country's modernist current. Thousands of religious university graduates in the 1970s and 1980s formed a new generation of cadres for the Wahhabi mission. The religious universities were important sites for updating the Wahhabi canon by asserting it formed part of the mainstream Sunni tradition. Professors and their graduate students published new editions of classical Islamic treatises that, according to their Saudi editors, represented the legacy of "the Pious Ancestors." This lexical move signaled the embrace of Salafism as the preferred label for their teachings and an attempt to distance the country's religious doctrine from the pejorative connotation that "Wahhabism" bore in much of the Muslim world.[46]

The Disruptions of 1979

In late 1978, the Saudi dynasty had a set of policies and relationships that cemented its rule and regional security. Partnership with the Wahhabi mission and cooperation with transnational Islamic organizations afforded symbolic legitimacy. Investment of oil revenues in national development signaled commitment to citizens' material welfare. Alignment with the United States offered a buffer against foreign threats. Those policies and relationships proved their worth in the face of multiple disruptions that unfolded in 1979.

Three major events that year altered the regional strategic balance. In February, a revolution in Iran overthrew the pro-Western monarchy. In March, Egypt and Israel signed a peace treaty, introducing a new cause of tension with Washington, which expected Riyadh to support Anwar al-Sadat's break with Arab ranks to pursue a separate deal.[47] In December, the Soviet Union invaded Afghanistan. In the midst of regional turmoil, two revolts against the Saudi monarchy erupted in late November at opposite ends of the country.

The Iranian revolution turned out to have the longest-lasting and most destabilizing impact on Saudi Arabia. The deposed ruler,

Muhammad Reza Pahlavi, rankled the Saudis with his pretensions to regional primacy and irredentist claim to Bahrain and small islands in the Gulf.[48] Nevertheless, he was a fellow monarch, a staunch anticommunist aligned with the United States, and a foe of Arab nationalists, particularly the Baathist regime in Iraq. His military intervention in Oman to defeat the Dhofar rebellion removed a leftist threat from Saudi Arabia's southern border. Furthermore, the shah's anticlerical posture meant that Iran's standing as a Shiite country was not a factor in relations with the Saudis and other Sunni countries. The revolution changed Iran from a strategic ally to a threat.

For Saudi Arabia, the revolutionary regime posed an ideological challenge that bore similarities to the Arab nationalist movement. The Islamic Republic and Arab nationalists stood for anti-imperialism, and they sought to overthrow monarchies, a goal that Arab nationalists achieved in Egypt, Iraq, Yemen, and Libya. Saudi Arabia's economic and strategic relationship with the United States made it vulnerable to charges that it betrayed Muslim solidarity, particularly on the Palestine cause. The revolution's significance for Sunni–Shiite dynamics is complicated. A new constitution, ratified in December 1979, enshrined Twelver Shiism as the official religion, but the leader Ayatollah Ruhollah Khomeini proclaimed solidarity with all Muslims—whether Shiite or Sunni. Thus, the Islamic Republic embraced the Palestinian cause against Israel. It also became the champion of Shiites living under governments dominated by Sunnis in Iraq, Bahrain, and Saudi Arabia, and it urged Shiites to overthrow rulers deemed corrupt puppets of Western powers. In doing so, Iran added political suspicion to perennial Wahhabi hostility toward the kingdom's Shiite minority. To combat the Islamic Republic, Riyadh mobilized clerics and allies in the transnational religious institutions established in the early 1960s to combat Arab nationalism to broadcast anti-Shiite rhetoric and conflate Iranian subversion with discontent at home, casting Saudi Shiites as agents of Iran.[49] Anti-Shiism was part of classic Wahhabi doctrine that now had political value for the dynasty. While the rivalry between Iran and Saudi Arabia played on religious allegiances (in addition to anti-imperialist tropes), the religious dimension was secondary to national interest.

While Iran's revolutionary turmoil held the world's attention, a dissident faction in the Salafi Group for Commanding Right and Forbidding Wrong was looking ahead to the dawn of the fifteenth century in the Muslim calendar (November 20, 1979), when they expected to play a part in a millenarian scenario that required them to take over the Grand Mosque in Mecca. In the early 1970s, the Salafi Group had spread around the country by recruiting religious youth who shared their disapproval of satanic inventions such as television. They formed residential enclaves where they devoted themselves to what they considered pure religious observance in daily life and ritual. Members of the Salafi Group took inspiration from Nasir al-Din al-Albani's conspicuous adherence to Prophetic Traditions, even when it meant breaking from Wahhabi positions. They shared Albani's disdain for the Muslim Brotherhood, and by extension the Awakening, viewing them as political opportunists not truly committed to religion. Albani also influenced the attitude of Salafi Group members toward the Wahhabi establishment. While some members remained loyal to their official patron Abd al-Aziz ibn Baz and his lieutenants, a dissident faction agreed with Albani that the clerics were too ready to compromise religious principles for the sake of placating the Sauds, whom Albani considered corrupt and unqualified for political allegiance because they were not from the Prophet's tribe Quraish, a criterion for the caliphate according to Sunni political theory.

The leader of the dissident faction was Juhaiman al-Utaibi (1938–1979), who hailed from the old Brethren colony of Sajir.[50] With his forceful personality, Juhaiman eclipsed the Salafi Group's founders. His enmity toward the Sauds stemmed from his belief that Abd al-Aziz had betrayed the Brethren and abandoned religion by permitting infidel ways to spread. In his essay, "Removing Confusion from Abraham's Community," he wrote:

> He [King Abd al-Aziz] called upon the Brethren, may God have mercy on them, those who migrated to various villages in a migration (*hijra*) to God. He called on them to pay him allegiance according to the Book and the Sunna. They were waging jihad and conquering towns in the belief that he was the legitimate leader of the Muslims. Then when he consolidated power and he achieved his aims, he allied with the Christians and prohibited jihad in God's path outside Arabia when they went to fight polytheists in Iraq, who were praying to Ali, Fatima and Hasan, along with God.[51]

In summer 1977, Ibn Baz sent a deputy to meet with Salafi Group leaders in Medina to persuade them to conform to mainstream religious practices rather than continue adhering to Albani's unusual opinions. The meeting caused a schism, with most members taking Juhaiman's side.[52] In the following months, Juhaiman toured the country to rally Salafi Group members against the government. He urged members to quit government jobs, and to boycott public schools and the lessons of official clerics.

In December 1978, Saudi police got a tipoff that the group was storing weapons and raided its properties. Juhaiman eluded arrest, thanks to a relative in the Medina police who warned him the authorities planned to detain him. He struck into the desert, where he spent the next year as a fugitive. During that year, he and his followers became consumed by millenarian beliefs and dreams about the Muslim messiah—in Arabic, the Mahdi—that led to their violent seizure of the Grand Mosque.[53]

On the morning of November 20, 1979, the first day of the Muslim New Year, Juhaiman and a band of around 300 men entered the Grand Mosque before the dawn prayer. They had prepared to seize control by smuggling weapons into the sacred precinct on shrouded funeral stretchers, disguising the arms as corpses. At the moment the prayer leader began reciting the dawn prayer, Juhaiman and his comrades shoved him aside and one of their number announced the advent of the Mahdi, as foretold in Prophetic Traditions, according to apocalyptic signs the group's members saw in their dreams. The Saudi government was completely unprepared for the messianic revolt. The first attempts to regain control over the Grand Mosque failed: Juhaiman's band included veteran National Guardsmen posted to minarets and parapets from which they drove back security forces in a hail of fire. The government resorted to inviting French special forces to direct Saudi forces in a two-week battle that ended on December 4 in the surrender of Juhaiman and a few dozen survivors from his band. The government put sixty-three members to death on January 9, 1980.[54]

In the midst of the Mecca uprising, anti-government protests erupted on the other side of the country in the Eastern Province, the center of the country's oil industry. Simultaneously, the symbol of the monarchy's religious standing and the core of its economy were in jeopardy. The Eastern Province protests had roots in the government's discrimination against Shiites and the ways that transnational Shiite networks afforded ideological inspiration for activists.

In the early years of the oil boom the Eastern Province's three main cities—Dammam, Dhahran, and Khobar—received large sums for urban infrastructure and commercial development. By contrast, Shiite towns and villages suffered neglect. In 1977, the interior ministry took note of the disparities and promised to improve conditions in Shiite towns, but the government's development agencies failed to follow up. In the first part of 1979, the major newspaper in Dammam reported on government failures. The municipal council of Qatif blamed the national government for failing to keep sewage systems in good repair, pointing to the problems that farmers faced from depleted wells and polluted water in contrast to the visible prosperity of the three major cities. It was the obverse of the legitimacy the state expected from spreading oil wealth: blame for failures from citizens excluded from the benefits of oil pumped from their home province.[55]

At the same that the oil boom passed by Eastern Province Shiites, the activist strain in transnational Shiite politics took root with the establishment of branches of the Shirazi movement. The old notable Shiite families who esteemed traditionalist clerics in Iraq worried that Shirazi activists might disrupt their relationship with the government. The leading Saudi proponent of the Shirazi movement, Hasan al-Saffar, criticized the notable families for failing to protest policies toward Shiites.[56] Since the Diriyya emirate first imposed Wahhabi authority over Hasa, Saudi rulers had discriminated against Shiites. The state's skewed allocation of resources added a material dimension to Shiite grievance. Sunnis enjoyed the fruits of oil revenue, be they modern medical facilities, jobs in the rapidly expanding public sector, or higher living standards. Furthermore, Wahhabi domination of the new national education system ensured that enmity toward Shiism became embedded in schools. By treating the Shiites as a single population, the state and the clerics defined Shiites as a marginal minority, turning theological sectarianism into political discrimination. With a network of religious centers throughout the Gulf, the Shirazi movement contributed to framing a transnational Shiite cause, by connecting Saudi Shiites to coreligionists throughout the region, and by providing a platform for mobilizing against discrimination and material deprivation on the basis of sectarian prejudice.

Anti-government protests erupted at a moment of regional strain defined in religious terms. On November 4, Iranian students seized the American embassy in Tehran, setting off a confrontation between the United States and Iran, which the students and their sympathizers in Shiite communities expected to bring about American military reprisals. Two weeks later, as Shiites prepared for the start of the Shiite Ashura religious holiday, Ayatollah Khomeini blamed Juhaiman's takeover of the Grand Mosque on the United States. In Pakistan, Khomeini's false statement sparked a mob to attack and burn the American embassy in Islamabad.

In the Eastern Province, Shirazi activists had recently established an underground group called the Organization of Islamic Revolution. Its leaders prepared to defy the government ban on public observance of Ashura, when Shiites gather to mourn the martyrdom of Imam Hussein, an event that the Iranian revolution framed as heroic resistance against tyranny.[57] On November 26, a crowd of 4,000 joined a religious procession in Safwa, a Shiite town north of Dammam. On the actual holiday two days later, religious processions turned into violent confrontations with Saudi National Guard units. The Organization of Islamic Revolution's leaflets attacked imperialism and royal corruption, criticized wasting money on weapons, and called for a constitution. Underground leftist groups wanted to join the protests, but Shiite religious leaders opposed cooperating with them, and therefore the leftists held separate protests where they condemned the Camp David Accords, called for ending sectarian discrimination in hiring for government jobs, and demanded the government take steps to improve health and sanitation in Qatif. It took security forces five days to suppress the protest movement. More than twenty demonstrators were killed. Opposition leaders who eluded arrest fled the country. The government responded to some of the grievances with improvements to sewage and roads, construction of hospitals and schools, and investment in modern commercial districts. Nothing was done to remedy religious discrimination.[58]

The 1979 uprisings in Mecca and the Eastern Province revealed religious subcultures that the Wahhabi mission and its royal sponsors unwittingly fostered with strategies designed to buttress the dynasty. The uprisings also reflected the splintering in opposition ranks. The religious dissenters in Juhaiman al-Utaibi's band had roots in fidelity to the exclusivist strain in Wahhabism, resentment in Brethren colonies toward Saudi betrayal, injured pride at the suppression of Bedouin independence, transnational religious currents imported to Medina by Albani and the Ahli Hadith, and a wild card element of millenarianism.[59] The Wahhabi mission's creation of transnational institutions and the establishment of religious institutes across the country were elements of internal and regional integration that made it possible to spread religious dissent through the same channels that Riyadh used to assert central political and religious authority. In the Eastern Province, the Organization of Islamic Revolution revived political demands first broached by leftists and nationalists more than two decades before, but it refused to join forces with the remnants of the region's leftist groups. The Eastern Province uprising fed Riyadh's suspicion that the Islamic Republic exploited the Shiite minority to destabilize the kingdom.

According to a common narrative, the monarchy was slowly opening society to Western influence and suddenly reversed course in a panicky reaction to the Mecca uprising with renewed enforcement of strict religious rules.[60] The royals funded individuals and institutions that promoted and exported an extremist version of Islam that was alien to the country's legacy of "moderate Islam." Al Qaeda's 2001 terrorist attack on the United States then spurred the royals to reverse course once again. On closer inspection, however, things were more complicated than the conservative backlash narrative.

The problem with the narrative is that the authorities were already taking steps to curb Western influence. In summer 1977, the interior ministry tightened restrictions on travel abroad for women, requiring that a male guardian (father, husband, brother, or son) accompany them. It meant that a woman would not be allowed to travel even if her husband were in hospital in another country.[61] In April 1979, the authorities enforced a prohibition on religious celebrations for non-Muslims, ending a long practice of allowing inconspicuous observances. A few months later, the Committee for Commanding Right and Forbidding Wrong announced that women would not be allowed in hotel swimming pools if men were present. In response, hotels in Riyadh and Jeddah closed their pools rather than deal with hot, frustrated guests. New regulations forbade women from trying on clothes in shops and male tailors from measuring women for clothes.

Religious police raided a Chinese restaurant in Riyadh and expelled foreign women not wearing veils. The Western reporter attributed the crackdown on small signs of departure from Wahhabi propriety to the government's nervousness about Iranian revolutionary propaganda and a sense that the royals needed to reinforce their reputation for piety.[62]

Wars in the Gulf and Afghanistan

Other than paying closer attention to the Shiite population in the Eastern Province, there was little the Saudi leaders could do about the revolutionary incitement issuing from Tehran. Iraqi leader Saddam Hussein, however, decided to go to war against the Islamic Republic, blaming it for inciting Iraqi Shiites to overthrow his Baath Party regime. On September 22, 1980, he ordered an invasion that he expected would bring down the Islamic Republic. Saddam may have assumed that Khomeini's purge of Iranian officers and the chaos surrounding the revolution would make it easy to achieve his aims. He miscalculated badly, and not for the last time. The war lasted nearly eight years, drained the two countries of blood and treasure, and produced a new strategic alignment in the Gulf. Fear of revolutionary incitement drove the Gulf Arab states to forget about years of Baathist anti-monarchy propaganda. They loaned Iraq billions of dollars to help pay war expenses. The United States was officially neutral, but because an Iranian victory could have destabilized the pro-Western monarchies, Washington supported Baghdad with economic, technological, and intelligence assistance. In the later phases of the war, the United States enlarged its naval presence in the Gulf to protect oil tankers from attack. By the end of the war in summer 1988, United States military forces had taken over the role Britain had relinquished in 1971 when it withdrew from the Gulf.

Tehran's calls for revolution resonated among Shiites in Saudi Arabia, Bahrain, and Kuwait. The spectre of a powerful patron inciting Shiites in the Arab Gulf states made them appear to be an instrument of subversion wielded by a foreign enemy. Henceforth, Gulf Shiites could not raise a grievance without appearing to be Iranian agents. The image of Shiite subversion gained plausibility from Iranian leaders, such as the ayatollah who proclaimed Iran would annex Bahrain if it did not become an Islamic republic. Arab Gulf rulers responded to the Iranian threat in February 1981 by agreeing to form the Gulf Cooperation Council (GCC) comprising Saudi Arabia, Kuwait, Bahrain, Qatar, the United Arab Emirates, and Oman. Its charter provided for cooperation in education, culture, and trade, but the council turned into a body focused on security matters.

The Iranian revolution was not the only event in 1979 that produced closer alignment between Riyadh and Washington. The Soviet Union's invasion of Afghanistan on December 24, 1979, had a similar effect, but waging a proxy war against Moscow came to hinge on collaboration with Islamic revivalist organizations. The Soviets intervened to stabilize the Marxist government in Kabul, where communists seized power the year before. The United States and conservative Gulf states feared the Soviets might turn Afghanistan into a base for a military thrust through western Pakistan to the Indian Ocean, where it could establish a position to threaten the flow of oil through the Persian Gulf and lend support to radical forces in the region. Afghan guerrilla bands fighting the Marxist regime called their military struggle a jihad and their fighters mujahidin, those who wage jihad. An anti-communist axis took shape bringing together Afghan mujahidin, Islamic revivalist movements, and the governments of Pakistan, Saudi Arabia, and the United States.[63] Pakistan lent the mujahidin safe haven while the United States and Saudi governments supplied funds and arms. The intelligence services of Saudi Arabia, the United States, and Pakistan coordinated the flow of arms to Afghan militias.[64]

For the Saudi leadership, support for the Afghan cause strengthened its standing with the public at a time when low oil prices impeded progress on national development. The Afghan cause also provided an opportunity to deflect Iranian criticism of the close relationship with Washington. A pan-Islamic volunteer campaign for the Afghan cause took shape through the efforts of transnational revivalists (the Muslim Brotherhood) and transnational organizations (the Muslim World League). The risk for both Riyadh and Washington was that Islamic transnational institutions had ties to groups beyond state control.[65]

The Afghan War spread enthusiasm for jihad from the fringes of radical Islamist groups striving to overthrow secular governments they deemed apostate to the political mainstream. The most influential individual promoting the cause was a Jordanian Muslim Brother, Abdallah Azzam.[66] He presented a novel legal argument for classifying jihad in defense of Afghanistan as an individual duty incumbent on Muslims everywhere, not only on Afghan Muslims. In classical legal doctrine, jihad has two purposes, either to expand territory under Muslim rule or to defend Muslims against non-Muslim attack. In the first, offensive kind of jihad, the duty to fight is collective: not all men are obliged to participate, only as many as needed to effectively take the fight to the enemy. In the second, defensive jihad, the duty to fight is individual and incumbent on most able-bodied men. Azzam's concept of a universal individual duty to defend any Muslim land under attack drew criticism from religious authorities. Wahhabi clerics neither endorsed Azzam's doctrine nor did they favor sending aid to Afghan groups known for failing to uphold correct belief. The leading Awakening shaikhs (Safar al-Hawali and Salman al-Awda) did not support the Afghan cause either: they agreed with Wahhabi clerics on doctrinal grounds and they found fault with the cause on political grounds, considering the Afghan resistance an instrument of United States geostrategic power.[67] Nevertheless, Azzam's jihad doctrine resonated beyond Afghanistan because it could apply to a Muslim population anywhere fending off non-Muslim aggression, and therefore Azzam's logic turned zones of conflict between Muslims and non-Muslims into zones of transnational jihad.

In Saudi Arabia, the Muslim Brotherhood was the primary agent for mobilizing public opinion to support the Afghan cause, exercising influence through the Muslim World League, the Islamic University of Medina, and the Awakening networks. In the first years of the war, a handful of Saudis went to Pakistan to join medical relief efforts through the Red Crescent Society. A camp to train Arab volunteers was set up near Pakistan's border with Afghanistan in 1984, at first hosting a dozen or so men. That same year, Osama bin Laden went to Pakistan to lend his support to Azzam's "Services Bureau," intended to coordinate distribution of resources and direct volunteers. The Services Bureau also extended assistance to Afghan refugees, providing medicine and food.[68]

The Saudi government encouraged charities and individual donors to send funds to the Afghan resistance. Osama bin Laden promoted the cause to friends in Jeddah and Medina, publicized Azzam's visits, and urged his acquaintances to lend support. For two years, he made regular trips between Pakistan and Saudi Arabia before he decided to stay in late 1986. At that time, he established a camp called the Lion's Den for Arab volunteers recruited through personal networks, publicity in Islamist magazines issued from Peshawar, and favorable coverage in the Saudi press. How many Saudis went to Pakistan or Afghanistan during the war is not documented. Estimates range from several thousand to 20,000. Whatever the correct figure, few Saudis spent more than a month or two in Pakistan; somewhere between 1,000 and 5,000 saw combat; estimates for Saudis killed in battle range from 50 to 300. Raw numbers, however, do not do justice to the impact of the Afghan jihad on religious culture in Saudi Arabia, where jihadist militancy had no foothold since the Brethren rebellion in the late 1920s. For years after the Afghan War ended in 1989, a jihadist current in Saudi Arabia connected militants throughout the Muslim world, from the Philippines to Nigeria.[69]

The Afghan War was the most conspicuous manifestation of religious solidarity that brought together Muslim governments (e.g., Saudi Arabia and Pakistan), transnational institutions (e.g., the Muslim World League), and revivalist movements. Accounts that simplify and reduce militancy's multiple agents and channels to Saudi Arabia's "export of Wahhabism" neglect the essential roles of other players, such as Pakistan's military dictator General Zia-ul-Haq, whose regime showered financial and logistical support on militant groups to shore up its domestic position and contest India for control of Kashmir. Saudi Arabia certainly did wield influence in Muslim societies, but the "Saudi impact" was not uniform. It could not be so because Saudi Arabia's religious landscape was not uniform. There were the classic Wahhabi call to purify worship and the Awakening movement's activist impulse, itself divided between reformist and militant strands. Furthermore, Saudi influence varied from one country to another, according to local demographic and political conditions. Funding for schools, hospitals, mosques, and religious publications intended to "win hearts and minds" needed local allies for leadership and staff. In Indonesia, the government created the Indonesian Council for Islamic Proselytizing in 1967, to collaborate with Saudi and transnational organizations.[70] In the case of West Africa, Saudi clerics collaborated with African religious scholars residing in the holy cities to design ways to spread Salafism.[71] Notwithstanding variable factors, Riyadh's alliance with foreign revivalist movements and government leaders did have common effects. One was an extension of the original Wahhabi mission's sectarian purpose to proselytize against denominational pluralism in other Muslim societies. A second effect that dovetailed with revivalist aims was to combat Western political domination and cultural influence, deemed idolatrous in the Wahhabi outlook. Finally, the alliance bolstered like-minded believers abroad against secular and religious rivals for whom it was convenient to blame outsiders for the growing influence of "foreign" religious ideas.

Culture Conflict

Saudi Arabia's diverse religious landscape of establishment clerics, Awakening preachers, and militant youth had latent tensions, as the Mecca uprising demonstrated. Alarm at the influence of cosmopolitan culture, however, tended to press pious Saudis to form a common front in a battle with secular Saudis over the country's direction. The population they all sought to influence reflected changes wrought by economic and social development. The new Saudi was urban, literate, in tune with political currents in other Muslim countries, and disposed to see the state as responsible for citizens' welfare. Apart from those common features, Saudis were divided between two camps, Islamist and modernist, when it came to how they thought of their country and its place in the world. The division was the fruit of how rulers had formed close ties with incompatible partners. On one side, foreign Arab advisers at the royal court, Aramco staff, and Western consultants contributed to the formation of a modernist tendency. On the other side, foreign Muslim educators, technicians, and workers shaped Islamist activists, who allied with the Wahhabi religious establishment to combat the modernist tendency. The creation of parallel university systems, secular and religious, reinforced divergent outlooks.

The division between Islamists and modernists had a generational facet. The modernists came of age in the 1960s and 1970s, attended Western universities, and returned to successful careers in government offices, benefiting from the rapid expansion of government during the oil boom. The Islamists were younger and came from Saudi religious universities that bore the Muslim Brotherhood's imprint. When members of the younger generation entered the job market in the 1980s, the boom years had given way to the austerity of a stretch of low oil prices, and the older generation blocked paths to career advancement. A sense of generational deprivation was exacerbated by cultural polarity between secular-leaning elders—marked by clean shaves, cigarettes, and lax piety—and Islamist youngsters, convinced that the country had fallen under control of an international Masonic cabal consisting of former Arab nationalists and leftists educated at American universities that trained Saudi students to do Washington's bidding.[72]

In the early 1980s, modernist writers had a monopoly on the cultural supplements of leading magazines and newspapers dedicated to discussing major Arab authors and Western thinkers: Syrian poet Adonis, Moroccan critic Abed al-Jabri, and Western theorists Jacques Derrida and Roland Barthes. Saudi writers participating in the modernist discourse included poets Ali al-Dumaini and Muhammad al-Ali, and novelists Raja Alim, Abdi Khazindar, and Saad al-Dawsari. In the mid-1980s, Awakening activists started challenging modernist speakers at meetings of literary clubs in Abha, Riyadh, and Jeddah. They also reacted against a royal initiative in 1985 to hold an annual event, the Janadriyya festival, to promote the country's status as part of modern Arab culture. The inaugural event featured several major Arab thinkers: Abed al-Jabri, Muhammad Arkoun, and Abd al-Wahhab Bayati. The Awakening camp regarded the festival as another sign of Western cultural invasion. In the festival's second year, Awakening activists attended to challenge modernist speakers. In the next few years, Awakening writers grew bolder in accusing modernists of waging a clandestine campaign against Islam. Mosque sermons, cassette recordings, and newspaper articles smeared modernists in terms implying they were connected to Jews and Satanists.[73] Around 1988, Awakening shaikhs started to criticize the government in pamphlets, cassettes, and sermons for permitting Western influences. The government responded by starting to favor Awakening speakers over modernists in granting access to platforms such as the Janadriyya festival, newspaper columns, and literary clubs.[74]

One of the most charged issues in the culture field was the status and roles of women. Investment in girls' education gave rise to expanding numbers of university graduates whose ranks included scholars who explored feminist ideas in the 1970s. Former leftists also supported women's rights. As the social climate came to allow different degrees of modest dress, conservatives expressed alarm at the spread of foreign contamination. Around 1973–4, calls for conformity to stricter norms triggered responses from women poets upholding "the right of women to make their own decisions, take control of their own lives."[75] In the early 1980s, state-sponsored media reinforced the conservatives by blaming the Western cultural invasion for turning Saudi women against their own society. Pamphlets appeared in public places (schools, malls, hospitals, airports) purporting to explain Islamic womanhood and rehearsing arguments for the legitimacy of polygamy.[76] Pious and modernist camps staked out rival visions of gender relations in a discourse that focused on marriage law, dress, driving, travel without a male guardian, and how mandatory gender segregation at workplaces affected options for women to work. All these questions were part of a collective redefinition of gender roles after recent social transformation, as people pondered whether urbanization and education brought progress or moral corruption.

In mundane terms, urbanization and education indeed altered everyday conditions. One study of women in the eastern city of Dammam found significant differences between old and young generations regardless of high or low social status. Most older women (over fifty-five, born before 1930) had arranged marriages at a young age, around fourteen years, and polygamy was common. Most of them were illiterate; a few attended Quranic school. They tended to live with extended families and seldom worked outside the home, having lost customary means of income such as making clothes and raising chickens to sell eggs.[77] Young women typically waited to finish school in their later teens before they got married, less frequently had arranged marriages, and rarely dealt with polygamy. While older women disliked polygamy, they were resigned to it. Younger women expressed clear opposition to the custom. School attendance had become universal, and some women pursued college degrees. There was a notable shift in living situations, with the nuclear family becoming the norm. Women reported feeling isolated compared to living with an extended family and they shouldered the burden of having to do all the household chores and childrearing on their own instead of having more women around to share tasks. Even though the expanding urban economy of the boom years created demand for labor, few women worked outside the home in modern occupations for two primary reasons. First, government investment in girls' education beyond the intermediate level was low and therefore few women acquired the qualifications for professional employment. Second, social norms limited women to a handful of occupations in health, social work, and education.[78]

The increase in girls' education created a growing audience of women eager for literature reflecting their experiences and aspirations. Newspapers issued weekly literary sections, while publishers, bookstores, and literary clubs stimulated and reflected an appetite for fiction.[79] In the 1950s and 1960s, a handful of women authors came from elite families that had the means and inclination for their daughters to pursue education. Women like Najat Khayyat and Samira Khashshogji published short stories and poetry in the literary sections of magazines and newspapers in the 1970s. The number of women authors expanded in the 1980s, resulting in pluralism in style and themes resembling those in other Arab countries.[80] Authors sketched the predicaments confronting educated women and men in new urban settings. Women characters frequently dealt with personal misfortunes rooted in subordination to male authority. In "Had I Been Male" by Najat Khayyat, the main character is an orphan girl whose uncle arranged for her to marry a much old man when she was fifteen years old. After finding life with her husband to be intolerable, the young bride runs away to her mother, but her mother urges her to be patient because nobody else will provide for her: "You are a female."[81] Other stories depict women's complicity in perpetuating male privilege, the notion that a bad man is better than no man at all,[82] the absurdity of requiring a male guardian or *mahram*,[83] and the hardships of "the second shift."[84] The stories do not look forward to individual solutions or escape from family. Instead, they dream of living among enlightened men. They give the impression that the authors yearn for a marriage that is not an arrangement between families or an expression of patriarchal power where polygyny, divorce, and loss of custody over children loom over wives. A married couple should share respectful understanding and a life that balances the family with professional endeavors.

In the early 1970s, changes in external conditions boded well for the Saudi monarchy. The Arab Cold War ended in defeat for the nationalists and the left. The sudden increase in the price of oil made Saudi Arabia an important player in the global economy and gave the state the means to deliver material comfort to citizens. Rising living standards along with the repression of nationalist and leftist movements ended a cycle of political contention going back to the labor protests in the 1940s.

The upheavals of 1979 reflected the integration of national and transnational spaces. The Persian constitutional revolution of 1905–11 did not make a ripple in Arabia while the 1979 Iranian revolution inspired the kingdom's Shiite population, only recently redefined as the "Saudi Shiite minority," to mobilize under the banner of transnational Shiite movements that took shape in the 1960s. The Mecca uprising mirrored national integration of demobilized Bedouin and transnational integration of religious institutions and currents through the Islamic University of Medina. The energetic popular and government responses to Soviet intervention in Afghanistan reflected integration with transnational Muslim causes and the global Cold War rivalry. The Afghan War ended on favorable terms for Riyadh, but the mobilization of national and transnational religious solidarity would soon give rise to a new cycle of political contention over the monarchy's commitment to the revivalist view of true Islamic society and solidarity with Islamic causes.

8

The Kuwait Crisis and Political Mobilization, 1990–2000

On August 2, 1990, Iraq invaded Kuwait and then declared its annexation. The brazen violation of international law set off a crisis that concluded with the United States leading a multinational military coalition of Western and Arab forces to expel Iraqi forces and restore Kuwaiti sovereignty. Coming at the end of the Cold War, the Kuwait crisis marked a new era of heightened power for the United States. Coming on the heels of the Iran–Iraq War, it marked a further escalation in United States military intervention in the Persian Gulf.

In Saudi Arabia, the event initiated the country's longest stretch of open dissident mobilization, most notably by the Awakening movement, but also by liberals, including the first public women's protest. Demands stemmed from a sense of Western cultural invasion, Western strategic domination, shortcomings in developmentalist projects, and autocratic resistance to accountability. The government refused to make substantial concessions and countered with a mix of tactics: repression, bureaucratic reorganization of religious agencies, and bolstering support for official clerics. The unexpected incapacitation of King Fahd by a stroke in November 1995 and transfer of effective power to Crown Prince Abdallah a month later made no dent in the dynasty's solid determination to deflect substantial modification to its grip on power. The militant stream in Saudi and transnational religious circles then became the focus of resistance to the country's integration into the Western-oriented political order under United States domination. From a long-term perspective, the Kuwait crisis underscored contradictions between the monarchy's dependence on the Western powers and its dependence on religious solidarity to mobilize support at home and in the very Muslim transnational networks it had played an important role in building.

The Kuwait Crisis

Saddam Hussein's decision to invade Kuwait was a strategic blunder akin to the invasion of Iran ten years earlier, this time driven by the pressing need to cope with postwar economic problems. Demobilized soldiers had to be absorbed into an economy where the public sector was a major employer and the war-torn south required reconstruction. Iraq's ability to manage these problems was constrained at a time of low oil prices. In addition, Iraq had borrowed tens of billions of dollars from Kuwait and Saudi Arabia to fund the war. While the Saudis accepted Saddam's position that Iraq had paid the price of thwarting Iran's efforts to export revolution in blood, Kuwait insisted on repayment. Furthermore, Iraq accused Kuwait of economic sabotage in two specific ways. First, Kuwait exceeded the production quota set by OPEC and thereby put downward pressure on prices. Second, Kuwait pumped oil from a field that straddled the border with lateral drilling pulling oil from the Iraqi side. Beyond immediate grievances, Saddam wanted to address a historic problem arising from the way Britain drew the Kuwait–Iraq boundary that left Iraq with a very narrow coastline on the Gulf.[1] He sought Kuwaiti agreement to lease two islands for development of port facilities, but Kuwait refused. Finally, Iraq had an irredentist claim to Kuwait since the days of the Hashemite monarchy that it reaffirmed shortly after Kuwait attained independence in 1961.

The invasion encountered immediate international condemnation. The day of the invasion, the United Nations Security Council adopted a resolution demanding the withdrawal of Iraqi forces from Kuwait. Iraq's superpower patron, the Soviet Union, was collapsing and no longer in a position to act as a check on the United States if Washington decided to intervene. Moscow attempted to persuade Saddam to withdraw his forces, but the Iraqi leader did not budge. In the arena of Arab public opinion, outside the Gulf states, the invasion was popular as a gesture of defiance of the West. Many Arabs applauded the way Saddam linked withdrawal from Kuwait to Israeli withdrawal from occupied Palestinian territory. Furthermore, many Arabs resented the wealthy Gulf states. The resentment was rooted in the feeling that the Gulf Arabs did not earn their wealth; that they were backward and did not deserve their wealth while other Arabs strove for technical education that made them indispensable to operating modern economies on behalf of their uneducated cousins; and that Gulf Arabs were hypocrites pretending to be more pious than other Arabs at home but abandoning morals when on vacation in Beirut, Cairo, and Damascus.

The Saudis worried that Saddam might use Kuwait as a launchpad for seizing the oil-rich Eastern Province. On August 7, a delegation of high-ranking American political and military officials convinced the Saudi king and senior princes that only a massive Western military intervention could protect their country. Confronting an Iraqi army numbering 900,000, the kingdom had 45,000 troops and about the same number of foreign military personnel: 10,000 troops from Pakistan, 30,000 advisers from the United States, another 7,000 or so from France and the United Kingdom. The Saudis had spent \$3 billion on US weapons since the early 1970s, but they still depended on foreign military power for protection.[2]

King Fahd understood that bringing non-Muslim troops to Saudi Arabia would be unpopular and he sought approval from the religious leadership. Shaikh Abd al-Aziz ibn Baz and his colleagues on the Board of Senior Clerics had to find a loophole in Islamic law that dodged the prohibition on seeking assistance from infidels against fellow Muslims. Like good lawyers everywhere, they found the language to frame a fatwa giving the king what he wanted: "expediency" permitted the government to bring "qualified" forces capable of deterring an aggressor. It was an awkward formulation to be sure, but it gave cover, if a fig leaf, for allowing Western forces to operate from Saudi soil. In the eyes of many Saudis, the fatwa laid bare the hypocrisy of the senior clerics. The Awakening current's leaders denounced it as a violation of Islamic law.[3]

The arrival of Western military forces and Kuwaiti refugees had the unanticipated consequence of challenging the customary ban on women driving motor vehicles. American military units included women soldiers who drove military vehicles down boulevards in Saudi cities. Kuwaiti women were accustomed to driving back home and continued to do so while in exile. The moment was propitious for Saudi women to assert their right to drive. On November 6, forty-seven women with drivers' licenses from foreign countries drove in a group around Riyadh. Traffic police pulled them over and male family members were summoned to retrieve "their women." Before the women were released, they were required to agree they would not repeat their demonstration. The women and their families then faced an ugly backlash from conservatives insulting them on radio and television broadcasts. Some of the women were suspended from their jobs.[4]

In late summer and fall 1990, the United States led an international operation to bring thousands of troops and massive stores of military equipment to Saudi Arabia. Prince Sultan Air Base at Kharj (50 miles south of Riyadh) was enlarged to handle squadrons of F-15E aircraft. By mid-January 1991, the base was a sprawling tent city accommodating 5,000 US Air Force personnel.[5] Egypt, Syria, and Morocco joined the coalition, making it possible to muddle the impression of a Western alliance against Iraq. In Jordan and Yemen, public sympathy for Iraq held the governments back from joining the alliance. Riyadh retaliated against Yemen by expelling more than 700,000 Yemeni workers. In November, the UN Security Council increased the diplomatic pressure on Saddam by passing a resolution authorizing the use of force against Iraq if it did not withdraw by January 15, 1991.

The Security Council deadline passed and the next day the international coalition attacked Iraqi military positions. In the next six weeks, the US and allied air forces carried out massive bombing attacks, but the Iraqis did not retreat. In fact, they launched a successful raid against Saudi Arabia and seized the border town of al-Khafji at the end of January. A joint force of Saudi and Kuwaiti troops was able to retake the town. The Iraqis also attacked Saudi Arabia with surface-to-surface Scud missiles.[6] The United States defended Saudi targets with the Patriot anti-missile system, but a number of Scuds broke through and killed Western troops at a base near Dhahran. On February 24, coalition forces launched a ground offensive. The battered Iraqi troops retreated in panic and thousands were killed in flight. In four days, multinational ground forces liberated Kuwait.

Saddam had gambled and lost again, but he kept his grip on power. The United Nations Security Council Resolution 687 for a permanent ceasefire stipulated conditions intended to prevent Saddam from threatening neighbors. Iraq had to admit United Nations inspectors to confirm elimination of the ability to make nuclear, biological, and chemical weapons. In addition, the resolution required Iraq to pay reparations to Kuwait, account for missing Kuwaitis, and renounce its claim to Kuwait. When Saddam resisted, the United Nations applied pressure by imposing economic sanctions that caused food and medicine shortages. For the rest of the decade, ordinary Iraqis suffered the effects of their leader's refusal to comply with the United Nations resolutions. Saddam exploited their suffering by blaming it on the West and pro-Western Arab governments such as Saudi Arabia. In the court of Arab public opinion, widespread hunger and illness in Iraq was the fault of the West and its regional lackeys. It was another exhibit in the case of Muslim suffering at the hands of the West.

In a separate initiative, the United States, France, and Britain declared "no-fly zones" over southern and northern Iraq to shield Shiite and Kurdish rebels from retaliation. US forces operating from Dhahran air base to defend Saudi Arabia against a foreign threat turned into a political liability as an implicit admission of dependence on Western power. The "expediency" of depending on "qualified" forces turned into a pillar of the kingdom's strategic security. It also became a fundamental grievance for dissidents.

National Protest

The Kuwait crisis laid bare the contradiction between the government's professed solidarity with fellow Muslims and its alignment with the United States. Many Saudis agreed with Saddam Hussein that it was sheer hypocrisy for the United Nations to sanction military force to expel Iraq from Kuwait and to turn a blind eye to Israel's occupation of Palestine. The senior clerics' fatwa allowing non-Muslim military forces made an unconvincing case for dodging the prohibition on alliance with infidels against believers. A few days after its publication, a leading Awakening cleric, Safar al-Hawali, issued a declaration faulting the fatwa for misinterpreting Islamic law, and Awakening preachers echoed his declaration from the pulpits. Shaikh Abd al-Aziz ibn Baz and other establishment clerics then issued fatwas defending the official fatwa, even though Ibn Baz had given a fatwa years before where he condemned Egyptian President Nasser for depending on foreign (Soviet) troops.[7] The hurried production of a pretext for inviting non-Muslim military forces also caused Saudis to question the government's stewardship of oil wealth. How could the government have spent billions of dollars on the latest weaponry and failed to develop the capacity to defend the country? Dissatisfaction with the government aroused both the religious and modernist camps to make demands for deep political and social reform.

The first initiative to call on the government to undertake thorough reforms came from liberal activists in December 1990. A group of merchants, professors, and government technocrats addressed a petition to King Fahd, calling on him to establish institutions that would ensure government accountability to the public: a consultative council with authority to draft laws and monitor government agencies; elected municipal councils; and professional associations. The petition also expressed frustration with the conservative social climate and called for easing censorship, giving women a role in public affairs, and limiting the scope of authority for the Committee for Commanding Right and Forbidding Wrong.[8]

The liberal petition spurred leaders of the Awakening movement to formulate its own agenda for political reform that it sent to the king in May 1991, a "Letter of Demands," urging the adoption of reforms guided by religious principles.[9] The Letter called for the creation of an independent advisory council to guide the rulers on adopting domestic and foreign policies in accordance with Islamic law, for increasing investment in religious institutions, for a comprehensive review of laws to ensure compliance with Islamic law, and for complete independence of the judiciary. To remedy the government's failure to deliver fair distribution of wealth, the letter urged abolishing the income tax and interest on loans, and establishing Islamic banks. There was a veiled attack on Western-educated Saudis in the call for monitoring the morality of government officials and for ensuring that media conform to Islamic morality. One point highlighted the need to strengthen the national army, presumably to dispense with the need for alliance with Western powers.[10] The Letter of Demands bore the imprint of twentieth-century revivalism's preoccupation with ordering society and politics rather than Wahhabism's emphasis on belief and worship. It reflected strides in national development since the 1950s: a banking system, modern media, and a government role in distributing wealth. One area of overlap with premodern Muslim political thought is the preoccupation with the moral qualities of individuals rather than devising institutions based on rules.

King Fahd took the Letter of Demands as an insult to his commitment to uphold Islam. Security forces arrested some signatories and barred others from preaching.[11] Nevertheless, agitation by religious and modernist camps did nudge the king in March 1992 to promulgate a document akin to a constitution designed to satisfy calls for political reform. The Basic Law of Government defined the system of government as a hereditary monarchy under the Saud clan responsible for upholding Islam and protecting Islam's Holy Places. It defined mutual obligations for citizens and government, where citizens had the duty to obey the government, and the government had the duty to safeguard citizens' welfare, defined as employment, medical care, and education. The Basic Law was essentially a restatement of Faisal's 1962 Ten-Point Program, and a succinct formula for the rentier bargain of benefits for compliance. It did not create mechanisms for representation or for balancing royal power. As such, it was an exercise in "ornamental constitutionalism."[12]

The Basic Law did not address the Awakening movement's sense that the country needed a firm commitment to the "Islamization" of society and politics. In September 1992, its leaders published a second document, the Memorandum of Advice, addressed not to the king but to the head of the religious establishment, Abd al-Aziz ibn Baz. At over one hundred pages, the Memorandum of Advice elaborated on the Letter of Demands with a long list specific measures for the government to take: strengthening military forces to end dependence on Western powers; calling alignment with the United States a betrayal of solidarity with the Palestinians; using oil revenue to guarantee education and health care; and abolishing interest on bank loans. Ibn Baz and the Board of Senior Clerics, acting at the government's behest, condemned the Memorandum, declared its authors had no qualifications to comment on such matters, and claimed that it had the potential to cause harm. Two months later, however, three establishment clerics defended the qualifications of the Memorandum's authors, signaling open dissent within senior clerical ranks.

In early 1993, Awakening activists took a new step to advance their cause by declaring the formation of the Committee for the Defense of Legitimate Rights (CDLR). The founders came from the Awakening movement's three factions: independent clerics, lay figures, and establishment clerics. The CDLR's definition of rights straddled a line between the international understanding of human rights and a religious understanding of rights under Islamic law. The organization's name incorporated the adjectival form of *shariʿa* (*sharʿiyya*), whose field of meaning includes legitimate, legal, and that which pertains to Islamic law. Soon after announcing the new organization on May 3, 1993, the lay leaders coordinated with an Islamist human rights association based in London to handle public relations with Western media organizations, giving the impression the committee was pursuing human rights in the Western understanding. Meanwhile, in Saudi Arabia, the Board of Senior Clerics denounced the CDLR, and security forces rounded up its organizers. Most of the Awakening shaikhs withdrew support to avoid confrontation with the government. Salman al-Awda and Safar al-Hawali, however, continued their support for CDLR from the pulpit.[13]

In October 1993, the government took a new step to show it was responsive to calls for change by creating a consultative council (*Majlis al-Shura*) to serve as an advisory body on policy. In a slight to the Awakening activists, King Fahd appointed sixty men with degrees from the country's secular universities and from Western universities. The government also took steps to marginalize the Awakening activists in national religious institutions with the first reorganization of that sector in two decades. A newly formed Ministry of Islamic Affairs, Endowments, Preaching, and Guidance removed supervision of the country's mosques, pulpits, and endowments (funds for religious purposes) from the hands of the Wahhabi establishment, then still headed by Ibn Baz. Then, the government created a High Council of Islamic Affairs under direct control of the Saud clan. The Awakening leaders had called for greater independence for religious institutions and instead they got the opposite. Universities too came under closer royal supervision. Henceforth, university presidents were appointed by the king rather than being chosen by university councils; and the Ministry of Education vetted the university presidents' appointments of faculty chairs and deans.[14]

The government reinforced loyal clerics by funneling resources to a faction that became known as the Jamis, named after Shaikh Muhammad Aman al-Jami, an Ethiopian shaikh. The Jamis often came from the ranks of foreign-born shaikhs from Ethiopia and Palestine, from lower social classes in Saudi Arabia, and from the country's geographical periphery in provinces such as Jizan. The abundance of resources and positions opened to the Jamis also drew opportunistic junior Saudi clerics. In treatises and cassettes, loyal clerics denounced the Awakening activists, praised the Saud clan for its dedication to religion, and reinforced support for the position that purification of beliefs must precede political reform or else a population holding corrupt beliefs will corrupt politics. Scuffles sometimes erupted between young backers of the Awakening shaikhs and Jami speakers, but over time, the Awakening shaikhs retreated from dissent to prove their loyalty, more frequently sprinkling their lessons with classic Wahhabi treatises and omitting mention of Muslim Brother writers.[15]

Alongside initiatives like the Basic Law and the Consultative Council, and reorganization of religious offices, the Saudi government reined in Awakening activists by gradually raising the price of dissent. Senior princes invited dissidents to meetings where they tried to persuade them to cease their protests. Then the government had Ibn Baz and other senior clerics give it a try. When persuasion did not work, the authorities resorted to firmer measures—suspending shaikhs from preaching at mosques, banning the sale of cassettes with subversive sermons, and barring foreign travel.[16] Lay professors were reassigned to administrative duties that cut them off from students. Arrests were a last resort, with detentions usually lasting a few months before release in return for a promise of "good behavior."

The two most prominent Awakening shaikhs in the CDLR, Safar al-Hawali and Salman al-Awda, continued to criticize the government until September 1994, when they were arrested by the authorities in Buraida, a center of dissent in the Qasim Province. Supporters marched to government offices to demand their release and the deputy governor agreed to do so. Then, when the protesters dispersed, the deputy governor ordered the police to detain several dozen men. Attempts by the CDLR from its exile in London to spur protests in solidarity with the protesters in March and May 1995 fizzled. The Awakening cycle of contention that began with optimism in fall 1990 had run out of steam.[17]

In the end, the monarchy used a combination of reward and punishment to wear down the Awakening protest. The dissidents tapped a reservoir of popular sentiment rooted in transnational Islamic solidarity and in Wahhabi doctrine's impulse to forbid contacts with infidels, even via indirect modernist influence. The dissidents, however, never formed an organized movement and they splintered in the face of government pressure; most of them wound up affirming loyalty to the government.[18]

The Awakening movement coincided with government steps to reconcile exiled Shiite activists and allow them to return to the country, where they adopted the posture of a loyal opposition.[19] The prospect of seeing the government offer improvements for Shiites alarmed Wahhabi clerics and they responded by putting forth new arguments for discriminating against Shiites. In 1993, Nasir al-Umar, a prominent Awakening shaikh, wrote "The Shiites in the Land of Monotheism."[20] Umar wanted to alert true believers to the threat that he imagined Shiites posed to Islam. He claimed that Shiite leaders encouraged large families to increase their share in the overall population. For proof, he pointed to collective marriage ceremonies held by Shiites, which in fact were meant to make marriage affordable to poor families. He claimed that Shiites were gaining influence in all spheres of public life. For instance, he found it alarming that Shiites sought to improve their social position through education, by attending technical institutes and universities in all parts of the country, not only in the Eastern Province, where one supposes he thought they should be confined. Shiites' robust participation in trade and agriculture was another worrisome indication for Umar that they were gaining economic influence. Opening the country's public sphere, as narrow as it was, to Shiites also alarmed Umar. He found it objectionable that newspapers permitted Shiite writers to publish, and especially outrageous that Shiites were permitted to hold book fairs where they peddled what he considered idolatrous writings. Finally, Shiites enjoyed too much religious freedom: They were allowed to operate their own religious schools, preach at their own mosques, go to their own law courts, and openly celebrate their religious ceremonies, not only in the Shiite majority town of Qatif but also at the Mosque of the Prophet in Medina. "The Shiites in the Land of Monotheism" became a reference in subsequent anti-Shiite writings that painted a threat of a rising minority bent not only on securing its rights but also on taking over the country through population growth, control of the economy, and educational achievement.

Militancy

While the government strove to defeat the Awakening dissidents, the militant current in transnational revivalism was thriving in different parts of the Muslim world, with support from Saudi clerics and activists. The Afghan War was the first transnational jihad, where volunteers from various Muslim countries fought against the enemies of fellow Muslims, perhaps akin to volunteers in the Spanish Civil War joining a common cause against fascism. The breakup of the Soviet Union soon after defeat in Afghanistan proved long and violent, with the eruption of civil wars in three zones that became causes for Muslim solidarity and transnational jihad: the former Yugoslavia, Chechnya, and Tajikistan.[21]

When Yugoslavia began to unravel in 1990, independence movements arose in Croatia and Slovenia. Ethnic conflicts between Serbs, Croats, and Slovenes were of no concern to Muslims. Fighting in Bosnia, however, was different. In the eyes of many Muslims, conflict in Bosnia was not ethnic but religious, and the call for defending beleaguered Muslims drew donations and fighters on the pattern of the Afghan cause. A headquarters for the transnational campaign was set up in Zagreb, Croatia, where the Islamic Benevolence Committee (modelled on Azzam's Services Bureau and built on personal ties established in Peshawar) coordinated the flow of volunteers and arms, raised funds, and disseminated propaganda in print and video. Alongside the committee, Saudi charities opened offices in Zagreb to support the Bosnian jihad. Back in Saudi Arabia, Wahhabi clerics endorsed the Bosnian cause as a jihad and promoted fundraising and recruitment of volunteers. From outbreak of fighting in 1992 to the signing of the Dayton Accords ending the conflict in 1995, between 1,000 and 6,000 Arabs, including an indeterminate number of Saudis, fought in the conflict. Many fighters went home while others dispersed to other battlefronts: Chechnya, the Philippines, Somalia, Algeria, Kashmir, Tajikistan, Eritrea. The two Chechen wars arising from efforts to secede from the Russian Federation were especially important in keeping the jihadist cause alive for the Saudi public. The second war, which began in 1999, deflected many Saudi volunteers to Al Qaeda's Afghan training camps because the Russians were able to block routes to Chechnya.[22]

The precise extent of Saudi participation in the Afghan and later jihad campaigns before 2001 is not documented.[23] Volunteers mentioned different reasons for joining jihad campaigns: the desire to defend fellow Muslims, the emotional response to images of Muslim suffering—"children crying, women widowed, and the high number of incidents of rape"—seeking martyrdom, religious rebirth, and aspiration to perform heroic feats. There is no evidence that volunteers held strong feelings against the United States or the Saudi government. Nor is there evidence that volunteers were driven by the desire to wipe out idolatry, the classic Wahhabi purpose.[24]

The first major terrorist attack against the United States in Saudi Arabia took place on November 13, 1995. A year earlier, a Saudi veteran of the Afghan jihad, Abdallah al-Hudhaif, had thrown acid in the face of a police officer. Hudhaif belonged to a band of militant moral vigilantes with cells in Riyadh and Qasim that vandalized video stores. It seems he was angry at the police over allegations they tortured religious dissidents, including his father, who had been arrested in the September 1994 sweep in the wake of the Buraida protests. On August 12, 1995, Hudhaif died in prison, either executed or under torture, according to fellow dissidents. Three months later, four of his friends, three of them veterans of the Afghan War, detonated a truck bomb outside the building of the United States mission for training the Saudi National Guard, killing five Americans and two Indians. The perpetrators were familiar with Osama bin Laden's writings, but they were not part of Al Qaeda, and Al Qaeda did not plan the bombing. The massive bombing jolted the Saudi government, and security forces responded by arresting around 200 dissidents. The four suspects in the bombing were executed in May 1996.[25]

The second major attack on a United States target took place on June 25, 1996. Terrorists exploded a truck bomb that demolished American barracks in Khobar, killing nineteen Americans and wounding around 400 Saudis, Americans, and people of other nationalities. At first, suspicion fell on Sunni militants, but investigators eventually concluded the attack was carried out by Shiite extremists. The United States relocated its headquarters for no-fly zone operations from Dhahran to the remote Prince Sultan Air Base. In response to the terrorist threat, personnel were mostly restricted to the base, women were required to wear the abaya, and they were not permitted to drive.[26]

A new wave of arrests detained around 2,000 dissidents, mostly Shiites but a small number of Sunnis as well. In 1998 and 1999, the authorities detected two plots to smuggle missiles from Yemen. One of the plots was intended to strike the American consulate in Jeddah. The authorities detained more than 1,000 dissidents suspected of ties to the missile plots. Many of the dissidents underwent torture in prison that intensified their fury at the government and sowed in their minds the feeling that government officials were as much of an enemy as the United States, and that the government had betrayed them by promoting volunteering for a moral cause in places like Bosnia then subjecting them to torture when they came home. In a sense, government brutality drove these men into the arms of Al Qaeda. During the bloody conflict between the Saudi government and Al Qaeda in the Arabian Peninsula from 2003 to 2007, jihadists targeted for assassination men they held responsible for their torture.[27] Comparison to the radicalization of Egyptian members of the Muslim Brotherhood such as Sayyid Qutb at the hands of Nasser's torturers is inescapable.

At the same time as the authorities intensified the repression of militants, they opened the media to Awakening veterans who adopted moderate views. Allowing independent expression, within limits, acknowledged the need to update Saudi media at a moment when new technologies were transforming media spaces, most notably with the launch of Qatar's satellite television network Al-Jazeera in 1996. Satellite television and the Internet came to Saudi Arabia in the mid-1990s. Despite an official prohibition on the satellite dish, it spread rapidly, blowing through a censorship curtain.[28] Limited Internet access for research had begun in 1993 at the King Fahd University for Petroleum and Minerals; two years later, it came to the King Abd al-Aziz City for Science and Technology and the King Faisal Specialist Hospital and Research Center. In 1997, the government issued a decree that made the King Abd al-Aziz City for Science and Technology in Riyadh responsible for regulating Internet access. The public was able go online starting in 1999. The government used control over access to block many websites, both political and non-political. Nevertheless, Saudis found ways to dodge censorship designed to quarantine them from political, social, and cultural influences. Access to entertainment was perhaps the most transgressive facet, drawing the attention of a swath of the public either content with or indifferent to the political status quo but curious, if not eager, to expand the bounds of permissible leisure.[29]

At the turn of the century, the Saudi religious field was in flux, with the Awakening shaikhs splitting into factions and the Wahhabi clerical leadership in transition after the deaths of Ibn Baz in 1999 and Ibn Uthaimin in 2001. The militant current simmering in clandestine networks found a symbolic center outside the country in August 1996, when Osama bin Laden seized the mantle of leadership in transnational jihad with a declaration of war on the United States and a call for the expulsion of American troops from the kingdom.

Bin Laden was born in Jeddah in 1957. His father Mohammed bin Laden immigrated from Yemen in the 1930s, scrapped his way to wealth in the construction sector, and established prosperous enterprises in manufacturing and real estate. Osama attended King Abd al-Aziz University in Jeddah, where he concentrated in business administration—a promising path for the son of a magnate—but he quit university to support the Afghan cause, using his family's business ties to raise funds and assist jihad volunteers. He established Al

Qaeda, literally "the base," in August 1988 to keep alive the jihad spirit on the model of Abdallah Azzam's Services Bureau.[30]

With the end of the war against the Soviet Union, Al Qaeda members scattered: some stayed in Peshawar, some set off for other zones of conflict, some like bin Laden returned to their homes. During the Kuwait crisis, he tried to persuade the government to rely on him to raise a Muslim force rather than Western armies to deter Iraqi aggression. In 1992, he relocated to Khartoum, where he spent four years turning Al Qaeda into a substantial organization with funds, structure, and staff, but lacking strategic focus: Egyptian members were bent on violent overthrow of the government in Cairo while bin Laden's priority was expelling United States forces from Saudi Arabia. Bin Laden also voiced support for the Awakening movement's efforts to press the monarchy to end its alignment with the United States.[31]

In the mid-1990s, militant groups were divided over strategy between a focus on "the near enemy," national governments they faulted for failing to rule according to Islamic law, and a focus on "the far enemy," the United States, whose power shielded such governments. The idea of making conflict with the United States the priority for Muslims became known as "global jihad." It marked a departure in the history of jihad doctrine. It was also a departure from Wahhabi doctrine because it required Muslims to elevate the duty to defend Muslims above unity on religious doctrine where disagreements could lead to excommunication. According to the global jihad idea, it was an individual duty for Muslims to join the anti-American jihad and it was permitted under Islamic law to attack American targets anywhere in the world. While bin Laden followed Wahhabi doctrine on correct worship, he was willing to ally with Muslims who did not.[32]

For bin Laden, the United States' military bases in Saudi Arabia violated the sanctity of the holy cities, allowed the Americans to dominate Muslims' oil resources, and enabled Washington to compel the Saudi government to spend oil revenue on expensive American weapons. The Americans were modern-day Crusaders turning Saudi Arabia into a base for bombing Afghanistan and Iraq and for reinforcing Jewish control in Palestine. Bin Laden asserted that Saudi rulers forfeited legitimacy when they agreed to allow American military bases. In his version of modern Saudi history, King Abd al-Aziz was the first to betray the Muslims by supporting the British in Palestine.[33] In 1990, King Fahd betrayed the Muslims by letting American military forces into the kingdom. Bin Laden's jihad was a recasting of the struggle between belief and unbelief onto a global plane, in a sense, claiming to remove the illusion that believers were fighting the main battle against unbelief when they targeted governments in Algeria, Egypt, or Syria.[34]

In 1996, the Sudanese government yielded to pressure from the United States and ordered bin Laden out of the country. The Taliban militia had recently seized power in Kabul and offered him a haven. Afghanistan became a meeting place for numerous militant groups waging jihad against local enemies in Tajikistan, Chechnya, and Kashmir. Bin Laden increased Al Qaeda's footprint in transnational militant circles by lending resources to other groups. In spite of his Saudi origin and the conspicuous part that Saudis played in major terrorist attacks, Al Qaeda did not have a large following in his home country. But it was not for lack of trying to gain one to carry out attacks on American targets. Rather, Saudi success at exposing plots in 1998 and 1999 resulted in the authorities capturing militants. Bin Laden decided to stop plotting attacks in Saudi Arabia and to use contacts there for fundraising and recruiting.[35]

Al Qaeda agents in Kenya and Tanzania carried out the first major attack against American targets on August 7, 1998, when they exploded massive truck bombs that destroyed US embassies, killed 224, and wounded more than 4,500. Two weeks later, Washington struck back, launching cruise missiles against targets in Sudan and Afghanistan. Recruitment of Saudis increased in the aftermath of the

East Africa bombings, thanks in part to the opening of the country to the Internet. Instantaneous dissemination of text and images put a potent propaganda, recruitment, and fundraising tool in the hands of Al Qaeda, which posted militant sermons and treatises alongside images of Muslims suffering around the globe.[36] Satellite television and the Internet broadcast horrific images from Kosovo and Chechnya, where the second war far surpassed the earlier conflict in intensity. The eruption of the second Palestinian intifada in fall 2000 increased anti-American feeling. In late 2000 and early 2001, scattered attacks on Western residents and their property in Saudi Arabia took six lives.[37] On October 12, 2000, Al Qaeda struck again with an attack against an American warship, the USS *Cole*, in Aden harbor, killing seventeen sailors. The next terrorist strike on September 11, 2001, precipitated American military invasions of Afghanistan and Iraq.

Economy and Society After the Oil Boom

In the midst of political turmoil at home and in the region, daily life for many Saudis reflected conditions of an economic plateau after the oil boom. Most Saudis no longer toiled in oasis gardens, desert encampments, or mudbrick markets. Instead, foreign workers performed menial tasks and a growing share of Saudis worked in offices. From the outside, the kingdom no longer looked like a poor land but an El Dorado. From the inside, Saudis came to expect a promising future of improvement in living conditions, a sign that government planners had succeeded in fashioning a modern economy.

During and after the boom years, demand for foreign labor grew, but the countries sending workers to Saudi Arabia shifted from Arab to Asian countries, a pattern that other Gulf states followed as well. In 1975, foreign Arabs comprised 90 percent of the foreign workforce; by 1996, their proportion had fallen to 30 percent. The Gulf state rulers considered Asian workers less likely to cause political disruption because of the ethnic divide from the Arab population. Employers believed that Asians were willing to work longer hours for lower wages, and if profits tightened, it was easier to fire a foreigner than a fellow Saudi. In addition, Asian governments favored "labor exports" because migrant workers sent home large sums of money, and their remittances became a significant portion of foreign exchange. Furthermore, a new profitable commercial sector emerged, comprising labor brokers who connected employment in the Gulf to jobseekers in Asia. While Gulf wages were much higher than in home countries, Asian jobseekers held the weakest position in the labor market: they had the least amount of information about conditions in the Gulf, they lacked financial and logistical resources to access work in the Gulf on their own, and in both the Gulf and their home countries, they had no legal protection from abusive sponsors.[38]

In the 1980s and 1990s, the kingdom's oil revenues rose and fell in tandem with shifts in the volatile global oil market. Royals and commoners expected oil sales to sustain the rentier economy, where the state supervised infrastructure development and provided employment and social services. At times of low demand and low prices, the economy contracted, leaving the government to choose between drawing on reserves and revising expenditure on defense, education, and infrastructure projects. Over the long term, the fat years were sufficient to pay for extensive investment in infrastructure (roads, ports, electricity) that supported new commercial and industrial activity and to bring material improvements to daily living (construction, water desalination) for much of the population. To modulate disruption caused by market cycles, government planners devised policies intended to wean the economy from dependence on external resources: oil sales and foreign workers.[39]

Efforts to raise cereal production in the 1980s and early 1990s by pumping large amounts of underground water to increase irrigated area were an example of ill-conceived investment. Some Saudi royals and their business allies supposed that food production offered opportunities for profit. In addition, expanding grain cultivation had the potential to achieve food security. Businessmen were drawn by the promise of subsidies to offset the cost of purchasing equipment and of hiring technical personnel to oversee large-scale cultivation of wheat. In the short term, the outcomes were promising. Saudi Arabia became a major exporter of wheat by 1992. Large absentee landowners prospered as long as the subsidies covered part of their costs. When those subsidies were cut in the early 1990s in response to low oil prices, the experiment in grain crops tailed off.[40] Apart from a new class of commercial farmers, some wealthy families in Najd maintained date farms as emblems of fidelity to national culture. Instead of relying on traditional irrigation and Saudi labor, they deployed mechanical pumps and hired workers from Egypt to manage the trees.[41]

Economic uncertainty and the rising cost of living stoked debate over government policy. Some observers believed it was time to reduce dependence on oil revenue and on employment in the public sector. Others asserted that the economy had already evolved to a great extent, pointing out that the percentage of oil in gross domestic product was declining, investment in national infrastructure had created an integrated domestic market, and the private sector's share in gross domestic product was steadily rising. In their view, it would suffice to reform the state institutions that guided economic development and to encourage the private sector to play a larger role in expanding investment and in hiring young Saudis entering the job market.[42] In 1998, Crown Prince Abdallah made an announcement that firmly sided with the view that it was time to decrease dependence on oil income. As Steffen Hertog put it, "the orthodox rentier state model, according to which states could forgo economic policy, did not apply to Saudi Arabia any longer."[43] Abdallah undertook three initiatives to strengthen the Saudi economy: promote foreign investment, gain membership in the World Trade Organization, and increase the employment of Saudi nationals in the private sector, known as "Saudization."

Economic liberalization after decades of state-led development turned out to be a tall order. Royal power had shaped state agencies into mechanisms for construction and distribution, mechanisms run by thousands of civil servants habituated to doing things a certain way. When the government took responsibility for national economic development, formally enunciated in the 1962 reform program, state institutions were geared to allocating shares in oil revenue. The crown prince's initiatives required state institutions to become regulatory agencies, but that kind of government function demands a high degree of trust between public agency and private individuals and companies as well as a high capacity for collecting and organizing information about them.[44]

When Abdallah decided to pursue these goals, the balance of resources between the state and business had changed since the early years of the oil boom in the late 1970s. The private sector played a much larger part in infrastructure investment, relied far less on government contracts, and was an important segment in the regional economy. The question in the late 1990s was whether the private sector could take the state's place in creating employment for the growing population and in modernizing infrastructure. In the past, power was expressed as a gift from the ruler to the tribesman, then it evolved to be expressed as a guaranteed job for the university graduate, and now power was to take the shape of a labor policy that induced, or compelled, businesses to "hire Saudi" because the state could no longer afford to give jobs to new cohorts of graduates.[45]

Measures to rebalance the ratio between Saudi and foreign workers went back to the 1980–4 five-year plan, with a goal to lower the number of expatriate workers by 1 million; instead, their numbers doubled, from 1.3 to 2.7 million, and reached 4.5 million in 1994. In the meantime, population growth and wider access to higher education meant that thousands of graduates flooded the public sector.

Bifurcation of employment by sector was striking, with nationals comprising 94 percent of public-sector workers and only 7 percent in the private sector. The skewed pattern was beneficial to Saudi workers and businesses. Public sector jobs paid well and offered security, while private sector employers preferred foreign workers, who in 1996 earned about 1,900 SR per month compared to 5,700 SR per month for Saudis: one-third the labor expense is a compelling reason for employers to avoid Saudization.[46] As for employees, how many people would turn down a good, steady salary to loaf in the office? Furthermore, Saudi Arabia and the Arab Gulf states offered the prospect of higher pay to workers from the Indian Ocean rim than at home. The planners in Riyadh hoped that spending on education would reduce reliance on foreign workers in technical fields, but the number of Saudis graduating from vocational institutes and pursuing technical fields in universities remained stagnant. By contrast, the religious universities increased their enrollments, but did not prepare graduates for careers in fields requiring scientific and engineering expertise.

The mismatch between workforce needs and preferences in university studies was widely known and the subject of satirical treatment in a short story by Hasan al-Nemi. "Rahwan and the Newspaper Vendor" is about a recent college graduate with a degree in history: "I am handicapped by my degree. I am not a scholar, I am no use at research, but I do intend to live and make a living from my degree." The whole family is miserable: his father expected the son to support him when he grew old; the protagonist feels he has no future. His father once feared that his daughter would be a burden, but she wound up getting married, so now his son was a burden. The protagonist thinks of finding a job washing cars or driving, but there are no jobs. In an encounter with a man peddling newspapers on the street, the vendor wants to know why he does not have a job:

"Because I have a degree in history."
"What's a job got to do with history?"

"They told me to study history to get a good job, so I did, but I couldn't find a job."

"Make a living out of history?" Pause. "Do you want a job?"

They agreed he would help sell newspapers. The mother was delighted, the father slightly relieved. The next day, as he went to work, he felt excited and hopeful; merely having a job made him feel better. He thought about how he had a university degree and no job while the vendor had a job and no degree. When he arrived at the place where he met the vendor the previous day, he was not there. He searched for him and did not find him, as he walked through street after street that looked the same, the buildings looked the same, the pedestrians looked the same. The story ends without him finding the vendor.[47]

To invigorate the Saudization policy, the cabinet issued Decree 50 in 1995. The decree required companies with more than twenty employees to increase the percentage of Saudis by 5 percent each year, or else they would lose their permits to hire foreign workers and government contracts. Subsequent years brought new decrees that reiterated, modified, and sometimes contradicted Decree 50. "Hire Saudi" became a buzz phrase, akin to "buy American" when Washington adopted free trade in the 1990s. Banks, accounting firms, hospitals, contractors for Saudi Aramco, and foreign airlines came under pressure from different state bodies to increase employment of Saudis, but the policy collided with basic economic interests favoring the bifurcated division of labor. In addition, implementation of policy foundered on confused, overlapping jurisdictions in the public agencies involved in issuing visas and managing labor programs. Coordination among provincial authorities and the ministries of labor, interior, defense, and health proved impossible. Furthermore, while businesses did not openly oppose Saudization, they were effective at dragging their feet. How was a civil servant in a labor office to know if a company had made a good-faith effort to hire Saudis when he seldom had the expertise to determine if Saudi job candidates possessed the right technical qualifications?[48]

Nevertheless, the number of Saudis in the workforce did rise, both in absolute numbers and as a percentage (rising from 33 to 38 percent). Two of the country's largest employers, Aramco and Saudi Basic Industries (SABIC), focused on hiring nationals and raised their representation to over 70 percent of their workforces. But in the national economy, the number of expatriate workers also grew by half a million (from 4.0 to 4.5 million) between 1990 and 1999. Most worrisome was the failure of the economy to absorb the rising number of educated Saudis. Unofficial estimates of unemployment rates suggest they grew from 12 percent in 1993 to 27 percent in 1999.[49]

The oil boom accentuated the forces that redistributed nomads, villagers, and townsmen across the country. Mobility was always deeply embedded in the fabric of Arabian life, with merchants and pilgrims trekking in caravans and herders pursuing pasture. In the late twentieth century, society followed new laws of motion. Thousands of Saudis jetted to Lebanon, Egypt, Europe, and North America for leisure and study. Townsfolk in large cities commuted daily from homes to offices, malls, and schools. By the early 1990s, roughly 70 percent of Saudis lived in cities, with perhaps one-third the population in major cities over 100,000. Urbanization also meant population growth in towns with fewer than 20,000 residents. In the two decades after the oil boom, their combined population rose from around 460,000 to 590,000, primarily in Najd and Asir, as the national government extended public services for education, medicine, road construction, and transportation.[50]

Demobilization of the Bedouin had been essential to consolidating central political authority. The shrunken ranks of pastoralists relied on a modern desert infrastructure to move livestock and water tanks in trucks. No longer following the seasonal rhythm of their ancestors, Bedouin migrated to cities where they frequently occupied the bottom of the social and economic hierarchy, but some did enter modern professions. Many others became sedentary residents of small towns and scattered farms where they retained distinctive tribal identities. Settlement and education improved the material conditions of everyday life, but at a price. According to a longtime observer of Bedouin life, women gave mixed assessments to the new dispensation. A woman from the Rwala tribe told her interlocutor:

> It's good that the young men study at universities, because they can get good jobs, and they widen their minds. They know about things that are important now and that we don't understand. But at the same time we lose them, they go too far away from us, especially if they study abroad for three or four years. Sometimes they marry abroad, they stay there and work. If they return here, they get a job in a city or a region far from us, and they visit maybe once a year. So we don't know all our grandchildren as we should. Their father and I are glad that A is married to a good man from our *jamaʿa* [relatives], and that their marriage is happy because she was educated at university as well, but we wish they didn't live on the other side of the country. But that's where his work is. We talk by telephone at least once a week; it isn't the same but it helps. Lots of women are in this position. But the future is the children's. That we are sometimes lonely, and our knowledge and skills are less valued is a part of modern life.[51]

Some Bedouin women appreciated that education had the potential to bring financial independence through a career in the modern professions, business, or civil service. But not everyone in the younger generation believed that modern education and career brought satisfaction. In the words of one educated woman:

> I went to school, I did well, I went to University in Riyadh and I have my degree. The only job I can do is teaching. I teach girls to get educated so they can go to university and learn to teach other girls

> ... For what purpose? There isn't one. I'm less happy than my mother and she can't read or write. My older sister can't [read and write] and she's far happier than I am. So I have a degree; I can't weave or spin; I don't know about local plant medicines; I can cook and make bread and sew, but I can't herd. I'm dependent on a town and the state, and I don't like it.[52]

Ethnographers William and Fidelity Lancaster found Rwala Bedouin grappling with how to reconcile their notion of self-reliance with modern political and economic conditions. Maintaining a sense of self-reliance was especially difficult, in part because of the hardening of international borders. Before the 1970s, Bedouin were able to migrate between Saudi Arabia, Syria, and Jordan and to claim more than one nationality. Then the states curtailed their movement and forced them to choose a nationality, which became a claim to education, health care, and the legal right to work. Control over external revenues, whether from oil or foreign aid, put the states in a position to dominate their respective populations. Local resources no longer drove the economy, leaving rural folk dependent on the state for jobs to have a share in oil revenue.[53]

Saudi Arabia passed through phases of political mobilization that interlocked with transnational currents. From the late 1940s to the early 1970s, labor, liberal, and anti-imperial Arab nationalist demands circulating in the Arab world connected to and magnified the same currents in Saudi Arabia. From the late 1970s, liberal, Islamist (Sunni and Shiite), and jihadist currents transcended national boundaries. The Awakening and jihadist currents both stemmed from the Wahhabi mission's integration with transnational Muslim forces. The activists sprang from Saudi soil, and they were faithful to Wahhabi theology, but they identified with different political projects, not with the Saud dynasty as protectors of belief, but with the welfare of the believers at large, the *umma*.

The Kuwait crisis created a dilemma for the monarchy: call on infidel troops or risk losing the oil province. The senior clerics' fatwa laid bare the rift between loyalty to the monarchy and solidarity with believers. By choosing the latter, the Awakening movement and the militants made the clerical estate seek ways to demobilize the Awakening movement and to delegitimize the militants without losing credibility in pious circles aggrieved at Muslim suffering at the hands of infidels. Although the religious establishment and Awakening shaikhs diverged on political priorities, they formed a solid phalanx against the modernist current. The divide between religious and modernist camps remained wide enough for the monarchy to deflect calls for accountability and contain the militant current. The Kuwait crisis and its aftermath also made clear Saudi Arabia's place in the global political and economic orders: it was unable to defend itself and too valuable for the Western powers not to intervene. For all of the state-building, national development, and social transformation underwritten by oil income, the country remained a weak player in the Gulf.

9

In the Midst of Regional Unraveling, 2001–15

Al Qaeda's September 11, 2001, attacks on the United States opened new chapters in American intervention in the Muslim world and in Saudi Arabia's relationship with Washington. Links between Saudi Arabia and Al Qaeda underscored the contradiction between Riyadh's close relationship with Washington and the religious strand in the monarchy's claim to legitimacy. If the monarchy were truly devoted to Muslim causes, then it would have to distance itself from Israel's patron. If the monarchy were truly a reliable partner of the United States, then it would have to end support for Wahhabi institutions in the kingdom and abroad. Crown Prince Abdallah leaned toward curbing the Wahhabi mission by promoting a public climate where conversations about reform were encouraged, but when it came to action, he moved inch by inch, trying the patience of Saudis eager for decisive steps toward political reform and the relaxation of religious restrictions on public life, especially in the areas of women's rights and discrimination against Shiites. The passing of King Fahd in August 2005 and Abdallah's succession reaffirmed the monarchy's stability and the new king's implementation of incremental opening of public life and economic reform.

The Aftermath of September 11

Tuesday morning, September 11, 2001. Osama bin Laden's global jihad struck the United States. Nineteen Al Qaeda terrorists hijacked four US passenger flights. They crashed two airliners into New York City's World Trade Center towers, one airliner into the Pentagon in Washington, DC, and one airliner into a field in western Pennsylvania. The attack killed nearly 3,000 people: airline passengers and crews; men and women working in the World Trade Center and the Pentagon. More than twenty years later, New York City firefighters who hurried to the rescue at the disaster site in Lower Manhattan were dying of illness caused by exposure to toxic dust. The worst attack on the United States since Pearl Harbor shocked the American public. Nine days after the attack, President George W. Bush announced to the US Congress he would lead the country in a "Global War on Terror," a political, diplomatic, and military campaign that changed relations between the West and the Middle East, including Saudi Arabia. The White House demanded the Taliban hand over Osama bin Laden. When they refused, the United States invaded Afghanistan to overthrow the Taliban, apprehend bin Laden, and destroy Al Qaeda. American forces and their Afghan allies in the Northern Alliance achieved the first objective, but bin Laden escaped to Pakistan, where Al Qaeda and the Taliban found refuge in the rugged frontier region.

Smashing Al Qaeda's Afghan headquarters did not stave off stunning terrorist attacks in Bali, Mombasa, Casablanca, Istanbul, and London. Explanations in Western outlets for the spate of terrorism frequently traced it to Wahhabi doctrine—specifically, to its incorporation into Saudi Arabia's education system and to its export to Muslim communities through official Saudi programs, transnational Islamic organizations, and charities. The Saudi government denied any connection to terrorism at the same time it took steps to promote a more liberal (for the Saudi context) public climate, promising to reform textbooks, nudging the clerics to retreat from puritanical and xenophobic stances, and choking off channels for funding transnational groups suspected of terrorism.[1]

Saudi Arabia had a unique role in the "Global War on Terror." In the eyes of many in the West and the Muslim world, Saudi mosques and schools instilled the hatred that inspired terrorists. In the eyes of many in Saudi Arabia and the Muslim world, the rulers sided with Western oppressors of Muslims. Hence, the Sauds had to find ways to balance ties to Western powers with commitment to Muslim causes. And they had to maintain that balance in the face of American invasions of Afghanistan and Iraq and of insurgencies waged by Al Qaeda offshoots that invoked religious reasoning that had much in common with Wahhabi doctrine. With so many challenges arising from religious militancy, it made sense for the Sauds to encourage the liberal current, but that posed the prospect that liberals might push for political participation, which the royals were loath to allow. Autocratic liberalism was not only an oxymoron; it was an impossibility.

One of the aims of the 9/11 attacks was to disrupt Saudi–US relations. The American public learned that fifteen of the nineteen hijackers came from Saudi Arabia, leading many to suspect the Saudi government of having a hand in the attack. At the very least, Americans concluded that Wahhabism fostered terrorism in Saudi classrooms and in Saudi-funded religious schools throughout the Muslim world, including the Muslim diaspora in the West.[2] American officials, journalists, and think tanks demanded that the Saudis purge their schools of religious bigotry against non-Muslims and make certain that Saudi institutions and individuals were not funding terrorist groups, such as Al Qaeda.

Western demands meshed with the aims of Saudi Arabia's liberal camp. In January 2003, 100 writers and businessmen submitted a petition to Crown Prince Abdallah calling on him to institute extensive reform of the political system. They called their agenda "A Vision for the Present and Future of the Homeland." In the tradition of

Islamic modernists since the late 1800s, the petitioners cited the principle of consultation (*shura*) as the foundation for leaders and the people to secure the general welfare. They wanted to see the conversion of the Consultative Council from an appointed body to an elected one, and the establishment of a body to ensure human rights, free speech, and free association.[3] Abdallah agreed on the need for change, but not institutional limits on royal power or liberal rights. He considered religious intolerance to be the root cause of the kingdom's problems that could be addressed by fostering a "national dialogue" among Saudis from different religious backgrounds. In June 2003, a three-day event for "Reinforcing National Unity" brought together Wahhabis, Twelver Shiites, Ismaili Shiites, Sufis, and non-Wahhabi Sunnis (Maliki and Shafii). The inclusion of Shiites made sense in view of Iran's moderate turn since the re-election in 2001 of the reformist President Muhammad Khatami, but the Awakening shaikhs were divided on agreeing to meet with the Shiite leader Hasan al-Saffar.[4]

After the event, Crown Prince Abdallah announced the establishment of the King Abd al-Aziz Center for National Dialogue to signal commitment to promoting a moderate religious climate. The second National Dialogue session, held in Mecca in late 2003, addressed ways to combat extremism. The session expanded the ranks of participants to include women, allowed to participate on the condition they gather in a separate room and join sessions through closed-circuit television. At the third session, held in Medina in June 2004, the dialogue focused on gender relations. Half of the seventy participants were women, albeit with conservatives outnumbering liberals. The organizers limited discussion to employment and domestic violence, leaving male guardianship and the right for women to drive off the agenda.[5]

Advocates of political reform viewed the National Dialogue sessions as a distraction from the need for limits on the monarchy. They pointed out that the authorities defined the agenda for each session and selected the participants, and that recommendations for follow-up action were ignored. Defenders of the National Dialogue argued that it advanced tolerance and provided the rulers important insight into issues such as education, health, and employment that mattered to all Saudis, be they Sunni or Shiite, men or women. The royal initiative expressed a preference for controlled change, an extension of development planning into the social sphere, for the sake of altering the religious climate, without conceding to demands for political change.

In the spirit of Crown Prince Abdallah's support for controlled change, the education system became the focus of calls for reform. For some years, plans to stimulate the economy required schools to begin emphasizing the skills and knowledge that would make Saudi workers competitive in the global economy, but doing so required reducing classroom time spent on religious lessons. The impetus to reduce religion's large part in children's education meshed with growing public criticism of the Wahhabi establishment, especially the Committee for Commanding Right and Forbidding Wrong for intrusive enforcement of strict conformity to Wahhabi norms.[6] Public frustration with clerical power in the education system escalated in March 2002, when a deadly fire engulfed a girls' school in Mecca and fifteen pupils perished. Eyewitness accounts blamed the girls' deaths on the religious police for blocking exits from school grounds because the pupils were not "dressed for public." In response to the public outcry, the government stripped the clerical establishment of responsibility for girls' education and assigned it to the Ministry of Education.[7] Soon after, the Ministry of Education started to revise schoolbooks, removing passages that taught hatred toward non-Muslims and inserting passages that highlighted inter-faith tolerance. Defenders of Wahhabi doctrine criticized the revisionist project as a concession to American interference.[8] Altering the cultural substance of education, however, required far more than writing and distributing new schoolbooks. Schools and universities operated in a climate of conformity and censorship, where errant teachers and administrators faced dismissal and recalcitrant students would be denied their degrees.[9]

In addition to education, the Saudi government responded to the 9/11 attacks by placing charities under tighter regulation in the face of accusations that organizations funneled donations to Al Qaeda. For example, the Haramain Islamic Welfare Association came under suspicion for money laundering to finance terrorism. A Saudi veteran of the Red Crescent Society had set up the association in Peshawar at the end of the Afghan War to provide assistance to Afghan refugees. In 1990, Haramain established headquarters in Riyadh to direct operations in Asia, Africa, Europe, and North America. Its activities included food kitchens, medical centers, and orphanages. Accusations by the United States government that it abetted terrorism were never substantiated. Nevertheless, after 9/11, Washington was able to persuade the Saudi authorities to ban Haramain and to regulate charities in general for the sake of suppressing money laundering.[10]

Suspicion of Saudi charities stemmed from concern about the role of religion in Riyadh's foreign policy. Measuring the scale and effects of "Saudi religious transnationalism"[11] with precision is impossible for three reasons. First, there was no central agency that managed proselytizing and charitable activities. Rather, there were an array of organizations and individuals supporting missionary activities: religious attachés, seconded from the Ministry of Islamic Affairs, in Saudi embassies; transnational organizations based in Saudi Arabia; gifts from members of the royal family and wealthy businessmen; and satellite television programs that broadcast lessons and sermons. Some writers put specific figures on the amount of money spent on foreign religious activities, but information about funding is fragmentary and inconsistent.[12] Second, Saudi Arabia's influence varied from one country to another according to several factors: the presence or absence of religious groups likely to welcome Saudi resources; rivalry with the religious diplomatic initiatives of other governments such as Iran and Turkey; the ability of national governments to regulate religious institutions; the balance between Muslim and non-Muslim populations; and the particular source in Saudi Arabia for religious projects. Different Saudi religious universities were dominated by one or another religious current: establishment clerics in some, Awakening shaikhs in others. Just as they competed for influence in the kingdom, so they did abroad. Thus, in Indonesia, the effects of Saudi proselytizing reproduced rivalry between disciples of Wahhabi clerics and pupils of Sururi instructors.[13] Third, research on the national and transnational connections and on the diverse doctrinal currents in contemporary Salafism is a young field. Untangling and gauging the precise role of a "Saudi effect" awaits fuller synthesis of the scholarship.[14]

The most commonly observed effects of Saudi proselytizing were the adoption of conservative gender norms (veiling and segregation), the spread of canonical worship at the expense of popular and Sufi practices, and the sharpening of tension between adherents to Wahhabi, or Salafi, beliefs and other Muslims.[15] The connection between Saudi proselytizing and militancy came from the migration of Wahhabi doctrine beyond the scope of the dynasty's authority. In countries where leaders did not uphold the mission's insistence on purging worship of idolatry, Wahhabi-Salafi groups felt they had cause to wage jihad.[16] Over time, however, the disruptive impact of Saudi proselytizing wore off. In the West African Sahel, rival religious currents gained ground against uncompromising hardliners. In Central Asia and Ethiopia, national governments took steps to constrict foreign religious influence.[17]

Around the world, Wahhabi proselytizers distributed translations of the Quran, including an English version published in 1985 and authorized by the Islamic University of Medina and the Fatwa Office. It is more precise to call the Saudi version of the Quran an edition rather than a translation because it adds words and phrases that are not part of the original Arabic text. For example, the Saudi edition adds words in parentheses to the last verse in the Quran's first *sura*, or chapter: "The Way of those on whom You have bestowed Your Grace, not (the way) of those who earned Your Anger (such as the Jews), nor of those who went astray (such as the Christians)." There is no indication in the Arabic text that the verse refers to Jews or Christians. Likewise, the translation of Sura 33, Verse 59, inserts phrases that describe Saudi beliefs about how women should dress: "O Prophet! Tell your wives and your daughters and the women of the believers to draw their cloaks (veils) all over their bodies (i.e. screen themselves completely except the eyes or one eye to see the way). That will be better, that they should be known (as free respectable women) so as not to be annoyed. And Allah is Ever Oft-Forgiving, Most Merciful." For a religious mission claiming to defend a fixed, literal text against distorted interpretation by other Muslims, it was peculiar to present the Quran in that way.[18]

The US Invasion of Iraq

The Bush administration viewed reforming Saudi Arabia's religious policies at home and abroad as important parts of the "Global War on Terror." The strategy to defeat terrorism took a wrong turn when Washington decided to invade Iraq in March 2003. The rationale for war rested on two false claims made by American officials: that Saddam Hussein had a part in Al Qaeda's 9/11 attacks (he did not), and that he operated a clandestine program to develop weapons of mass destruction that posed a threat to the United States (he did not). White House officials frightened the American public with the specter of a "suitcase bomb" and "a mushroom cloud" rising over a devastated American city. The public mood in the United States was seething in the wake of 9/11 and deaf to voices that questioned the administration's faulty assertions. Thus, with strong public support, a joint Anglo-American force invaded Iraq on March 20, 2003. Baghdad fell on April 9. The military forces did their job, but the

White House had no plan for the insurgency that materialized. An invasion intended to stabilize the region and to suppress terrorist groups boomeranged, although there was one gain for relations between Saudi Arabia and the United States: Saddam Hussein no longer posed a threat, and the United States withdrew military forces from Saudi soil.[19]

From the perspective of Saudi Arabia, the Western invasion of a neighboring Arab Muslim country was bound to create problems. The government feared Saddam's overthrow would strengthen Iran, in part because the Americans planned to turn Iraq into a democracy that pro-Iranian Shiite groups would likely dominate. From 2003 to 2006, American officials held elections for an interim Iraqi government, then a transitional national assembly, followed by a referendum on a constitution, and finally the election of a parliament under the new constitution. As the Saudis expected, Iraq's first elected government was dominated by pro-Iranian Shiite political parties. King Abdallah considered Prime Minister Nuri al-Maliki a proxy for Tehran, while Maliki suspected Saudi Arabia of secretly backing the anti-government insurgency.[20]

Ordinary Saudis sympathized with the anti-American insurgency, viewing it as a clear case of defensive jihad (never mind that the US worked with Iraqi Muslims to set up a new, independent Iraqi government). The torture of Arab detainees by American military personnel at Abu Ghraib prison replicated the scenario at the US naval base at Guantanamo, Cuba, where the United States indefinitely detained Muslims captured in Afghanistan and mistreated them. Religious solidarity prompted hundreds of young men to head for Iraq. In the first two years of the war, as many as 1,500 Saudis joined the anti-American insurgency. The Saudi government discouraged young men from enlisting in jihad. Security forces intercepted volunteers heading to Iraq, while Wahhabi clerics and Awakening shaikhs declared that it was legitimate for Iraqis but not for Saudis to fight the Americans in defense of their homeland. On the other side, jihadists argued that sincere Muslims would not allow artificial national boundaries to compromise Muslim solidarity. Clandestine networks smuggled volunteers to Iraq, especially to the militia led by a Jordanian national, Abu Musʿab al-Zarqawi, a one-time street criminal who converted to Salafi doctrine in prison in Jordan. Zarqawi's strategy for his band, Al Qaeda in Iraq, marked a departure from Al Qaeda's focus on the West to an obsession with Shiism that became a hallmark of the Islamic State, which evolved from his organization after American forces killed him in June 2006.[21]

Zarqawi's fixation on Shiism fit the post-Baathist context in Iraq, where Iran exercised influence through political parties and militias claiming to represent the interests of the country's Shiite majority. In Saudi Arabia, Sunni paranoia took hold as clerical hardliners in Iran buried the liberal movement led by President Muhammad Khatami, who had represented the desire to temper the Islamic Republic's revolutionary tendencies. To replace him in 2005, hardliners engineered the election to the presidency of Tehran's populist mayor, Mahmud Ahmedinejad, a firebrand prone to inflammatory anti-Western declarations that recalled Khomeini's belligerent language threatening pro-Western governments. With a heightened sense of Iran as a threat, Riyadh embraced a strategy that claimed Shiites were plotting to undermine Sunni Islam.

The new "sectarian" strategy differed from the Wahhabi mission's theological sectarianism, which notably put other Sunnis into the same basket of infidels as Shiites. It still played on religious difference, but now other Sunnis were fellow believers for the sake of serving three political purposes. In the region, the strategy supplied a common cause to align conservative pro-Western governments (Egypt, Jordan, the Gulf) against Iran and its allies in Iraq, Lebanon, Syria, and Yemen. At home, the strategy delegitimized calls to end discrimination put forth by Saudi Shiites, and it portrayed them as agents of a hostile foreign power that sought to weaken the monarchy as a defender of Sunni Islam. Finally, the sectarian strategy discredited liberal efforts to forge a cross-sectarian campaign for political reform. Establishment clerics and Awakening shaikhs were ready to remind believers that Shiites were idolaters bent on undermining Islam. The problem with encouraging anti-Shiism was that it invoked classical Wahhabi hostility toward infidels, whether Shiite or Christian. Thus, stoking the anti-Shiite clerics also strengthened anti-Western voices.[22]

Al Qaeda in the Arabian Peninsula

Recruitment to the anti-American insurgency tapped clandestine militant networks in Saudi Arabia led by dissident clerics and veterans of the Afghan jihad. Dissident clerics issued online statements arguing the 9/11 attacks were permissible under the law of jihad, breaking with the Wahhabi establishment and Awakening shaikhs who denounced the attacks. In June 2002, veterans of the Afghan jihad used a shoulder-held missile in an attempt to shoot down an American plane operating at Prince Sultan Air Base.[23] The militants were divided into two separate networks. One network was neutralized in November 2002 when its leader, Abd al-Rahim al-Nashiri, the organizer of the 2000 attack on the USS *Cole*, was arrested in the United Arab Emirates. A second network was led by Yusuf al-Uyairi. He proved adept at using the Internet for propaganda, with a website, *al-Neda* (*The Call*) that became the unofficial outlet for Al Qaeda. His network of several hundred militants used desert farms as training camps, where volunteers learned to assemble bombs and practiced detonating truck bombs. The network had safe houses to store weapons and explosives in Riyadh, Mecca, Medina, Buraida, Jeddah, Dammam, Ha'il, and Jizan.[24]

In March 2003, Saudi security forces uncovered a militant hideout in Riyadh where they found weapons and documents outlining plans for attacks on Western targets in the kingdom. The police followed clues in the documents to track down militants, who engaged in gun battles rather than surrender. On May 6, police in Riyadh came across papers that had the last wills of volunteers for suicide attacks. To head off an attack they believed was imminent, the authorities published the names of nineteen wanted militants.[25] On May 12, 2003, Uyairi's men struck: fourteen terrorists in five vehicles attacked three residential compounds for expatriates in Riyadh, killing thirty-five and wounding more than 160. The victims came from the United States, Australia, Jordan, and the Philippines, as well as Saudi Arabia.[26] It was the first blow in a terrorist insurgency that lasted three and a half years. Before May 12, few Saudis believed that Al Qaeda had carried out the 9/11 attacks. Popular conspiracy theories pinned the attacks on Israel's Mossad (to trigger violence between the United States and Muslims) or the Central Intelligence Agency (to legitimize United States military action against Muslims). Not that conspiracy theories were limited to Saudi Arabia: the United States had its own "9/11 Truthers" who were certain the attacks were "an inside job" perpetrated by a clandestine "deep state."

After the May 12 attack, the militants declared their goal to expel the Americans but did not announce their secondary aim of overthrowing the government, because it would be unpopular with the public. A wave of arrests, raids, and shootouts took the lives of Yusuf al-Uyairi and other leading figures. In a November Internet posting, the terrorists called themselves Al Qaeda in the Arabian Peninsula (AQAP). The next major operation fell on November 8, 2003, with an attack on a residential compound in Riyadh that killed seven and injured more than 120. The carnage horrified the public, and tips from the public soon helped the government arrest more members.[27]

Between April and August 2004, AQAP carried out a wave of killings against Western residents and revenge attacks on Saudi security forces, including a car bomb that killed six outside a police headquarters in Riyadh on April 21. Ten days later, terrorists killed five Westerners at a company in the Red Sea port of Yanbu; at the end of May, an attack on a residential compound in Khobar killed twenty-two people. The mayhem continued in June with the abduction and beheading of an American and then with attacks in December against the United States consulate in Jeddah and the Saudi interior ministry in Riyadh. In April 2005, police and militants fought a gun battle for days at a farm in the Qasim Province. The government was getting the upper hand. On February 24, 2006, an attack on an oil refinery failed, and three days later its perpetrators were killed in a shootout in Riyadh. The police were able to disrupt other plans for attacks that year. The last attack was the murder of four French nationals on a desert excursion on February 26, 2007.[28]

Security forces played the major part in the counter-terrorism effort, with support from the religious establishment and Awakening shaikhs who condemned the bombings. State television broadcast images of Muslim children killed and injured in bombings. The government offered amnesty to deserters who went on television to repent and renounce violence.[29] In the final analysis, the Saudi public would support jihad for the sake of Muslims under attack in Afghanistan, Bosnia, and Chechnya, but few saw justice in terrorist attacks on foreign civilians or security forces in their own country. AQAP members were mostly men who had spent time at training camps in Afghanistan, where they assimilated violent anti-Americanism.[30] As the security forces whittled down AQAP's ranks, it was not able to recruit Saudis who did not have the Afghan experience. In addition, the government found ways to counter AQAP's use of the Internet to solicit support. The authorities monitored the Internet and bolstered an unofficial initiative, "Sakinah Campaign," that infiltrated militant chatrooms and refuted religious arguments that justified violence.[31] The moment for violent armed struggle came and went, leaving the Saud clan firmly in power, making no dent on the country's political structure, perhaps reinforcing a cautious mood stirred by the bloody chaos in Iraq. It did not, however, mean the end of political opposition. In fact, for some Saudis, AQAP was evidence that the country was in dire need of liberal reform.

Social and Cultural Opening

By initiating the National Dialogue, the monarchy veered from support for the Wahhabi mission to official recognition of the country's pluralist character and of the need for social change, including women's roles. In brief, Crown Prince Abdallah's gesture toward a less restrictive public climate planted the seeds of a cultural flowering. Journalists, academics, and writers from the modernist camp felt encouraged to advance their vision of a more open society. The rapid spread of access to satellite television, the Internet, and social media broadened the range of voices as well as the size of the audience. Saudis tuned into a far wider communications network than ever before, both inside and outside the country, digesting, pondering, embracing, questioning views on politics and society. Satellite television played a part in propagating a "moderate" interpretation of religion with programs featuring popular televangelists from Egypt who emphasized religious coexistence while preserving conservative morality.[32]

Taking its cue from the palace, the modernist current broke new ground in cultural expression. The governor-prince of Asir, Khalid al-Faisal, lent support to a local visual arts movement that breached religious taboos and gained an international audience and market when the country connected to the Internet.[33] A latent yearning for humorous entertainment got an outlet on a popular television program and through standup comedy shows performed at small venues and disseminated on YouTube.[34] Saudis eager to try their hand at film and television production took advantage of the technological and cultural openings.[35] In 2013, Haifaa al-Mansour became the first woman to make a film, *Wadjda*, the story of a young girl testing gender norms by seeking to purchase a bicycle.[36]

Al-Mansour's film attested to how the position of women remained a central point of contention between modernists and conservatives. A generation of educated women who grew up with a system of national public education had come of age and they were ready to put their stamp on gender relations. Saudis debated male guardianship, family law, the right to drive cars, restrictions on where women could work, and segregation of men and women in public places.[37] A flood of stories circulated about women suffering physical abuse, abandonment, and mistreatment that were blamed on old-fashioned customs and wrongheaded interpretation of religion.[38]

The government took steps to present a new face to the world consonant with Western norms by trotting out representatives of the successful educated Saudi woman. Princesses, professionals, and businesswomen started showing up at international meetings. These Saudi women were accomplished and fluent in several languages; they provided proof the kingdom was not a cloistered, backward land that oppressed women. In addition, the government opened the country to Western journalists and arranged for them to meet and write about professional Saudi women. For the first time, the king appointed a woman to the post of deputy minister. Government planners lent implicit backing to the campaign.[39] The eighth five-year plan aimed to increase women's participation in the economy with more opportunities and fewer obstacles to employment.[40]

Not all women embraced the modernist agenda. Conservative women writers, many of them graduates of the religious universities, expressed support for preserving restrictions in the name of protecting women (from men) and resisting pressure from Western powers to abandon inherited ways. In their view, individual women's safety and the integrity of an imagined national culture hinged on rejecting liberal norms. Conservative writers and activists expressed a range of perspectives, with some amplifying the opinions of establishment clerics while others embedded their views in an Islamist outlook that pitted the Muslim world against a Western conspiracy to weaken Islam.[41]

In everyday life, young women were carving new ways of inhabiting the country's urban landscapes. Going to school, attending university, and working in an occupation were recently established options in the lives of girls and women that entailed navigating family and government lines of the permitted and the prohibited. Young women were not the passive, obedient subjects of authority often portrayed in Western accounts. Rather, they pushed limits and made the most of homosocial (female-only) public places, seizing on trendy self-help thinking and bourgeois consumption habits.[42] The debates over women's roles and changing habits made it indisputable that Saudi Arabia was a very different place compared to fifty years earlier, when the first public schools for girls opened. Patriarchy was not a static system of male domination imposed on oppressed women. Rather, it had always been and remained a fluid field of relations where notions of what is acceptable and unacceptable were negotiated, contested, stretched, and reshaped.

If it was conceivable to remake social relations, liberals might also look forward to revising the political field, introducing some degree of accountability and participation. A cohort of articulate advocates for liberal rights framed in Islamic terms (rehearsing familiar reasoning dating in other Muslim societies to the nineteenth century) hoped the government would begin a gradual transition to representative government with local elections.[43] Their hopes seemed fulfilled in 2005 when the government announced it would hold municipal elections for the first time since 1960. In the early 2000s, other authoritarian regimes in the Arab world held elections that did not lead to a change in power. Also known as "facade elections," going through the motions of a democratic practice played a part in prolonging authoritarian rule, rendering visible to authorities the relative popularity of the government and its critics, and easing internal and external pressures for liberalization.[44]

The firsthand account of the municipal election campaign by French scholar Pascal Menoret reports different attitudes toward a "cosmetic, incomplete, patronizing democratic experiment." The exiled dissident Awakening cleric Saad al-Faqih defined the election as part of the government's counter-terrorism strategy. Other critics pointed out that municipal councils had no authority over the decisions of officials in the Ministry of Municipal and Rural Affairs and that half the council seats were reserved to appointed members. Nevertheless, the prospect of exercising choice enticed some Saudis to register and cast ballots. More than 9,000 candidates ran for around 600 seats. One man reasoned that even if the elections had no bearing on the exercise of power, they were worthwhile as an expression of popular will. A prominent Awakening shaikh, Nasir al-Umar, endorsed the election as a means to thwart the secular current that, in his view, was a tool of Western domination and indifferent to the spread of moral corruption. While the election rules prohibited candidates from combining on lists, to prevent the formation of political parties, Awakening activists circumvented the ban by creating slates endorsed by prominent shaikhs and circulating their candidate lists via cell phone.[45]

Menoret's account makes it clear that candidates, election monitors, and voters, while only a fraction of the eligible electorate, took the campaign seriously. In Riyadh, an unofficial list of Islamic activist candidates swept the seven seats, handily defeating academics and businessmen. The assortment of Awakening voluntary associations that took root in the 1960s and 1970s—Quran memorization clubs, summer camps, and the like—served as a latent social network that became activated for the movement to rally to candidates, defeating the government's effort to prevent the election from taking political and ideological overtones.[46]

The rulers were not ready to lift restraints on open political activity, but in the relaxed climate after 9/11, grassroots activism for social causes increased. With historical roots in religious endowments, charities came under government regulation in 1962. Saudi welfare associations channeled Islam's emphasis on generosity to the less fortunate as social change created a new class of urban poor. The social opening after 9/11 contributed to a rapid increase in the number of welfare associations from a few dozen to more than 700 by 2012.[47] The potential for the charitable impulse to mobilize collective action became visible in the aftermath of a rainstorm that caused devastating flooding in Jeddah on November 25, 2009. Video clips of destruction in poor neighborhoods spread via cell phones. Saudis blamed the local government for failing to install adequate drainage and to assist poor residents whose homes were destroyed. The public responded. Young people coordinated relief efforts through Facebook, the volunteer organization Muwatana (Homeland) spearheaded a campaign to collect donations, and the Jeddah Chamber of Commerce and Industry assisted with the conversion of a conference center into an emergency relief site to triage donations, volunteers, and beneficiaries. Soon, around 2,000 volunteers were going to the relief site each day to hand out food, blankets, household supplies, and medicine. Nine official charity associations and several informal groups banded together to form the Committee for the People of Jeddah.[48] Emergency disaster response was a popular cause throughout the country. Not all Saudis agreed with welfare associations that challenged common assumptions about the privileges of citizenship by ignoring legal regulations that restricted their work to Saudi nationals. Instead, they extended support to the needy without regard for nationality. In doing so, they validated the residence of around a million foreigners who either overstayed their work visas or entered the country illegally.[49]

Shifts in the Economy

The work of welfare associations with the country's poor and needy drew attention to shortcomings in national economic development. Crown Prince Abdallah put the spotlight on the plight of poor Saudis in November 2002 when he visited a low-income neighborhood in Riyadh and declared a campaign to wipe out poverty. Government technocrats from different ministries announced a National Strategy to Eradicate Poverty based on the assumption that unemployment was the root cause of poverty. The government's strategy had a short-term element, increasing benefits for the poor, and a long-term element, improving education to train Saudis to replace foreign workers, thus renewing the call for Saudization of the workforce. Whether or not the government made progress was impossible to know because the many surveys, studies, and reports it carried out were not released to the public, and government offices did not share information with each other. According to one estimate, 30 percent of the population was living in poverty in 2010.[50]

The anti-poverty campaign signified the success and the failure of state-led development. In a generation, central planning had transformed an agrarian economy, rearranged livelihoods, and invented a completely different expectation of comfort and consumption, changing what had always been the common miserable lot into poverty. Large numbers of Saudis attained high levels of material comfort and health. Judging by rise in per capita income, spending on cars, electronics, and household goods, the spread of commercial advertising, and the multiplication of shopping malls, Saudi Arabia had become a consumer society.[51] At the same time, state-led development had left millions of Saudis and foreign workers mired in poverty.

In the late 1990s, planners became concerned that middle-class Saudis would begin to suffer declining living standards if the government did not take steps to end the economy's dependence on oil production. To maintain living standards required structural reform along the lines of the Washington Consensus prescription for neoliberalism: expand the private sector, open up to foreign investment, and diversify the economy. The seventh five-year plan (2000–4) was notable for embedding priorities in a time horizon stretching to 2020. Officials set goals that reflected pressure on the government to meet the needs of a fast-growing population for housing, services, and employment. If the plan succeeded at spurring private-sector growth and investment, the government could begin to increase revenue for public investment from taxes and fees and decrease reliance on oil revenue.[52] By 2005, a few companies were competitive on global scale, but most were struggling to enter the global market, a sign of uneven results in the early stages of shifting the economy from public to private investment and employment.[53]

The idea that improving education in science and technology was essential to make companies and their workers competitive in the global economy was hardly new. In 1990, businessmen had petitioned for education reform for the sake of improving the labor force.[54] The government decided to bypass established universities that would prove difficult to reform, and to start fresh with new ones: between 2003 and 2010, the number of public universities tripled, from eight to twenty-four, and the government provided scholarships for graduate study at overseas institutions to 90,000 students. In 2009, King Abdallah University of Science and Technology (KAUST) offered graduate-level studies to both men and women, busting the taboo on coeducation. While it had the potential to improve higher education in STEM subjects, few students were Saudis. Notwithstanding the government's focus on science and technology, high enrollment for degrees in humanities and social sciences was persistent even though graduates faced dismal job prospects. In August 2010, around 200 graduates with degrees to become Arabic teachers gathered before the Ministry of Education to demand teaching jobs.[55]

The five-year plan for 2010–14 addressed the need to reorient K–12 education if higher education reform was to fulfill its purpose. The Ministry of Education would spend 30 percent of its budget on retraining teachers to improve learning in mathematics and science. In addition, the curriculum would devote less time to religious lessons. The plan looked beyond public education to vocational training as a way to improve the workforce and allotted $200 billion for vocational training.[56]

Even if central planning resulted in educational improvement, there was no guarantee the private sector would quit the habit of employing foreign workers and "hire Saudi." The Seventh Plan did raise the percentage of Saudis in the workforce from 37 to 42 percent by 2004, but the number of foreign workers continued to rise, from 4.5 to 4.7 million.[57] Bureaucratic confusion hampered efforts to change the workforce. Multiple state agencies were responsible for visas, sponsorship, and business regulations. Because they did not coordinate their efforts, they issued different, sometimes contradictory guidelines, and even if they were streamlined, state agencies had little capacity to monitor compliance: in 2005, twenty inspectors at the Ministry of Labor were charged with overseeing 300,000 companies. The risks for employers to dodge "hiring Saudi" were low.[58] Furthermore, it was common for workers to stay in the country after their visas expired and for pilgrims to seek work in the underground economy. In the early 2000s, there were approximately 1 million "overstayers."[59] Many small enterprises depended on low labor costs and found ways to evade quotas: not reporting newly hired foreign workers, using personal connections in state agencies to obtain worker visas, paying civil servants for documents affirming the fulfillment of quotas. Men with connections in the government obtained visas in bulk and sold them to employers. To fill a "Saudization" quota, some businesses employed Saudis "on paper," hiring them at a low wage and not requiring they come to work.[60]

Expatriate workers were pervasive throughout the country, including the settlements and towns of former Bedouin. They had become part of the national economy of production and consumption. Sudanese herders tended camels on the range[61] and drove water tanker trucks to herding stations that were often staffed by cooks and servants from Nepal, Bangladesh, or Indonesia. The population of the Murrah tribal town Jabrin was divided between one clan, Al Jabir, and foreign workers, mostly Asians, employed in health and education, or working at cafes, shops, and gas stations.[62]

A conspicuous feature of the country's adjustment to a large foreign population was the terminology used to refer to expatriates: they were called "foreign workers" rather than immigrants or migrant workers, a lexical move tantamount to "immigration denial."[63] Asian women domestic workers occupied the lowest rung of the labor hierarchy. In the early 2000s, the average monthly pay for Sri Lankan women was $100 to $140, which was two to ten times higher than women earned in their home country's garment industry, agriculture, or domestic work. In the Saudi context, Sri Lankan domestic workers earned roughly one-fifth the prevailing minimum wage for a Saudi national.[64] With the typical workday lasting sixteen to twenty hours, the hourly rate was between fifteen and twenty-two cents.[65] For some women, the work proved worthwhile: it was the only way to make enough money for materials to build a house back home. Even before leaving Sri Lanka, exploitation began with labor agents misleading jobseekers about positions, wages, living conditions, and even the destination country.[66] In Saudi Arabia and other Gulf countries, Sri Lankan women frequently endured mistreatment: cramped sleeping space, withholding food, nonpayment of wages, confinement to the employer's residence, verbal abuse, physical beatings, and sexual assault.[67]

The Shiite Question

The National Dialogue's gestures for religious moderation did not bring about practical measures to ease discrimination against Shiites. In April 2003, Shiite activists submitted a petition seeking legal standing for the Shiite law school in Saudi courts, ending anti-Shiite incitement, opening positions in the foreign service, security forces, and high-level bureaucracy to Shiites, appointment to seats on the Consultative Council (Majlis al-Shura), and a special branch for Shiites in the Ministry of Endowments and Islamic Affairs. The streak of anti-Shiite bigotry in Sunni clerical ranks was evident in an essay by Awakening shaikh Safar al-Hawali, "When the Minority Rules the Majority," that condemned the Shiite petition. Hawali borrowed from modern political ideas to frame anti-Shiism as a matter of defending majority rights against minority rule. In his view, the Shiite desire to prohibit fatwas, sermons, and publications condemning Shiism was a step toward achieving domination over Sunnis. He cited the 1992 Basic Law's stipulation that the purpose of education in Saudi Arabia was to teach the Islamic creed. In the Saudi context, Wahhabi doctrine is the Islamic creed; therefore, Shiite calls for removing Wahhabi doctrine from the classroom violate the constitution. The Basic Law also states that law courts are to apply Islamic law. Hawali considered Shiite law a corruption of Islamic law; therefore, to allow Shiites to establish their own law courts would violate the constitution.[68] Anti-Shiism amounted to scapegoating a minority that refused to assimilate.

The prospect of Iraq coming under Iranian domination magnified perceptions of a foreign "Shiite threat" on the part of the palace, where some suspected a secret American plan to support Shiite interests throughout the Gulf.[69] This made Shiites the one segment in the country that had the misfortune to have its calls for equal rights appear to be a national security problem. The conflation of Iran and the Shiite minority as a single threat weakened the liberal cause by driving a wedge between Sunni and Shiite activists, justifying the government's resistance to demands for accountability, and making clerical opponents to reform who revived classic Wahhabi images of Shiites as idolaters valuable to the rulers.

A fresh round of government confrontation with Shiite citizens erupted in February 2009 when police and Shiite pilgrims in Medina clashed. The pilgrims were gathered to celebrate the Prophet's birthday (a religious holiday that Wahhabi clergy consider an illegitimate innovation) and they became angry when they noticed a man they believed to belong to the Committee for Commanding Right and Forbidding Wrong making a videotape of the women pilgrims.

For the next five days, pilgrims clashed with government security forces. The authorities arrested a few dozen pilgrims. The incident in Medina triggered protests in the Eastern Province, where patience with promises to improve conditions was dwindling. In mid-March, a Shiite cleric, Nimr al-Nimr, called for throwing off Saudi rule. His sermon, which became known as "the Dignity Speech," spread on the Internet. The government arrested him and some of his followers and declared a curfew in Nimr's hometown, Awamiyya, a few miles north of Qatif.[70] Rather than calming the situation, the arrests in Medina and Awamiyya set off a cycle of contestation in the Eastern Province that simmered before igniting during the 2010–11 Arab uprisings.[71]

The Arab Uprisings and Their Aftermath

On December 17, 2010, a young Tunisian food vendor set himself on fire to protest harassment at the hands of police and municipal officials. The incident sparked a wave of demonstrations that engulfed the country and swept through the Arab world, from North Africa to the Gulf. The longtime presidents of Tunisia and Egypt were forced to step down. Regimes in Syria, Libya, and Yemen lost control and their countries fell into civil war. Saudi Arabia emerged as a leader of counter-revolution determined to preempt protests in the kingdom and to suppress them in neighboring Bahrain.

King Abdallah was in the United States to have back surgery when the Tunisian uprising broke out. By the time he got home in late February, demonstrators had driven Tunisia's President Zine El Abidine Ben Ali and Egypt's Hosni Mubarak from power. Suddenly hopes for breaking the grip of corrupt, brutal authoritarian regimes surged, and quickened the Arab world's fragmented activist circles. In Saudi Arabia, young Shiites joined with young Sunnis to form the Free Youth Coalition. Older, reformist Shiite activists joined a cross-sectarian petition calling for the country's conversion into a constitutional monarchy, granting women the rights to vote and hold elected office, and establishing procedures to rein in corruption. A sprinkling of demonstrations in Riyadh and Jeddah called for better job opportunities and the release of political detainees.[72]

Divergent agendas between provincial-sectarian and national concerns weakened the opposition. Shiite activists formed a separate group, the Eastern Region Revolution, to call for the release of Tawfiq al-Amir, a cleric "guilty" of advocating constitutional government.[73] Disagreement on tactics—petitions or demonstrations—also divided opposition to the monarchy. Nevertheless, from afar, it appeared possible that the regional mood might stoke the Saudi public to join the protest wave. Activists living in exile issued a call on Facebook for Saudis to mark March 11 as a Day of Rage, with demonstrations to demand their rights.

To preempt protest, the government resorted to its well-tested repertoire of rent, religion, and repression. It announced it would spend billions of riyals to alleviate a housing shortage, unemployment, and stagnant wages in the public sector.[74] Establishment clerics denounced public demonstrations as violations of Islamic law because they would damage national unity and play into the hands of the Iranian government's scheme to undermine Sunni Islam. The government prepared for demonstrations by flooding the streets with police and security forces. According to press reports, on March 11, a single protester showed up in Riyadh.

In the Eastern Province cities of Qatif and Hofuf, Shiite activists continued their movement for equal rights and for the release of political prisoners, some of whom had been detained since the late 1990s. As the year wore on, the government reinforced security forces with armored cars and helicopters. Armed protesters ambushed police patrols. In June 2012, the authorities arrested the most outspoken shaikh, Nimr al-Nimr, after a car chase and exchange of gunfire.[75] The cycle of protest and repression had no end in sight as long as the monarchy refused to rein in sectarian clerics, give Shiites more than token representation in state offices, and remedy economic deprivation.

Trying to confine unrest to the Eastern Province dovetailed with a well-worn Sunni narrative that portrays Shiite treachery. The narrative hearkens back to the Mongol conquest of Baghdad in 1258, when the Shiite vizier of the last Abbasid caliph supposedly supported the infidel Mongols: Shiite treachery is to blame for the end of the caliphate. According to the narrative, claims of mistreatment by Saudi Shiites are disingenuous, and any effort to foster cooperation between Shiite and Sunni activists for the sake of liberal political reforms is illegitimate. In 2010, authorities imprisoned a Sunni activist for speaking out against attacks on Shiites. In May 2011, Sunni and Shiite reformers came together to issue a declaration urging the government to refrain from using force in the Eastern Province. In response, the government charged Sunni signatories with undermining national unity. The irony of accusing Sunnis and Shiites working together of weakening unity was lost on the authorities bent on silencing Sunni voices for political reform. In fall 2012, the police arrested founders of the Saudi Civil and Political Rights Association for setting up an unlicensed association and "breaking allegiance to the ruler." The court found Muhammad Fahd al-Qahtani, a professor of economics, and Abdallah al-Hamid, a professor of literature, guilty and sentenced them to more than ten years in prison. Hamid died in prison in 2020.[76]

Viewing events through sectarian and authoritarian lenses, Riyadh was bound to do all it could to defeat the democratic movement in Bahrain, where a Sunni clan had ruled the Twelver Shiite majority since conquering the island in 1783. After Bahrain became independent in 1971, it became a constitutional monarchy with an elected parliament. The monarchy suspended the constitution in 1975. Throughout the 1990s, activists pressed for restoration of the constitution, and in early 2002, the monarchy issued a revised constitution with articles that strengthened the court's powers. The 2011 protest movement represented a continuation of the decades-long movement striving for accountable government; it was not an Iranian plot.

But in the official narratives promoted by the hereditary rulers of Bahrain and Saudi Arabia, protesters at Pearl Square in Bahrain's capital of Manama were part of the Shiite conspiracy hatched in Tehran. Likewise, Shiite demonstrations in the Eastern Province calling for equality and the release of political prisoners were tools of the Islamic Republic. From Riyadh's perspective, sending military units to Bahrain on March 14 to stand guard while Bahrain security forces crushed the demonstrators' camp at Pearl Square prevented an Iranian takeover.[77]

The Shiite populations in Bahrain and Iraq belong to the same branch of Shiism as Iran and there are deep historical connections among their Twelver Shiite communities. Therefore, applying the sectarian narrative to those three countries possessed a superficial validity, even though it papered over diversity and tensions within Twelver Shiism. Likewise, reducing political conflict in Syria and Yemen to sectarian strife conflated all Shiites into a single body and distorted the modern political history of the two countries. Syria's Alawite minority belongs to a cluster of sects referred to as *ghulat* Shiites. Ghulat means "extremists," not in a political sense but in a doctrinal sense coined by medieval Sunni theologians characterizing groups that ascribed divine status to Ali. One such group followed the teachings spread in the late ninth century by Muhammad ibn Nusair. In northern Syria, his followers were known as Nusairis, until modern times, when Alawite became the more common term, implying worship of Ali. The Alawites have no connection to the Twelver Shiite tradition of Lebanon, Iraq, Iran, and the Gulf—no common doctrine, no common ritual, no common clerical leadership.[78]

In religious terms, there was nothing Alawite about the Syrian regime of Bashar al-Asad. He inherited power from his father, Hafiz al-Asad, who led a military coup by one faction of the Arab nationalist Baath Party against another in 1970. Hafiz al-Asad came from the Alawite minority, and he depended on some fellow Alawites to fill sensitive intelligence and security positions in his regime. Families of those Alawites in the regime exploited their position to enrich themselves, but, contrary to a common narrative, most Alawites did not profit from the Asad regime. Rather, Sunni Islamists painted the Asad regime as Alawite to stir up popular opposition to its secular measures and violent repression of dissent (features of the two Baath Party regimes that ruled from 1963 until Asad seized power).

The sectarian narrative cannot account for the improvement in Saudi Arabia's relations with Syria when Hafiz al-Asad seized power: he dropped the previous regime's revolutionary hostility toward monarchy in favor of a pragmatic foreign policy. Asad's decision to support Iran's religious republic against Iraq's Baath Party regime during the Iran–Iraq War was rooted in enmity between rival factions of the Baath Party. Strategic logic explains the Islamic Republic's refusal to support the Islamist insurgency that fought Asad from 1979 to 1982.[79] Likewise, Asad had strategic reasons to cooperate with Iran to combat Israel's 1982 invasion of Lebanon, recalling that Syria and the rest of the Arab states had recently lost Egypt's military weight to counter Israeli power after President Sadat signed the peace treaty with Israel.

In 2011, the protests in Tunisia and Egypt inspired Syrians to demand their rights. Asad reacted to peaceful demonstrations with detentions, torture, and bullets. Violent suppression stoked the rise of rebel militias, including Sunni Islamist groups whose slogans framed the battle in sectarian terms. As civil war engulfed Syria, the Asad regime summoned support from Iran and Hizballah while the Saudis and other Gulf Arab states supplied funds and arms to rebel militias. The sectarian narrative transformed Bashar al-Asad from a Baathist president to a conspirator in a Shiite campaign to suppress Sunni Islam. Applying sectarian terms to Yemen distorted the true picture as well. The main Shiite militia in conflict with Saudi Arabia, the Houthis, belongs to the Zaidi branch of Shiism, not the Twelver Shiite branch present in the Gulf countries. Wahhabi theologians distinguish Zaidis from Twelver Shiites, not regarding Zaidis as the *rafida*, a pejorative term that they apply to Twelvers for "rejecting" (*rafada*) the first three caliphs.[80] Furthermore, in the 1960s, Saudi Arabia supported the Zaidi monarchy of Yemen against the Free Officers, backed by Egyptian President Nasser. At that time, Wahhabi clerics did not criticize the government's backing for the Zaidi cause. Iran's secular monarchy also supported the Zaidi monarchy, not out of Shiite solidarity but out of opposition to the spread of revolutionary Arab nationalism.

The end of Yemen's civil war led to the abandonment of the Zaidi monarchy and the installation of a republic troubled by instability until Ali Abdallah Salih became president in 1978. Part of the complex web of Saudi–Yemeni relations is rooted in the 1934 Ta'if agreement that marked the conclusion of hostilities between Abd al-Aziz and Imam Yahya. The agreement recognized that strict enforcement of an international border would create hardship for people living on either side of it; therefore the governments agreed not to impede perennial trade and tribal connections. The agreement also recognized a special status for Yemenis that made it easy for them to work and live in Saudi Arabia. By the 1980s, their number had grown to around 800,000. Iraq's invasion of Kuwait in August 1990 disrupted Yemen–Saudi relations because the Yemeni government expressed sympathy for Iraq. Riyadh retaliated by expelling Yemenis en masse, costing the economy of Yemen's northern district dearly. Many uprooted Yemeni traders turned to smuggling over the rugged, poorly patrolled border. In the early 2000s, Riyadh's struggle against AQAP drew attention to the Yemen border region as a conduit for smuggling weapons and for infiltration, leading the Saudis to reinforce border security.[81]

In the 1980s and 1990s, Saudi proselytizing in the Saada region, the historical center of Zaidi Shiism, made advances, thanks in part to the arrival of Yemenis who studied at the Islamic University of Medina, where they became enthusiastic proponents of Salafism (as Wahhabism had become known).[82] Zaidis blamed President Salih for doing nothing to block the spread of Saudi influence. In the early 1990s, defenders of the Zaidi tradition gathered behind a cleric named Badr al-Din al-Houthi. His son Hussein and other Zaidi revivalists founded the Association of Believing Youth and set up branches of the association in villages in the Saada region. The national government viewed the Believing Youth, usually referred to as the Houthis, as a potential source of instability. At times, it accused the Houthis of seeking to revive the Zaidi imamate; at times, it claimed the group abandoned traditional Zaidism in favor of slogans and practices borrowed from Iran. In turn, the Houthis accused the government of persecuting Zaidis in order to placate its putative Saudi sponsors.[83]

Armed conflict between the Houthis and the national government broke out in June 2004, when the government tried to arrest Hussein al-Houthi for allegedly attempting to restore the Zaidi monarchy. He evaded capture but was killed some months later in fighting between his militia and the Yemeni army.[84] In the next five years, Houthi militiamen and government forces engaged in several rounds of fighting in the Saada region. In August 2009, President Salih announced Operation Scorched Earth to eliminate the Houthis. During the fighting, Houthi and Saudi forces clashed near the border, with both sides blaming the other for escalating the conflict.[85] Fighting spilled over the Saudi border, sparking two months of inconclusive battles that resulted in more than 100 Saudi combat deaths. The combination of Houthi opposition to Wahhabi proselytizing and its radical anti-Western slogans made it seem reasonable, from a Saudi point of view, to suspect that the Houthis were not primarily concerned with local conditions as much as Iran's scheme to achieve regional domination.[86] Wahhabi clerics responded to the political moment with declarations that Houthis are not traditional Zaidis at all but instead are converts to Twelver Shiism allied with Iran.[87]

The struggle between the Houthis and the national government became embroiled in the massive protest movement that swept Yemen in late January 2011, with crowds demanding the fall of

President Ali Abdallah Salih. The protest movement made his position untenable, and in November, he agreed to resign in accord with the terms of an initiative by the Gulf Cooperation Council that paved the way for a transitional government under his vice-president, Abd Rabbu Mansur Hadi. The GCC initiative also provided for a process to undertake constitutional reform through a National Dialogue Conference.[88] While those talks proceeded, the Houthis battled Salafi militias in the north and succeeded in gaining full control in Saada governorate by the middle of 2014. In September, Houthi forces occupied Sanaa, benefiting from the inability of other Yemeni factions to close ranks. At the end of 2014, Yemen was on the precipice of all-out civil war.[89]

Saudi Arabia's posture as a defender of Sunni interests was complicated by the turn of events in Egypt during the 2011 uprising. After President Hosni Mubarak resigned, a caretaker military government called the Supreme Council of the Armed Forces held elections to parliament in December 2011–January 2012. The Muslim Brotherhood received nearly half the votes. In June, the Muslim Brotherhood candidate, Muhammad al-Morsi, won the presidential election. Riyadh already mistrusted the Muslim Brotherhood for its opposition to Western military intervention against Iraq's annexation of Kuwait, as well as for inspiring the Awakening movement. Morsi's visit to Iran shortly after his election doomed the prospect for establishing good relations with Saudi Arabia.

Morsi's position weakened in Egypt as political instability caused economic conditions to deteriorate, and on July 3, 2013, the Supreme Council of the Armed Forces abruptly removed him from power. In Saudi Arabia, Awakening shaikhs condemned the coup against an elected leader. By contrast, King Abdallah immediately applauded the generals and pledged $12 billion in economic aid. On August 14, Egyptian police fired on pro-Morsi demonstrators in Cairo, killing between 600 and 1,000 people. The massacre triggered outrage in Europe and North America, but the Saudi government was ready to support the generals' steps to crush the staunchly Sunni Muslim Brotherhood. In March 2014, the monarchy passed a law that declared the Muslim Brotherhood an illegal terrorist organization and made it a crime to show sympathy or support it, a clear warning to the Awakening movement.[90]

The Arab uprisings coincided with the failure of Iraq's hardline Shiite prime minister to placate the country's Sunni citizens. He squandered the gains made by American forces in a military-political campaign known as "the Surge," which drove Al Qaeda in Iraq out of Sunni districts and forged a tentative reconciliation of militant Sunnis and the Baghdad government. When United States military forces withdrew at the end of 2011, Baghdad's Shiite leadership adopted harsh measures toward the Sunni minority. Al Qaeda in Iraq, rebranded as the Islamic State in Iraq, exploited Sunni grievances to reestablish itself. When the Syrian government withdrew forces from the region bordering Iraq to combat the insurgency threatening Damascus, the Islamic State in Iraq moved into Syria and proclaimed the Islamic State in Iraq and Syria. In June 2014, its forces conquered Raqqa and it proclaimed the revival of the caliphate.

The Islamic State presented two challenges to Saudi Arabia. First, it undercut the Sauds' religious legitimacy by claiming to be the true heir to the teachings of Muhammad ibn Abd al-Wahhab. The Islamic State expressed admiration for the Diriyya emirate's zealous implementation of Wahhabi doctrine and contempt for the modern kingdom's failure to enforce Islamic law, its toleration of Shiism, and its alignment with the infidels (the West). Republishing and citing treatises by Muhammad ibn Abd al-Wahhab bolstered the Islamic State's religious credentials and undermined Riyadh's. At the same time, the Islamic State diverged from the Wahhabi tradition in its focus on reviving the caliphate and apocalyptic scenarios.[91]

The second challenge from the Islamic State was a terrorist campaign, preceded by the recruitment of volunteers for jihad in Syria and Iraq. From November 2014 to November 2015, militants carried out nearly twenty shooting and suicide bomb attacks against security forces and Shiite targets that took about ninety lives. The Saudi government deployed the counter-terrorism apparatus it had built up in its fight against AQAP. Between interdicting the flow of volunteers and breaking up cells plotting attacks in the country, the authorities rounded up about 4,000 militants by the end of 2015.

The renewal of violence on Saudi soil put Wahhabi clerics in a bind. On one side, the Islamic State accused them of hypocrisy for tolerating Shiite idolatry. On another side, liberal critics condemned the clerics for refusing to renounce Wahhabi doctrine. King Abdallah scolded clerics at a gathering for their failure to condemn the Islamic State. Taking a cue from the king, liberal critics renewed their denunciation of the clerics, and a clerical dissident named Hatim al-Awni called on peers to abandon the doctrine of *takfir*. Few clerics were willing to bend, but they did deny there was a connection between the Islamic State and the teachings of Muhammad ibn Abd al-Wahhab.[92] In retrospect, Abdallah foreshadowed the dramatic demotion of the religious establishment under his successor King Salman, in the sense that the royals concluded that Wahhabism was impossible to reform and, more importantly, when not restrained by Riyadh's golden handcuffs, harmful to stability.

Attaining equilibrium at home, in the region, and in relations with the West was a matter of constant adjustment. The question could be framed as: how does Saudi Arabia fit into the international political system? Al Qaeda pursued religious purity and separation from the West for the sake of solidarity with fellow Muslims. The Sauds, however, were deeply invested in economic and strategic ties with the United States and other Western powers. It is important to take note of a major shift in the twentieth century in how the monarchy defined its religious commitments. Muslim solidarity replaced the Wahhabi mission's hostile stance toward the Muslim world; the "Other" was now "the West." Preoccupation with doctrinal purity and idolatry was a vestige, replaced by the imperative to rescue Muslims suffering oppression. Washington's "Global War on Terror" put severe strains on Riyadh's posture as a defender of fellow Muslims. Nevertheless, the post-1973 dispensation under the developmentalist state held steady in the face of multiple challenges, allocating oil income to sustain the rentier economy's division of labor and benefits. The state maintained its position as the largest employer and guarantor of material welfare.[93] Yet time and again, demands for reform issued from different directions: Awakening and militant currents on the religious side, women, liberals, and Shiites on the secular side. The opposition's diverse currents represented the country's chronic strains over imperialism and national culture, individual rights versus dynastic prerogative and Sunni male privilege.

10

Striving for Transformation, Since 2015

When King Abdallah died in January 2015 and his brother Salman succeeded him, it appeared the bloc of allied senior princes was bound to last awhile longer. Two years earlier, Abdallah had designated Prince Muqrin, a former provincial governor, to follow Salman. But it turned out the new king was determined to bring the fifty-year-old custom of collective fraternal rule to an end and concentrate royal authority in his own line. Eliminating the need to arrive at consensus among princes allowed him to move fast on what he considered urgent matters. He undertook extensive reorganization of national government, announced a program for economic transformation to a post-petroleum era, intensified repression of dissidents, sidelined the religious establishment, loosened restrictions on public life, and abandoned the country's customary caution in regional affairs.

Succession

Clan strife has disrupted the Saud line at different moments. The Riyadh emirate witnessed three episodes of violent conflict: Turki's assassination, the expulsion of Khalid at the end of the second Egyptian occupation, and the civil war after Faisal. King Abd al-Aziz established the line of succession twenty years before he died, but that did not prevent a political struggle between Saud and Faisal that consumed a full decade. For a half-century, one son of Abd al-Aziz after another reigned. By the time King Fahd died in 2005, however, the few remaining members of his generation were advanced in years (truly senior princes), and the question of how the throne would pass to a member of the next generation, the grandsons of Abd al-Aziz, became pressing. In 2007, King Abdallah took a stab at fashioning a mechanism that would preserve clan harmony by establishing the Allegiance Council, a body that would also serve to balance the power of the Sudairi faction in the clan.[1] As it turned out, the Allegiance Council was no more than a facade for the king's supremacy. The council rubber-stamped his choices for a successor when Prince Sultan died in 2011 and when Prince Naif died in 2012. After all, the 1992 Basic Law of Governance gave the king full power over naming a successor. Thus, when Salman ascended to the throne, there was no institutional check on how he would decide the monarchy's future.

In King Salman's first days on the throne, he indicated that leadership would soon pass to the next generation. He named a second-in-line, Prince Muhammad ibn Naif, renowned for his leadership of the campaign to defeat AQAP. He also appointed his son Muhammad to head the Ministry of Defense and a new council for the economy and development. As head of the council, the young prince was in charge of the two major public companies—Saudi Aramco and Saudi Basic Industries—the Public Investment Fund, and public companies responsible for telecommunications and civil aviation. Salman balanced moves that, in the Saudi context, were disruptive, with gestures to assure the monarchy's customary constituencies. He confirmed senior princes at the heads of key ministries; he brought conservative clerics back to influential positions on religious bodies; he distributed bonus allowances to tribal leaders and enlarged the circle of tribal beneficiaries; he awarded two-month salary and payment bonuses for public-sector employees, the military, and students; and he announced new spending on public utilities.[2]

Salman followed political consolidation with steps to concentrate bureaucratic power. He restructured government offices and functions, forming new councils, trimming others, and shuffling ministers to install his own clients. Clan politics were part of the reorganization: King Abdallah's sons were dismissed as governors of Riyadh and Mecca. Having stacked the Allegiance Council with his own men, on April 29, he removed Muqrin as crown prince, elevated Muhammad ibn Naif to that position, and named his son Muhammad deputy crown prince.

More than a year would pass before Salman took the next major step on June 4, 2017, ordering the crown prince to yield his position to Muhammad ibn Salman. There are different accounts about the circumstances, with some sources reporting the isolation of the king's nephew, and other sources indicating that senior princes persuaded him to concede. One way or another, he relented, Muhammad ibn Salman became the next-in-line to the throne, and the king refrained from naming a new deputy crown prince.[3]

The final step in securing full control over all organs of coercion took place on November 4, 2017, when Salman dismissed the late King Abdallah's son Mitʿib from command of the National Guard. The move was part of an extensive purge of potential dissent in the royal family in the name of rooting out corruption. Salman created the Supreme Committee for Combating Corruption and put his son Muhammad in charge. The committee corralled more than 300 princes, businessmen, and present and former ministers, and detained them at Riyadh's Ritz-Carlton hotel. Security agents blindfolded the detainees, subjected some of them to beatings, and interrogated them to uncover the extent and location of ill-gotten wealth. The harsh treatment landed seventeen men in hospital; one man died.[4]

The shakedown's targets included the sons and entourage of the late King Abdallah. Prince Mitʿib surrendered his assets to obtain his release at the end of November and disappeared from public view. Prince Turki, recently governor of Riyadh, remained in indefinite detention until 2023, when he was sentenced to seventeen years on corruption charges. The country's most famous prince-businessman, Prince Walid, also landed in the Ritz-Carlton. His octogenarian father Talal, the former Free Prince, was a member of the Allegiance Council and had opposed elevating Muhammad ibn Salman to be the crown prince. Prince Walid parted with $6 billion, around one-third of his fortune, in exchange for release in January 2018.[5] The anti-corruption committee claimed it clawed back for the national treasury more than $100 billion in assets, mostly real estate and business holdings, from around ninety detainees; according to some accounts, the haul was less than $30 billion.[6] The anti-corruption campaign satisfied a populist appetite for humbling the arrogant, and the demonstration of royal power was a clear message that Salman's line was in full control.

Saudi Vision 2030

Salman, his son, and their entourage were able to accomplish the dynastic shuffle in a few years. Transforming the economy would take longer, but the blueprint was ready in April 2016 when the government announced Saudi Vision 2030. The king decided to abort preparations for the tenth five-year plan in favor of an ambitious fifteen-year project aiming to shift the economy from dependence on oil and foreign labor to one where capital reserves spurred the formation of a high-technology economy grounded in private-sector entrepreneurship and national labor. To put together the Vision, Salman used American consulting firms, much as he had done when he was governor of Riyadh to obtain a "master plan" for urban development.[7] Saudi Vision 2030 relied on a formula for bolstering royal power that went back to the 1930s: leverage foreign expertise (foreign Arabs, British advisers, American technicians) and technology (military, communications, oil extraction, construction). It also represented continuity with the developmentalist state's agenda going back to the 1962 Ministerial Statement, where the government acts as the guarantor of national welfare.

The five-year plans and Saudi Vision 2030 shared the political purpose of winning the population's allegiance in return for securing material welfare, the heart of the rentier bargain, where the government delivers benefits in exchange for the population's compliance. Vision 2030 sweetened the five-year plan's economic dish, promising abundant diversions in a package that meant not only the end of clerical surveillance and restrictive Wahhabi norms, but also the country's arrival as a member of the global vanguard in expensive technological innovations, albeit imported from abroad. Part of the excitement for young Saudis was the lure of some freedom to pursue the arts: painting, sculpture, television, and film. Far more people were able to participate in creative endeavors than the early generation of authors whose writings laid the foundations of Saudi modernist literature. Introducing political participation was not on the Vision's horizon.

To solicit public enthusiasm, the government and foreign consultants painted an exciting future that would lead the world in building zones that combine residence, work, and leisure, wrapped in fantastic notions of ecological harmony and almost psychedelic technological dreams. Under the rubric of "megaprojects," the government advertised the opening of a vast entertainment-sports-shopping complex outside Riyadh (al-Qiddiya), a couple of luxury resorts on the Red Sea, and a half-trillion-dollar city called NEOM (the new future) to materialize in the country's northwest corner where the Gulf of Aqaba meets the Red Sea.[8]

Progress toward realizing the elements of Saudi Vision 2030 has been uneven. On the positive side, the king's men did reorganize and streamline government bodies, in part by getting rid of the old princely fiefdoms that reflected the diffusion of political power after King Faisal, making possible improved governance.[9] The government made modest strides toward revising legal and regulatory regimes to favor private enterprise. Female labor participation and non-oil revenue grew rapidly.[10] Reducing subsidies for water and energy made some dents in demand and modified the blanket allocation of oil revenue that allowed the wealthy Saudis to pay the same low rates as the poor.[11] On the negative side, foreign investment declined as a result of Western revulsion at the Khashoggi murder (see below, p. 277) and doubts about the feasibility of the NEOM project.[12] Measures to reduce wages and benefits for public-sector workers provoked a Twitter campaign that succeeded in getting the government to rescind reductions.[13] Notwithstanding some stumbles, according to the World Economic Forum's measure of global competitiveness, Saudi Arabia made impressive strides in reshaping government agencies and regulations to pursue national goals.[14]

Achieving economic transformation by 2030 faced daunting obstacles. Restructuring the economy required reducing the public sector as the primary source of employment (around two-thirds of Saudi workers) and cutting the private sector's reliance on inexpensive expatriate labor. According to one assessment, that would have meant quadrupling the size of the private sector's Saudi labor force, a feat that likely would take decades. Restructuring would also require a shift from oil revenue to taxation as the main source for government revenue. How to manage that without deep cuts in social benefits that could foment unrest was an open question.[15] Climate change was another disruptive variable. Saudi Arabia and its Gulf neighbors were confronting a dismal climate future of extreme heat, flash floods, drought, depletion of groundwater, and coastal flooding that will impose heavy costs on infrastructure and government resources.[16]

Repression

Saudi Vision 2030 had no room for popular mobilization, dissent, or even debate on public issues. While King Abdallah allowed discussion of public matters in the media, he never endorsed steps to protect freedom of speech or assembly. As dark as the political climate was in 2014, it got worse under King Salman. The handful of venues for public expression—the Consultative Council and elected municipal councils—were sidelined.[17] On January 2, 2016, the government carried out the largest mass execution since it put to death Juhaiman al-Utaibi and his followers in 1980. Forty-seven condemned men were beheaded, all but four of them on charges arising from the AQAP terrorist campaign. The best-known figure in the group was the Shiite dissident Shaikh Nimr al-Nimr.[18] In response to his execution and that of three other Shiites, Iranian crowds attacked and set fire to the Saudi embassy in Tehran. Riyadh retaliated by severing diplomatic relations.[19]

Repression intensified after Muhammad ibn Salman became crown prince in June 2017. In September, the government arrested twenty activists from across the political spectrum—liberals, Awakening shaikhs, and women's rights activists.[20] In November, the government issued a new counter-terrorism law that so vaguely defined offenses that just about any public comment might be construed as a crime. According to an analysis by Human Rights Watch, "disturbing the public order," "exposing national unity to danger," and "to bring religion or justice into disrepute" were defined as terrorist acts.[21] In short order, writers, academics, and journalists found themselves detained or banned from leaving the country.[22] In May 2018, twelve women activists were arrested for having the gall to be in contact with foreign human rights groups.

In March 2022, the government issued a revised personal status law that set a minimum age for marriage but did not alter stipulations that a wife obey her husband and that a woman must obtain permission from her male guardian to get married. The new law kept men's advantages in divorce, inheritance, and custody.[23] When a young woman called for lifting male guardianship on social media, she was arrested, even though she applauded the easing of social restrictions.[24] The climate of fear resulted in an increase in the number of Saudis seeking political asylum in Europe and North America, climbing from a handful to more than 2,000 between 2015 and 2018. By the end of 2018, around 1,500 activists were under detention.[25]

The murder of a journalist in exile, Jamal Khashoggi, drew widespread condemnation from forcign governments and human rights organizations. A confidant of high-ranking princes, Khashoggi fell afoul of King Salman and his son for writing critical pieces in *The Washington Post* following the arrest of activists in fall 2017. He disappeared after entering the Saudi consulate in Istanbul in October 2018 to obtain documents to record his marriage to a Turkish woman. According to Western media reports, the Turkish government had installed surveillance equipment at the consulate that obtained evidence that Saudi government officials murdered Khashoggi and dismembered his corpse. The Saudi government asserted that rogue agents were responsible for the crime, while Western media broadcast allegations that senior officials in Riyadh may have ordered the operation. Khashoggi was not the only victim of measures to silence dissidents in exile. A ring of government agents known as the Rapid Intervention Group kidnapped dissidents, including princes and business rivals, from Switzerland, France, and Morocco.[26] Authorities in the United States, Canada, and Norway became aware that dissidents in their countries were under threat from Saudi intelligence agents. With a cloud of suspicion hanging over the Saudi government, businesspeople shied away from investing in new projects and journalists started paying closer attention to the reports of repression.[27]

The intelligence apparatus surrounding the crown prince included an agency called the Center for Studies and Media Affairs that engaged United States firms to consult on surveillance and deployed Israeli-developed spyware. The US Department of Justice filed complaints against Saudi agents for infiltrating the social media company Twitter to access information from 6,000 accounts.[28] A message was sent from the crown prince's WhatsApp account that is believed to have planted spyware on the cell phone of Amazon and *Washington Post* owner Jeff Bezos, perhaps to gain leverage over the newspaper's coverage of Saudi Arabia.[29] A 2019 report on "computational propaganda" rated Saudi Arabia as one of the top seven governments to deploy cyber troops to sway foreign public opinion, drown out opposition voices inside the country, and harass critics.[30]

Instilling fear is a blunt instrument for suppressing dissent. King Salman's regime also devised legal, regulatory, and bureaucratic ways to prevent political mobilization emerging from collective endeavors for charitable purposes. From the 1990s, traditional welfare associations proliferated and the range of nongovernment actors grew to include advocacy associations for causes such as HIV/AIDS, breast cancer, the environment, domestic violence, and addiction. Under King Abdallah's regime of limited reform, nongovernment organizations increased in number and succeeded at engaging young Saudis in projects targeting residents, Saudi and non-Saudi, in need.[31]

In December 2015, the government issued a law on nongovernmental organizations to revise older regulations dating to 1976 and amended in 1990. The purpose of the new law was to better organize "the Third Sector," groups outside the government and private business sectors that constituted civil society. One thing that better organization meant under the law was close government oversight by the Ministry of Human Resources and Social Development (formerly the Ministry of Social Affairs). Associations were required to submit to the ministry annual financial reports, advance notice of meetings, and minutes of meetings. The decisions of associations were subject to ministry approval. The law banned activity outside the country and contact with members of international organizations in the country. While the law gave the government extensive oversight, it was largely ink on paper: in 2020, responsibility for regulation of associations in the entire country fell to a staff of thirty.[32]

A New Social Bargain

For Saudis willing to leave politics alone and eager to have fun, King Salman's policy to allow a measure of social freedom fulfilled long-sought aspirations to be like Arabs in the rest of the Gulf states. In 2018–19, the government lifted the ban on women driving, ended enforcement of separation between men and women in malls and restaurants, and rescinded the requirement that a male guardian travel with a woman.[33] Young people, attuned to cosmopolitan norms and tastes through virtual media, enjoyed the freedom to go to the movies, attend concerts and sports events, and mingle at cafes and restaurants. New tourist destinations in the country made holidays more affordable compared to trips to the Gulf and Europe. They also opened a new sector for private-sector employment.[34] The government put a "guided" stamp on leisure activities. Since 2010, young people in Jeddah had taken up hiking to raise money for charity, to enjoy the outdoors, and to escape restrictions on gender mixing. Under King Salman, the government regulated hiking. Participants had to register to go on a hike with a guide possessing a government license, obtained at great expense, that was passed along to tourists and excursionists. Hiking became a luxury pastime.[35]

The new climate of greater social freedom meant the religious establishment lost its authority to enforce conformity to its conception of proper conduct. In the early 1990s, the royals reacted to the Awakening protests by reshaping religious institutions and bolstering the authority of establishment clerics. Twenty years later, King Abdallah expressed his ire at senior clerics for refusing to renounce some of the classic Wahhabi doctrines that ISIS claimed for inspiration.[36] King Salman decided it was time to impose the monarchy's will on the religious establishment in order to enact sweeping changes in public life. If the bans on women driving, mingling between men and women, public entertainment venues, and creative arts were to be lifted, then religious police patrols had to end.

King Salman framed the new public order in terms of a new narrative that claimed the country's original, moderate religious heritage was in harmony with a more liberal social life. The narrative asserted that extremist religious ideology infiltrated the country at the hands of the Muslim Brotherhood and that the 1979 Mecca uprising was the result of foreign influence. The government reacted to the uprising by reversing liberal social trends and by appeasing the extremist current with funding for its agenda at home and abroad. King Salman was determined to restore a putative moderate religious life. The 1979 backlash narrative was a convenient way to frame the new dispensation, where the rulers wanted to allow the public to enjoy social freedom and entertainment. The Committee for Commanding Right and Forbidding Wrong was sidelined and redirected to emphasizing obedience to political authority and acting to support national unity.[37]

The king and his advisers appointed clerics willing to advocate "moderate" religious views to lead religious agencies. The Board of Senior Clerics still included members of the old guard, tokens of the Wahhabi legacy, but the rulers no longer took their expertise and opinions into consideration. Under the leadership of the liberal cleric Muhammad al-Isa, the Board endorsed the decision to allow women to drive.[38] When called on to condemn the Muslim Brotherhood, the Board performed its role dutifully.[39] As a gesture to the Wahhabi heritage, a pragmatic member of Al al-Shaikh was chosen to head the Ministry of Islamic Affairs. The ministry reined in critics of social freedom, kept an eye on mosque personnel to guard against political agitation, preached the fight against terrorism, and reminded believers of their duty to obey the ruler. Clerics unhappy with the imposition of "moderate Islam" held their tongues or went into exile.[40]

Some of the most extensive changes took place in the legal field. The religious establishment's resistance to codification of the law crumbled and religious courts faced a shrinking sphere of jurisdiction as the government strove toward a legal system marked by uniform, consistent, and transparent enforcement of laws.[41] The old guard, however, was able to hold the line to keep women off the bench.[42] In education, the king's officials undertook an extensive campaign to uproot the Muslim Brotherhood influence with a purge of teachers and administrative leadership at religious universities. The education ministry excised lessons in schoolbooks that implied support for activism in support of Muslim solidarity on the grounds it entailed extremism and deviancy.[43] The king withdrew substantial financial resources from the clerical establishment when he relocated responsibility for religious endowments from the Ministry of Islamic Affairs to a new agency, the General Authority for Endowments.[44]

Ever since the 9/11 attacks on the United States, Saudi Arabia had been suspected of supporting international terrorism by failing to regulate charitable and humanitarian organizations. A few months after coming to the throne, King Salman set up the King Salman Humanitarian Aid and Relief Center, or KSRelief, to gain full control over all charitable initiatives directed outside the country. The new royal agency represented a departure from the mechanisms and rhetoric at work in Saudi soft diplomacy that operated through multiple agencies (royal, private, government) and employed religious idioms to solicit and distribute assistance. As a matter of asserting the state's authority over charity, KSRelief's antecedents date to the creation in 1951 of an office in the Ministry of Finance to collect zakat. The rise in oil revenue in the 1970s bolstered private religious organizations that combined proselytizing with relief in the name of Muslim solidarity. After 9/11, the government tightened control over fundraising and cash transfers abroad, and it formed the Financial Investigation Unit to join an international effort to interdict funds destined to militant and terrorist groups, with legitimate charities suffering collateral damage. In terms of rhetoric, KSRelief emphasized humanitarian terms and norms emanating from Europe and North America, and it highlighted cooperation with the United Nations and United States rather than with Islamic institutions.[45]

How expatriate workers fit into the new social bargain was unclear. In November 2020, they came under new regulations that reduced but did not abolish an employer's ability to prevent a worker from changing jobs or leaving the country; domestic and farm workers were excluded from the new regulations.[46] Moreover, migrant workers were still at the mercy of agents in their home countries able to dodge government regulation and of employers in Saudi Arabia.[47] A 2024 report on workers from Nepal indicated that nothing had changed in recruitment and employment. Tens of thousands of Saudi labor-contracting companies imported Asian workers for construction on the Vision 2030 megaprojects and low-wage jobs in coffee shops, warehouses, and factories. Recruiters in Nepal lied to workers about the prospective employer, salary, and living conditions.[48]

Expatriate workers were caught between contradictory government policies. On one hand, the government had plans to expand sectors that depended on low-wage labor, namely construction projects and everyday leisure, and on the other hand, the government aspired to increase the proportion of Saudi nationals in the private sector. Furthermore, government officials undertook periodic campaigns to clear out undocumented residents who overstayed their work or pilgrimage visas. In summer 2021, the government raided neighborhoods with large expatriate populations and arrested 80,000 migrants who had overstayed work and pilgrimage visas, mostly from Yemen and Ethiopia.[49] The following year, an urban redevelopment project razed a Jeddah neighborhood with around a half million residents to make way for a luxury resort district.[50] During the COVID pandemic, expatriate workers in Mecca contracted the infection at a high rate because they lived in cramped quarters. Government officials relocated many of them to underused buildings and tightened housing standards to render residences less prone to spreading infection.[51]

The COVID Pandemic

Saudi Vision 2030 called for increasing the number of annual pilgrims as part of the plan to expand religious tourism. The COVID-19 pandemic put that plan on hold. Saudi health officials detected the first case of COVD-19 on March 2, 2020. A few days earlier, the government had suspended international travel for Muslims performing the lesser pilgrimage to Mecca. Like the rest of the world, the Saudi government grappled with how to contain the new virus. The Ministry of Health responded with an urgency that reflected the country's encounter in 2012 with Middle East respiratory syndrome (MERS), a different coronavirus. On March 17, the government closed mosques to prayer, and clerics exhorted people to perform prayer in their homes. In April, the government banned travel between provinces, enforced shutdowns in the major cities, and rolled out a program to test for infection.[52]

While officials from the Ministry of Health and the World Health Organization assessed the risk of holding the hajj, international flights from countries with high infection rates were suspended on March 23. At the beginning of April, the government announced curfews in Mecca and Medina, as COVID shutdowns spread around the world. By the time of the hajj at the end of July, the country had recorded more than 250,000 cases and nearly 3,000 deaths from the pandemic. The Ministry of Health decided to allow only 1,000 residents to perform the pilgrimage: 700 foreign residents and 300 Saudi nationals. In normal years, more than 2 million Muslims gathered in Mecca, the majority coming from abroad. Pilgrims were required to isolate and take PCR tests before and after the hajj. While performing the rituals, pilgrims were required to wear masks, observe social distancing, and refrain from touching the Kaaba. The government supplied sterilized prayer mats and pebbles for the ritual stoning of pillars representing Satan. With strict public health measures, there were no reports of COVID cases.[53]

When the vaccine became available in 2021, the government offered free vaccinations and by the time of that year's hajj, around half the population had received one dose. The quota was increased to 60,000 pilgrims, all fully vaccinated residents. In 2022, the government opened the pilgrimage to international visitors and the numbers surged to around 1 million. From the global perspective of recovery from the pandemic, it was the largest mass gathering event since the start of the COVID-19 outbreak. The lifting of restrictions on age and vaccination status in 2023 resulted in a record number of pilgrims, exceeding 2.5 million. One sign of return to normal was that foreign Muslims complained about a virtual platform intended to facilitate acquisition of a visa and reserving lodging.[54]

Foreign Relations

Foreign policy was not part of Saudi Vision 2030. It was, however, part of King Salman and his son's agenda for countering threats from Iran and the Muslim Brotherhood: they blamed both for stoking internal unrest. The Arab uprisings had exacerbated the rivalry between Riyadh and Tehran, with the Saudi leadership bundling distinct political forces into one threat: Shiite dissent, the Bahrain reform movement, the Houthi movement in Yemen, and Iranian expansionism. The Muslim Brotherhood undermined the monarchy's standing with Sunni communities. The situation resembled the challenge Riyadh faced in the 1950s and 1960s when opposition groups were part of the Arab nationalist wave. The task before King Salman, then, was to devise ways to untangle and deflect forces that challenged royal power.

One of his frustrations was Washington's ambivalent attitude toward the monarchy. On one hand, the kingdom's massive influence on oil markets and its appetite for US weapons were reasons for policymakers to favor Saudi interests. On the other hand, the American public did not identify with a monarchical system of government that backed a sectarian religious establishment. Saudi relations with the United States were strained during President Barack Obama's administration. When Arab uprisings broke out, Washington favored transitions from autocratic to democratic regimes in Tunisia, Egypt, Bahrain, and Libya. Members of the Saudi government took a firm stance in support of the autocrats: they did not want democracy fever spreading to their country, and they worried that Iran might be able to extend its influence through support for anti-government movements in Bahrain and Yemen. The Saudi government was also frustrated with Obama's decision to refrain from retaliating against Syria's Bashar al-Asad for a chemical weapon attack on Syrian rebels in 2014. Obama's policy toward Iran was yet another irritant for the Saudis. They favored the Bush administration's hard line toward Tehran and believed that moderate tactics invited Iranian expansionism. The US worked with the permanent members of the UN Security Council, Germany, and the European Union to reach an agreement with Iran to limit its nuclear program in July 2015.

The Saudis felt they had very good reason to be alarmed at Iran's growing influence in the region. In neighboring Yemen, the Houthi rebels seized control of Sanaa in September 2014 and forced the transitional president to flee a few months later. In March 2015, Saudi Arabia and the United Arab Emirates intervened in Yemen with the aim of defeating the Houthis.[55] The United States supplied logistical support to the Saudi air force and the United Nations passed a resolution that demanded the Houthis withdraw from Sanaa. Seven years of brutal bombardment, strategic starvation, and economic destruction failed to dislodge the Houthis, who attacked Saudi Arabia with missiles and drones, largely targeting oil installations and airports. By the time a fragile truce between the Houthis and Saudi Arabia took hold in April 2022, nearly 400,000 Yemenis had lost their lives to Saudi bombings, with munitions supplied by the United States, starvation tactics, and disease, including a massive cholera epidemic caused by the destruction of water and sanitation infrastructure.[56]

The failure of Riyadh's intervention to dislodge the Houthis underscored deficiencies in the country's military capacities and the prospect of continued dependence on Washington for strategic security.

Iran was not the only threat that loomed in the Yemen war. The two jihadist organizations, Al Qaeda in the Arabian Peninsula and the Islamic State, established footholds. The jihadist current appeared in Yemen in the early 1990s, when veterans of the Afghan jihad created the Islamic Jihad Movement.[57] A second jihadist organization was founded in the mid-1990s called the Aden-Abyan Islamic Army. While Yemen's leadership was preoccupied with the Houthis in the early 2000s, Al Qaeda was able to attract fresh recruits and in January 2009 its leaders announced the revival of AQAP. The United States gained President Salih's cooperation to carry out a drone war against AQAP cells. During the 2011 uprising, AQAP created a militia, Supporters of Islamic Law (Ansar al-Sharia), which briefly occupied some towns in the southern Abyan province. A few years later, when Yemen fell into civil war, the Islamic State drew Sunni fighters to its banner and carried out attacks on Shiite (Houthi) targets.

In an attempt to stabilize its northern front, the Saudis took steps to mend relations with Iraq. Riyadh wanted to support Baghdad's campaign to defeat ISIS and to contend with Iran for influence. The Saudis adopted a nonsectarian strategy, seeking ties with Shiite politicians such as Muqtada al-Sadr, known for his independent streak, and bidding for roles in economic projects. From Iraq's perspective, good relations with both Saudi Arabia and Iran made sense as a strategy to balance its neighbors.[58]

In contrast to the light-touch strategy in Iraq, Riyadh resorted to strongarm tactics toward Qatar and Lebanon. In June 2017, Saudi Arabia, the United Arab Emirates, Bahrain, and Egypt severed diplomatic, travel, and trade ties with Qatar over its stance toward Iran and the Muslim Brotherhood. Qatar was a refuge for Muslim Brotherhood members and maintained unofficial relations with Iran as part of a foreign policy designed to assert independence of

Riyadh.[59] Saudi Arabia and its allies justified their move by pointing to reports that Qatar's ruler, Emir Tamim, expressed sympathy for Iran, Hizballah, and Hamas. According to one deep analysis of allegations about Emir Tamim, they were a piece of digital disinformation planted at the behest of the United Arab Emirates.[60] The anti-Qatar coalition members wanted to smash the Brotherhood. The Egyptian military regime had overthrown the country's elected Muslim Brother president in 2013; leaders in the United Arab Emirates and Saudi Arabia considered the Brotherhood a source for domestic unrest. The boycott ended in failure in 2020: Qatar did not yield to the coalition's demands to shutter the Al-Jazeera satellite television network and expel members of the Muslim Brotherhood. In one respect, the boycott backfired: Qatar developed closer relations with Iran.

Another attempt to fight Iranian influence failed as well. In November 2017, the prime minister of Lebanon, Saad al-Hariri, visited Riyadh at the invitation of Muhammad ibn Salman, with the understanding they would discuss a new aid package. Instead, Saudi security agents confined and rough handled him, apparently to get him to announce his resignation. The aim of detaining the prime minister was allegedly to incite conflict between Lebanese Sunni Muslims loyal to him and Hizballah, as a way to end Iranian influence in Lebanon. The ham-fisted plot only convinced the outside world the new Saudi leadership was erratic.[61]

When Donald Trump became president of the United States in 2017, the Saudis had reason to expect a notable shift in Washington's policy. He made Riyadh the destination for his first trip abroad and announced agreement on a lucrative arms deal. Secretary of State Rex Tillerson, former chief executive officer at ExxonMobil, described a common US–Saudi vision of economic and strategic cooperation, including support for Saudi Arabia's military intervention in Yemen. The Saudi leadership was relieved that Trump abandoned the Obama administration's concern about human rights. President Trump's decision to withdraw from the Iran nuclear agreement in 2018 was welcomed in Riyadh as a sign that the US was ready to roll back Tehran's influence in the region. Trump disappointed Riyadh when he did not take action to match his bellicose rhetoric. On September 14, 2019, Iran carried out a drone and missile attack on Saudi oil installations that knocked out half of its oil production capacity, but Trump did not authorize retaliation against Iranian targets.[62] The Trump administration shared with the Obama administration the view of Saudi Arabia as a customer for massive arms purchases: close to $140 billion during Obama's presidency.[63] The newest weapons, however, did not translate to military power or security, as demonstrated by Riyadh's fumbling intervention in Yemen. And Trump was no more eager for military intervention than Obama.

The outlook for relations with the United States changed when Joseph Biden was elected president in 2020. During the election campaign, he referred to Saudi Arabia as a pariah because of the government's alleged complicity in Jamal Khashoggi's murder. Weeks after Biden's inauguration as president, he announced the US was ending support for Riyadh's war in Yemen. There was less to the new policy than met the eye because Biden promised to support Saudi Arabia against terrorist and regional threats and therefore continued to supply military equipment to the Saudis and their partner in the conflict, the United Arab Emirates. The Biden administration attempted to revive the Iran nuclear agreement, but talks to that end foundered. Nevertheless, strains between Washington and Riyadh worsened in spring 2022, when OPEC announced production cuts that pushed up oil prices at a time the United States (and the global economy in general) was struggling with inflation.

The Saudi leadership decided to pursue new lines in foreign relations to contain rivalry with Iran. In 2021 and 2022, the governments of Oman and Iraq facilitated meetings between Saudi and Iranian officials to explore the possibility of restoring diplomatic relations and ways to stabilize the region. During a visit to Riyadh for an Arab–

China summit in December 2022, President Xi Jinping suggested that the Saudis and the Iranians hold talks in Beijing. The time was ripe for both countries, and they sent officials for talks in the first week of March 2023, resulting in the Joint Trilateral Statement announcing their agreement to restore diplomatic relations.[64] While the United States perceived China's role as encroachment on its sphere of influence, Iran's mistrust of Washington meant that another country would have to mediate a rapprochement, and China was ready to step in. Riyadh and Tehran exchanged ambassadors and cooperated on removing obstacles to Iranians wishing to perform the pilgrimage. Whether détente would result in commercial and cultural contacts or cooperation on regional security was an open question.[65]

In early 2023, Saudi Arabia made a dramatic offer to the United States to normalize relations with Israel on two conditions. First, Israel would have to make a firm commitment to implementing a two-state solution to its conflict with the Palestinians. Second, the United States would have to upgrade its commitment to Saudi Arabia's security and assist it to develop a civilian nuclear energy program. Such an agreement had the potential to establish a strategic security alignment that would resolve the Palestinian–Israeli conflict and solidify the front of Egypt, Jordan, Israel, the GCC, and the United States against Iran and the Muslim Brotherhood. Saudi Arabia's integration into the United States' global security order would be deeper than ever.[66]

The prospects for Saudi Arabia to normalize relations with Israel were damaged by the terrorist attack against Israel carried out by Hamas on October 7, 2023, and the subsequent war in Gaza. Hamas terrorists massacred 1,200 Israelis and took around 250 hostages back to Gaza. Israel then invaded Gaza in a campaign to destroy Hamas, and the Palestinian organization went underground, using hundreds of miles of tunnels to elude Israeli forces and hide the hostages. In a year of fighting, the war took the lives of around 40,000 Palestinians in Gaza and 400 Israeli soldiers. Israeli shelling and bombardment created a humanitarian disaster and reduced most of Gaza to rubble. Qatar, Egypt, and the United States attempted to arrange a ceasefire and the release of hostages (they achieved a tenuous agreement in late January 2025). At the regional level, support for Hamas from Iran, Hizballah, the Houthis, and pro-Iranian militias in Iraq threatened to turn the Gaza conflict into a regional war. The Houthis attacked commercial shipping in the Red Sea and fired missiles against Israel. Clashes between Hizballah and Israel flared on the Israel–Lebanon border. Israel killed Hamas, Hizballah, and Iranian commanders in Lebanon and Syria. In April 2024, Iran launched a large missile attack against Israel, rendered ineffective by its antimissile shield. In the next few months, Israeli military forces killed the leaders of Hamas and Hizballah and inflicted heavy damage on Hizballah. A dramatic side effect of the war came at the end of 2024, when the Asad regime in Damascus suddenly collapsed in the face of an offensive by Syrian rebel forces. Israel's battering of Hizballah and Iran had whittled away Asad's external support and exposed his regime's hollowness. Asad's fall may end Iranian influence in the Levant and set the stage for a new constellation of powers. What course events in Syria would take and how it would affect Riyadh's strategic position were impossible to foresee. In the broader scope of Saudi Arabia's position in the global arena, Donald Trump's return to the White House for a second term in 2025 makes it appear likely that Saudi–US relations will remain centered on strategic security for Riyadh and energy security for Washington.

Epilogue

In the twenty-first century, it was becoming clear that the volatility of oil prices, the prospect of falling demand for oil in the global economy, and strains on the budget imposed by mass public-sector employment could erode the monarchy's position. Under King Salman and his son Muhammad, government planners and Western consultants devised a new formula to legitimize dynastic power that celebrated youth, technology, creativity, and the promise of a prosperous future where Saudi Arabia would become an advanced economy, a regional power, a society open to artistic expression, providing abundant outlets for diversion and entertainment, and, perhaps above all, a country on par with global leaders in the G20.[1] The country would shake loose from its subordinate place in the world and become the author of its destiny. In this scenario, the state would become efficient, step away from its position as the economy's dominant investor and employer, end dependence on foreign workers, and retreat from transnational religious solidarity. The king and his son liberated public space from religious oversight and severed the monarchy's perennial alliance with transnational revivalist currents. In Saudi Arabia's culture war dating to the annexation of Hijaz, the modernists prevailed. If the government stays the course,

Wahhabi doctrine will become a part of national heritage, and perhaps reshaped into moderate Islam for the pulpits and the schoolbooks. It seems the implication of Saudi Vision 2030 is that the citizenry will be so grateful for being able to enjoy relief from puritanical restrictions that they will overlook the reign of surveillance, digital disruption, and repression against calls for rights and accountability. The megaprojects spurring a construction boom mean that it will be some time before the country can possibly dispense with expatriate workers. With a few years remaining before the benchmark year of 2030, two elements in the kingdom's history remain constant: absolute power for the palace and close alignment with the United States. At the same time, a persistent historical pattern is the way dynastic plans have encountered pockets of dissent and unintentionally produced new challengers. For all the power and wealth on the side of the monarchy, ordinary Saudis will have a hand in their country's future.

Timeline

1741	Muhammad ibn Abd al-Wahhab begins religious reform mission
1744/5	Muhammad ibn Abd al-Wahhab moves to Diriyya
1745–1811	The Diriyya emirate
1811–18	Mehmet Ali Pasha's invasion and destruction of Diriyya emirate
1824–38	Restoration of Saudi power at Riyadh
1838–43	Mehmet Ali Pasha's invasion and occupation of Najd
1843–91	Second restoration of Saudi power at Riyadh
1891	Fall of Riyadh emirate
1902	Recapture of Riyadh
1924	Conquest of Mecca
1930	Suppression of the Brethren rebellion
1932	Declaration of the Kingdom of Saudi Arabia
1933	Oil concession agreement
1943	US extends Lend-Lease assistance to Saudi Arabia
1953	Major labor protest against US oil company
1962	Ten-Point Program for National Development
1973–4	Oil revolution

TIMELINE

1979	Iranian revolution
	Uprisings in Mecca and the Eastern Province
1980–8	Jihad against Soviet forces in Afghanistan
	Iran–Iraq War
1990–1	Kuwait crisis
2001	Al Qaeda attacks on the United States
2003	US invasion of Iraq
2003–7	Al Qaeda in the Arabian Peninsula terrorist wave
2011	Arab uprisings
2016	Announcement of Saudi Vision 2030
2017	King Salman names his son Muhammad the heir to the throne

Endnotes

Introduction

1. Hanna Ziady, "Jamie Dimon and other top bankers visit Saudi Arabia as Israel-Hamas war rages." October 24, 2023. CNN Business. https://www.cnn.com/2023/10/24/investing/saudi-davos-in-the-desert-jamie-dimon/index.html, accessed September 17, 2024.
2. On the accumulation of external resources by empires, Frederick Cooper and Jane Burbank, *Empires in World History: Power and the Politics of Difference*, Princeton, NJ: Princeton University Press, 2010, 9.

1 Old Najd

1. For discussion of the elastic meanings of "tribe," see Dale Eickelman, *The Middle East and Central Asia: An Anthropological Approach*, fourth edition, Englewood Cliffs, NJ: Prentice Hall, 2002, 115–39; Richard Tapper's introduction to his edited volume, *The Conflict of Tribe and State in Iran and Afghanistan*, London: Croom Helm, 1983; Philip S. Khoury and Joseph Kostiner, *Tribes and State Formation in the Middle East.*
2. From north to south, there are eight districts on the eastern slope: al-Sudair, al-Mihmal, al-Shaʿib, al-Arid (Riyadh and Diriyya), al-Kharj, al-Furʿ, al-Aflaj, and Wadi al-Dawasir. On the northwest slope is a densely populated district, al-Washm. Just beyond the northern end of the Tuwaiq Ridge is al-Qasim, a region of oases fed by the extensive Wadi al-Rummah network that drains smaller wadis throughout northern Najd. The Shammar Mountain is the northernmost part of Najd, bounded by the Nafud sands. Uwaidah M. Al-Juhany, *Najd before the Salafi Reform Movement*, 24–31.
3. Juhany, 35–7.
4. Juhany, 35–6.

5. Muhammad A.H. Abdallah, "Climate Fluctuation and Natural Disasters in Arabia between Mid-17th and Early 20th Centuries," *GeoJournal* 37:1 (September 1995): 176–80. "Hijri" refers to the Islamic calendar.
6. On different techniques in runoff farming, see Benjamin Reilly, *Slavery, Agriculture, and Malaria in the Arabian Peninsula*, 31–7; Saad Abdullah Sowayan, *Nabati Poetry: The Oral Poetry of Arabia*, 19.
7. For different techniques that were used to draw water from wells, see Reilly, 43–7; Sowayan, 19.
8. Jérémie Schiettecatte and Abdulaziz Alghazzi, *Al-Kharj: Report on Two Excavation Seasons in the Oasis of Al-Kharj, Saudi Arabia, 2011–2012*, Riyadh, 2016, 89–91.
9. Reilly, 26.
10. Eickelman, 64. Some Bedouin were semi-nomads who combined raising livestock with cultivation. Studies of specific Bedouin tribes demonstrate variation in ecology, herding practices, and social organization. A monograph about the Al Murrah in the Empty Quarter is Donald Powell Cole, *Nomads of the Nomads*. A monograph about the Rwala in the north and straddling the border with Syria is William Lancaster, *The Rwala Bedouin Today*.
11. For background on the history of nomadism's early development in the Middle East, Beatrice Forbes Manz, *Nomads in the Middle East*, Cambridge: Cambridge University Press, 2021, 3–27.
12. Sowayan, 31. On the gender division of labor in a modern Bedouin tribe, Lancaster, 70–1; Cole, *Nomads*, 37–8, 64.
13. Sowayan, 38.
14. Alexei Vassiliev, *The History of Saudi Arabia*, 35.
15. For a discussion of conceptions of the tribe in Arabia, Eickelman, 65, 75–7.
16. Sowayan, 23.
17. Sowayan, 38–44.
18. Sowayan, 21–4.
19. Marcel Kurpershoek, *Arabian Satire: Poetry from 18th-Century Najd*, 91, vv. 18–23.
20. Michael Cook, "The Historians of Pre-Wahhabi Najd," *Studia Islamica* 76 (1992): 163–76; Juhany, 4–9.
21. Eickelman, 117; Lancaster, 24–35.
22. Abdulaziz H. Al-Fahad, "The *Imama vs.* the *Iqal*: *Hadari*–Bedouin Conflict in the Formation of the Saudi State," in *Counter-Narratives: History, Contemporary Society, and Politics in Saudi Arabia and Yemen*, edited by Madawi Al-Rasheed and Robert Vitalis, New York: Palgrave Macmillan, 2004, 38–9.
23. On the nuances of gender relations based on modern ethnographic observation, Lancaster, 58–72.
24. Juhany, 95–6.
25. Reilly, 50–3, 66–70.
26. Juhany (95) indicates control over land in emirates rested with dominant clans.
27. The evidence about control over land and fighting manpower suggests the emirs of Najd considered trade a lucrative source for taxation, not that the emirs were traders, in contrast to Gulf coast emirs who were merchants. Humaidan's poetry describes honorable and dishonorable merchants. There is no hint that they were oasis emirs. Kurpershoek, 43–5.

28. Kurpershoek, 47–9.
29. Juhany, 96–100. See below on this dynamic at work in the history of the Saud clan.
30. Juhany, 99–100.
31. Lancaster, 73–7, 87, 128–31.
32. Juhany, 146. His count for conflicts in Najd covers the period from 1690 to 1736.
33. Abdullah Al-Askar, *Al-Yamama in the Early Islamic Era*, 3.
34. Askar, 67–8. Adversaries of the Wahhabi mission used the association to discredit it as just another Najdi heresy.
35. W. Montgomery Watt, "Musaylima," in P. Bearman (ed.), *Encyclopaedia of Islam New Edition Online (EI-2 English).* https://referenceworks.brill.com/display/db/eieo.
36. Askar, 68–72. The Kharijite leader was Najda ibn ʿAmir.
37. Juhany, 42–7; W. Madelung, "Al-Ukhaydir," in Bearman (ed.), *Encyclopaedia of Islam New Edition Online.*
38. Juhany, 144–8.
39. Juhany, 148–9. These outcomes were obtained at different times during the initial Saudi expansion.
40. Juhany, 150–2, mentions Uyaina, Tharmada, Dilam, Julajil, and Unaiza.
41. Juhany, 92, 105–8.
42. Abdallah, "Climate Fluctuation," 176–8.
43. Juhany, 92, 103–5.
44. A. Kevin Reinhart, "On Sunni Sectarianism," in *Living Islamic History: Studies in Honour of Professor Carole Hillenbrand*, edited by Yasir Suleiman and Adel Al-Abdul Jader, Edinburgh: Edinburgh University Press, 2010.
45. James Grehan, *The Twilight of the Saints*, New York: Oxford University Press, 2014, 14–19. He applies the concept to his study of the Syria–Palestine region in the late Ottoman period. To anticipate a later historical phase, Wahhabi proselytizing (the "export of Wahhabism") was an extension of a sectarian campaign against agrarian religion's tolerance for non-canonical customs.
46. Juhany, 128–9.
47. For examples of non-canonical customs in Najd, Juhany, 153–4. With respect to Ottoman Syria, the focus of Grehan's study, Muslims, Christians, and Jews shared customs because they lived in villages too poor to afford fulltime religious specialists (ulama, priests, and rabbis) and religious structures (mosques, churches, and synagogues). Grehan, 20–61.
48. For an extensive discussion of scholastic treatises condemning innovations, Maribel Fierro, "The Treatises against Innovations (*kutub al-bidaʿ*)," *Der Islam* 69:2 (1992): 204–46.
49. Reinhart, 216.
50. Reinhart, 212. The Wahhabi mission is an expression of the sectarian attitude.
51. Grehan notes it was the advent of modern conditions, primarily urbanization and mass literacy, that sounded the death knell of agrarian religion because its economic and social foundations dissolved. In later chapters, we will see how the sectarian Wahhabi mission contributed to and adapted to the decline of agrarian religion. Grehan, 196–208.

2 The Diriyya Emirate: A Sectarian Empire, 1744–1818

1. Emphasis in original. Rodney Stark and William Sims Bainbridge, "Of Churches, Sects and Cults: Preliminary Concepts for a Theory of Religious Movements," *Journal for the Scientific Study of Religion*, 18:2 (1979): 117–33; citation on 125.
2. For analysis of Muhammad ibn Abd al-Wahhab in the framework of a scholastic interpretive tradition, Samira Haj, *Reconfiguring Islamic Tradition: Reform, Rationality, and Modernity*, Stanford, CA: Stanford University Press, 2008.
3. Cole M. Bunzel, *Wahhabism*, 128–45. His thorough analysis identifies the points where Ibn Abd al-Wahhab follows and departs from Ibn Taimiyya.
4. Cole Bunzel presents a persuasive interpretation of his teachings that underscores the definition of monotheism (*tawhid*) to include excommunication, exhibiting enmity toward infidels, and waging jihad. Bunzel, *Wahhabism*, 127. Michael Crawford, *Ibn Abd al-Wahhab*, gives an overview of Shaikh Muhammad's writings, 48–58. For summaries of his main treatises, Abd Allah Salih Uthaymin, *Muhammad ibn ʿAbd al-Wahhab: The Man and His Works*, London: I.B. Tauris, 2009.
5. Bunzel, 145–62. For Crawford's discussion of *takfir* and how later Wahhabis relented on collective excommunication, 61–5; on secondary excommunication and the duty to emigrate, 65–9.
6. Crawford, 59.
7. Bunzel, 162–73.
8. Bunzel (173–85) compares the positions of Shaikh Muhammad and Ibn Taimiyya on jihad. Crawford discusses jihad, 69–71.
9. Crawford, 37–8.
10. Crawford, 74.
11. Crawford, 85.
12. Crawford, 86–8.
13. Crawford, 76–80. The Bedouin denied women a share in inheritance in contrast to Islamic law that assigns female heirs half the share of a male heir.
14. Nabil Mouline sees a direct line from Hanbali teachings to the Wahhabi mission. Nabil Mouline, *The Clerics of Islam*. For Hanbali critics of the mission, David Commins, "Traditional Anti-Wahhabi Hanbalism in Nineteenth-Century Arabia," in *Ottoman Reform and Muslim Regeneration: Studies in Honour of Butrus Abu-Manneh*, edited by Itzchak Weismann and Fruma Zachs, London: I.B. Tauris, 2005.
15. For the idea that Wahhabism was part of a wave of religious reform in the eighteenth century and a critique of that idea, Ahmad S. Dallal, *Islam without Europe: Traditions of Reform in Eighteenth-Century Islamic Thought*, 20–55, Chapel Hill, NC: University of North Carolina Press, 2018.
16. We know very little about when Shaikh Muhammad studied at these places or for how long. Bunzel, 33–6; Crawford, 23–6.
17. Bunzel, 41, 63.
18. According to some sources, Ibn Abd al-Wahhab's father disapproved of his views. Bunzel, 39. Crawford, 28–9.
19. Crawford, 30–2; Bunzel, 42–3.

20. Bunzel, 43–4, 48. The mission's adversaries liked to cite a Prophetic tradition from the Sahih Collection of Muslim ibn al-Hajjaj, *Kitāb al-fitan wa-ashrāṭ al-sāʿa*, number 2905: *Bāb al-fitan min al-mashriq min ḥayth yaṭlaʿu qarn al-shayṭān*. "The turmoil would appear from this side [the east]; verily, the turmoil would appear from this side; verily, the turmoil would appear from this side - the side where appear the horns of Satan."
21. Bunzel, 56–8; Crawford, 31.
22. Emine O. Evered, "Rereading Ottoman Accounts of Wahhabism as Alternative Narratives: Ahmed Cevdet Pasa's Historical Survey of the Movement," *Comparative Studies of South Asia, Africa and the Middle East* 32:3 (2012): 625.
23. Bunzel, 76–8. David Commins, *The Mission*, 22–4.
24. Bunzel, 75–9.
25. Bunzel, 63–4.
26. On Ottoman views, Evered, 626. For a summary of anti-Wahhabi images, Crawford, 52.
27. Crawford, 32.
28. George S. Rentz, "Muhammad ibn ʿAbd al-Wahhab (1703/4–1792) and the Beginnings of the Unitarian Empire in Arabia," University of California, doctoral dissertation, 1948, 50.
29. The account is in Uthman ibn Bishr's chronicle, composed about a century after Shaikh Muhammad's arrival in Diriyya. Crawford, 35–7. Bunzel, 67, n. 167.
30. For a detailed study of how Saudi forces wore down resistance in one district, see Michael Cook, "The Expansion of the First Saudi State: The Case of Washm," in *The Islamic World from Classical to Modern Times: Essays in Honor of Bernard Lewis*, edited by C.E. Bosworth, et al., Princeton, NJ: Darwin Press, 1989.
31. Bunzel, 200–2.
32. Crawford, 40.
33. Shaikh Muhammad claimed that he resorted to arms only to ward off attacks and that he did not begin to wage jihad until his enemies excommunicated and attacked him. Bunzel, 68, 199. Dahham ibn Dawwas remained a thorn in Diriyya's side for nearly thirty years even though Muhammad ibn Saud helped him rise to power. Rentz, 57–61.
34. On the assassination of Uthman ibn Muʿammar, Crawford, 41–2. The shaikh may have thought that the emir's wavering loyalty made him a hypocrite deserving death.
35. Rentz, 71–2, 76.
36. Rentz, 106–12.
37. Rentz, 133–7.
38. Rentz, 149–56.
39. Rentz, 157–61, 172–4, 183, 187–90. Members of the old ruling clan were expelled.
40. Rentz, 128–31, 150–1, 156, 175–81.
41. At the time, nobody imagined the world's largest oil reserves lay beneath the district.
42. Crawford, 76–88. Bunzel, 211–15.

43. Rentz, 100–3.
44. Rentz, 195–202, 210–14.
45. Samer Traboulsi, "An Early Refutation of Muhammad ibn ʿAbd al-Wahhab's Reformist Views," *Die Welt des Islams*, New Series 42 (2002): 373–415.
46. Crawford, 31, 39.
47. Bunzel, 215–16. Rentz, 183–4, 215–18.
48. Bunzel, 216. Vassiliev, 91–3.
49. Samer Traboulsi, "'I Entered Mecca . . . And I Destroyed All the Tombs': Some Remarks on Saudi–Ottoman Correspondence," in *The Islamic Scholarly Tradition*, edited by M. Bonner and B. Sadeghi, Leiden: Brill, 2011 (citing Ahmad ibn Zayni Dahlan), 203.
50. Traboulsi, 204–11.
51. Traboulsi, 211 n. 51. Vassiliev, 98–105.
52. Bunzel, 213–14. Vassiliev, 93–6.
53. Bunzel, 218–19.
54. Vassiliev, 106–9. David Commins, *The Gulf States: A Modern History*, London: I.B. Tauris, 2012, 70–1. The English East India Company and the ruler of Muscat, Sayyid Sultan, signed a treaty in 1798 pledging mutual support. The treaty was the first in a series of pacts between London and Gulf rulers that converted the Gulf into a British sphere of influence.
55. Michael Crawford refers to Shaikh Muhammad's aim as the establishment of "a regime of godliness," 89–106.
56. Crawford, 93, 97. Neither the Quran nor the Prophetic traditions define political institutions.
57. Crawford, 101. The *bayʿa* doctrine went back to the Prophet Muhammad; the *bayʿa* to a political leader other than the Prophet went back to the first caliph Abu Bakr. E. Tyan, "Bayʿa," in Bearman (ed.), *Encyclopaedia of Islam New Edition Online.*
58. The Saudi chronicles say little about Muhammad ibn Saud. George Rentz suggests that Shaikh Muhammad was the mastermind behind military expansion and that by the early 1800s, few in Diriyya recalled much about the first Saudi emir. Rentz, 116, n. 6.
59. Crawford, 101.
60. Signs of clan dissent appeared well after Shaikh Muhammad's time. In 1810/11, three of Emir Saud's sons were reportedly dissatisfied with their roles and set off on an independent military adventure in the direction of Oman. There were also reports that some of Saud's brothers resented his rule and he had them sent away. Vassiliev, 142.
61. The Saudi chronicles do not explain how Abd al-Aziz became the second emir instead of his brother Abdallah. Shaikh Muhammad announced Saud's succession in 1788.
62. Bunzel, 220–4.
63. Crawford, 102–3.
64. Shaikh Muhammad and members of the Saud married women from Uyaina's Muʿammar clan. Emir Abd al-Aziz married a daughter of Emir Uthman ibn Muʿammar: their son Saud became the leader of the Diriyya emirate. Crawford, 42.

65. One member of Diriyya's Suwailim clan became the governor of Thadiq and a second member of the clan became governor of Mahmal district, with its seat in Huraimila.
66. Sulaiman ibn Ufaisan was the emir of Dilam and later expanded the scope of his authority to Wadi al-Dawasir in the far south when Saudi forces annexed it. In addition, he commanded expeditions to Qatar. Bayly Winder, *Saudi Arabia in the Nineteenth Century*, 21, 30–1, 65. In Qasim, Emir Hujailan led loyalist forces to quell a revolt in 1782 and organized defense against an expedition from Iraq in 1786/7. He was the leader of Saudi forces that conquered Jabal Shammar. Rentz, 175–81, 195–228.
67. Bunzel, 206–7.
68. M.S.M. El-Shaafy, "The Military Organisation of the First Saʿudi State," *The Annual of Leeds University Oriental Society* 7 (1969–73): 61–74; Jerzy Zdanowski, "Military Organization of the Wahhabi Amirates," *New Arabian Studies* 2 (1994): 130–9.
69. For comparative perspective on premodern fiscal practices, Peter F. Bang, "Tributary Empires and the New Fiscal Sociology: Some Comparative Reflections," in *Fiscal Regimes and the Political Economy of Premodern States*, edited by Andrew Monson and Walter Scheidel, Cambridge: Cambridge University Press, 2015, 540–3.
70. Crawford, 36, citing Ibn Bishr. Vassiliev, 113, sees Diriyya as a military machine consuming plunder. On how plunder substituted for taxation in the Roman Republic, Bang, 545.
71. Ibn Ghannam barely mentions the subject. Ibn Bishr wrote that proceeds from plunder far exceeded revenue from the alms tax. Vassiliev, 112. Bunzel, 207.
72. Vassiliev, 113–14.
73. The Saudis imposed punitive terms of surrender for the first time in 1758/9 on the district of Mahmal. Revolts in Sudair in 1780 ended in similar measures.
74. Vassiliev, 116–17. The regular mention of zakat in Saudi chronicles suggests it had importance as a sign of religious legitimation.
75. Vassiliev, 112, 121–2. Hasa's revenues went to maintain defenses, allowances for the governor's retinue and for clerics, and a share reserved for Diriyya.
76. William Facey, *Dirʿiyya*, 48.
77. Facey, *Dirʿiyya*, 80–95.
78. Vassiliev, 118–21.
79. Jorg Determann, *Historiography in Saudi Arabia*, 27–8.
80. A.M. Abu-Hakima, "Ibn Ghannam," in P. Bearman (ed.), *Encyclopaedia of Islam New Edition Online*. Bunzel, 41.
81. Crawford, 78–82. Bunzel, 206. The argument that Diriyya pacified the Bedouin or that they converted to the mission rests on a few mentions in the chronicles. Al-Fahad, "The *Imama vs.* the *Iqal*," 44, 50–1.
82. Eleanor Doumato, *Getting God's Ear*, 40, 127–8, 213–15. The hypothesis is related to Doumato's effort to explain the difference between the greater scope for religious expression in the Gulf before Saudi annexation and in Najd.
83. Hala Fattah argues the emirate was a mercantile enterprise but admits the evidence is insufficient to firmly establish that notion. *The Politics of Regional Trade in Iraq, Arabia, and the Gulf*, Albany, NY: State University of New York Press, 1997, 45–61.

84. Michael Crawford, *The Imam, the Pasha, and the Englishman*, 27–8. F.E. Peters, *Mecca: Literary History of the Muslim Holy Land*, Princeton, NJ: Princeton University Press, 1994, 306, 314, 317. Vassiliev, 143–5.
85. Peters, 319–24. John Lewis Burckhardt, *Notes on the Bedouins and Wahabys: Collected During his Travels in the East*, New York: Johnson Reprint Corp., 1967, 371–2.
86. Vassiliev, 150–5. Peters, 325–7. Crawford, *The Imam*, 44–7. For the story of Emir Abdallah's captivity, transport to Cairo and Istanbul, and public execution, Crawford, *The Imam*, 47–53, 70–110.
87. Vassiliev's survey of Saudi history represents the most ambitious attempt to assemble as much source material as possible to form as full a picture as possible. His assessment of the sources for the emirate's expansion is a sensible summary of factors. On close inspection, however, generalizations about several decades are based on the account in a source for a single year.
88. Paul Dresch's modification of Ibn Khaldun's emphasis on pure tribal solidarity. Dresch, "Imams and Tribes: The Writing and Acting of History in Upper Yemen," in Khoury and Kostiner, 266. Khalid al-Dakhil refutes the application of Ibn Khaldun's concepts to the Diriyya emirate. *Al-Wahhabiyya bayna al-shirk was tasaddu' al-qabiliyya*, Beirut: Al-Shabaka al-Arabiyya li al-Abhath wa al-Nashr, 2013, 22–7.
89. Juhany, 147. Khalid S. Dakhil, "Wahhabism as an Ideology of State Formation," in *Religion and Politics in Saudi Arabia: Wahhabism and the State*, edited by Hasan Kosebalaban and Mohammed Ayoob, Boulder, CO: Lynne Rienner, 2009, 34–5. Al-Fahad, "The *Imama vs.* the *Iqal*," 42–5. Madawi Al-Rasheed, *A History of Saudi Arabia*, 18–22. Other Saudi historians have proposed explanations that cite changes in economic, social, and religious conditions. Determann, *Historiography*, 191–202.
90. For a recent astute discussion of different explanations for Saudi expansion, Leor Halevi, "Arabians for Guns: Wahhabi Matchlocks, World Trade, and the Rise of the First Saudi State," *Journal of the Royal Asiatic Society* Series 3 (2023): 26–42.

3 The Riyadh Emirate: A Sectarian Enclave, 1821–91

1. Winder, 52–6.
2. As if Mehmet Ali's punishments were not enough, Najd witnessed its first cholera epidemic in 1821.
3. Turki was a nephew of Emir Abd al-Aziz.
4. William Facey, *Riyadh, the Old City: From Its Origins until the 1950s*, 122–3. Winder, 56–64.
5. Winder, 29–30, 51, 64–8, 75–9, 81–3.
6. Ibn Bishr reports Turki gave the speech in 1832, at a camp in the Dahna sands while en route from Hasa to Riyadh. Cited in Winder, 85–6. Vassiliev (166) also cites the speech, with different translation.
7. Winder, 65, 83–4, 92–4.
8. Winder, 96–9, 109–20. Faisal's sons Abdallah and Muhammad, and his cousin Jalwi joined him in exile.

9. Winder, 122–3. Mehmet Ali's officials carried out the same measures in Syria in the early 1830s.
10. J.B. Kelly, "Mehemet Ali's Expedition to the Persian Gulf 1837–1840, Part II," *Middle Eastern Studies* 2:1 (Oct. 1965): 53. According to some reports, the Egyptians allowed Faisal to return, supposing he would become a strategic ally. Shortly after regaining Riyadh, Faisal had Ibn Thunayan imprisoned, where guards killed him, reportedly to avenge kinsmen he had put to death. Winder, 131–48.
11. Winder, 157–82.
12. Winder, 185–91.
13. Winder, 191–203.
14. Winder, 238–9. On speculation about Saud's motives, Winder 229–30. Crawford refutes J.B. Kelly's idea that the civil war reflected Wahhabi vs non-Wahhabi Bedouin elements. M.J. Crawford, "Civil War, Foreign Intervention, and the Question of Political Legitimacy: A Nineteenth-Century Saʿudi Qadi's Dilemma," *International Journal of Middle East Studies* 14:3 (1982), 243, citing Kelly, *Britain and the Persian Gulf, 1795–1880*, Oxford: Clarendon Press, 1968, 717. Kelly based his interpretation on William Palgrave's account of his brief visit to Riyadh in 1863.
15. Winder, 245–8.
16. Winder, 248–63.
17. Madawi Al-Rasheed, *Politics in an Arabian Oasis*, 34–6, 40–5, 96–102, 108, 147–52. Michael Baran, "The Rashidi Amirate of Hayl: The Rise, Development and Decline of a Premodern Arabian Principality," University of Michigan, doctoral dissertation, 1992, 41–2.
18. Al-Rasheed, *Politics*, 123–4.
19. Winder, 242–4, 266–78. Al-Rasheed, *Politics*, 153–4.
20. Commins, *The Mission*, 42–5. When Abd al-Rahman ibn Hasan died in 1869, his son Abd al-Latif followed him as leader of the religious estate. Abd al-Rahman ibn Hasan and Abd al-Latif ibn Abd al-Rahman composed numerous treatises and dozens of epistles. When Abd al-Latif died in 1876, there appears to have been a hiatus in Al al-Shaikh leadership until his son Abdallah assumed the role in 1879, which he filled for over forty years until he died in 1922.
21. David Commins, "Contestation and Authority in Wahhabi Polemics," in *Religion and Politics in Saudi Arabia*, edited by Kosebalaban and Ayoob, 41–3.
22. Of Najdi ulama born in the first quarter of the century, ten traveled to study at Riyadh; all of them attended Abd al-Rahman ibn Hasan's lessons; and nine of them became qadis for the Riyadh emirate. Commins, "Contestation," 41–2.
23. Commins, *The Mission*, 45. The "suspicious scholar" was Hasan al-Shatti, a conventional Ottoman Hanbali scholar, meaning he considered Wahhabism a misguided set of teachings. On Hasan al-Shatti's career and anti-Wahhabi writings, see Itzchak Weismann, *Taste of Modernity: Sufism, Salafiyya, and Arabism in Late Ottoman Damascus*, Leiden: Brill, 2001, 65–7.
24. Commins, *The Mission*, 58–61.
25. "There occur among you matters that cause pain for the believers and joy for the hypocrites . . . most of you honor Daud the Iraqi even though he is famous

for enmity toward monotheism and its supporters . . . This man enjoys friendly relations with your town and is accustomed to going there. Among its nobility and dignitaries are some who honor, befriend, and support him, and who accept his specious arguments. The reasons for this are hatred, heretical tendencies, and refusing to accept Allah's light and guidance, which are known in [the Riyadh district]." Commins, *The Mission*, 59.

26. Commins, *The Mission*, 52–8. The full discussion of Unaiza's resistance to Wahhabi conformity is in David Commins, "Why Unayza? Ulema Dissidents and Nonconformists in the Second Saudi State," paper presented at conference on Religion and Society in the Late Ottoman Empire, UCLA, April 12–13, 2002.
27. For a meticulous examination of the debate among Wahhabi clerics and its relationship to the writings of Ibn Taimiya, see Crawford, "Civil War." A summary is in Commins, *The Mission*, 61–4. On the legal discussion of seeking assistance from infidels, Abdulaziz H. Al-Fahad, "From Exclusivism to Accommodation: Doctrinal and Legal Evolution of Wahhabism," *New York University Law Review* 79:2 (May 2004): 500–4. Bunzel, 241–7.
28. Crawford, "Civil War," 232–6.
29. On the dissident shaikh Ibn Ajlan and Abd al-Latif's response, Crawford, "Civil War," 236–8.
30. Bunzel, 250.
31. Commins, *The Mission*, 131–7.
32. Commins, *The Mission*, 144–5. Mouline, 90–2.
33. Buraimi was under the Sudairis from 1857 to 1869. Winder, 190–230. On district-level appointments to the emirate of Mahmal, and the treasurer of Sudair, Winder, 66.
34. Winder, 21. Ibrahim ibn Ufaisan is the builder of Ibrahim Palace in Hofuf, a UNESCO World Heritage Site candidate; he led raids into Qatar in 1790s. Abdallah ibn Ufaisan governed Qatif, Qatar, and Bahrain for Emir Saud. Winder, 30–1. Sulaiman ibn Ufaisan was governor of Kharj. Winder, 65. Muhammad ibn Ufaisan was a military commander for Emir Turki. Winder, 75–8. Umar ibn Muhammad Ufaisan was a military commander for Emir Turki and governor of Kharj, Buraimi, and Hasa. Winder, 61, 65, 75–8, 94 n. 1.
35. Winder, 36, 37 n. 1, 140, 151–2. Ibn Bishr refers to Bilal as Faisal's "ghilam." Uthman ibn Bishr, *Unwan al-majd fi Tarikh najd*, Riyadh: Dar al-Habib, 1999, 2:161. The English traveler William Palgrave also mentions Bilal as the governor of Hasa with his seat at Hofuf. William Gifford Palgrave, *Narrative of a Year's Journey through Central and Eastern Arabia (1862–63)*, vol. 2, reprint edition, London: Macmillan and Co., 1865, 150. Palgrave mentions another slave of Faisal's named Farhat as the governor of the port town of Qatif, vol. 2, 189–90.
36. Faisal's son Saud was governor of Kharj. Faisal's brother was governor of Wadi al-Dawasir. Winder, 152–4, 157.
37. Winder, 157–64. For Jalwi's background, Winder, 52 n. 3. When Turki ibn Abdallah fled Ibrahim Pasha's forces in 1818, he found refuge with a friendly clan in the Ajman tribe and married an Ajman woman. He named the son "Jalwi," which means exile, founding the branch of the family that rose to authority in Hasa, which was part of the Ajman tribe's domain. The common pronunciation of the name is "Jiluwi."

38. Winder, 173. After his visit to Riyadh in 1865, Pelly reported a general distribution of territory between Faisal's sons: the south was under Saud, the north was under Muhammad, and the center was under Abdallah. Winder, 204.
39. Winder, 84–5.
40. The British official Lewis Pelly reported five different arrangements where the variables were payment of taxes or tribute, grazing rights, and military assistance: 1) pay taxes in return for grazing rights or dates; 2) pay taxes and adhere to mutual defense against adversaries; 3) enjoy grazing rights and not have a claim to military support from Riyadh if a tribe that was not aligned with Riyadh attacked them; 4) a nonaggression agreement; 5) pay tribute to Riyadh and no obligation from Riyadh to defend them. Lewis Pelly, "A Visit to the Wahhabee Capital, Central Arabia," *Journal of the Royal Geographical Society of London* 35 (1865): 187. Winder, 206.
41. On reports of tribes not yet adhering to Wahhabism, Lewis Pelly, *Report on a Journey to Riyadh in Central Arabia (1865)*, Cambridge: Oleander/Falcon, 1978 reprint edition, 29–30. Winder, 208.
42. For instance, when Emir Faisal sent military expeditions to punish Bedouin tribes for raids on pilgrim caravans and towns, see Winder, 152–3, 170–2.
43. We have a different set of figures from William Palgrave, who visited in 1863, vol. 2, 84–6. Historians are divided on the veracity of his account. Nonetheless, while his figures are much higher than those reported by Pelly, the ratio of settled and nomadic populations and contributions to the treasury do correspond.
44. That would convert to 6 MT dollars per capita from the settled population and 5.7 MT dollars from Bedouin.
45. Qasim and Sudair each generated 70,000 MT dollars.
46. Qahtan, Utaiba, Mutair, and Dawasir.
47. This may have been a recitation to Pelly of canonical taxation.
48. Pelly, *Report*, 26.
49. Pelly, *Report*, 48–9.
50. Pelly's report includes a table with figures for the population of districts and tribes as well as the revenue raised from them. Pelly, *Report*, Appendix IX, 85–6. Winder, 211–14.
51. Pelly, "A Visit," 188. Winder 208–9.
52. Determann, 30–2. Bunzel, 22–3.
53. Sowayan, 70–1.
54. Sowayan, 72–3.
55. William Ochsenwald, *Religion, Society, and State in Arabia: The Hijaz under Ottoman Control, 1840–1908*, Columbus, OH: Ohio State University Press, 1984, 8.
56. Ochsenwald, 75, 79–80.
57. On the social and economic history of Jeddah, Ulrike Freitag, *A History of Jeddah: The Gate to Mecca in the Nineteenth and Twentieth Centuries*, Cambridge: Cambridge University Press, 2020.
58. A different sharifian clan in Medina held the prestigious post of custodian of the Mosque of the Prophet.
59. Ochsenwald, 60–2, 101–6.
60. Ochsenwald, 41–7.

61. Matthiesen, *Other Saudis*, 29–36.
62. Mattthiesen, 37–40.
63. The Babi movement that burst on the scene in Iran in 1844 and its later offshoot the Bahai religion emerged from Shaikhi tradition.
64. Matthiesen, 40–4.

4 The Opening of Najd, 1902–32

1. Frederick F. Anscombe, *The Ottoman Gulf: The Creation of Kuwait, Saudi Arabia, and Qatar*, New York: Columbia University Press, 1997, 87–90, 155.
2. Vassiliev, 211–13. Standard accounts for the revival of Saudi power in the twentieth century include Leslie J. McLoughlin, *Ibn Saud: Founder of a Kingdom*, New York: St. Martin's Press, 1993; David Howarth, *The Desert King: A Life of Ibn Saud*, New York: McGraw-Hill, 1964.
3. The Ottoman expedition had 2,000 troops, equipped with light artillery seldom seen in Najd. Vassiliev, 214–16.
4. In one battle against the Ottomans, Abd al-Aziz suffered shrapnel wounds. Anscombe, 155–7; Lacey, *The Kingdom*, 77–9; Vassiliev, 216–18; Baran, 147–52.
5. Baran, 153–6; Lacey, 81–2; Vassiliev, 216–21.
6. Vassiliev, 222–3.
7. The British agent at Bahrain was under the authority of the Political Resident for the Gulf.
8. Goldberg argues that the Kuwait meeting changed Abd al-Aziz's strategy. He previously sought assurance of British protection before trying to seize Hasa, but now he decided to seek protection after expelling the Ottomans. Jacob Goldberg, "The 1913 Saudi Occupation of Hasa Reconsidered," *Middle Eastern Studies* 18:1 (Jan. 1982): 25–7. For a biography of Captain Shakespear, see Alan Dillon, *Captain Shakespear: Desert Exploration, Arabian Intrigue, and the Rise of Ibn Saʿud*, Surbiton: Medina Publishing, 2019.
9. Anscombe, 150–61.
10. Goldberg, 25–7; Anscombe, 162.
11. Matthiesen, 45–9.
12. Anscombe, 162.
13. Anscombe, 163–4; Lacey, 113. According to Vassiliev, however, Abd al-Aziz expelled foreign traders from the ports and set the tax on imports at 8 percent.
14. Daniel Silverfarb, "The Anglo-Najd Treaty of December 1915," *Middle Eastern Studies* 16:3 (1980): 169–71; Vassiliev, 327; Lacey, 115–17.
15. Jacob Goldberg, *The Foreign Policy of Saudi Arabia: The Formative Years, 1902–1918*, 136; Joseph Kostiner, *The Making of Saudi Arabia, 1916–1936: From Chieftaincy to Monarchical State*, 14; Lacey, 125.
16. The agreement is known both as the Treaty of Darin and the Treaty of Qatif. At the time, Percy Cox was British Political Resident in the Persian Gulf, the highest-ranking British government official in the region.
17. Kuwait, Bahrain, Qatar, and the Trucial shaikhs.
18. Silverfarb, 172–3; Lacey, 124; Vassiliev, 238. Abd al-Aziz went on the offensive against the Ajman in early 1916 when reinforcements arrived from Riyadh. Vassiliev, 239.
19. Silverfarb, 174.

20. Daniel Silverfarb, "The Philby Mission to Ibn Sa'ud, 1917–18," *Journal of Contemporary History* 14:2 (April 1979): 270.
21. Silverfarb, "Anglo-Najd Treaty," 176, citing Philby, *Arabian Jubilee*.
22. Silverfarb, "The Philby Mission," 269. Silverfarb's article examines different assessments by British officials in the Gulf and Cairo of Abd al-Aziz and Sharif Hussein.
23. The Arabic term for the movement, *Ikhwan*, is commonly used in histories of Saudi Arabia.
24. This discussion of the Brethren relies on John S. Habib, *Ibn Sa'ud's Warriors of Islam*; Kostiner, *The Making of Saudi Arabia*; Christine Moss Helms, *The Cohesion of Saudi Arabia: Evolution of Political Identity*; and Al-Fahad, "The *Imama vs.* the *Iqal*."
25. The first colony at al-Artawiya was in the domain of the Mutair tribe, along the route between Qasim and Kuwait. We do not know who had the idea to settle Bedouin in colonies. Some accounts indicated Abd al-Aziz initiated the scheme in order to domesticate Bedouin tribes. According to other accounts, the idea came from Wahhabi clerics wishing to indoctrinate the Bedouin. Our sources are non-Saudi Arabs (Zirikli and Wahba) who entered Abd al-Aziz's circle years later and British visitors to Riyadh passing along hearsay. For discussion of this question, Habib, 16–24.
26. Roger Webster, "Hijra and the Dissemination of Wahhabi Doctrine in Saudi Arabia," in *Golden Roads: Migration, Pilgrimage, and Travel in Mediaeval and Modern Islam*, edited by Ian Richard Netton, Richmond: Curzon Press, 13.
27. Habib, 42–3.
28. Registers held information for each colony. Habib, 227–8.
29. Habib, 54, 107. Helms, 132–4. Helms suggests mistrust of outsiders may have stemmed from the settlement of tribal sections in their own colonies in their home regions, a practice that reinforced tribal solidarity. Helms, 135–6, citing Ahmed A. Shamekh, *Spatial Patterns of Bedouin Settlement in al-Qasim Region Saudi Arabia*, Lexington, KY: University of Kentucky Press, 1975.
30. Commins, *The Mission*, 85–6. Abd al-Aziz first tried to uproot religious figures spreading extremist beliefs in 1916. Webster, 14. Helms, 132–4. Al-Fahad, 52–5. Abd al-Aziz paid to have a treatise by the Wahhabi cleric Sulaiman ibn Sihman published in Cairo. Cole Bunzel is the first scholar to analyze in detail Ibn Sihman's treatises. *Wahhabism*, 264–6, 274–92, 307–15, 317–21.
31. Habib, 82–3, citing Rihani, *Najd wa mulhaqatihu*, Beirut: Dar al-Rihani, 1964, 434.
32. Bunzel, 310–11. Habib, 81–3. Al-Fahad, 52–3.
33. Habib, 66–7, 79.
34. Al-Fahad, 71 n. 95 and n. 96. He cites Ubayyid, a Qasimi trader who became the prayer leader for the emir of Khurma, Khalid ibn Luway.
35. Al-Rasheed, *Politics*, 56, 63–4; Lacey, 161–2.
36. Al-Rasheed, *Politics*, 224–5.
37. Al-Rasheed, *Politics*, 229–31; Lacey, 161–2.
38. One example of Sharif Hussein's clumsy political touch was his effort to annex the Khurma oasis, located 200 miles east of Mecca. The leader, Khalid ibn Luway, belonged to a minor sharifian clan and considered himself independent of outside authority. During the First World War, he sided with Sharif Hussein's

revolt against the Ottomans, as an ally, not as a subject. Meanwhile, Brethren preachers won converts to the mission, including Khalid. When sharifian forces attempted to gain control over Khurma in May 1919, Khalid inflicted a humiliating defeat on them. Joshua Teitelbaum, *The Rise and Fall of the Hashimite Kingdom of Hijaz*, 254–60; Kostiner, 17–19; Lacey, 147–50. For a concise analysis of how rival claims to religious authority and bidding for support from London affected the contest between Sharif Hussein and Abd al-Aziz, see Haifa Alangari, *The Struggle for Power in Arabia: Abd al-Aziz, Hussein and Great Britain, 1914–1924*, Reading: Ithaca Press, 1998, 191–246.

39. Kostiner, 63–6; Lacey, 185–8.
40. Lacey has Jeddah merchants forming a council to urge Hussein to abdicate, 188–9.
41. Lacey, 190–5.
42. Lacey, 192–3.
43. Medina surrendered to forces commanded by Muhammad ibn Abd al-Aziz, the third oldest son. Lacey, 199–200; Kostiner, 66–70. Adam Mestyan, *Modern Arab Kingship: Remaking the Ottoman Political Order in the Interwar Middle East*, Princeton, NJ: Princeton University Press, 2023, 188. Mestyan traces the diplomatic interactions with London that surrounded changes in the official name of the Saudi realm, from Sultanate of Najd to the Kingdom of Saudi Arabia declared in 1932.
44. Vassiliev, 259–60, 283–6. In the final Saudi military campaign, Abd al-Aziz's two older sons led two prongs of the expedition: Emir Saud led forces into Najran and Emir Faisal led forces into Hodeida.
45. Ash Rossiter, "The Yemeni–Saudi Border: From Boundary to Frontline," in *Yemen and the Gulf States: The Making of a Crisis*, edited by Helen Lackner and Daniel Martin Varisco, Berlin: Gerlach Press, 2018, 30.
46. For a meticulous revisionist analysis of the early history of relations between Saudi Arabia and Iraq, see Joshua Yaphe, *Saudi Arabia and Iraq*, especially for different conceptions of borders 47, 59–60, and for the series of negotiations between 1921 and 1941 to determine Iraq–Saudi Arabia relations, 31–41.
47. H.R.P. Dickson, *Kuwait and Her Neighbours*, London: Allen & Unwin, 1956, 271–80. Helms, 210–11.
48. Helms, 213.
49. Lacey, 196–7.
50. Helms, 219–21.
51. Holmes went to Uqair at the behest of Dr. Alex Mann, a physician Abd al-Aziz engaged on the recommendation of Percy Cox. In 1922, Abd al-Aziz asked Dr. Mann to purchase medical supplies as well as to locate a prospector for oil. Paul Lunde, "A King and a Concession," *Aramco World* 35:3 (May/June 1984).
52. Lacey, 168–72.
53. Daniel Silverfarb, "The Treaty of Jiddah May 1927," *Middle Eastern Studies* 18:3 (1982): 276–7.
54. Silverfarb, "Treaty of Jiddah," 277–80.
55. Suzanne Miers, "Diplomacy versus Humanitarianism: Britain and Consular Manumission in Hijaz, 1921–1936," *Slavery and Abolition* 10:3 (1989): 103.

56. Matthew S. Hopper, "Slaves of One Master: Globalization and the African Diaspora in Arabia in the Age of Empire," in *Indian Ocean Slavery in the Age of Abolition*, edited by Robert Harris et al., New Haven, CT, and London: Yale University Press, 2013, 224, 227.
57. Miers, 110–11. On the tensions between Britain and the Ottoman empire over slavery in Hijaz, see William Ochsenwald, "Muslim–European Conflict in the Hijaz: The Slave Trade Controversy, 1840–1895," *Middle Eastern Studies* 16:1 (Jan. 1980): 115 26. He points out that European powers did not begin the controversy in Hijaz. Instead, it was the attempt by an Ottoman governor in Jeddah to implement an imperial ban on the slave trade that triggered an anti-Western backlash in 1855; 118–19. An overview of slavery and the slave trade in Mecca during the nineteenth century, with excerpts from observations by European travelers, is Peters, 266–79.
58. "Slavery Still Flourishes: European Powers Charged with 'Winking' at Traffic in Arabia and Abyssinia," *The New York Times*, July 3, 1927. The article claims a European consul remarked that the annual traffic in 2,000 slaves a year "doesn't amount to anything anymore."
59. Miers, 117–21.
60. A rare firsthand account of the lives of concubines at the court of the sultan of Oman and Zanzibar in the mid-1800s, Emily Ruete, *Memoirs of an Arabian Princess from Zanzibar*, New York: Marcus Wiener, 1989.
61. Alaine Hutson, "Enslavement and Manumission in Saudi Arabia 1926–38," *Critique: Critical Middle East Studies* 11:1 (Spring 2002): 62–3. It is impossible to know whether the enslaved individuals who appeared at the British consulate were representative of slavery in Saudi Arabia at that time. Nevertheless, the records offer rare glimpses of their lives otherwise absent from historical records.
62. Hutson, 54–66.
63. Hutson, 70.
64. Suzanne Miers, "Slavery and the Slave Trade in Saudi Arabia and the Arab States on the Persian Gulf, 1921 to 1963," in *Abolition and its Aftermath in the Indian Ocean, Africa, and Asia*, edited by Gwyn Campbell, London: Routledge, 2004, 131.
65. Al-Fahad, 54. The British resident in Kuwait, Dickson, observed this difficulty. Helms, 211–12; Kostiner, 85. In the words of a diehard Bedouin warrior, why would "God punish him for 'the killing of [a mere] fifteen Mutayri and three Harbi tribesmen, while not punishing King Abd al-Aziz for the killing of thousands of men?'" Abdulaziz H. Al-Fahad, "Raiders and Traders: A Poet's Lament on the End of the Bedouin Heroic Age," in *Saudi Arabia in Transition*, edited by Bernard Haykel, Thomas Hegghammer, and Stephane Lacroix, Cambridge and New York: Cambridge University Press, 2014, 232–3.
66. Ugo Fabietti, "State Policies and Bedouin Adaptations in Saudi Arabia, 1900–1980," in *The Transformation of Nomadic Society in the Arab East*, edited by Martha Mundy and Basim Musallam, Cambridge: Cambridge University Press, 2000, 84–5; Donald P. Cole, "Where Have the Bedouin Gone?" *Anthropological Quarterly* 76:2 (Spring 2003): 239.
67. Anthony Toth, "Conflict and a Pastoral Economy: The Costs of Akhwan Attacks on Tribes in Iraq, 1922–29," *Critique: Critical Middle Eastern Studies* 11:2 (2002): 205–7.

68. Estimate of losses to Brethren attacks in Iraq, Kuwait, Jordan from 1921 to 1931: 2,200 men and women, 140,000 sheep, 11,200 camels—an undercount since not all losses reached British officials. Toth, 203–4, 224; Anthony B. Toth, "Last Battles of the Bedouin and the Rise of Modern States in Northern Arabia: 1850–1950," in *Nomadic Societies in the Middle East and North Africa: Entering the Twenty-First Century*, edited by Dawn Chatty, Boston, MA: Brill, 2006, 68–70.
69. Dickson, 266–7.
70. Helms, 261–3.
71. Al-Fahad, "The *Imama* vs the *Iqal*," 73 n. 112. On the Ajman resistance to Abd al-Aziz, Habib, 121. Some suspected Iraq's Emir Faisal of plotting with the Mutair leader Faisal al-Duwish to get rid of Abd al-Aziz and take his place. Helms, 238–42.
72. The three leaders were Faisal al-Duwish, Sultan ibn Bijad, and Dhidan ibn Hithlain. Helms, 253; Habib, 122–3. Bunzel (92) cites a fatwa issued by the clerical leaders.
73. An eyewitness account of the raid is in Toth, "Conflict and a Pastoral Economy," 212–14. Abd al-Aziz had protested that the post violated the 1922 Uqair Protocol that prohibited military fortifications in the "vicinity of the border." Neither the 1925 Bahra Agreement nor the March 1927 Jeddah Treaty specified the meaning of "vicinity of the border." Daniel Silverfarb, "Great Britain, Iraq, and Saudi Arabia: The Revolt of the Ikhwan, 1927–1930," *International History Review* 4:2 (May 1982): 222–7. Habib, 125, puts the attack on September 5. For analysis that takes into account multiple perspectives represented by Bedouin tribes in Saudi Arabia and Iraq, the Iraqi and Saudi governments, and British officials, see Yaphe, 44–8, 83–93. His discussion avoids the pitfall of assuming the state is the harbinger of progress and the tribe is a vestige of primitive ways.
74. Habib, 129–35; Helms, 254–6.
75. Silverfarb, "Great Britain," 244–5. There is evidence that British officials did not act in unison and that some cooperated with Iraqi officials to provoke rebellion. Yaphe, 88–91.
76. Habib, 137–41; Helms, 256–9; Lacey, 211–13. There are various accounts of last-minute efforts to avoid battle. After the battle, Sultan ibn Bijad surrendered and went to prison. Faisal al-Duwish suffered serious wounds and was allowed to return to his colony.
77. Habib, 142–4.
78. Lacey, 217–19.
79. Helms, 266–71; Habib, 144–55. Al-Duwish and Ibn Bijad both died in prison.
80. Habib, 151–60.
81. Habib, 141. Published in the April 12, 1929, issue of *Umm al-Qura*, less than two weeks after the battle.
82. Sowayan, 75. For his career, 75–87.
83. Amin al-Rihani, *Ibn Sa'oud of Arabia*, Boston, MA: Houghton Mifflin Company, 1928, 297–9.
84. Ahmad Suba'i, *My Days in Mecca*, edited and translated by Deborah Akers and Abubaker A. Bagader, Boulder, CO: Lynne Riener, 2009. "Suba'i" is the spelling of his name in the published edition of his memoir.
85. Muhammad al-Shamikh, *The Rise of Modern Prose in Saudi Arabia*, Riyadh: King Saud University, 1984, 21–9.

86. Al-Shamikh, 37–47.
87. Known as the *mahjar*.
88. *Beyond the Dunes: An Anthology of Modern Saudi Literature*, edited by Salma Jayyusi, London: I.B. Tauris, 2005, 11–13.
89. Al-Shamikh, 73–4. The Meccan writer Ahmad al-Sibai describes in his memoir the electrifying effect made on him by Amin al-Rihani and Gibran Khalid Gibran. *My Days in Mecca*, 99–100. See below for Rida's influence.
90. Rihani, 285–6.
91. Naif Khalaf Althaqeel, "The Beginning of Theatre in Saudi Arabia," *Performing Islam* 6:1 (2017): 30–1. While Salih was teaching at a school in Bahrain, students staged a historical play about the encounter between the Arabs and the Persian emperor, *An Arab Delegation to Chosroes*.
92. The dissident emirs became known as the *ara'if*, the term for camels recovered years after they were stolen in a raid. Abd al-Aziz arranged matches between three of his sisters and three of the cousins. His favorite sister, Nura, married Saud al-Kabir. Saud's mother belonged to the Hithlain clan, leaders of a powerful section of the Ajman tribe. His marriage to Nura created an affinal relationship between the Ajman and the Abd al-Aziz line in the Saud clan. The Ajman coined the moniker Saud al-Kabir. Lacey, 96–101, 123, 131; Dickson, 259, 415. Alexander Bligh, *From Prince to King*, 17–18.
93. According to some accounts, Muhammad sympathized with the Brethren's religious outlook perhaps because he married the daughter of Sultan ibn Bijad.
94. Bligh, 18–38; Al-Rasheed, *History of Saudi Arabia*, 72–4.
95. Wahba played roles in starting modern schools and representing Riyadh at the Vatican and London. Yasin published the official government newspaper in Mecca. Vassiliev, 299. Adam Mestyan's suggestion of a heavy Ottoman imprint on interwar invention of new Arab monarchies invites attention to the central part that Syrian anti-French activists played in Saudi Arabia's early diplomacy and state consolidation. *Modern Arab Kingship*, 173–201.
96. Mohammed Almana, *Arabia Unified: A Portrait of Ibn Saud*, London: Hutchinson Benham, 1980, 190–1.
97. Nelida Fuccaro, "Between *Imara*, Empire, and Oil: Saudis in the Frontier Society of the Persian Gulf," in *Kingdom without Borders*, edited by Madawi Al-Rasheed, 54–61.
98. Agents in Bahrain produced and dispatched translations of Reuters reports. Rihani, 46; Dickson, 268.
99. Charles Tilly, "How Empires End," in *After Empire*, edited by Karen Barkey and Mark Von Hagen, London: Routledge, 2018, 3–4.
100. Vassiliev, 309.
101. Kostiner, 118.
102. Kostiner, 101.
103. Almana, 181–2. Muhammad Almana served as the court interpreter for nine years. He does not describe the documents. Rasheed speculates they included correspondence with his district heads, tribal chiefs, and the British. *History of Saudi Arabia*, 84.
104. Rihani, 164.

105. Rihani, 125, 133–4; Facey, *Riyadh*, 245, 250, provides a similar description by a British visitor to the court in 1920.
106. Rihani, 154–6.
107. That amount was roughly the expenditure in 1911 of Wolverhampton, UK, a city of 160,000. Correspondence with Professor Nicky Tynan.
108. An overview of the scant evidence for taxation during this period is in Helms, 161–71; Vassiliev, 303–6; Rasheed, *History of Saudi Arabia*, 89.
109. Figures for the number of pilgrims represent very rough estimates. There is a discussion of "counting" pilgrims in David Long, *The Hajj Today*, Albany, NY: State University of New York Press, 1979, 125–6. His table on 127–8 divides the pilgrims between those who arrived by sea and by land. It is not clear how many of the latter came from other countries. William Ochsenwald modifies Long's table, "Islam and Loyalty in the Saudi Hijaz, 1926–1939," *Die Welt des Islams* 47:1 (2007): 12.
110. Peter Sluglett and Marion Farouk-Sluglett, "The Precarious Monarchy: Britain, Abd al-Aziz ibn Saud and the Establishment of the Kingdom of Hijaz, Najd and its Dependencies, 1925–1932," in *State, Society, and Economy in Saudi Arabia*, edited by Niblock, 46–7. The Slugletts use figures from British government documents. There are no records for a regular budget before 1934. Joshua Yaphe's discussion of fiscal strains examines taxation of Bedouin and the possibility that district authorities accepted plundered livestock as payment for the zakat. *Saudi Arabia and Iraq*, 101–5.
111. Doumato, 103–4, citing Philby.
112. Commins, *The Mission*, 93. On the appointments to positions in Mecca, see Nadav Samin, "Saudi Primary Education and the Formation of Modern Wahhabism," *Die Welt des Islams* New Series 58 (2018): 448.
113. An excellent recapitulation of this theme in the history of Wahhabism is in Al-Fahad, "From Exclusivism to Accommodation."
114. Hafiz Wahba, *Arabian Days*, London: A. Barker, 1964, 57–60, 132.
115. Wahba, 54–5.
116. Guido Steinberg, "The Shiites in the Eastern Province of Saudi Arabia (Al-Ahsa'), 1913–1953," in *The Twelver Shia in Modern Times: Religious Culture and Political History*, edited by Rainer Brunner and Werner Ende, Leiden: Brill, 2001, 245–8.
117. Habib, 38.
118. Steinberg, 248–54. On the uprising in Awwamiya in late 1929, see Matthiesen, *The Other Saudis*, 50–2.
119. Mark J.R. Sedgwick, "Saudi Sufis: Compromise in the Hijaz, 1925–1940," *Die Welt des Islams* New Series 37:3 (1997): 349–68.
120. William Ochsenwald, "Islam and Loyalty in the Saudi Hijaz," *Die Welt des Islams* New Series 47:1 (2007): 21–4. On the reaction of Shiites outside Saudi Arabia to the destruction of ornamentation over tombs in a venerated cemetery in Medina, see Werner Ende, "The *Nakhawila*, a Shiite Community in Medina Past and Present," *Die Welt des Islams* New Series 37:3 (1997): 265–6, 284, 318.
121. During the 1926 pilgrimage, the Brethren brawled with Egyptian pilgrims for playing bugles during the ceremonial draping of the Kaaba. Habib, 115–18. D. Van der Meulen, *The Wells of Abd al-Aziz*, London: John Murray, 1957, 104–5.

For descriptions of the pilgrimage business in the nineteenth century, with excerpts from travelers' accounts, Peters, 256–7, 262–3, 284–5.

122. Ochsenwald, "Islam and Loyalty," 10–18, 26–7.
123. Ahmad A. Nasr and Abu Bakar A. Bagader, "Al-Ges: Women's Festival and Drama in Mecca," *Journal of Folklore Research* 38:3 (Sept.–Dec. 2001): 243–62. Ulrike Freitag, "Playing with Gender: The Carnival of *al-Qays* in Jeddah," in *Women and the City, Women in the City: A Gendered Perspective on Ottoman Urban History*, edited by Nazan Maksudyan, New York and Oxford: Berghahn Books, 2014, 71–85. Hamza Bogary, *The Sheltered Quarter: A Tale of a Boyhood in Mecca*, translated by Olive E. Kenny and Jeremy Reed, Austin, TX: Center for Middle East Studies, University of Texas, 1991, 93.
124. Farquhar, *Circuits of Faith*, 48–9, 55–6; Samin, "Saudi Primary Education," 449–50.
125. Wahba, 49–51.
126. *The Book of God's Unity* and a commentary on it by Shaikh Muhammad's grandson.
127. A number of the Scholastic Institute's directors and teachers came from Rashid Rida's circle. Henri Lauziere, *The Making of Salafism*, 71–9, 92; Farquhar, 50–6.
128. The definitive study on the subject is Michael Cook, *Commanding Right and Forbidding Wrong in Islamic Thought*, Cambridge: Cambridge University Press, 2001. On the duty's minor place in Wahhabi writings, 169–75. On its implementation in Mecca in the early 1800s, 168 and n. 18. On the Riyadh emirate, 175–9. The verse in the Quran is 3:104. In A.J. Arberry's translation, "Let there be one nation of you, calling to good, and bidding to honor, and forbidding dishonour." One version of the hadith is, "Whoever sees a wrong and is able to put it right with his hand, let him do so; if can't, then with his tongue; if he can't, then with his heart, which is the bare minimum of faith." Cook, 33.
129. Cook, 181–4, identified the first specific information about such committees as a 1926 announcement in the official newspaper. Mouline, 207–9. Ayman al-Yassini indicates there were committees in Najd and Hasa before the conquest of Hijaz. *Religion and State in the Kingdom of Saudi Arabia*, Boulder, CO: Westview Press, 1985, 68–9.
130. *Umm al-Qura*, no. 1, December 12, 1924. *Umm al-Qura*, Mother of Cities, is a nickname for Mecca. Abd al-Aziz put a Syrian adviser, Yusuf Yasin, in charge of *Umm al-Qura*. On Yusuf Yasin's connection to Rashid Rida, see Kostiner, 105.
131. *Umm al-Qura*, no. 27, June 26, 1925. The same point is in no. 59, February 12, 1926. Also see a speech that Abd al-Aziz gave to Indian pilgrims in 1925: *Umm al-Qura*, no. 28, July 10, 1925. He expressed the same idea in his annual address to pilgrims in later years. Muhammad ibn ʿAbd al-Rahman al-Khamis, *ʿInayat al-Malik ʿAbd al-ʿAziz bi-l-ʿaqida al-salafiyya*, Riyadh: al-Amana al-ʿAmma li-l-Ihtifal bi-Murur Miʾat ʿAmm, 1999, 20–2.
132. Lauziere, 62–7.
133. Lauziere, 68, n. 30.
134. Lauziere, 71–9.

135. Published in the United Kingdom as *Ibn Sa'oud of Arabia: His People and His Land*. Rihani had already published a similar work in Arabic.
136. "Rihani Welcome at Ibn Saud's Court," *The Daily Boston Globe*, June 24, 1928, B7.
137. *The New York Times*, April 28, 1928. The reporter, Joseph M. Levy, was born in New Jersey, grew up in Jerusalem, and attended the American University in Beirut. He wrote for the *Times* from 1928 to 1947. Jewish Telegraph Archive notice on his death in 1965. In the article, he refers to the religious current in Najd as Brethrenism.
138. Donald P. Cole and Soraya Altorki, "Was Arabia Tribal? A Reinterpretation of the Pre-Oil Society," *Journal of South Asian and Middle Eastern Studies* 15:1 (Summer 1992): 79–84.
139. J.B. Mackie, "Hasa: An Arabian Oasis," *The Geographical Journal* 63:3 (March 1924): 194–204.
140. Rihani, 180–2. By 1930, car races were on the way to replacing horse racing. Facey, *Riyadh*, 261.
141. Cole, "Where Have the Bedouin Gone?," 241.
142. Ajman, Awazim, and Mutair were the tribes most affected by the blockade.
143. Anthony Toth, "Tribes and Tribulations: Bedouin Losses in the Saudi and Iraqi Struggles over Kuwait's Frontiers, 1921–1933," *British Journal of Middle East Studies* 32:2 (2005): 150–4, 159.
144. Toth, "Tribes and Tribulations," 155–8, 158 n. 55.
145. Hala Fattah, *The Politics of Regional Trade*, 185–94.
146. For a similar picture of how Iraq killed the Bedouin way of life, Toth, "Tribes and Tribulations," 160–6.

5 Petroleum and Its Discontents, 1932–53

1. Cyrus Veeser, "A Forgotten Instrument of Global Capitalism? International Concessions, 1870–1930," *International History Review* 35:5 (October 2013): 1137–40.
2. Veeser, 1141.
3. J.E. Peterson, *Saudi Arabia under Ibn Saud*, 46–51. Irvine Anderson, *Aramco, the United States and Saudi Arabia*, 21–6.
4. Robert Vitalis excavates continuities in labor relations in mineral extraction enterprises, from mining companies that preceded the oil industry to the Saudi oil fields. On the roots of racist operations in the American Southwest, *America's Kingdom*, 42–50; and in Venezuela and Colombia, 55–6. Aramco concocted a version of history that glorifies its role as a benevolent corporation using its private resources for the Saudi public good to put the country on the path to modernization and prosperity. Robert Vitalis dissects the Aramco version with forensic exactitude through a careful, exhaustive reading of private letters and memos from the pens of "Aramcons" and review of United States government documents. His book reveals how public relations specialists on the company's payroll invented the narrative and traces Aramco's efforts to conceal racist practices and attitudes so bold they made American diplomats blush.
5. Ian J. Seccombe, "'A Disgrace to American Enterprise': Italian Labour and the Arabian American Oil Company," *Immigrants and Minorities* 5:3 (1986): 241.

6. I.J. Seccombe & R.I. Lawless, "Foreign Worker Dependence in the Gulf, and the International Oil Companies, 1910–1950," *The International Migration Review* 20:3 (Autumn 1986): 548–74, esp. 550–5.
7. Seccombe and Lawless, 570; Seccombe, 233–8, 241. The earliest reported worker action took place in 1931 in Mecca, where chauffeurs threatened to strike over arrears in pay. The authorities had them arrested and beaten. Yaphe, 203 n. 29.
8. Seccombe, 242–7.
9. Seccombe, 248–51.
10. Seccombe and Lawless, 571.
11. Seccombe, 253–4.
12. Seccombe and Lawless, 571–2.
13. Robert Vitalis, *America's Kingdom*, 153. Had Chaplin heard about the incident, he probably would not have been surprised: following the film's opening in London, the US government obstructed his return, because of his political views, and he spent the next twenty years in Europe.
14. For a compelling account of the 1953 strike and analysis of the oil company's perception of its causes, see Vitalis, 145–53.
15. Suzanne Miers, *Slavery in the Twentieth Century*, 254–5; on slavery in agriculture, Reilly, 24.
16. Miers, *Slavery in the Twentieth Century*, 255.
17. Miers, *Slavery in the Twentieth Century*, 255–60.
18. Miers, *Slavery in the Twentieth Century*, 319–23; on abduction and deceit, 343; on Makran Baluchis to Oman to Saudi trade, Miers, "Slavery and the Slave Trade," 126–7.
19. Marianne Alireza, *At the Drop of a Veil*, Boston, MA: Houghton Mifflin, 1971, 139–40. William Lancaster describes the slaves of the Bedouin tribe he studied as members of the tribe and not particularly obedient to an owner's whims. *The Rwala Bedouin Today*, 12–13, 82–3.
20. Anthony B. Toth, "Last Battles of the Bedouin and the Rise of Modern States in Northern Arabia: 1850–1950," in *Nomadic Societies in the Middle East and North Africa*, edited by Chatty, 71; and Anthony Toth, "Control and Allegiance at the Dawn of the Oil Age: Bedouin, Zakat, and Struggles for Sovereignty in Arabia, 1916–1955," *Middle East Critique* 21:1 (2012) 57–79.
21. Peterson, 71–4.
22. The British government paid for a little more than half of the budget; the balance came from local revenues, the US government, and a loan from the oil company. Peterson, 77–90. In assessing the Saudi budget, a British official estimated that expenses probably comprised five times more than it could expect in revenues, with half the revenues from the pilgrimage, about a quarter each from oil payments and customs, and very little from zakat. Peterson, 86.
23. For the evolution of United States government positions on Saudi Arabia and Aramco as parts of global strategy during the Second World War, Anderson, 199–202.
24. Fred Lawson, "The Iranian Crisis of 1945–46 and the Spiral Model of International Conflict," *International Journal of Middle East Studies* 21:3 (August 1989): 310–11.

25. Peterson, 98. The US Congress established the Lend-Lease program in March 1941, giving the president authority to allocate financial and material assistance to countries he deemed vital to national interest. During the war, the United States delivered nearly $50 billion in goods, of which Saudi Arabia received approximately $20 million. "Lend-Lease," *Encyclopedia Britannica* online.
26. Peterson, 97, 102–4. Abd al-Aziz's meetings with Roosevelt and with Winston Churchill a few days later get a lot of attention in the literature on Saudi Arabian–United States relations. The eyewitness account is a slim book by the first American ambassador to Saudi Arabia, William Alfred Eddy, *F.D.R. Meets Ibn Saud*, New York: American Friends of the Middle East, 1954. No formal agreement issued from the meeting and to celebrate it as a major development is perhaps an exaggeration.
27. James L. Gormly, "Keeping the Door Open in Saudi Arabia: The United States and the Dhahran Airfield, 1945–46," *Diplomatic History* 4:2 (1980): 193–4, 198.
28. Gormly, 199, citing the State-War-Navy Coordinating Committee. Additional statements on the oil interest, Lawson, 311, 314.
29. The British resented what they regarded as American encroachment on their sphere of influence. They welcomed an American presence to reinforce Britain's dominant influence, not to replace it. A point of friction arose from rival ambitions to dominate international civil aviation after the war. Gormly, 195–6. The Americans grew frustrated with British obstruction, but as one Washington official noted, "If we tickle the palms of the foreigners [other than British] with a few billions," we will get our way. Gormly, 190 n. 4. The American carrier, Trans World Airlines (TWA), acquired the contract to operate the civilian part of Dhahran airfield and to assist the establishment of a Saudi carrier. Gormly, 200–2.
30. On the loan, Lawson, 314. On Dhahran airfield, Gormly, 203–5. On how the Cold War shaped Washington's perspective on Saudi Arabia, Anderson, 202–5.
31. Kostiner, 177–83.
32. The May 1931 agreement, Kostiner, 151–2. The one area that the 1936 treaty left unresolved was the status of the neutral zone. Kostiner, 179.
33. Kostiner, 154–8, 165–6, 178–9.
34. H.R.P. Dickson in October 1937. An overview of the official Saudi narrative, of how Abd al-Aziz gave priority to relations with London, his apprehension of Hashemite ambition, and the 1948 war, is in Madawi Al-Rasheed, "Saudi Arabia and the 1948 Palestine War: Beyond Official History," in *The War for Palestine: Rewriting the History of 1948*, edited by Eugene Rogan and Avi Shlaim, Cambridge: Cambridge University Press, 2001, 228–47.
35. Dickson, 389–92.
36. On contacts between Abd al-Aziz and the United States, Maurice Jr. Labelle, "'The Only Thorn': Early Saudi–American Relations and the Question of Palestine, 1945–1949," *Diplomatic History* 35:2 (April 2011): 262–6.
37. Stephanie Cronin, "Tribes, Coups, and Princes: Building a Modern Army in Saudi Arabia," *Middle Eastern Studies* (2013): 14.
38. Labelle, 273–9.
39. Peterson, 20.

40. Vassiliev, 293–4; Steffen Hertog, *Princes, Brokers, and Bureaucrats*, 42. During Dickson's 1937 visit to Riyadh, he observed a palace official give a report on political news from radio broadcasts. Dickson, 393.
41. Vassiliev, 305.
42. Kiren Chaudhry, *The Price of Wealth: Economies and Institutions in the Middle East*, Ithaca, NY: Cornell University Press, 1997, 63–8, 68 n. 47.
43. Hertog, 43. He paid back the loans, unlike Sharif Hussein.
44. Hertog, 42. See Hertog for extensive refutation of Chaudhry's view that a centralized state emerged in this period. Saudi Arabia was not the only Middle East country lacking organized fiscal mechanisms. Iran brought a team of United States experts in the early 1920s to set up a Treasury Department. For the Millspaugh mission, Arthur Millspaugh, *Americans in Persia*, Washington, DC: The Brookings Institution, 1946.
45. Yaphe, 67.
46. Hertog, 42.
47. Cronin, 12–14.
48. Vassiliev, 294; Yaphe, 68; Matthiesen, 53.
49. On governance in the provinces, Vassiliev, 294; Kostiner, 165.
50. Hertog, 41.
51. Hertog, 43.
52. Hertog, 42.
53. Vassiliev, 294–5; Chaudhry, 71–2. In 1933/34, the Saudis invested in new waterworks to improve purity and increase the supply for Jeddah. Peterson, 64–5.
54. Vassiliev, 296; Hertog, 42.
55. Peterson, 59, 67.
56. Hertog 43–4, sees rentierism going back to royal gifts in the late 1940s.
57. Al-Rasheed, *History of Saudi Arabia*, 91, citing Fuad Hamzah.
58. Bunzel, *Wahhabism*, 324–5.
59. *Saudi Arabia Enters the Modern World: Secret U.S. Documents on the Emergence of the Kingdom of Saudi Arabia as a World Power, 1936–1949, Part I*, edited by Ibrahim al-Rashid, Salisbury, NC: Documentary Publications, 1980, 201–3. Anderson, 112–13. Mouline, 118.
60. Salafi means "following the Pious Ancestors," the "founding fathers" of Islam.
61. David Commins, "From Wahhabi to Salafi," in *Saudi Arabia in Transition*, edited by Haykel, Hegghammer, and Lacroix, 155–8; Muhammad Hamid al-Fiqi, *Athar al-daʿwa al-wahhabiyya fi al-islah al-dini wa-l-ʿumrani fi jazirat al-ʿarab wa ghayriha*, Cairo: Matbaʿat al-Nahda, 1935, 6, 33, 43–6.
62. ʿAbdallah ibn ʿAli al-Qasimi, *al-Thawra al-Wahhabiyya*, Cairo: al-Matbaʿa al-Rahmaniyya, 1936, 1, 3.
63. Al-Qasimi, *al-Thawra*, 26, 66. On Wahhabi ulama opposition to wireless telegraphy at the time al-Qasimi was writing, see Wahba, *Arabian Days*, 57–60. Observing the ostensible paradox of positing compatibility between Wahhabism and nationalism, Werner Ende referred to a "mismatch of national consciousness and neo-Hanbalite convictions." Ende, *Arabische Nation und islamische Geschichte. Die Ummayyaden im Urteil arabischer Autoren des 20. Jahrhunderts*, Beirut, 1977, 92. Cited by Hamadi Redissi, "The Refutation of Wahhabism in

Arabic Sources, 1745–1932," in *Kingdom without Borders*, edited by Al-Rasheed, 174–5, n. 57.

64. Grehan, 196–208.
65. Aziz Dawud, *al-Jamʿiyyat al-islamiyyah fi misr wa dawruha fi nashr al-daʿwah al-islamiyyah* (*The Islamic Groups in Egypt and their Role in Spreading the Islamic Call*), Cairo: Al-Zahra li-iʿlam al-ʿArabi, 1992. A separate Sudanese organization inspired by the Egyptian group adopted the same name.
66. Mouline, 208.
67. On the history of the Muslim Brotherhood, Richard P. Mitchell, *The Society of the Muslim Brothers*, Oxford: Oxford University Press, 1993. In the second half of the twentieth century, the Muslim Brotherhood conception of religion, society, and politics became highly influential in the Awakening movement.
68. For studies of how other states in the region subjugated nomadic populations, see Stephanie Cronin, "Re-Interpreting Modern Iran: Tribe and State in the Twentieth Century," *Iranian Studies* 42:3 (2009): 357–88. On Transjordan, Ricardo Bocco, "The Settlement of Pastoral Nomads in the Arab Middle East: International Organizations and Trends in Development Policies, 1950–1990," in *Nomadic Societies*, edited by Chatty, 302–30.
69. Wilfred Thesiger, *Arabian Sands*, New York: E.P. Dutton & Co., 1959, 329–30.
70. Dickson, 355–6.
71. Dickson, 92–6.
72. Dickson, 456–7.
73. Dickson, 405–8.
74. Richard Bulliet, *The Camel and the Wheel*, Cambridge, MA: Harvard University Press, 1975, 87–110.
75. Thesiger, 66.
76. Thesiger, 140.
77. Thesiger, 60.
78. Louis Dame, "From Bahrain to Taif: A Missionary Journey across Arabia," *Moslem World* 23:2 (April 1933): 168.
79. Dickson, 386–7.
80. Dickson, 569–73, citing William Harold Storm, *Whither Arabia*.
81. Thesiger, 233.
82. Alireza, *At the Drop of a Veil*. During a 1952 visit to Kharj district in southern Najd, Daniel van der Meulen, a former Dutch diplomat, described the pursuit of game in cars as the "new way of hunting" that foreign residents in Jeddah had introduced years earlier. D. van der Meulen, *The Wells of Ibn Saud*, London: John Murray, 1957, 209–10.
83. Van der Meulen, 213–16.
84. The old palace was still used by government officials. Facey, *Riyadh*, 272, 291, 302, 311–12.
85. Facey, *Riyadh*, 300, 305–9. Riyadh got an airfield in 1953.
86. Dickson, 569–73, citing Storm, *Whither Arabia*.
87. Nelida Fuccaro, "Introduction: Histories of Oil and Urban Modernity in the Middle East," *Comparative Studies of South Asia, Africa, and the Middle East* 33:1 (2013): 4–5.

88. On his early years, Richard N. Farmer, "Local Entrepreneurship in Saudi Arabia," *Business History Review* 33:1 (1959): 73–86. In 1950, the government moved the provincial seat from Hofuf and Dammam when it created the Eastern Province, which incorporated Hasa into a larger territory that stretches from Oman to Kuwait. Toby Craig Jones, "Rebellion on the Saudi Periphery: Modernity, Marginalization, and the Shiʿa Uprising of 1979," *International Journal of Middle East Studies* 38 (2006): 216.
89. Fuccaro, 5–6. Atef Alshehri and Lulu Almana, "Khobar City Plan and the New Public Space in Saudi Arabia," *Journal of Public Space* 6:1 (2021): 216–24.
90. Jones, *Desert Kingdom*, 139–40. For the Aramco version of the company's role in Saudi Arabia, Wallace Stegner, *Discovery! The Search for Arabian Oil*, Beirut: Middle East Export Press, 1971.
91. Jones, 97–8.
92. George Linabury, "The Creation of Saudi Arabia and the Erosion of Wahhabi Conservatism," in *Religion and Politics in the Middle East*, edited by Michael Curtis, Boulder, CO: Westview Press, 1981, 281.
93. Van der Meulen, 147–8.
94. A first-person account of the first student mission to Egypt, Hasan Naseef, "Memoirs of a Student," in *Beyond the Dunes*, edited by Jayyusi, 456–73.
95. Different accounts trace soccer to the oil company camps in Hasa or to Western sportsmen in Jeddah.
96. David Holden and Richard Johns, *The House of Saud*, 169–70.
97. It later became a daily newspaper in 1953, and in 1959 it was renamed simply *The Land* (*al-Bilad*). Al-Shamikh, 73–4.
98. Al-Shamikh, 81–96.
99. Translations of works from Urdu, Turkish, Japanese, English, and French. *Beyond the Dunes*, edited by Jayyusi, 21–2; Al-Shamikh, 76–8. The interwar press in Hijaz included an outlet for local news and history of Medina, *Madina the Illuminated* (*al-Madina al-Munawwara*), published by Uthman Hafiz starting in 1937. There was also a short-lived joint venture of Meccans and Malays to publish a bilingual newspaper for pilgrims who stayed in Mecca. *The Islamic Call* (*al-Nida al-Islami*) lasted from 1937 to 1938, perhaps until 1941, and was probably the first publication devoted to a non-Arab audience in the kingdom. Al-Shamikh, 77–8.
100. Al-Shamikh, 101–3
101. Al-Shamikh, 106–7.
102. Mansur al-Hazimi, "Introduction," *Beyond the Dunes*, edited by Jayyusi, 20.
103. Al-Shamikh, 111–16.
104. Naif Althaqeel mentions school plays in Medina, Mecca, Jeddah, Ta'if, Hasa, Jizan, and Qunfidha. Naif Khalaf Althaqeel, "The Beginning of Theatre in Saudi Arabia," *Performing Islam* 6:1 (2017): 30–3.
105. This was the school Hasan Naseef attended before his study in Egypt.
106. Althaqeel, 33.
107. For controversy over the introduction of theater in early twentieth-century Damascus, David Commins, *Islamic Reform: Politics and Social Change in Late Ottoman Syria*, New York: Oxford University Press, 1990, 122.
108. Mansour Ben Muhammad al-Khiraiji, *Beyond the Glamour of the Job: Snaps from My Earlier Life*, in *Beyond the Dunes*, edited by Jayyusi, 445–55.

109. Abd al-Aziz al-Rabee', "Memories of a Pliant Child," in *Beyond the Dunes*, edited by Jayyusi, 474–81.
110. Hasan Naseef, "From Memoirs of a Student," in *Beyond the Dunes*, edited by Jayyusi, 456.
111. Dickson, 569–73.

6 Hereditary Monarchy in the Age of Revolution, 1953–70

1. For earlier bodies in Hijaz preceding the council and for early "ministries on paper," Charles W. Harrington, "The Saudi Arabian Council of Ministers," *Middle East Journal* 12:1 (1958): 1–19.
2. Bligh, 56–83. A full account of the contest for power between Saud and Faisal is in Sarah Yizraeli, *The Remaking of Saudi Arabia: The Struggle Between King Saud and Crown Prince Faysal, 1953–1962*. Yizraeli's interpretation aligns with the position that Faisal was a more effective leader.
3. The Arabic slogan *al-wahda, al-hurriyya, wa al-ishtirakiyya* (unity, freedom, and socialism) has a rhyming ring.
4. Malcolm Kerr, *The Arab Cold War, 1958–1964: A Study of Ideology in Politics*, London: Oxford University Press, 1965. Gregory Gause summarizes Malcolm Kerr's analytical frame for the Arab Cold War: "The power of the major protagonists in the Arab cold war was measured in their ability to affect domestic political struggles in neighboring states where weak regimes had trouble controlling their own societies and local players sought regional allies against their own domestic opponents. Non-state actors played major roles. The contending camps themselves were not always united, with tactical alliances crossing what appeared to be the lines of conflict." F. Gregory Gause, III, *Beyond Sectarianism: The New Middle East Cold War*, Washington, DC: Brookings Institution, 2014, 1, 3–4.
5. The emergence of modern political opposition in Saudi Arabia conforms to patterns across the globe, where capitalism and the modern state concentrated and connected populations that created and shared modular forms of protest against grievances, and where the modern state served as both target and fulcrum for mediating demands arising from grievances. Sidney Tarrow, *Power in Movement: Social Movements and Contentious Politics*, third edition, Cambridge: Cambridge University Press, 2011, 71–91.
6. Hertog, 81, considered the opposition movements too small to threaten dynastic rule. For a revisionist account proposing a more robust and widespread leftist movement, see Rosie Bsheer, "A Counterrevolutionary State: Popular Movements and the Making of Saudi Arabia," *Past and Present* 238:1 (2018): 233–77.
7. In 1954 and 1955, more than 200 Palestinians were arrested for labor activism; many of them were deported. John Chalcraft, "Migration and Popular Protest in the Arabian Peninsula and the Gulf," *International Labor and Working Class History* 79 (Spring 2011): 41.
8. Mohammed Turki A. Al-Sudairi, "Marx's Arabian Apostles: The Rise and Fall of the Saudi Communist Movement," *Middle East Journal* 73:3 (Autumn 2019): 446–7; Vassiliev, 339.

9. Toby Matthiesen, "Migration, Minorities, and Radical Networks: Labour Movements and Opposition Groups in Saudi Arabia, 1950–1975," *International Review of Social History* 59 (2014): 478.
10. Matthiesen, "Migration," 480–2. For a discussion of the network of activists, merchants, and writers as an expression of urban civic engagement, see Claudia Ghrawi, "In the Service of the Whole Community? Civic Engagement in Saudi Arabia (1950s–1960s)," Jadaliyya.com, May 6, 2015.
11. Jones, 149.
12. Jones, 141.
13. Jones, 143–4, 161–5, 170.
14. Jones, 151–8.
15. Toby Matthiesen, "Centre–Periphery Relations and the Emergence of a Public Sphere in Saudi Arabia: The Municipal Elections in the Eastern Province, 1954–1960," *British Journal of Middle Eastern Studies* (2014): 3–7. The reason for the government's decision to hold elections is not known.
16. Matthiesen, "Centre–Periphery," 11–13.
17. Vassiliev, 160–1. On Ibn Muʿammar, Vitalis, 161–2, citing US government reports.
18. Vitalis, 159–60, citing US government reports and investigation by the US Air Force Office of Special Investigations.
19. Claudi Ghrawi, "Structural and Physical Violence in Saudi Arabian Oil Towns," in *Urban Violence in the Middle East: Changing Cityscapes in the Transition from Empire to Nation*, edited by Ulrike Freitag et al., New York: Berghahn Books, 2015, 254–6. Vitalis, 182–4, citing US government reports; Matthiesen, "Migration, Minorities, and Radical Networks," 489–91. The harsh repression in 1953 and later years contradicts the idea that King Saud represented a progressive alternative to Faisal.
20. On Baathist activism in the 1960s, see Claudia Ghrawi, "A Tamed Urban Revolution? The 1967 Riots in Saudi Arabia's Oil Conurbation," in *Violence and the City in the Modern Middle East*, edited by Nelida Fuccaro, Stanford, CA: Stanford University Press, 2016, 14. On Saudi Baathists, their tribulations with arrests, imprisonment, and deaths, Matthiesen, "Migration, Minorities, and Radical Networks," 494–7.
21. Matthiesen, "Migration, Minorities, and Radical Networks," 492–3.
22. Vassiliev, 368.
23. For an interim assessment of the budget measures, Arthur N. Young, "Financial Reforms in Saudi Arabia," *Middle East Journal* 14:4 (Autumn 1960): 466–9. He attributed the riyal's devaluation to "varying far from the canons of sound finance" (466).
24. Lacey, 319–24.
25. Lacey, 335–44.
26. Bruce Riedel, *Kings and Presidents*, 39–41.
27. Riedel, 37–8, 41; Lacey, 340–4.
28. The English translation is in *Middle East Journal* (1963), issue 1. For a comparison of Faisal's ministerial statement to Nasser's May 1962 National Action Charter proposing they represent a "social contract moment" in the region, Relli Shechter, "A Social Contract Moment: Egypt's National Action Charter and Saudi Arabia's Ten-Point Program Compared," *Middle East Journal* 75:4

(2021/2): 574–90. The declaration of a major reform agenda at a moment of domestic and international crisis has a familiar ring to Middle East historians: Ottoman sultans announced the Tanzimat reforms at the height of crises in 1839 and 1856, and the constitution in 1876 in the midst of the Balkan crisis.
29. Al-Sudairi, 451–4.
30. The Trucial States (later the United Arab Emirates) in 1964, Oman in 1970, and Mauritania in 1981.
31. Miers, *Slavery in the Twentieth Century*, 347–50; Miers, "Slavery and the Slave Trade," 128–30; Shirley Kay, "Social Change in Modern Saudi Arabia," in *State, Society, and Economy in Saudi Arabia*, edited by Niblock, 178–9; Holden and Johns, *The House of Saud*, 221, 230–1. According to their account, there were roughly 30,000 slaves when emancipation came.
32. Nora Derbal, *Charity in Saudi Arabia: Civil Society under Authoritarianism*, Cambridge: Cambridge University Press, 2022, 220, 226. Madawi Al-Rasheed, *The Son King*, 204–7.
33. Riedel, 39–42.
34. Raihan Ismail, *Saudi Clerics and Shi'a Islam*, 63–5.
35. Lacey, 344–5.
36. Mouline, 121–4; Lacey, 353–4.
37. Lacey, 355–6.
38. Lacey, 299–301.
39. Bsheer, 233–77. In Bsheer's interpretation, Faisal and his faction framed and broadcast the negative image of Saud.
40. The nephew was Faisal ibn Musa'id. Al-Rasheed, *The Son King*, 60–2; Holden and Johns, 379–83. Lacey, 425–7.
41. Bligh, 90–1.
42. Jesse Ferris, *Nasser's Gamble: How Intervention in Yemen Caused the Six-Day War and the Decline of Egyptian Power*, Princeton, NJ: Princeton University Press, 2013, 190.
43. Ghrawi, "A Tamed Urban Revolution," 17–21.
44. Vassiliev, 371.
45. Joseph Mann, "King Faisal and the Challenge of Nasser's Revolutionary Ideology," *Middle Eastern Studies* 48:5 (2012): 756.
46. Vassiliev, 371. Nasir Said's Union of the Peoples of the Arabian Peninsula reported the arrests in September 1969, *Middle East Journal* 24:1 (1970): 65.
47. Exiles in Kuwait set up the Saudi Communist Party in 1975. Toby Matthiesen, "The Cold War and the Communist Party of Saudi Arabia," *Journal of Cold War Studies* 22:3 (Summer 2020): 35. One of its leaders, Mustafa Hafiz Wahba, was the son of Abd al-Aziz's Egyptian adviser Hafiz Wahba. The younger Wahba joined the leftist current in the 1950s and briefly held the post of deputy finance minister under Prince Talal in 1960. King Faisal expelled him in 1968 because of his leftist views. On the origins of communist activism in the 1940s, Al-Sudairi, 443–4. The remnants included the Socialist Action Party in the Arabian Peninsula, with no more than 100 members in Beirut, Damascus, and Aden. Matthiesen, "Migration, Minorities, and Radical Networks," 499–500.
48. Matthiesen, "The Cold War," 36.

49. Activism sometimes goes underground and into exile before resurfacing with new leaders, networks, grievances, and demands, initiating a new "cycle of contention." Tarrow, 195–214.
50. Some historians propose earlier dates for the establishment of formal government institutions. Joseph Kostiner suggests they took shape from the early 1920s to the mid-1930s. Kostiner, 187–91. Kiren Chaudhry, in *The Price of Wealth*, sees state-building commencing in the late 1920s after the annexation of Hijaz when "changing modes of domestic taxation, and the social struggles attending them, influenced the construction of the state bureaucracy and the national military," 44. For the elaboration of her argument, 43–83. Steffen Hertog argues, with persuasive abundant evidence, that the establishment of formal government offices commenced when Faisal seized the reins in the early 1960s. Hertog, 33–83.
51. Mounira M. Charrad and Julia Adams, "Introduction: Patrimonialism, Past and Present," *Annals of the American Academy of Political and Social Science* 636 (July 2011): 6–15; Gero Erdman and Ulf Engel, "Neopatrimonialism Reconsidered: Critical Review and Elaboration of an Elusive Concept," *Commonwealth & Comparative Politics* 45:1 (2007): 95–119.
52. Madawi Al-Rasheed writes, "The redistributive role of central power in Arabia . . . Surplus appropriated from one group as a result of tribute/zakat or raids had always been partially redistributed among other groups . . . The rest had always been used to buy loyalty. Oil revenues allowed generosity to surpass the regular feast of lamb and rice and the occasional gifts of cloth, dates, and weapons." Al-Rasheed, *History of Saudi Arabia*, 125–6.
53. Hertog, 74. Faisal's circle is the most likely source for this part of his reputation.
54. Hertog, 51.
55. Hertog, 28, 56–7. On the establishment of the Saudi Arabian Monetary Authority, Arthur Young, "Financial Reforms in Saudi Arabia," *Middle East Journal* 14:4 (Autumn 1960): 466–9. On the financial advisory mission that advised Saudi Arabia in 1951–2, Arthur Young, "Saudi Arabian Currency and Finance," *Middle East Journal* 7:3 (Summer 1953): 361–80; Arthur Young, "Saudi Arabian Currency and Finance, Part II," *Middle East Journal* 7:4 (Autumn 1953): 539–56.
56. Stephanie Cronin, "Tribes, Coups, and Princes: Building a Modern Army in Saudi Arabia," 2–5, 15–22.
57. Air force officers were more difficult to coopt. They felt proud of their technical prowess and resented the promotion of princes whose chief qualification was descent. Cronin, "Tribes, Coups, and Princes," 17–21.
58. Hertog, 50, 72.
59. Hertog, 64. For thumbnail descriptions of the twenty-one ministries established by 1990, see Fouad Al-Farsy, *Modernity and Tradition: The Saudi Equation*, London: Kegan Paul, 1990, 52–83.
60. Hertog, 80–1, 82 n. 163.
61. Hertog, 78.
62. Vassiliev, 310.
63. Mouline, 136–8. Sarah Yizraeli, *Politics and Society in Saudi Arabia*, 261, on a 1965 proposal from Muhammad al-Mubarak, a Syrian Muslim Brother, for a

national education network from elementary to university level that blended religious lessons with modern subjects.

64. Yizraeli, *Politics and Society*, 227, describes the background to creating a national system of public education but does not mention the imprint left by foreign Arab teachers who spread Muslim Brotherhood ideas.
65. For an overview of codification in Islamic law, Rudolph Peters, "From Jurists' Law to Statute Law or What Happens When the Shariʿa is Codified," in Rudolph Peters, *Shariʿa, Justice and Legal Order: Egyptian and Islamic Law: Selected Essays*, Leiden: Brill, 2020, 531–45.
66. Mouline, 143–4, 164–70. The most extensive study of law in Saudi Arabia up to the 1980s is Frank E. Vogel, *Islamic Law and Legal Systems: Studies of Saudi Arabia*, Leiden: Brill, 2000. A summary treatment based on Vogel is Commins, *The Mission*, 113–22.
67. On the history of fatwas in the Wahhabi tradition, Muhammad Al-Atawneh, *Wahhabi Islam Facing the Challenges of Modernity: Dar al-Ifta' in the Modern Saudi State*, Leiden: Brill, 2010, 10–16. He refers to the new body, *Dar al-Ifta'*, as the Institute for the Issuance of Fatwas and the Supervision of Religious Affairs and places its establishment in 1953, 8. According to Mouline, it was established in 1955, 138.
68. Mouline, 138–40.
69. Atawneh, 10, 17–20. The body is sometimes referred to as the Council of Grand Ulama.
70. Mouline, 151–3.
71. For the budgets of religious agencies, Yizraeli, *Politics and Society*, Table 12, 192; Table 13, 223; Table 14, 224; and Tim Niblock with Monica Malik, *The Political Economy of Saudi Arabia*, Table 2:3, 42. The figures reported in these tables show the committee's staff and budget roughly doubled from 1963 to 1973, contrary to the impression in Aramco reports that King Faisal constrained the committee's growth. Yizraeli, 218, 220. Mouline reports that the agency's budget and staff grew in the late 1950s and early 1960s before King Faisal halted expansion in favor of allowing cinema, foreign publications, soccer, and photography, 210–11.
72. On cooperation among Muslim Brothers, Pakistan's Jamaati Islami, and the Saudi government to spread conservative religious views, Olivier Roy, *The Failure of Political Islam*, Cambridge, MA: Harvard University Press, 1994, 110, 117. Roy observes that the desire of Wahhabis and Muslim Brothers to preserve morality and religious practice provided a common platform for cooperation despite their differences on doctrine.
73. The revivalist groups at the university came from Egypt (the Muslim Brotherhood and Ansar al-Sunna) and from South Asia (Ahli Hadith and Jamaati Islami). Farquhar, *Circuits of Faith*; Mouline, 132–3. A concise overview of the university's history, Christopher Anzalone and Yasir Qadhi, "From Dir'iyya to Riyadh: The History and Global Impact of Saudi Religious Propagation and Education," in *Wahhabism and the World*, edited by Peter Mandaville, 53–75.
74. Reinhard Schulze, "Transnational Wahhabism: The Muslim World League and the World Assembly of Muslim Youth," in *Wahhabism and the World*, edited by

Mandaville, 93–113. Abdullah M. Sindi, "King Faisal and Pan-Islamism," in *King Faisal and the Modernisation of Saudi Arabia*, edited by Willard A. Beling, London: Croom Helm, 1980. On the Muslim World League's efforts to combat Sufism, Elizabeth Sirriyeh, *Sufis and Anti-Sufis: The Defence, Rethinking and Rejection of Sufism in the Modern World*, Richmond: Curzon, 1999,158–60. On its activities in Nigeria, Alexander Thurston, *Salafism in Nigeria*, Cambridge: Cambridge University Press, 2016, 68–91. The Muslim World League paid salaries for imams at mosques in Europe and North America. Roy, *The Failure of Political Islam*, 116. On the World Assembly of Muslim Youth, Schulze, 101–2. The World Assembly of Muslim Youth and the Muslim Brotherhood had close ties in European countries. Jørgen S. Nielsen and Jonas Otterbeck, "Muslim Organisations," in *Muslims in Western Europe*, fourth edition, Edinburgh: Edinburgh University Press, 2016, 133–68.

75. On the general trend for state-led development in the Middle East, James Gelvin, *The Modern Middle East: A History*, fifth edition, New York: Oxford University Press, 2020, 262–5, 275–80.
76. Jones, 56.
77. Kuwait offered a model of a hereditary shaikhdom spending oil revenues for development.
78. Toby Jones interprets the program as a logical extension of how Abd al-Aziz distributed subsidies to win loyalty. *Desert Kingdom*, 61–3.
79. Niblock, 38, 41.
80. For a revisionist interpretation of how the outlook of technical experts played out in Saudi Arabia from the 1940s to the 1970s, see Jones.
81. Abdal-Majeed Daghistani and Colin Lee, "Urban Planning and Development in Saudi Arabia," in *The Arab City: Its Character and Islamic Cultural Heritage*, edited by Ismail Serageldin, Richard R. Herbert, and Samir El-Sadek, Riyadh: Arab Urban Development Institute, 1982, 142–3. On the ratio of rural and urban populations, Yizraeli, *Politics and Society*, 167.
82. Michael L. Ross argues oil production has social effects that restrict women's participation in the economy and reinforce patriarchy. *The Oil Curse: How Petroleum Shapes the Development of Nations*, Princeton, NJ: Princeton University Press, 2012, 111–44. For discussion of the ways oil wealth affected gender norms and women's participation in the labor force, see Madawi Al-Rasheed, *A Most Masculine State*, 22–5.
83. Donald P. Cole and Soraya Altorki, "Production and Trade in North Central Arabia: Change and Development in ʿUnayzah," in *The Transformation of Nomadic Society in the Arab East*, edited by Martha Mundy and Basim Musallam, Cambridge: Cambridge University Press, 2000, 149. By the early 1970s, the share of Unaiza's workforce in manufacturing and trade fell from a large majority to less than 20 percent. Cole and Altorki, 149–51.
84. Unaiza did not see any large agriculture projects before the oil boom. Cole and Altorki, 151–2.
85. Jones, 64–9.
86. Niblock, 51. Ismail Serageldin has a lower estimate for the ratio of expatriates in the workforce in 1970 at around one-fourth. *Saudis in Transition*, New York: Oxford University Press, 1984, 22.

87. In Bedouin custom, *kafala* refers to an agreement to sponsor safe passage through territory. William and Fidelity Lancaster, "Integration into Modernity: Some Tribal Rural Societies in the Bilad Ash-Sham," in *Nomadic Societies*, edited by Chatty, 339.
88. For a discussion of the legal principle in Sunni legal traditions, Y. Linant de Bellefonds, "Kafala," *Encyclopaedia of Islam New Edition Online*. Ray Jureidini and Said Fares Hassan, "The Islamic Principle of *Kafala* as Applied to Migrant Workers: Traditional Continuity and Reform," in *Migration and Islamic Ethics: Issues of Residence, Naturalization and Citizenship*, edited by Ray Jureidini and Said Fares Hasan, Leiden: Brill, 2020, 92–7. For the application of *kafala* in the modern Gulf, Omar Al Shehabi, "Policing Labour in Empire: The Modern Origins of the Kafala Sponsorship System in the Gulf Arab States," *British Journal of Middle East Studies* 48:2 (2012): 291–300.
89. Ricardo Bocco, "The Settlement of Pastoral Nomads in the Arab Middle East: International Organizations and Trends in Development Policies, 1950–1990," in *Nomadic Societies*, edited by Chatty, 304–6, 308–11. In 1957, the International Labor Organization tasked Arab experts with studying nomadic populations in Saudi Arabia, Jordan, Iraq, and Egypt. The experts, none of whom came from a nomadic background, recommended settlement projects. From 1960 to 1980, the Jordanian government implemented eleven settlement projects, believing that eroding tribal solidarity by settling nomads would benefit national integration. Bocco, 319–20.
90. For an overview of changes and attitudes on the eve of the oil boom for one Bedouin tribe, Cole, *Nomads of the Nomads*, 105–11, 136–63.
91. Khaled Al-Radihan, "Adaptation of Bedouin in Saudi Arabia to the 21st Century: Mobility and Stasis among the Shararat," in *Nomadic Societies*, edited by Chatty, 848–9.
92. Al-Radihan, 849–62. See Jones, 80–3 for an abortive effort to settle Murrah Bedouin at the Haradh oasis in the late 1960s and early 1970s. The Real Estate Development Fund's programs were part of the rearrangement of land control and ownership going back to sweeping land appropriations in the 1950s, that according to Bernard Haykel, played a major part in how the Sauds consolidated power. "Oil in Saudi Arabian Culture and Politics: From Tribal Poets to Al-Qaeda's Ideologues," in *Saudi Arabia in Transition*, edited by Haykel, Hegghammer, and Lacroix, 135 n. 21.
93. Motoko Katakura, *Bedouin Village: A Study of a Saudi Arabian People in Transition*, Tokyo: University of Tokyo Press, 1977, 110–11. Shirley Kay, "Social Change in Modern Saudi Arabia," 174.
94. Donald P. Cole, "New Homes, New Occupations, New Pastoralism: Al Murrah Bedouin, 1968 to 2003," in *Nomadic Societies*, edited by Chatty, 374–7; Cole, "Where Have the Bedouin Gone?," 242–9; Al-Radihan, 856–8.
95. Thesiger, 202.
96. Cole, "Where Have the Bedouin Gone?," 251–2; Bocco, 324.
97. Al-Fahad, "Raiders and Traders," 231–3.
98. James Buchan, "Secular and Religious Opposition in Saudi Arabia," in *State, Society, and Economy*, edited by Niblock, 108–12.
99. Yizraeli, *Politics and Society*, 219–20.

100. Thomas Hegghammer and Stephane Lacroix, "Rejectionist Islamism in Saudi Arabia: The Story of Juhayman al-ʿUtaybi Revisited," *International Journal of Middle East Studies* 39:1 (February 2007): 106–7.
101. Karamuddin Amin, "Nasiruddin al-Albani on Muslim's *Sahih*: A Critical Study of his Method," *Islamic Law and Society* 11:2 (2004): 149–76. On Albani's standing in the Islamic scholastic tradition compared to Wahhabi doctrine, Daniel Lav, *Radical Islam and the Revival of Medieval Theology*, Cambridge: Cambridge University Press, 2012, 107–14.
102. Stephane Lacroix, *Awakening Islam: The Politics of Religious Dissent in Contemporary Saudi Arabia*, 85.
103. Nasir al-Huzaimi, *The Mecca Uprising: An Insider's Account of Salafism and Insurrection in Saudi Arabia*, translated by David Commins, London: I.B. Tauris, 2022, 83–4; Hegghammer and Lacroix, "Rejectionist Islamism," 106–7.
104. Lacroix, *Awakening Islam*, 104–9.
105. This discussion of the Muslim Brotherhood's influence is based on Lacroix, *Awakening Islam*, 40–55, 63–70.
106. Toby Matthiesen, *The Other Saudis*, 93; Laurence Louer, *Transnational Shia Politics: Religious and Political Networks in the Gulf*, New York: Columbia University Press, 2009, 83–99, 143–9; Laurence Louer, *Shiism and Politics in the Middle East*, New York: Columbia University Press, 2012, 14–18, 27–45.
107. Hertog, 60 n. 120, citing S.N. Eisenstadt, *Traditional Patrimonialism and Modern Neopatrimonialism*, Beverley Hills, CA: Sage Publications, 1973, 56.
108. Abd al-Aziz ibn Baz, "Critique of Nationalism," 1961, cited in Mouline, 126–7.

7 The Oil Boom and Rapid Development, 1970–90

1. Bruce Riedel, "Fifty Years after 'Black September' in Jordan," *Studies in Intelligence* 64:2 (2020): 35–41.
2. Roham Alvandi, "Nixon, Kissinger, and the Shah: The Origins of Iranian Primacy in the Persian Gulf," *Diplomatic History* 36:2 (April 2012): 337–72.
3. David Commins, *The Gulf States: A Modern History*, London: I.B. Tauris, 2012, 202.
4. Christopher W. Dietrich, *Oil Revolution, Anticolonial Elites, Sovereign Rights, and the Economic Culture of Decolonization*, Cambridge: Cambridge University Press, 2017.
5. On Abdallah al-Tariqi's part in the effort by oil producing countries to assert the sovereign right to natural resources, Dietrich, 68–71, 78–9, 92–5, 115–20. Ellen R. Wald, *Saudi, Inc.: The Arabian Kingdom's Pursuit of Profit and Power*, New York: Pegasus Books, 2018, 125–33. Vitalis, 116–17, 133–40.
6. On the formation of OPEC and its part in the 1973–4 oil crisis, Zuhayr Mikdashi, "The OPEC Process," *Daedalus* 104:4 (Fall 1975): 203–15.
7. Edith Penrose, "The Development of Crisis," *Daedalus* 104:4 (Fall 1975): 40–4.
8. Dietrich, 252–5. On the terms of Saudi Arabia's takeover of Aramco, Wald, 206–9.
9. Penrose, 44–7.
10. Penrose, 45–50.

11. The Saudi members included Crown Prince Fahd and the ministers of oil, finance, and planning. They met with President Nixon, Kissinger, and the secretaries of the treasury and commerce. Holden and Johns, 357–8. For a report on the Joint Commission's projects for economic and administrative development in the first fifteen years, see "Status of U.S.–Saudi Arabian Joint Commission on Economic Cooperation," Report to the Chairman, Subcommittee on Europe and the Middle East, Committee on Foreign Affairs, House of Representatives, United States General Accounting Office, 1983. The Joint Commission was terminated in 2000 by mutual agreement. An overview of the Commission's history is by Thomas Lippman, "Cooperation under the Radar: The US–Saudi Arabian Joint Commission for Economic Cooperation (JECOR)," Middle East Institute, October 1, 2009. https://www.mei.edu/publications/cooperation-under-radar-us-saudi-arabian-joint-commission-economic-cooperation-jecor.
12. Holden and Johns, 359–66. Iran was by far the largest customer for US arms, purchasing $15 billion in five years.
13. A concise description of the arrangement is in Holden and Johns, 366–7. William Glenn Gray, "Learning to 'Recycle': Petrodollars and the West," in *Oil Shock: The 1973 Crisis and Its Economic Legacy*, London: I.B. Tauris, 2016, 172–97. Toby Matthiesen, "Saudi Arabia and the Cold War," in *Salman's Legacy*, edited by Madawi Al-Rasheed, 219–20. Matthiesen relies on David E. Spiro, *The Hidden Hand of American Hegemony: Petrodollar Recycling and International Markets*, Ithaca, NY: Cornell University Press, 1999.
14. William B. Quandt, *Saudi Arabia in the 1980s: Foreign Policy, Security, and Oil*, Washington, DC: Brookings Institution Press, 1981, 118–20.
15. Niblock with Malik, *The Political Economy of Saudi Arabia*, 54-65. For a summary of five-year plans from 1970 to 1990, Al-Farsy, *Modernity and Tradition*, 145–71.
16. Commins, *The Gulf States*, 215.
17. An overview of the exceptional scale of investment and expansion of public sector employment is Steffen Hertog, "National Cohesion and the Political Economy of Regions in Post-World War II Saudi Arabia," in *Saudi Arabia in Transition*, edited by Haykel, Hegghammer, and Lacroix, 98–102.
18. Niblock with Malik, *The Political Economy of Saudi Arabia*, 15.
19. Niblock with Malik, *The Political Economy of Saudi Arabia*, 15–17.
20. Niblock with Malik, *The Political Economy of Saudi Arabia*, 50.
21. Niblock with Malik, *The Political Economy of Saudi Arabia*, 18–21; Hertog, 18, 83, 264–75. For a summary of recent critical assessments of the model's value, shortcomings, and potential for extension, Michael Herb and Marc Lynch, "Introduction: The Politics of Rentier States in the Gulf," in POMEPS Studies 33: *The Politics of Rentier States in the Gulf*, January 2019. For discussion of how oil fosters the rentier state, neopatrimonialism, and state capitalism, see Matthew Gray, *The Economy of the Gulf States*, Newcastle upon Tyne: Agenda Publishing, 2018, 40–3; Matthew Gray, "A Theory of 'Late Rentierism' in the Arab States of the Gulf," Center for International and Regional Studies occasional paper no. 7, Doha: Center for International and Regional Studies, Georgetown University School of Foreign Service in Qatar, 2011. An extended critique is Islam Yasin Qasem, *Oil and Security Policies: Saudi Arabia 1950–2012*, Leiden: Brill, 2016.

22. Serageldin, *Saudis in Transition*, 29–39.
23. Niblock with Malik, *The Political Economy of Saudi Arabia*, 83–9.
24. Monera Nahedh, "The Sedentarization of a Bedouin Community in Saudi Arabia," University of Leeds, doctoral dissertation, 1989, 588, 599.
25. Nahedh, 549. For a 1981 study of half a dozen settlements in Hijaz and government efforts to improve access to health services, Zohair A. Sebai, *The Health of the Family in a Changing Arabia: A Case Study of Primary Health Care*, Jeddah: Tihama, 1981.
26. Nahedh, 151–5.
27. Donald P. Cole, "New Homes, New Occupations, New Pastoralism: Al Murrah Bedouin, 1968 to 2003," in *Nomadic Societies*, edited by Chatty, 380–1. A snapshot of the Murrah in 1980 is in Donald Cole, "The Bedouin and Social Change in Saudi Arabia," *Change and Development in Nomadic and Pastoral Societies* (1981): 133–47.
28. Cole, "New Homes," 378–9. Similar dynamics were at play in the north. See Al-Radihan, 857.
29. Al-Radihan, 859–63, 860 n. 1.
30. Nahedh, 555–9. An increase in polygamy may have correlated with the change from nomadism to settlement. Reports on polygamy's frequency are not consistent. During fieldwork among the Rwala Bedouin in the early 1970s, William Lancaster found "polygamy almost totally absent." *The Rwala Bedouin Today*, 132.
31. *New Voices of Arabia: The Short Stories*, edited by Abdulaziz al-Sebail and Anthony Calderbank, London: I.B. Tauris, 2012, 224–8. The aura of fearful superstition brings to mind passages in Sayyid Qutb's memoir, *A Child from the Village*, edited and translated by John Calvert and William Shepard, Syracuse, NY: Syracuse University Press, 2004.
32. *New Voices*, edited by al-Sebail and Calderbank, 174–5.
33. Shirley Kay remarks on phased migration where first the men move to the city while women and children remain in the village engaged in farming for some time before they follow. "Social Change in Modern Saudi Arabia," 172.
34. Fahd Atiq, *Life on Hold*, translated by Jonathan Wright, New York: American University in Cairo Press, 2012, 45–52. For a summary of the critical attitude in fiction toward materialism and social alienation, see Abdulaziz Al-Sebail, "Introduction," in *New Voices*, edited by al-Sebail and Calderbank, xi–xvii.
35. Atiq, 30–1. For additional passages related to the spread of consumerism, 53, 96.
36. Atiq, 13–14, 18.
37. Atiq, 90–1.
38. Bernard Haykel, "Oil in Saudi Arabian Culture and Politics: From Tribal Poetics to Al-Qaeda's Ideologues," in *Saudi Arabia in Transition*, edited by Haykel, Hegghammer, and Lacroix, 127. Al-Fahad, "Raiders and Traders," in *Saudi Arabia in Transition*, 236–7, 258.
39. Lacroix, *Awakening Islam*, 15–16.
40. Lacroix, *Awakening Islam*, 17–20.
41. Naif Khalaf Althaqeel, "The Beginning of Theater in Saudi Arabia," *Performing Islam* 6:1 (2017): 23–40. His information is based on interviews with older men recalling their school days, 35–6.

42. Nazeer El-Azma, "Saudi Arabia," *World Encyclopedia of Contemporary Theatre, Volume 4: The Arab World*, London: Routledge, 1999.
43. Serageldin, *Saudis in Transition*, 45.
44. Doumato, 2–5.
45. Huzaimi, 72.
46. David Commins, "From Wahhabi to Salafi," in *Saudi Arabia in Transition*, edited by Haykel, Hegghammer, and Lacroix, 161–4; Lauziere, 199–230.
47. Quandt, 68–9.
48. He claimed the islands when the British left the Gulf in 1971 and sent his military forces to seize two islands from the United Arab Emirates. For studies of Saudi–Iranian relations, W. Andrew Terrill, "The Saudi–Iranian Rivalry and the Future of Middle East Security," in *Rivalry in the Middle East: Saudi Arabia and Iran*, edited by M. Tyler and A.M. Boone, New York: Nova Science, 2012, 1–51. Fahad Muhammad Alsultan and Pedram Saeid, *The Development of Saudi–Iranian Relations since the 1990s: Between Conflict and Accommodation*, New York: Routledge, 2017. Simon Mabon, *The Struggle for Supremacy in the Middle East: Saudi Arabia and Iran*, Cambridge: Cambridge University Press, 2023.
49. "There were some who saw Khomeini's efforts must be countered by similar sectarian thrust from Saudi Arabia." Prince Turki ibn Faisal in *Bitter Rivals: Iran and Saudi Arabia*, *Frontline*: Season 36, Episode 8, 2018.
50. Huzaimi, 81–3. Hegghammer and Lacroix, "Rejectionist Islamism," 109.
51. Huzaimi, 117–18.
52. Huzaimi, 89–90. Hegghammer and Lacroix, "Rejectionist Islamism," 108.
53. Huzaimi, 90–1.
54. Huzaimi, 101–4. The government spared the lives of men who did not have physical signs of participating in the fighting; it rounded up and imprisoned Salafi Group members in other parts of the country; some members escaped punishment by fleeing the country. Hegghammer and Lacroix, "Rejectionist Islamism," 112–13; Yaroslav Trofimov, *The Siege of Mecca*, 238–41; Robert Lacey, *Inside the Kingdom*, 21–36.
55. Jones, 193–9.
56. Matthiesen, *The Other Saudis*, 97–100. On Saffar's background and initial encounters with the Shirazi current, Louer, *Transnational Shia Politics*, 145–6.
57. Jones mentions that protesters and police in Awamiyya clashed the previous year. Jones, "Rebellion on the Saudi Periphery," 222.
58. Jones, "Rebellion on the Saudi Periphery," 218–28.
59. For interpretation of Juhaiman's band as an apocalyptic sect, see David Commins, "Introduction to the English Edition," in Huzaimi, *The Mecca Uprising*, 54–64. For a study of apocalyptic beliefs, Jean-Pierre Filiu, *Apocalypse in Islam*, Berkeley, CA: University of California Press, 2012.
60. Doumato describes the billowing conservative reaction, 12–16. I have not traced the origin of the narrative that views the Mecca uprising as the turning point, but it is ubiquitous in accounts after the September 2001 attacks on the United States. It is not in the earliest history after the uprising by Robert Lacey, published in 1981. On the contrary, Lacey ends the book with anecdotes to suggest the gradual infiltration of less conservative ways: *The Kingdom*, 512–13. The narrative is not in Madawi Al-Rasheed's 2002 history. When she describes

a conservative religious reaction in the 1980s, she discusses it in connection with the increasing visibility of women in the workplace, *The History of Saudi Arabia*, 152–3. Very brief suggestions that the rulers deliberately curbed social openings are in Hegghammer and Lacroix, "Rejectionist Islamism," 113; Trofimov, 241–3.

61. David Hirst, "Saudis Draw a Veil over Women's Travel," *The Guardian*, July 16, 1977. James Buchan observed increasing enforcement of Wahhabi norms before the Mecca uprising; "Return of the Ikhwan," in Holden and Johns, 519.
62. "Saudi Purdah Hits Western Women," *The Observer*, August 12, 1979.
63. A compelling and thorough account of the Afghan crucible is Steve Coll, *Ghost Wars*, New York: Penguin, 2004.
64. Thomas Hegghammer, *Jihad in Saudi Arabia*, 26–7. For background on the politics in Washington, George Crile, *Charlie Wilson's War: The Extraordinary Story of How the Wildest Man in Congress and a Rogue CIA Agent Changed the History of Our Times*, New York: Grove Press, 2003.
65. Hegghammer, *Jihad*, 23–4.
66. Thomas Hegghammer, *The Caravan: Abdallah Azzam and the Rise of Global Jihad*, Cambridge: Cambridge University Press, 2020. A brief description of his reinterpretation of jihad is in Quintan Wiktorowicz, "The New Global Threat: Transnational Salafis and Jihad," *Middle East Policy* 8:4 (December 2001): 18–38, at 23–4.
67. Hegghammer, *Jihad*, 29.
68. Hegghammer, *Jihad*, 40–3.
69. Hegghammer, *Jihad*, 44–8.
70. Noorhaidi Hasan, "Salafism, Education, and Youth: Saudi Arabia's Campaign for Wahhabism in Indonesia," in *Wahhabism and the World*, edited by Mandaville, 138–40.
71. Alexander Thurston, *Salafism in Nigeria: Islam, Preaching, and Politics*, Cambridge: Cambridge University Press, 2016, 64–91. Thurston's meticulous study demonstrates the variety and dynamism in Salafism. Another exemplary study of the interplay between Saudi and local conditions is Laurent Bonnefoy, *Salafism in Yemen: Transnationalism and Religious Identity*, New York: Columbia University Press, 2011.
72. Lacroix, *Awakening Islam*, 20, 129–32; Mouline, 242–3.
73. Lacroix, *Awakening Islam*, 134–43. The prominence of modernists in the 1980s is another problem with the narrative that sees a sharp conservative turn after the Mecca uprising.
74. Lacroix, *Awakening Islam*, 154–7.
75. Hatoon Ajwad el-Fassi, "Does Saudi Feminism Exist?," in *Arab Feminisms: Gender and Equality in the Middle East*, edited by Jean Said Makdisi et al., London: I.B. Tauris, 2014, 125–6. El-Fassi mentions volumes of poetry published in 1975 by Fawzia Khalid (*Until When Will They Continue to Kidnap You on Your Wedding Night*) and Badia Kashgari (*My Own Image and Others*).
76. El-Fassi, 126–7.
77. A means of earning some money for the mother in Hamza Bogary's *The Sheltered Quarter*.
78. Siham A. Alsuwaigh, "Women in Transition: The Case of Saudi Arabia," *Journal of Comparative Family Studies* 20:1 (Spring 1989): 67–78.

79. Deborah Akers, "The Short Story in the Arabian Gulf Region: Origins and Development," in *Oranges in the Sun: Short Stories from the Arabian Gulf*, edited and translated by Deborah Akers and Abu Bakr Ahmad Bagader, Boulder, CO: Lynne Rienner, 2008, 2–4.
80. Al-Sebail, "Introduction," in *New Voices*, edited by al-Sebail and Calderbank, xi–xvii; Akers, "The Short Story," 4.
81. Najat Khayyat, "Had I Been Male," in *Voices of Change: Short Stories by Saudi Arabian Women Writers*, edited and translated by Abubakr Ahmad Bagader, Ava M. Heinrichsdorff, Deborah S. Akers, and Abd al-Aziz al-Subayyil, Boulder, CO: Lynne Rienner, 1998, 19–22.
82. Badriyyah al-Bishr, "School Diaries," in *Voices of Change*, 23–7; Bishr, "Wednesday Night," in *Voices of Change*, 77–82.
83. Sharifah ash-Shamlan, "Complete Calm," in *Voices of Change*, 47–52.
84. Wafa Munawwar, "The Duties of a Working Wife," in *Voices of Change*, 43–6.

8 The Kuwait Crisis and Political Mobilization, 1990–2000

1. On the history of the border dispute, Richard N. Schofield, *Evolution of the Shatt al-Arab Boundary Dispute*, Wisbech: Middle East & North African Studies Press, 1986.
2. Cronin, "Tribes, Coups, and Princes," 24.
3. For discussion and analysis of the fatwa and translation of the text, Al-Fahad, "From Exclusion to Accommodation," 485–6, 514–19.
4. Ben Hubbard, *MBS: The Rise to Power of Mohammed Bin Salman*, 159–62; Robert Lacey, *Inside the Kingdom*, 134–40.
5. Rebecca Grant, "The Short Strange Life of PSAB," *Air Force Magazine* online, July 1, 2012.
6. A comprehensive study of the Scud attacks estimated nineteen Scuds targeted the Eastern Province in eleven attacks; eighteen Scuds targeted the Riyadh district in eleven attacks; nine Scuds targeted a military zone near Hafr al-Batin in four attacks; forty-two Scuds targeted Israel. The Scuds carried conventional warheads; none had chemical or biological agents. Federation of American Scientists, Information Paper, "Iraq's Scud Ballistic Missiles," https://nuke.fas.org/guide/iraq/missile/scud_info/index.html, accessed April 8, 2024.
7. Lacroix, *Awakening Islam*, 160–4. On the earlier fatwa, Mouline, 244.
8. Richard Dekmejian, "The Liberal Impulse in Saudi Arabia," *Middle East Journal* 57:3 (Summer 2003): 85–6; Anders Jerichow, *The Saudi File: People, Power, Politics*, New York: St. Martin's Press, 1998, 50–4.
9. Lacroix, *Awakening Islam*, 177–9. Daryl Champion, *The Paradoxical Kingdom: Saudi Arabia and the Momentum of Reform*, London: Hurst, 2002, 222–3. R. Hrair Dekmejian, "The Rise of Political Islamism in Saudi Arabia," *Middle East Journal* 48:4 (Autumn 1994): 630–2. For a full discussion of the religious dissident movement during the 1990s, Mamoun Fandy, *Saudi Arabia and the Politics of Dissent*, New York: St. Martin's Press, 1999.
10. Lacroix, *Awakening Islam*, 179–81.
11. Lacroix, *Awakening Islam*, 183–4.

12. Abdulaziz H. Al-Fahad, "Ornamental Constitutionalism: The Saudi Basic Law of Governance," *Yale Journal of International Law* 30 (2005): 376–96.
13. Lacroix, *Awakening Islam*, 188–92. In early 1993, the senior clerics issued a fatwa declaring that organizations like the Muslim Brotherhood caused division among Muslims. Mouline, 248.
14. Lacroix, *Awakening Islam*, 207–9.
15. Lacroix, *Awakening Islam*, 211–18.
16. According to Mouline, 243, Prince Salman met with the ministers of interior, information, and pilgrimage to discuss ways to control content of sermons and cassettes sold at stores.
17. Lacroix's sources estimate 50 to 100 arrests: *Awakening Islam*, 232–5.
18. Lacroix, *Awakening Islam*, 202–5, 225–6, 230–1. His analysis treats the rise and fall of the Awakening as an Islamist mobilization and demobilization, 151–236.
19. Louer, *Shiism and Politics in the Middle East*, 106–7.
20. Nasir al-Umar, "Waqiʿ al-rafida fi bilad al-tawhid," no date, http://ar.islamway.net/book/3165, accessed June 2016.
21. For an astute and succinct analysis of the early phases in transnational jihad, see Wiktorowicz, "The New Global Threat: Transnational Salafis and Jihad."
22. Hegghammer, *Jihad in Saudi Arabia*, 48–57.
23. Hegghammer's assessment of the evidence puts the likely figure closer to 1000. *Jihad in Saudi Arabia*, 59.
24. Hegghammer, *Jihad in Saudi Arabia*, 61–4.
25. Hegghammer, *Jihad in Saudi Arabia*, 71–3. On the circumstances of Hudhaif's death, Hegghammer cites reports by Amnesty International and the CDLR.
26. Grant, "The Short Strange Life of PSAB."
27. Hegghammer, *Jihad in Saudi Arabia*, 74–6.
28. The prohibition was issued in 1994. Mai Yamani, "Saudi Arabia's Media Mask," in *Kingdom without Borders*, edited by Al-Rasheed. Robert Lacey, *Inside the Kingdom*, 165–6, describes how Awakening shaikhs condemned satellite television at first on moral grounds, and how the royals figured out they could gain influence by investing in satellite television stations. For more about Saudi Arabia's assertion in Arab media, Andrew Hammond, "Maintaining Saudi Arabia's *Cordon Sanitaire* in the Arab Media," in *Kingdom without Borders*, 335–52. For the debate on allowing general public access to the Internet, see Joshua Teitelbaum, "Dueling for *Daʿwa*: State vs. Society on the Saudi Internet," *Middle East Journal* 56:2 (2002): 238–9, which has a translation of the February 2001 Council of Ministers Resolution on the Internet that set forth guidelines for accessing and using it, prohibiting the dissemination of material against the government and religion.
29. Hamad A. Alshahrani, "A Brief History of the Internet in Saudi Arabia," *Tech Trends* 60 (2016): 19–20. The Saudi Telecommunications Company developed the Internet infrastructure. Half the population had an Internet connection by 2013.
30. Hegghammer, *Jihad in Saudi Arabia*, 100. For a compelling, full account of Al Qaeda's origins and its 2001 attack on the United States, see Lawrence Wright, *The Looming Tower*.
31. Hegghammer, *Jihad in Saudi Arabia*, 100; Lacroix, *Awakening Islam*, 194–6.

32. Hegghammer, *Jihad in Saudi Arabia*, 101–2. For extensive study of the emergence of global jihad, see Fawaz Gerges, *The Far Enemy*. For theological debates between proponents of jihad and "quietest" Salafis, see Lav, 120–66.
33. In contrast to Juhaiman al-Utaibi's accusation that Abd al-Aziz betrayed religion by turning against the Brethren.
34. Following the careful analysis in Hegghammer, *Jihad in Saudi Arabia*, 102–8.
35. Hegghammer, *Jihad in Saudi Arabia*, 108–14. According to Hegghammer, 116, the Saudi government did not pay bin Laden to refrain from attacking Americans, as some writers have suggested.
36. Hegghammer, *Jihad in Saudi Arabia*, 122–3.
37. Hegghammer, *Jihad in Saudi Arabia*, 78–83.
38. Andrzej Kapiszewksi, *Nationals and Expatriates: Population and Labor Dilemmas of the Gulf Cooperation Council States*, Reading: Ithaca Press, 2001, 59–67. Hélène Thiollet, "Migrants and Monarchs: Regime Survival, State Transformation and Migration Politics in Saudi Arabia," *Third World Quarterly* 43:7 (2022): 1645–65. A fictional depiction of the bleak lot of a young man from Kerala dispatched to tend a goat herd in the desert is Benyamin, *Goat Days*, translated by Joseph Koyippally, London: Seagull Books, 2016.
39. Niblock, 94–9; Hertog, 117–19.
40. Peak years for irrigating wheat crops were 1985 to 1995. Eli ElHadj, *Camels Don't Fly, Deserts Don't Bloom: An Assessment of Saudi Arabia's Experiment in Desert Agriculture*, Occasional Paper No. 48, Water Issues Study Group, School of Oriental and African Studies (SOAS) / King's College London, University of London, May 2004, 2–4. He analyzes intensive use of water in the 1990s and early 2000s that depleted sub-surface water. Elie Elhadj, "Saudi Arabia's Agricultural Project: From Dust to Dust," *Middle East Review of International Affairs* 12:2 (June 2008): 35.
41. Donald P. Cole and Soraya Altorki, "Production and Trade in North Central Arabia: Change and Development in ʿUnayzah," in *The Transformation of Nomadic Society in the Arab East*, edited by Mundy and Musallam, 152–3.
42. Rodney Wilson, with Abdullah al-Salamah, Monica Malik, and Ahmed Al-Rajhi, *Economic Development in Saudi Arabia*, London: Routledge Curzon, 2004, 1–5.
43. Hertog, 138.
44. Hertog, 272.
45. Hertog, 137–40.
46. Niblock, 91, 140; Hertog, 186–8.
47. *New Voices*, edited by al-Sebail and Calderbank, 191–3.
48. Hertog, 192–7.
49. Niblock, 139–41; Hertog puts the 4.5 million figure in 1994, 186–7.
50. Mohammed Al-Gabbani, "Growth Trends and Changes in Small Towns in Saudi Arabia (1974–1993)," *Geojournal* 37:1 (1995): 105–12. On how Saudis reworked conceptions of tribal identity in urban settings, Nadav Samin, *Of Sand or Soil: Genealogy and Tribal Belonging in Saudi Arabia*, Princeton, NJ: Princeton University Press, 2013. Sebastian Maisel, "The New Rise of Tribalism in Saudi Arabia," *Nomadic Peoples* Special Issue: Reshaping Tribal Identities in the Contemporary Arab World, 18:2 (2014): 100–22.

51. William and Fidelity Lancaster, "Integration into Modernity: Some Tribal Rural Societies in the Bilad Ash-Sham," in *Nomadic Societies in the Middle East and North Africa*, edited by Chatty, 345.
52. William and Fidelity Lancaster, 345.
53. William and Fidelity Lancaster, 346.

9 In the Midst of Regional Unraveling, 2001–15

1. For the idea that Wahhabism fosters terrorism, see Dore Gold, *Hatred's Kingdom: How Saudi Arabia Supports the New Global Terorrism*, Washington, DC: Regnery, 2003. Stephen Schwartz, *The Two Faces of Islam*, New York: Doubleday, 2002. The idea that Wahhabism bred terror mixed modern Islamophobia with an earlier era's denominational Muslim hostility. For credible studies about the influence of Wahhabism in other Muslim societies based on extensive research, see *Wahhabism and the World*, edited by Mandaville, and *Kingdom without Borders*, edited by Al-Rasheed. For the broader context of Salafism and militancy, see *Global Salafism: Islam's New Religious Movement*, edited by Roel Meijer; Raihan Ismail, *Rethinking Salafism: The Transnational Networks of Salafi ʿUlama in Egypt, Kuwait, and Saudi Arabia*, New York: Oxford University Press, 2021.
2. The Western press fixated on the Arabic word for school, *madrasa*, supposing it applied only to religious schools. The question at stake was the school curriculum. There were madrasas that taught science, or science and religion, or only religion. Then, if a madrasa taught only religion, it might teach a sectarian conception of religion, a politicized conception, or a denominational one. In other words, the "problem" was not the madrasa.
3. Toby Jones, "Seeking a 'Social Contract' for Saudi Arabia," *MERIP* 228 (Fall 2003); Madawi Al-Rasheed, *Muted Modernists*, 31–5.
4. Salman al-Awda attended; Safar al-Hawali boycotted.
5. International Crisis Group, "Can Saudi Arabia Reform Itself?," Middle East Report No. 28, July 14, 2004, 16–18.
6. Frank E. Vogel observed that Saudi religious police went far beyond classical Sunni definitions of their duty. "The Public and the Private in Saudi Arabia: Restrictions on the Powers of Committees for Ordering the Good and Forbidding the Evil," *Social Research* 70:3 (Fall 2003): 764–5.
7. On the March 11 fire: Lacey, *Inside the Kingdom*, 237–9; David Commins, *Islam in Saudi Arabia*, London: I.B. Tauris, 2015, 96–7.
8. Eleanor Abdella Doumato, "Saudi Arabia: From 'Wahhabi' Roots to Contemporary Revivalism", in *Teaching Islam: Textbooks and Religion in the Middle East*, edited by Eleanor A. Doumato and Gregory Starrett, Boulder, CO: Lynne Rienner, 2006, 163–4, 171, 173.
9. Lacey, *Inside the Kingdom*, 50–1.
10. Derbal, *Charity*, 82–5. *Al-Haramain* is the Arabic term for the two holy places, Mecca and Medina. The founder of the Haramain Islamic Welfare Association, Aqil Abd al-Aziz al-Aqil, became enmeshed in multiple trials and lawsuits in the United States and Saudi Arabia over his alleged involvement in money laundering. On the Haramain and charges against it, Yusra Bokhari, Nasim Chowdhury, and Robert Lacey, "A Good Day to Bury a Bad Charity: The Rise

and Fall of the Al-Haramain Islamic Foundation," in *Gulf Charities and Islamic Philanthropy in the "Age of Terror" and Beyond*, edited by Jonathan Benthall and Robert Lacey, Berlin: Gerlach Press, 2014, 199–229. In June 2008, the US Treasury Department designated the Haramain Foundation and Aqil al-Aqil for supporting terrorism. "Treasury Designates Al Haramain Islamic Foundation," https://home.treasury.gov/news/press-releases/hp1043, accessed November 26, 2024.

11. Madawi Al-Rasheed coined the term in "Saudi Religious Transnationalism in London," in *Transnational Connections and the Arab Gulf*, edited by Madawi Al-Rasheed, London: Routledge, 2005.
12. *Wahhabism and the World*, edited by Mandaville, 7–9, 14–18. For case studies of Saudi proselytizing in Nigeria, Kosovo, and Indonesia, Krithika Varagur, *The Call: Inside the Global Saudi Religious Project*, New York: Columbia Global Reports, 2021.
13. Noorhaidi Hasan, "Ambivalent Doctrines and Conflicts in the Salafi Movement in Indonesia," in *Global Salafism*, edited by Meijer, 171–83.
14. For an outstanding collection of studies on Salafism in different Muslim and European countries, *Global Salafism*, edited by Meijer.
15. *Wahhabism and the World*, edited by Mandaville, 6–9, 20–3.
16. Mandaville refers to "denationalization and recontextualization of Wahhabism," in *Wahhabism and the World*, 23.
17. Alexander Thurston, "Wahhabi Compromises and 'Soft Salafization' in the Sahel," 238–54; Emil Nasritdinov and Mametbek Myrzabaev, "Saudi Influence in Kyrgyzstan: Beyond Mosques, Schools, and Foundations," 158–85; Terje Østebø, "Ethiopia and Saudi Arabia: Between Proximity and Distance," 221–37, all in *Wahhabism and the World*, edited by Mandaville.
18. Taqi al-Din al-Hilali and Muhammad Muhsin Khan, translators, *Interpretation of the Meanings of the Noble Qur'an in the English Language: A Summarized Version of at-Tabari, al-Qurtubi and Ibn Kathir with comments from Sahih Al-Bukhari, summarized in one volume*, Riyadh: Maktaba Dar-us-Salam, 1994. The preface to the 1985 edition, included in the 1994 edition cited here, states that "Some additions, corrections, and alterations have been made to improve the English translation and to bring the English interpretation very close to the correct and exact meanings of the Arabic," Hilali and Khan, vi. For the translation of Sura 1, Hilali and Khan, 2. For the translation of Sura 33, Hilali and Khan, 657. Discussions of the Saudi edition and its wide distribution are in Khaleel Mohammed, "Assessing English Translations of the Quran," *Middle East Quarterly* 12:2 (Spring 2005): 64–5; *Wahhabism and the World*, edited by Mandaville, 17; Nora Derbal, "Humanitarian and Relief Organizations in Global Saudi *Daʿwa*," in *Wahhabism and the World*, edited by Mandaville, 120.
19. The United States relocated to al-Udaid in Qatar between April and September 2003. Grant, "The Short Strange Life of PSAB."
20. Katherine Harvey attributes Riyadh's refusal to engage with the new Iraqi government to King Abdallah's belief it was beholden to Iran. Harvey, *A Self-Fulfilling Prophecy: The Saudi Struggle for Iraq*, London: Hurst, 2021. Eric Davis, in his review of Harvey for the *Journal of South Asian and Middle Eastern Studies*, sees underlying political calculations for Abdallah and Maliki as the cause. He points out that Maliki needed Iran's support for economic recon-

struction of his battered nation and that Maliki's Shiite coalition deeply mistrusted Sunni politicians.

21. Thomas Hegghammer thinks the figure of 3,000–5,000 Saudi volunteers cited by some authors is much too high. Hegghammer, "Combattants saoudiens en Irak: modes de radicalization et de recrutement," *Cultures et conflits* 64 (2006): 111–7. Cole Bunzel, "From Paper State to Caliphate: The Ideology of the Islamic State," Brookings Project on US Relations with the Islamic World, Analysis Paper, No. 19, March 2015, 13–17. On Abu Musʿab al-Zarqawi, Joby Warrick, *Black Flags: The Rise of ISIS*, New York: Doubleday, 2015. Jean-Charles Brisard and Damien Martinez, *Zarqawi: The New Face of Al-Qaeda*, New York: Other Press, 2005. On the background to the development of the jihadist strain in Salafism, see Joas Wagemakers, *A Quietist Jihadi: The Ideology and Influence of Abu Muhammad al-Maqdisi*, Cambridge: Cambridge University Press, 2012, 213–36.
22. For recent discussion of how Western scholars understand sectarianism, Morten Valbjorn, "Observing (the Debate on) Sectarianism: On Conceptualizing, Grasping and Explaining Sectarian Politics in the Middle East," *Mediterranean Politics* 26:5 (2021): 612–34. I thank one of my anonymous readers for referring me to this article.
23. Hegghammer, *Jihad in Saudi Arabia*, 143–50, 157–9, 163–73. The dissidents were known as the Shuʿaibi clerics. Hegghammer estimates that between 300 and 1,000 Saudis returned from Afghanistan after the United States' invasion.
24. Hegghammer, *Jihad in Saudi Arabia*, 167–79. According to Nelly Lahoud's thorough study of the "Bin Laden papers," computer files United States forces obtained in the raid that killed Osama bin Laden in May 2011, there is no evidence that he had a role in setting up a network in Saudi Arabia or directed it to carry out a terrorist campaign in 2003. *The Bin Laden Papers: How the Abbottabad Raid Revealed the Truth about Al-Qaeda, Its Leader and His Family*, New Haven, CT, and London: Yale University Press, 2022, 68–71. Hegghammer estimates that 300–700 men were in Uyairi's network: *Jihad in Saudi Arabia*, 181, 181 n. 46.
25. Hegghammer, *Jihad in Saudi Arabia*, 159–60. In the lingo of Islamic militants, suicide attacks were martyrdom operations.
26. Hegghammer, *Jihad in Saudi Arabia*, 184–5. See Lahoud, *The Bin Laden Papers*, 71, for the argument that the first attack was a response to the announcement of nineteen wanted men.
27. Hegghammer, *Jihad in Saudi Arabia*, 200–5. Roel Meijer, "Yusuf al-Uyairi and the Transnationalisation of Saudi jihadism," in *Kingdom without Borders*, edited by Al-Rasheed, 221–41.
28. Hegghammer, *Jihad in Saudi Arabia*, 206–15.
29. Hegghammer, *Jihad in Saudi Arabia*, 217–20.
30. Hegghammer, *Jihad in Saudi Arabia*, 189–90.
31. Christopher Boucek, "The Sakinah Campaign and Internet Counter-Radicalization in Saudi Arabia," CTC *Sentinel* 1:9 (August 2008).
32. Salwa Ismail argues that the promotion of "moderate" Islam was part of a larger US strategy for "global governance" that government agencies and US think tanks framed in terms for the Saudi government to adopt. Salwa Ismail, "Producing 'Reformed Islam': A Saudi Contribution to the US Projects of

Global Governance," in *Kingdom without Borders*, edited by Al-Rasheed, 128–30.

33. Sean Foley, *Changing Saudi Arabia: Art, Culture, and Society in the Kingdom*, Boulder, CO: Lynne Rienner, 2019, 36–45. Foley's book offers a granular portrait of the arts scene under King Abdallah.
34. Foley, 73–112.
35. Foley, 113–62.
36. Maria Garcia, "A Woman's Voice Is Her Nakedness: An Interview with Haifaa Al-Mansour," *Cinéaste* 38:4 (Fall 2013): 34–7; Rebecca Keegan, "Meet Haifaa Al-Mansour, the Saudi Woman Challenging Riyadh—and Hollywood—to Evolve," *Vanity Fair*, summer 2018.
37. For an extensive treatment of the debates on women and gender relations after 9/11, see Al-Rasheed, *A Most Masculine State*, 134–74.
38. An example of writing by Saudi women on domestic violence is Rania Al-Baz, *Disfigured: A Saudi Woman's Story of Triumph over Violence*, translated by Catherine Spencer, Northampton, MA: Olive Branch Press, 2009.
39. Al-Rasheed, *A Most Masculine State*, 134–47.
40. Niblock, 184.
41. For an overview of conservative Saudi women's positions in the early 2000s, see Al-Rasheed, *A Most Masculine State*, 244–79.
42. For a close examination of young women based on fieldwork in Riyadh, see Amelie Le Renard, *A Society of Young Women: Opportunities of Place, Power, and Reform in Saudi Arabia*, Stanford, CA: Stanford University Press, 2014. On the spread of shopping malls in the 1990s and 2000s, and their significance as locations for women to gather, see Le Renard, 46–9. On how consumption habits figure in the formation of conceptions of femininity, 131–57. For data on growing consumerism, see Soraya W. Assad, "The Rise of Consumerism in Saudi Arabian Society," *International Journal of Commerce and Management* 17:1/2 (2007): 73–104. For an overview of how young Saudis viewed social questions around this time, Caryle Murphy, *A Kingdom's Future: Saudi Arabia Through the Eyes of Its Twentysomethings*, Washington, DC: Woodrow Wilson International Center for Scholars, 2013.
43. For analysis of the factions in the liberal trend, Stephane Lacroix, "Islamo-Liberal Politics in Saudi Arabia," in *Saudi Arabia in the Balance: Political Economy, Society, Foreign Affairs*, edited by Paul Aarts and Gerd Nonneman, London: Hurst, 2005, 35–56. For profiles of the leading figures in the liberal trend, Lacroix, "Between Islamists and Liberals: Saudi Arabia's New Islamo-liberal Reformers," *Middle East Journal* 58:3 (2004): 345–64. The Saudi Association for Civil and Religious Rights, frequently referred to as HASM, its Arabic acronym, promoted an indigenous liberal model that bridged the religious-secular currents. A detailed study of the association and its leader Abdallah al-Hamid is Peter Enz-Harlass, *Peaceful Jihad: The Islamic Civil Rights Movement in Saudi Arabia*, London: I.B. Tauris, 2022. See also Al-Rasheed, *Muted Modernists*, 55–74. Al-Rasheed's book captures the terrain of reformist thought in the Arab uprisings period.
44. Jason Brownlee, *Authoritarianism in an Age of Democratization*, Cambridge: Cambridge University Press, 2007, 6–9, 25.

45. Pascal Menoret, *Graveyard of the Clerics*, 76–96; Menoret, "The Municipal Elections in Saudi Arabia 2005," Arab Reform Initiative, https://www.arab-reform.net/publication/the-municipal-elections-in-saudi-arabia-2005, accessed April 11, 2024.
46. Menoret, *Graveyard*, 76–8, 94. Writing in 2019, Menoret posited that Islamic activism would retain political potential, even though his account underscored how the state was able to defuse and contain opposition activism through deflection and fragmenting urban spaces. *Graveyard*, 209.
47. Derbal, *Charity*, 26–7.
48. Derbal, *Charity*, 1–5.
49. Derbal, *Charity*, 221–5.
50. Derbal, *Charity*, 146–62. The poverty level at the time was 3,800 SR (€780) per month. Derbal summarizes a few Saudi studies of poverty in Jeddah and Riyadh. Pascal Menoret traces how Western city planners produced "the slum" in Riyadh, in *Joyriding in Riyadh: Oil, Urbanism, and Road Revolt*, Cambridge: Cambridge University Press, 2014, 74–87.
51. Assad, "The Rise of Consumerism in Saudi Arabian Society."
52. Niblock, 181–3.
53. Niblock, 202.
54. Michaela Prokop, "The War of Ideas: Education in Saudi Arabia," in *Saudi Arabia in the Balance*, edited by Aarts and Nonneman, 59.
55. Ursula Lindsey, "Saudi Arabia's Education Reforms Emphasize Training for Jobs," *Chronicle of Higher Education* 57:7 (October 8, 2010): 31–2; Commins, *Islam in Saudi Arabia*, 60–1.
56. Lindsey.
57. Niblock, 198–9, 203.
58. Hertog, 198, 213.
59. Hertog, 199.
60. Hertog, 199–202, 215. For discussion of changes in the ways Asian and Gulf Arab governments and companies managed migrant labor and labor remittances since the 1980s, see Hélène Thiollet, "Managing Migrant Labour in the Gulf: Transnational Dynamics of Migration Politics since the 1930s," Working Paper 131, July 2016, International Migration Institute, Oxford Department of International Development, University of Oxford.
61. No longer raising camels for subsistence or to serve caravans, but for racing and camel shows (akin to dog shows in the West).
62. Donald P. Cole, "New Homes, New Occupations, New Pastoralism: Al Murrah Bedouin, 1968 to 2003," in *Nomadic Societies in the Middle East and North Africa*, edited by Chatty, 383–92.
63. Hélène Thiollet, "Migrants and Monarchs: Regime Survival, State Transformation and Migration Politics in Saudi Arabia," *Third World Quarterly* 43:7 (2022): 1650. Thiollet notes the resemblance to terminology in the United States (*braceros*) and Germany (guestworkers), and she argues the pejorative connotation of "immigration" stems from government circles.
64. *Exported and Exposed: Abuses against Sri Lankan Domestic Workers in Saudi Arabia, Kuwait, Lebanon, and the United Arab Emirates*, Human Rights Watch, November 2007, 51.
65. *Exported and Exposed*, 13–14, 46.

66. *Exported and Exposed*, 29–34.
67. *Exported and Exposed*, 43–4. Some recent studies of Asian migrant workers in the Arab Gulf states include *Migrant Labor in the Persian Gulf*, edited by Mehran Kamrava and Zahra Babar, New York: Columbia University Press, 2012; Rakkee Thimothy and S.K. Sasikumar, *Migration of Women Workers from South Asia to the Gulf*, New Delhi: V.V. Giri National Labour Institute, NOIDA, and UN Women South Asia Sub Regional Office, 2012; "Viewpoints: Special Edition: Migration and the Gulf," Middle East Institute Viewpoints, February 2010.
68. Matthiesen, *The Other Saudis*, 182–4.
69. Louer, *Shiism and Politics*, 108–9.
70. Frederic Wehrey, *The Forgotten Uprising in Eastern Saudi Arabia*, Washington, DC: Carnegie Endowment for International Peace, 2013.
71. On the decade of uncoordinated, unsynchronized protests from North Africa to the Gulf preceding the Arab uprisings, Gelvin, *The Modern Middle East*, 335–9.
72. Caryle Murphy, "Saudi Arabia's King Abdallah Promises $36 Billion in Benefits," *Christian Science Monitor*, February 23, 2011.
73. Wehrey, *The Forgotten Uprising*.
74. Murphy, "Saudi Arabia's King Abdallah"; F. Gregory Gause, *Saudi Arabia in the New Middle East*, Council on Foreign Relations (2011): 6.
75. Wehrey, *Forgotten Uprising*.
76. "Saudi Arabia Ramps Up Clampdown on Human Rights Activists," Amnesty International, June 18, 2012, https://www.amnesty.org/en/latest/news/2012/06/saudi-arabia-ramps-up-clampdown-on-human-rights-activists, accessed September 16, 2024; "Saudi Arabia: Prisoner of Conscience Dr. Abdullah al-Hamid Dies While in Detention," Amnesty International, April 24, 2020, https://www.amnesty.org/en/latest/news/2020/04/saudi-arabia-prisoner-of-conscience-dr-abdullah-alhamid-dies-while-in-detention, accessed September 16, 2024.
77. Simon Mabon, "The End of the Battle for Bahrain and the Securitization of Bahraini Shi'a," *Middle East Journal* 73:1 (Spring 2019): 29–50. For analysis of the Saudi government's sectarian strategy, see Madawi Al-Rasheed, "Sectarianism as Counter-Revolution: Saudi Responses to the Arab Spring," *Studies in Ethnicity and Nationalism* 11:3 (2011): 513–26. Critical analysis of the sectarian frame to describe regional political rivalry and conflict is in Gause, *Beyond Sectarianism*.
78. Martin Kramer, "Syria's Alawis and Shi'ism," in *Shi'ism, Resistance, and Revolution*, edited by Martin Kramer, Boulder, CO: Westview Press, 1987, 237–54.
79. On the Islamic insurgency, see Umar F. Abd Allah, *The Islamic Struggle in Syria*, Berkeley, CA: Mizan Press, 1983.
80. Ismail, *Saudi Clerics*, 63–5, 189–97.
81. Ash Rossiter, "The Yemeni–Saudi Border: From Boundary to Frontline," in *Yemen and the Gulf States*, edited by Lackner and Varisco, 30–6. Rossiter considers it plausible that the mass expulsion contributed to economic hardship in Yemeni districts along the border and may have contributed to friction between the national government and the region.
82. Bonnefoy, in *Salafism in Yemen*, argues that the role of Saudi clerics in spreading Salafism in Yemen was minimal. The most influential Yemeni Salafi was

Muqbil ibn Hadi al-Wadiʿi (c.1933–2001), born into a Zaidi family and converted to Salafism during his years of work and study in Saudi Arabia. In the early 1980s, he founded a Salafi religious center, with substantial funding from the Saudi religious establishment, in Saada province.

83. David Pinault, "Sunni, Shia, Zaydi: Religious Identity and Sectarian Proselytizing in Contemporary Yemen," *Journal of South Asian and Middle Eastern Studies* 33:1 (Fall 2009): 1–19. Pinault, 17, cites one Zaidi source, "Zaydis are concentrated in the north, Shafii Sunnis in the south, and they get along and respect each other . . . But the Wahhabis don't respect anyone, and they're like a cancer: they're growing everywhere."
84. On the Zaidis and the Houthi movement, Bernard Haykel, "A Zaydi Revival?," *Yemen Update* 36 (1995); J.E. Peterson, "The al-Huthi Conflict in Yemen," *Arabian Peninsula Background Notes*, August 2008; James Robin King, "Zaydi Revival in a Hostile Republic: Competing Identities, Loyalties and Visions of State in Republican Yemen," *Arabica* 59 (2012): 404–45; Christopher Boucek, "War in Saada: From Local Insurrection to National Challenge," Carnegie Endowment for International Peace, Middle East Program No. 110, April 2010; Barak A. Salmoni, Bryce Loidolt, and Madelein Wells, "Regime and Periphery in Northern Yemen," National Defense Research Institute, 2010; International Crisis Group, "Yemen: Defusing the Saada Time Bomb," Middle East Report No. 86, May 27, 2009.
85. Boucek, "War in Saada," 9–12. Rossiter, "The Yemeni–Saudi Border," 36–7.
86. Peterson, "The Al-Huthi Conflict in Yemen;" International Crisis Group, "Yemen: Defusing the Saada Time Bomb."
87. Ismail, *Saudi Clerics*, 195–6.
88. International Crisis Group, "Yemen: Enduring Conflicts, Threatened Transitions," Middle East Report No. 125, July 3, 2012.
89. International Crisis Group, "The Huthis: From Saada to Sanaa," Middle East Report No. 154, June 10, 2014; April Longley Alley, "Yemen's Houthi Takeover," International Crisis Group, December 22, 2014.
90. Stephane Lacroix, *Saudi Arabia's Muslim Brotherhood Predicament*, POMEPS Studies 25, March 25, 2014, 16–18.
91. Cole Bunzel notes that the Islamic State was also distinctive for its adoption of extreme violence based on a treatise written by an Egyptian in Afghanistan. Cole Bunzel, "The Kingdom and the Caliphate: Duel of the Islamic States," Carnegie Endowment for International Peace, February 2016.
92. Bunzel mentions that Jamal Khashoggi and Mansur al-Nuqaidan had called on clerics to revise doctrine since 2003. Bunzel, "The Kingdom and the Caliphate," 15.
93. The Saudi government far exceeded other Arab Gulf states as the source of salaries for its nationals. Steffen Hertog, "National Cohesion and the Political Economy of Regions in Post-World War II Saudi Arabia," in *Saudi Arabia in Transition*, edited by Haykel, Hegghammer, and Lacroix, 98–102.

10 Striving for Transformation, Since 2015

1. Madawi Al-Rasheed, "Mystique of Monarchy: The Magic of Royal Succession in Saudi Arabia," in *Salman's Legacy*, edited by Al-Rasheed, 56; David Rundel, *Vision or Mirage: Saudi Arabia at the Crossroads*, 61–2.

2. Rundel, 65–6.
3. Hubbard, 127–30; Rundel, 68–9.
4. US Department of State, "2018 Country Reports on Human Rights Practices: Saudi Arabia," 3. United States government officials provided information to Western journalists about the treatment of detainees. Hubbard, 186–202; Rundel, 243–7.
5. Hubbard, 186–8; David B. Ottaway, *Mohammed bin Salman: The Icarus of Saudi Arabia?*, 34–6.
6. Martin Chulov, "'Night of the Beating': Details Emerge of Riyadh Ritz-Carlton Purge," *The Guardian*, November 19, 2020, https://www.theguardian.com/world/2020/nov/19/saudi-accounts-emerge-of-ritz-carlton-night-of-the-beating, accessed May 17, 2024.
7. Hubbard, 66–7; Al-Rasheed, *The Son King*, 88–9. For a succinct outline of the main elements, see Nader Habibi, "Implementing Saudi Arabia's Vision 2030: An Interim Balance Sheet," Middle East Brief No. 27, April 2019. Crown Center for Middle East Studies, Brandeis University. Habibi, 3, remarks on the similarity between Vision 2030 and the earlier Metropolitan Development Strategy for Al-Riyadh, abbreviated as MEDSTAR. The major work on the early history of Western consultants in Saudi Arabia's economic planning is Toby Jones, *Desert Kingdom*.
8. Hubbard, 168–70. Ottaway, 100–3; Laleh Khalili, *Sinews of War and Trade: Shipping and Capitalism in the Arabian Peninsula*, London: Verso, 2020, 110. Malise Ruthven cites a *Le Monde* article that traces the seeds of NEOM to a 2014 science fiction movie, *Guardians of the Galaxy*. Malise Ruthven, *Unholy Kingdom: Religion, Corruption and Violence in Saudi Arabia*, London: Verso, 2025. Ruthven's chapter "Terraforming Arabia" offers an extensive critique of plans for large construction projects that draws on architects' perspectives. For a sanguine view of the feasibility of these projects, see the interview with a Saudi engineer involved in developing them, Faisal Alzaibag, "Saudi Arabia's Mega Projects," *Journal of International Affairs* 74:1 (Fall/Winter 2021): 365–72. For perspectives of young Saudi men toward the top-down changes and what they considered urgent issues, see Mark Thompson, *Being Young, Male and Saudi: Identity and Politics in a Globalized Kingdom*.
9. Habibi, 5.
10. Derbal, *Charity*, 281–2.
11. Jim Krane, *Energy Kingdoms: Oil and Political Survival in the Persian Gulf*, New York: Columbia University Press, 2019, 116–35. Krane, 125, makes the remarkable observation that the Saudi program to cut subsidies was similar to measures taken by Iran's President Mahmud Ahmedinejad.
12. Habibi, 6.
13. The government had made headway in reducing the share of oil in exports, from more than 90 percent in 1985 to around 75 percent in 2015. Makio Yamada, "Can Saudi Arabia Move beyond 'Production with Rentier Characteristics?' Human Capital Development in the Transitional Oil Economy," *Middle East Journal* 72:4 (Autumn 2018): 597–609. Yamada's analysis considers the effort to develop productive sectors independent of the oil industry through the lens of Human Capital Development (education), which is necessary to meet rising demand for employment from the growing young

population. His article gives an overview of development of education and vocational training since the 1960s and policies under King Salman.

14. "Saudi Arabia: Concluding Statement of the 2024 Article IV Mission," International Monetary Fund, June 14, 2024, https://www.imf.org/en/News/Articles/2024/06/13/mission-concluding-statement-saudi-arabia-concluding-statement-of-the-2024-article-iv-mission, accessed September 20, 2024.
15. Steffen Hertog, "What Would the Saudi Economy Have to Look Like to be 'Post-Rentier?'," in *The Politics of Rentier States in the Gulf*, POMEPS Studies 33, January 2019, 29–33.
16. Justin Dargin, "Beyond 'Green Pledges': Saudi Arabia and Society-Centered Climate Reforms," Climate Change and Vulnerability in the Middle East, Carnegie Endowment for International Peace, July 6, 2023, https://carnegieendowment.org/posts/2023/07/climate-change-and-vulnerability-in-the-middle-east?lang=en#sa, accessed October 22, 2024.
17. Rundel, 248.
18. "Saudi Arabia: Events of 2016," Human Rights Watch World Report 2017, https://www.hrw.org/world-report/2017/country-chapters/saudi-arabia, accessed May 17, 2024. The Saudi government carried out two additional mass executions. In April 2019, it put thirty-seven men to death. In March 2022, it surpassed the previous high count for executions in one day by putting eighty-one people to death. "Saudi Arabia: Mass Execution of 81 Men: Rampant Abuses in Criminal Justice System Make Fair Trials Highly Implausible," Human Rights Watch, March 15, 2022.
19. Ben Hubbard, "Iranian Protesters Ransack Saudi Embassy after Execution of Shiite Cleric," *The New York Times*, January 2, 2016; Ben Hubbard, "Saudi Arabia Cuts Ties with Iran Amid Fallout from Cleric's Execution," *The New York Times*, January 3, 2016. In March 2023, the two countries restored official relations.
20. The Awakening shaikhs Salman al-Awdah and Awadh al-Qarni had called for easing tensions with Qatar. See below on Saudi Arabia's campaign to force Qatar to change its policies. Ottaway, 78.
21. "Saudi Arabia: New Counterterrorism Law Enables Abuse," Human Rights Watch, November 23, 2017, https://www.hrw.org/news/2017/11/23/saudi-arabia-new-counterterrorism-law-enables-abuse, accessed September 16, 2024.
22. Derbal, *Charity*, 289–90.
23. Amnesty International, "Saudi Arabia: Personal Status Law Codifies Discrimination against Women," March 8, 2023.
24. Fitness enthusiast Manahel al-Utaibi was also charged for appearing on social media in exercise clothing that supposedly violated standards of modest dress. At a secret hearing in January 2024, she was sentenced to an eleven-year prison sentence on terrorism charges. She underwent physical abuse and beatings. Amnesty International, April 30, 2024.
25. Ottaway, 84–7; Rundel, 247.
26. Reda El Mawy, "Saudi Arabia's Missing Princes," BBC World Service, August 14, 2017; Hubbard, *MBS*, 144.
27. Al-Rasheed, *The Son King*, 101–38; Ottaway, 113–36; Hubbard, *MBS*, 70–8, 131–6, 147–55, 237–76; Jonathan Rugman, *The Killing in the Consulate:*

Investigating the Life and Death of Jamal Khashoggi, London: Simon & Schuster, 2019.

28. Diane Bartz and Katie Paul, "US Accuses Two Former Twitter Employees of Spying for Saudi Arabia," Reuters, November 7, 2019. Hubbard, *MBS*, 143. Rundel, 247.
29. "UN experts calls for investigation into allegations that Saudi Crown Prince involved in hacking of Jeff Bezos' phone," United Nations Human Rights Office of the High Commissioner, January 22, 2020. Annex One: Analysis of the evidence of surveillance of Mr. Bezos' personal phone: Key Technical Elements. Mandate of the Special Rapporteur on extrajudicial, summary or arbitrary executions and mandate of the Special Rapporteur on the promotion and protection of the right to freedom of opinion and expression.
30. Samantha Bradshaw and Philip N. Howard, "The Global Disinformation Order: 2019 Global Inventory of Organised Social Media Manipulation," Computational Propaganda Research Project at the Oxford Internet Institute, University of Oxford; Hubbard, *MBS*, 137–44.
31. Derbal, *Charity*, 278–80. Derbal's book considers the question of whether the creation of such associations indicated the emergence of civil society in authoritarian conditions.
32. Derbal, *Charity*, 270–80, 284.
33. Derbal, *Charity*, 281–2.
34. Ottaway, 100–1.
35. Derbal, *Charity*, 281.
36. Bunzel, "The Kingdom and the Caliphate: Duel of the Islamic States," 19–20.
37. Yasmine Farouk and Nathan Brown, "Saudi Arabia's Religious Reforms Are Touching Nothing but Changing Everything," https://carnegieendowment.org/2021/06/07/saudi-arabia-s-religious-reforms-are-touching-nothing-but-changing-everything-pub-84650, accessed October 25, 2024. See 197–8 for questions about the 1979 narrative.
38. Raihan Ismail, "Saudi Salafi Clerics under MBS: Reform and Survival," Crown Center for Middle East Studies, Brandeis University, October 2023, 5. Senior clerics also reversed the Wahhabi prohibition on performing music, lifting the taboo on holding and attending concerts.
39. Farouk and Brown, 13. Salman also retained the board's non-Hanbali Sunnis that King Abdallah had installed.
40. Abd al-Latif Al al-Shaikh was the new minister. Farouk and Brown, 14. On clerics choosing exile, Ismail, "Saudi Salafi Clerics," 6.
41. Reminiscent of Reza Shah's bureaucratic strategy to truncate the legal authority of clerics during the 1930s. Shahrough Akhavi, *Religion and Politics in Contemporary Iran: Clergy-State Relations in the Pahlavi Period*, Albany, NY: State University of New York Press, 1980, 38–40, 55–8.
42. Farouk and Brown, 16–17. Restricting judgeships to men was still the case in 2021. Samah al-Agha, "Female Judges in Saudi Arabia, Hope versus Reality," *Arab Law Quarterly* 37:3 (2021): 288–310.
43. Farouk and Brown, 23–5.
44. Derbal, "Humanitarian and Relief Organizations in Global Saudi *Da'wa*," 120.
45. Derbal, *Charity*, 115, 122–3. Salman put the liberal cleric Muhammad ibn Isa in charge of the Muslim World League and directed it to promote interfaith dialogue. Farouk and Brown, 27–8.

46. "Saudi Arabia: Labor Reforms Insufficient; Abusive Elements Remain; Changes Exclude Domestic Workers," Human Rights Watch, March 25, 2021.
47. "Saudi Trafficking Victim's Struggles Continue Even after Escape," Migrant-Rights.org, August 23, 2017.
48. Pramod Acharya, "Saudi Companies Opt for Subcontracting over Direct Hires, Resulting in Acute and Unchecked Exploitation," Migrant-Rights.org, March 3, 2024.
49. "Over 80,000 Undocumented Migrants in Saudi Arrested in Recent Raids," Migrant-Rights.org, September 3, 2021.
50. "Out with the Old: Half a Million Migrants Ejected in Jeddah's New Development Project," Migrant-Rights.org, March 9, 2022.
51. Noor Tayeh, "COVID-19 and Urban Marginalization in Saudi Arabia," Jadaliyya.com, August 27, 2020, https://www.jadaliyya.com/Details/41639, accessed April 25, 2024. Tayeh reports how one early reaction to the high infection rate in migrant worker neighborhoods was to refer to them as "places of danger."
52. Abdullah A. Algaissi et al., "Preparedness and Response to COVID-19 in Saudi Arabia: Building on MERS Experience," *Journal of Infection and Public Health* 13:6 (June 2020): 834–8; Hashim Talib Hashim et al., "The Hajj and COVID-19: How the Pandemic Shaped the World's Largest Religious Gathering," *American Journal of Tropical Hygiene and Medicine* 104:3 (2021): 797–9.
53. Hashim et al.; Jomana Karadsheh and Tamara Qiblawi, " 'Unprecedented' Hajj Begins—with 1,000 Pilgrims, Rather Than the Usual 2 Million," CNN.com, July 20, 2020, accessed February 22, 2024; "Epidemic and Pandemic-Prone Diseases: Learning from Saudi Arabia's COVID-19 Response amid Its Health Sector Transformation," World Health Organization, Regional Office for the Eastern Mediterranean, October 31, 2021, https://www.emro.who.int/pandemic-epidemic-diseases/news/learning-from-saudi-arabias-covid-19-response-amid-its-health-sector-transformation.html, accessed February 22, 2024.
54. Fione Andre, "New Hajj Booking Process Frustrates Many Foreign Pilgrims," *The Washington Post*, June 28, 2023.
55. Other members of the coalition were GCC members Kuwait, Bahrain, and Qatar; Egypt, Jordan, and Morocco. Ottaway, 185, describes the purposes of the coalition as being to thwart Iranian expansion, suppress the Muslim Brotherhood, and eradicate terrorist movements.
56. Isa Blumi, *Destroying Yemen: What Chaos in Arabia Tells Us about the World*, Berkeley, CA: University of California Press, 2018. "Yemen: Events of 2022," Human Rights Watch, https://www.hrw.org/world-report/2023/country-chapters/yemen, accessed November 27, 2024. Hubbard, *MBS*, 86–99.
57. International Crisis Group, "Yemen's Al Qaeda: Expanding the Base," Middle East Report No. 174, February 2, 2017, 2–3.
58. International Crisis Group, "Saudi Arabia: Back to Baghdad," Middle East Report No. 186, May 22, 2018, 8–12.
59. Lina Khatib, "Qatar's Foreign Policy: The Limits of Pragmatism," *International Affairs (Royal Institute of International Affairs)* 89:2 (March 2013): 417–31.
60. Marc Owen Jones, *Digital Authoritarianism in the Middle East*, London: Hurst, 2022, 141–61.

61. Hubbard, *MBS*, 175–85.
62. Ottaway, 175–6.
63. Ottaway, 173–4.
64. "How Beijing Helped Riyadh and Tehran Reach a Détente," International Crisis Group, March 17, 2023.
65. International Crisis Group, "Great Expectations: The Future of Iranian–Saudi Détente," Briefing No. 92 / Middle East & North Africa, June 13, 2024.
66. For an expert discussion of Saudi Arabia's relationship with the United States at that time, see Christopher Blanchard, "Saudi Arabia: Background and US Relations," *Current Politics and Economics of the Middle East* 9:2–3 (2018): 432–503.

Epilogue

1. A century ago, Reza Shah strove to elevate Iran's place in the international political order through "sartorial engineering." Houshang Chehabi, "Staging the Emperor's New Clothes: Dress Codes and Nation-Building under Reza Shah," *Iranian Studies* 26:3–4 (Summer/Fall 1993): 209–33.

Select Bibliography

Aarts, Paul, and Gerd Nonneman. *Saudi Arabia in the Balance: Political Economy, Society, Foreign Affairs*. London: Hurst, 2005.

Askar, Abdallah Al-. *Al-Yamama in the Early Islamic Era*. Reading: Ithaca Press, 2002.

Atawneh, Muhammad Al-. *Wahhabi Islam Facing the Challenges of Modernity: Dar al-Ifta in the Modern Saudi State*. Boston, MA: Brill, 2010.

Anderson, Irvine. *Aramco, the United States and Saudi Arabia: A Study of the Dynamics of Foreign Oil Policy*. Princeton, NJ: Princeton University Press, 1982.

Bagader, Abubaker A., Ava Molnar Heinrichsdorff, and Deborah S. Akers, eds. *Voices of Change: Short Stories by Saudi Arabian Women Writers*. Boulder, CO: Lynne Rienner, 1998.

Bligh, Alexander. *From Prince to King: Royal Succession in the House of Saud in the Twentieth Century*. New York: New York University Press, 1984.

Blumi, Isa. *Destroying Yemen: What Chaos in Arabia Tells Us about the World*. Berkeley, CA: University of California Press, 2018.

Bunzel, Cole M. "The Kingdom and the Caliphate: Duel of the Islamic States." Washington, DC: Carnegie Endowment for International Peace, 2016.

———. *Wahhabism: The History of a Militant Islamic Movement*. Princeton, NJ: Princeton University Press, 2023.

Chatty, Dawn, ed. *Nomadic Societies in the Middle East and North Africa: Entering the Twenty-First Century*. Boston, MA: Brill, 2006.

Cole, Donald Powell. *Nomads of the Nomads: The Al Murrah Bedouin of the Empty Quarter*. Chicago: Aldine, 1975.

Commins, David. *The Mission and the Kingdom: Wahhabi Power Behind the Saudi Throne*. London: I.B. Tauris, 2016.

Crawford, Michael. *Ibn Abd al-Wahhab*. London: Oneworld, 2014.

———, *The Imam, the Pasha and the Englishman: The Ordeal of Abd Allah ibn Saud, Cairo 1818*. Cowes: Arabian Publishing, 2021.

Determann, Jorg. *Historiography in Saudi Arabia: Globalization and the State in the Middle East*. London: I.B. Tauris, 2014.

Doumato, Eleanor Abdella. *Getting God's Ear: Women, Islam, and Healing in Saudi Arabia and the Gulf*. New York: Columbia University Press, 2000.

Enz-Harlass, Peter. *Peaceful Jihad: The Islamic Civil Rights Movement in Saudi Arabia*. London: I.B. Tauris, 2022.

Facey, William. *Dir'iyyah and the First Saudi State*. London: Stacey International, 1997.

———. *Riyadh, the Old City: From Its Origins until the 1950s*. London: IMMEL, 1992.

Fandy, Mamoun. *Saudi Arabia and the Politics of Dissent*. New York: St. Martin's Press, 1999.

Farquhar, Michael. *Circuits of Faith: Migration, Education, and the Wahhabi Mission*. Stanford, CA: Stanford University Press, 2016.

Foley, Sean. *Changing Saudi Arabia: Art, Culture, and Society in the Kingdom*. Boulder, CO: Lynne Rienner, 2019.

Goldberg, Jacob. *The Foreign Policy of Saudi Arabia: The Formative Years*. Cambridge, MA: Harvard University Press, 1986.

Habib, John S. *Ibn Sa'ud's Warriors of Islam: The Ikhwan of Najd and their Role in the Creation of the Sa'udi Kingdom, 1910–1930*. Leiden: Brill, 1978.

Haykel, Bernard, Thomas Hegghammer, and Stephane Lacroix, eds. *Saudi Arabia in Transition: Insights on Social, Political, Economic and Religious Change*. New York: Cambridge University Press, 2015.

Hazimi, Mansour I. al-, Ezzat A. al-Khattab et al., eds. *Beyond the Dunes: An Anthology of Modern Saudi Literature*. London: I.B. Tauris, 2006.

Hegghammer, Thomas. *Jihad in Saudi Arabia: Violence and Pan-Islamism since 1979*. New York: Cambridge University Press, 2010.

Hegghammer, Thomas, and Stephane Lacroix. *The Meccan Rebellion: The Story of Juhayman al-Utaybi Revisited*. Bristol: Amal Press, 2011.

Helms, Christine Moss. *The Cohesion of Saudi Arabia: Evolution of Political Identity*. Baltimore, MD: Johns Hopkins University Press, 1981.

Hertog, Steffen. *Princes, Brokers, and Bureaucrats: Oil and the State in Saudi Arabia*. Ithaca, NY: Cornell University Press, 2010.

Holden, David, and Richard Johns. *The House of Saud: The Rise and Rule of the Most Powerful Family in the Arab World*. New York: Holt, Rinehart, and Winston, 1982.

Hubbard, Ben. *MBS: The Rise to Power of Mohammed Bin Salman*. New York: Crown, 2020.

Ismail, Raihan. *Saudi Clerics and Shi'a Islam*. New York: Oxford University Press, 2016.

Jones, Toby. *Desert Kingdom: How Oil and Water Forged Modern Saudi Arabia*. Cambridge, MA: Harvard University Press, 2010.

Juhany, Uwaidah M. al-. *Najd before the Salafi Reform Movement: Social, Political, and Religious Conditions during the Three Centuries Preceding the Rise of the Saudi State*. Reading: Ithaca Press, 2002.

Kamrava, Mehran, and Zahra Babar, eds. *Migrant Labor in the Persian Gulf*. London: Hurst, 2012.

Katakura, Motoko. *Bedouin Village: A Study of a Saudi Arabian People in Transition*. Tokyo: University of Tokyo Press, 1977.

Khoury, Philip S. and Joseph Kostiner, eds. *Tribes and State Formation in the Middle East*. Berkeley, CA: University of California Press, 1990.

Kostiner, Joseph. *The Making of Saudi Arabia, 1916–1936: From Chieftaincy to Monarchical State*. New York: Oxford University Press, 1993.

Krane, Jim. *Energy Kingdoms: Oil and Political Survival in the Persian Gulf*. New York: Columbia University Press, 2019.

Kurpershoek, P. Marcel. *Arabian Satire: Poetry from 18th-Century Najd*. New York: New York University Press, 2018.

Lacey, Robert. *Inside the Kingdom: Kings, Clerics, Modernists, Terrorists, and the Struggle for Saudi Arabia*. New York: Viking, 2009.

——. *The Kingdom: Arabia and the House of Saud*. New York: Avon, 1983.

Lacroix, Stephane. *Awakening Islam: The Politics of Religious Dissent in Contemporary Saudi Arabia*, translated by George Holoch. Cambridge, MA: Harvard University Press, 2011.

Lahoud, Nelly. *The Bin Laden Papers: How the Abbottabad Raid Revealed the Truth about Al-Qaeda, Its Leader and His Family*. New Haven, CT, and London: Yale University Press, 2022.

Lancaster, William. *The Rwala Bedouin Today*. New York: Cambridge University Press, 1981.

Lauziere, Henri. *The Making of Salafism: Islamic Reform in the Twentieth Century*. New York: Columbia University Press, 2016.

Le Renard, Amélie. *A Society of Young Women: Opportunities of Place, Power, and Reform in Saudi Arabia*. Stanford, CA: Stanford University Press, 2014.

Louer, Laurence. *Transnational Shia Politics: Religious and Political Networks in the Gulf*. New York: Columbia University Press, 2009.

Mabon, Simon. *The Struggle for Supremacy in the Middle East: Saudi Arabia and Iran*. Cambridge: Cambridge University Press, 2023.

Mandaville, Peter, ed. *Wahhabism and the World: Understanding Saudi Arabia's Global Influence on Islam*. New York, Oxford University Press, 2022.

Matthiesen, Toby. *The Other Saudis: Shiism, Dissent, and Sectarianism*. New York: Cambridge University Press, 2014.

Meijer, Roel, ed. *Global Salafism: Islam's New Religious Movement*. New York: Columbia University Press, 2009.

Menoret, Pascal. *Graveyard of the Clerics: Everyday Activism in Saudi Arabia*. Stanford, CA: Stanford University Press, 2020.

—— *Joyriding in Riyadh: Oil, Urbanism, and Road Revolt*. New York: Cambridge University Press, 2014.

Miers, Suzanne. *Slavery in the Twentieth Century: The Evolution of a Global Problem*. Walnut Creek, CA: Alta Mira Press, 2003.

Mouline, Nabil. *The Clerics of Islam: Religious Authority and Political Power in Saudi Arabia*, translated by Ethan S. Rundell. New Haven, CT, and London: Yale University Press, 2014.

Mundy, Martha and Basim Musallam, eds. *The Transformation of Nomadic Society in the Arab East*. New York: Cambridge University Press, 2000.

Murphy, Caryle. *A Kingdom's Future: Saudi Arabia Through the Eyes of Its Twentysomethings*. Washington, DC: Woodrow Wilson International Center for Scholars, 2013.

Niblock, Tim, ed. *State, Society and Economy in Saudi Arabia*. London: Routledge, 1982.

Niblock, Tim, and Monica Malik. *The Political Economy of Saudi Arabia*. Abingdon: Routledge, 2007.

Ottaway, David B. *Mohammed bin Salman: The Icarus of Saudi Arabia?* Boulder, CO: Lynne Rienner, 2021.

Peterson, J.E. *Saudi Arabia under Ibn Saud: Economic and Financial Foundations of the State*. London: I.B. Tauris, 2018.

Al-Rasheed, Madawi. *A History of Saudi Arabia*, second edition. New York: Cambridge University Press, 2010.

——, ed. *Kingdom without Borders: Saudi Arabia's Political, Religious and Media Frontiers*. New York: Columbia University Press, 2008.

——. *A Most Masculine State: Gender, Politics, and Religion in Saudi Arabia*. New York: Cambridge University Press, 2013.

——. *Muted Modernists: The Struggle over Divine Politics in Saudi Arabia*. London: Hurst, 2015.

——. *Politics in an Arabian Oasis: The Rashidi Tribal Dynasty*. London: I.B. Tauris, 1991.

——, ed. *Salman's Legacy: The Dilemmas of a New Era in Saudi Arabia*. New York: Oxford University Press, 2018.

——. *The Son King: Reform and Repression in Saudi Arabia*. New York: Oxford University Press, 2021.

Reilly, Benjamin. *Slavery, Agriculture, and Malaria in the Arabian Peninsula*. Athens, OH: Ohio University Press, 2015.

Rentz, George S. *The Birth of the Islamic Reform Movement in Saudi Arabia: Muhammad ibn Abd al-Wahhab (1703/4–1792) and the Beginnings of the Unitarian Empire in Arabia*. London: Arabian Publishing, 2004.

Riedel, Bruce. *Kings and Presidents: Saudi Arabia and the United States since FDR*. Washington, DC: Brookings Institution Press, 2018.

Rundel, David. *Vision or Mirage: Saudi Arabia at the Crossroads*. London: I.B. Tauris, 2021.

Samin, Nadav. *Of Sand or Soil: Genealogy and Tribal Belonging in Saudi Arabia*. Princeton, NJ: Princeton University Press, 2013.

Sebail, Abdulaziz al-, and Anthony Calderbank, eds. *New Voices of Arabia: The Short Stories. An Anthology from Saudi Arabia*. London: I.B. Tauris, 2012.

Sowayan, Saad. *Nabati Poetry: The Oral Poetry of Arabia*. Berkeley, CA: University of California Press, 1985.

Suba'i, Ahmad. *My Days in Mecca*, translated and edited by Deborah S. Akers and Abubaker A. Bagader. Boulder, CO: Lynne Rienner, 2009.

Teitelbaum, Joshua. *The Rise and Fall of the Hashimite Kingdom of Arabia*. New York: New York University Press, 2001.

Thompson, Mark. *Being Young, Male and Saudi: Identity and Politics in a Globalized Kingdom*. New York: Cambridge University Press, 2019.

Trofimov, Yaroslav. *The Siege of Mecca: The Forgotten Uprising in Islam's Holiest Shrine and the Birth of al Qaeda*. New York: Doubleday, 2007.

Vassiliev, Alexei. *The History of Saudi Arabia*. New York: New York University Press, 2000.

Vincent, Peter. *Saudi Arabia: An Environmental Overview.* London: Taylor & Francis, 2008.

Vitalis, Robert. *America's Kingdom: Mythmaking on the Saudi Oil Frontier.* Stanford, CA: Stanford University Press, 2007.

Vogel, Frank E. *Islamic Law and Legal Systems: Studies of Saudi Arabia.* Boston, MA: Brill, 2000.

Wagemakers, Joas. *A Quietist Jihadi: The Ideology and Influence of Abu Muhammad al-Maqdisi.* New York: Cambridge University Press, 2012.

Wald, Ellen R. *Saudi, Inc.: The Arabian Kingdom's Pursuit of Profit and Power.* New York: Pegasus, 2019.

Winder, Bayly. *Saudi Arabia in the Nineteenth Century.* New York: Octagon, 1980.

Wright, Lawrence. *The Looming Tower: Al Qaeda and the Road to 9/11.* New York: Knopf, 2006.

Yaphe, Joshua. *Saudi Arabia and Iraq as Friends and Enemies: Borders, Tribes, and a History Shared.* Brighton: Sussex Academic Press, 2022.

Yizraeli, Sarah. *Politics and Society in Saudi Arabia: The Crucial Years of Development, 1960–1982.* New York: Columbia University Press, 2012.

———. *The Remaking of Saudi Arabia: The Struggle Between King Saud and Crown Prince Faysal, 1953–1962.* Tel Aviv: Moshe Dayan Center for Middle Eastern and African Studies, 1998.

Index

Entries for maps are in *italics*.
Saudi leaders before 1900 are referred to as emirs and after 1900 as kings.

INDEX

INDEX

INDEX

INDEX

INDEX

INDEX